Wes Reilay
P.O. Box 1043
Seguin, Tx. 78156

Power Graphics
Using Turbo C®++

Wiley's Coriolis Group Books are designed as practical, hands-on guides that show programmers how to get the most out of programming. They feature a step-by-step approach that will be welcomed by programmers whether they are new to programming or experienced.

Other Coriolis Group Books:

Windows Graphics Programming with Borland C++, Loren Heiny

Power Graphics Using Turbo C, Namir Shammas, Keith Weiskamp, Loren Heiny

Power Graphics Using Turbo Pascal 6, Namir Shammas, Keith Weiskamp, Loren Heiny

Object-Oriented Programming Using Turbo C++, Keith Weiskamp, Loren Heiny, Bryan Flamig

Turbo C++: Self-Teaching Guide, Bryan Flamig

Turbo Pascal: Self-Teaching Guide, Keith Weiskamp

To order our Coriolis Group books, call Wiley directly at 1-800-CALLWILE or check your local bookstore.

 CORIOLIS GROUP BOOK

Power Graphics Using Turbo C®++

Second Edition

Loren Heiny

John Wiley & Sons, Inc.

New York • Chichester • Brisbane • Toronto • Singapore

Library of Congress Cataloging-in-Publication Data

Heiny, Loren.
    Power graphics using Turbo C++ / Loren Heiny. -- 2nd ed.
      p. cm.
    Rev. ed of: Power graphics using Turbo C++ / Keith Weiskamp.
c1991.
    "Coriolis Group book."
    Includes Index.
    ISBN 0-471-30929-X (paper)
    1. Computer graphics. 2. Turbo C++. I. Weiskamp, Keith. Power graphics using Turbo C++. II. Title.
T385.W457 1994
    008.8'782--dc20

93-36768
CIP

Printed in the United States of America

10 9 8 7 6 5 4 3 2 1

Contents

Preface

Graphics programming used to be a luxury—but not anymore. Today's computer users expect and demand more visual and intuitive programs. This is one reason that Microsoft Windows is sweeping the PC market. But even with Windows, there's still the need for simple and sleek, DOS-based graphics programs. And with tools such as Turbo C++ and the Borland Graphics Interface (BGI) there's never been a better time to venture into the world of graphics programming.

In this updated edition of *Power Graphics Using Turbo C++*, you'll learn how to develop useful graphics tools and substantial, real-world, graphics applications, covering such topics as presentation graphics, icon editors, paint and CAD programs, and three-dimensional graphics. Like its earlier edition, this book is a hands-on guide to practical graphics programming techniques. In addition, the tools and applications are designed to take advantage of the power and flexibility of C++ and object-oriented programming (OOP).

However, the book also includes several important changes. The larger programs have been updated to give them a more modern look-and-feel and make them easier to use. I've also expanded the sections on three-dimensional graphics programming with a new chapter on solid modeling. This should give you a good foundation for your own experiments with virtual reality. In addition to these changes, there are numerous smaller ones sprinkled throughout the book.

Here are some of the highlights of *Power Graphics Using Turbo C++*:

- In-depth discussions of the major BGI functions
- Sidebars that present special graphics-related topics including BGI programming tips
- Hands-on approach to building object-oriented graphics tools
- Techniques for designing graphics-based user interfaces (GUIs)
- The fundamentals of two- and three-dimensional graphics programming
- Real-time animation
- Presentation graphics
- Interactive drawing tools

• Four major applications, including a paint program, a CAD application, a three-dimensional wire-frame viewer, and a virtual reality, solid modelling program.

WHO SHOULD READ THIS BOOK

If you've always wanted to know how to master the BGI, develop your own practical set of object-oriented graphics tools, or write a major graphics application such as a CAD program, you'll enjoy *Power Graphics Using Turbo C++*. Whether you're new to graphics programming or experienced with its fundamentals, this book shows you, step-by-step, how to design practical graphics tools and applications.

If you've never written a Turbo C++ graphics application, the first three chapters are designed to help you get acquainted with C++ and the BGI. Although we'll cover some of the key issues involved in C++ and object-oriented programming (OOP), you may want to use this book with other texts such as Bryan Flamig's *Turbo C++: Step-by-Step* (John Wiley & Sons).

WHAT YOU'LL NEED

To use this book you'll need Turbo C++, or Borland C++ for DOS, as well as an IBM PC XT, AT, PS/2, or a compatible computer system capable of displaying graphics. Most of the programs are designed to work with a CGA, EGA, VGA, or Hercules graphics adapters. The programs have also been tested on several Super VGA adapters using third-party BGI video drivers. Because of the flexibility of the BGI and the programs presented, you can easily customize them to run on your own system. You'll also probably want to have a Microsoft compatible mouse installed. Several of the programs in this book are designed around the mouse and work best if one is available.

A LOOK INSIDE

This book progresses from fundamental graphics programming techniques to more advanced topics such as building interactive drawing tools and three-dimensional graphics programming. Whenever possible, the programs are written using the object-oriented features of C++ so that you can more easily modify and extend them. Although we had to limit the features of some of the programs because of space, you'll find that they are complete, well explained, and highly useful—unlike the typical "toy" programs found in most graphics programming books.

Here's a quick run-down of each chapter:

Chapter 1: Introducing the Borland Graphics Interface
This chapter shows you how to use the BGI tools and C++ to access your graphics hardware and write complete stand-alone graphics programs. Along the way, we'll also cover some of the OOP features of Turbo C++. After we cover the essentials, we'll show you how to develop a program to create fractal images.

Chapter 2: BGI Drawing Functions
Find out how to use the major BGI drawing commands. This chapter will also teach you how to work with colors and various predefined and user-defined fill patterns.

Chapter 3: BGI Fonts and Text
This chapter presents the tools for displaying text in graphics mode. You'll learn how to work with the bit-mapped and stroke fonts and how to magnify and clip characters. We'll also create some custom functions for supporting text input in graphics mode.

Chapter 4: Presentation Graphics
Experiment with developing programs for generating high-quality presentation graphics. In this chapter, you'll learn how to combine the BGI fonts and drawing routines to display pie, bar, and coin charts.

Chapter 5: Two-Dimensional Graphics Techniques
In this chapter I cover a variety of techniques for working with two-dimensional graphics, including transforming and rotating graphic objects.

Chapter 6: Animation
Learn how to add animation effects to your two-dimensional graphics. You'll see how to use the **getimage( )** and **putimage( )** functions to move graphics images and how to use color palettes to simulate animation.

Chapter 7: Creating Mouse Tools
This chapter presents a hands-on discussion of how to build a set of tools to control a Microsoft compatible mouse. In later chapters, we'll use the mouse tools to support graphics drawing programs.

Chapter 8: Working with Icons
In this chapter, we'll build a useful icon editor, which we'll use to create the icons necessary to support our interactive drawing programs in Chapters 11 through 14.

Chapter 9: Pop-Up Windows in Graphics
In this chapter, we'll explore a set of tools for supporting pop-up windows in graphics mode.

Chapter 10: Interactive Drawing Tools

Learn how to build a useful toolset of interactive drawing routines.

Chapter 11: A Paint Program

This presents a powerful painting program that includes a mouse-based user interface.

Chapter 12: A CAD Program

You will build your own object-oriented, drawing or CAD program.

Chapter 13: Three-Dimensional Graphics

You will be introduced to the fundamentals of three-dimensional graphics programming, such as clipping, projection and three-dimensional representation. The chapter also presents a three-dimensional toolkit and a wire-frame viewing program.

Chapter 14: Solid Modeling

In this chapter, we'll step into the realm of virtual reality by extending the three-dimensional tools in Chapter 13 to display solid objects. We'll construct a solid modeling program that you can use as the engine to your own virtual reality system.

WHERE'S THE CODE?

This book includes a substantial amount of code. To save you typing time, the software is available in electronic form. A disk order form is located in the back of the book for your convenience. Alternatively, you can download the files from the BBS listed on the disk order page.

Introducing the Borland Graphics Interface

T his chapter will help you get started writing your own graphics programs. We'll take a look at the basic tools that the Borland Graphics Interface (BGI) provides and introduce a few of C++'s object-oriented programming (OOP) features. In later chapters, we'll cover the BGI tools and OOP in much greater detail as we develop a collection of useful graphics tools and eventually several significant applications, including an icon editor, CAD and drawing programs, and a three-dimensional viewer.

We'll begin our introduction by discussing the basic structure of a Turbo C++ graphics program, and then we'll show you how to use several of the BGI graphics functions. Some of the routines that we'll present include pixel-plotting functions, line-drawing commands, polygon-plotting routines, and text-manipulation routines that work in graphics mode. At the end of the chapter, we'll develop an interesting program that combines what we've learned into a very simple fractal program that displays computer generated, fractal landscapes.

Using the BGI

Out of the box, most PCs normally reside in text mode. This is fine for word processing and database applications; however, when you need to display a chart, floorplan, or digital image, you have to turn to graphics mode. So how do you write a graphics program?

In many ways, graphics programming is no different than text mode programming. The main problem is that there are many "standard" graphics adapters and graphics modes on the market—each operating a little differently from the others. You could write your programs to support all the graphics adapters; however, this is a lot of work. A better approach is to write your programs using a library, such as the Borland Graphics Interface, that provides a package of graphics functions so that you can focus on your application's details. The BGI library is located in the file GRAPHICS.LIB that comes with your Borland compiler.

The GRAPHICS.LIB file, however, is only part of the story. The BGI separates the low-level code to manipulate the graphics cards into *driver files.* Each driver file supports a specific class of graphics adapters and manages all the details for drawing on the screen for those graphics cards. The GRAPHICS.LIB library only contains the high-level graphics routines that call the lower-level routines in the drivers. When a graphics program begins, the BGI determines which driver you need (or uses the one you specify), and then normally loads the routines from that driver to access the screen. In Turbo C++, the driver files end with a .BGI extension. The EGAVGA.BGI driver file, for instance, supports the standard EGA and VGA graphics modes.

To access the BGI's functions, you must link your programs with the GRAPHICS.LIB library. You'll also need to place an **#include <graphics.h>** statement at the beginning of your programs to gain access to the constants, data structures, and functions defined in the BGI. If you haven't explored this file, you might want to take a few minutes and view it with the Turbo C++ built-in editor. You can find GRAPHICS.H in the INCLUDE subdirectory of your Turbo C++ compiler's directory. In the following section, we'll show you the basic components of a typical Turbo C++ graphics program.

Initializing the BGI

The first step in almost every graphics program is to switch the video display hardware into graphics mode. It's at this time that the BGI loads the proper BGI driver. Once in graphics mode, you can call the BGI's functions to draw figures to the screen. You must initialize the graphics hardware by calling the BGI function **initgraph()**:

```
void far initgraph(int far *gdriver, int far *gmode, char far *driver_path);
```

The **gdriver** and **gmode** parameters are pointers to integers that specify the graphics driver and mode to use. The **driver_path** parameter is a NULL-terminated string that specifies the path name where Turbo C++'s graphics driver files are stored.

The easiest way to use **initgraph()** is to let it automatically configure your video adapter. If the first argument is a pointer to an integer containing the constant **DETECT**, **initgraph()** will configure your graphics system to its highest resolution mode. The macro constant **DETECT** is declared in the GRAPHICS.H header file. The second argument in **initgraph()** does not need to be initialized to any value in this case; however, you do need to pass a pointer to an integer. After calling **initgraph( )**, you can examine the value of this argument to determine which graphics mode the BGI initialized. As a last requirement for setting your PC's video adapter, you'll need to specify the path to the BGI driver files in **initgraph( )**'s third argument.

The path name to the driver files can be represented as a full path name such as:

```
initgraph(&driver, &mode, "\\tcpp\\bgi");
```

or it can be a partial path name, such as:

```
initgraph(&driver, &mode, "graphics\\drivers");
```

In the second example, **initgraph( )** searches the directory DRIVERS, which is a subdirectory of the directory GRAPHICS, which is in turn a subdirectory of the current directory. Note that when specifying a path name you must use two slashes to represent one, since C++ interprets a single slash as a special character.

Alternatively, if the BGI graphics driver files are stored in the directory where you are executing your program, you can call **initgraph( )** with:

```
initgraph(&driver, &mode, "");
```

Here, the path name is specified as the NULL string. This approach may work the best if you need to move your graphics program from machine to machine.

It's important to specify the correct path name in the call to **initgraph( )**. If you supply an invalid path, or a directory that does not contain the proper BGI drivers, **initgraph( )** will not switch your program to graphics mode. We'll get back to this in a minute.

Exiting Graphics Mode

When you are writing a graphics program, **initgraph( )** is not complete without its companion routine **closegraph( )**. You should use the function **closegraph( )** at the end of all your programs to shut down the BGI system and restore the monitor to the video mode it was in before the call to **initgraph( )**. This function does not take any arguments nor does it return a value.

Writing the Basic BGI Program

To illustrate the initialization steps we have been discussing, let's write a simple graphics program that uses **initgraph( )** and **closegraph( )**. The following program is probably the shortest graphics program we can write in Turbo C++. It's shown here to emphasize the basic structure of the typical Turbo C++ graphics program. You can use it as a skeleton for your programs.

```
#include <graphics.h>                           // Turbo C++ graphics header
main()
{
  int gdriver = DETECT;                         // Use autodetection of
                                                // the graphics adapter
  int gmode;                                    // For autodetection, use a
                                                // variable placeholder
                                                // for the graphics mode
  initgraph(&gdriver, &gmode, "\\tcpp\\bgi");   // Initialize graphics
  // ... put your drawing commands here  ...
  closegraph();                                 // Exit graphics mode
}
```

If you're an experienced C programmer but a newcomer to C++, the first thing that might look different to you about this program is the syntax we've used to list the comments. In C++ the // characters are used to instruct the compiler that a comment string is about to follow. These characters augment the standard C comment delimiters /* and */. For example, the C comment statement

```
/* Exit graphics mode */
```

is similar to the C++ comment

```
// Exit graphics mode
```

Although Turbo C++ supports either style, we'll use the C++ commenting convention throughout this book.

Let's take a closer look at the program. The call to **initgraph( )** automatically configures your video adapter because **DETECT** is passed as the value for the first argument. The second parameter, which references the video mode, is not given a value; it simply acts as a placeholder in this example. Once again, note that the first two arguments are passed as pointers to integer values. After **initgraph( )** is called, you can examine **gdriver** and **gmode** to see which video adapter has been loaded and which mode was initialized. The third parameter to **initgraph( )** specifies the directory where the BGI driver files are kept. If you don't specify the correct directory, your program will fail to be initialized to graphics mode and won't display any graphics. We'll show you how to check for this and other potential errors when loading driver files in an upcoming section.

Compiling the Basic BGI Program

It's a good idea to try compiling the program presented in the last section to ensure that you have everything set up properly with your compiler. Besides making sure that your compiler has all its path settings correct (to your compiler's include files and libraries), you'll also want to tell the compiler to link in the BGI's GRAPHICS.LIB library file. If you are using your compiler's integrated environment, to compile and build your programs, you'll find an option to link in the GRAPHICS.LIB file. Refer to your compiler's documentation if you're not sure where to look for this option. Once you've set up the compiler correctly, you can build the program like any other. Just select the Make or Build menu options.

If you run this program without adding any graphics drawing commands, you'll see a couple of flashes on the screen and that's about it. The screen flicker is caused by your PC switching from its normal text mode to graphics mode and then back again to text mode (assuming the screen was in text mode before the call to **initgraph( )**).

A LOOK AT ERROR CHECKING

It's quite possible that the program discussed in the previous sections compiled, but did not run properly. Generally, it's a good idea to check for this possibility in your code. The BGI provides two functions for handling graphics error conditions: **graphresult()** and **grapherrormsg()**. The **graphresult()** routine obtains the error condition of the last graphics function called, and **grapherrormsg()** takes the value returned by **graphresult()** and returns a string containing an appropriate error message. We'll use these error-detection functions in the next program we write to show you how to construct a much more robust version of our first program.

The most common error that occurs in a BGI graphics program is caused when the required graphics driver cannot be found. Usually, this is because the third argument of **initgraph( )** specifies the wrong path. In our first sample program, the path to the graphics drivers is set to the directory \TCPP\BGI. If your BGI files are not in this location, you'll need to set this path to the directory where they are stored.

Here's a modified version of our last program that performs error checking. You should key in, compile, and execute the program to verify that everything is working correctly on your system. To compile the program, follow the instructions outlined earlier in *Compiling the Basic BGI Program*.

```
// ERRTEST.CPP: This program demonstrates how errors can be detected when
// initializing the graphics system.
#include <graphics.h>
#include <stdio.h>
#include <conio.h>
#include <stdlib.h>

main()
{
    int gmode, gerror, gdriver = DETECT;
```

```
initgraph(&gdriver, &gmode, "\\tcpp\\bgi");  // Autodetect and initialize
                                             // graphics adapter and mode
gerror = graphresult();                      // Get error flag value
if (gerror < 0) {                            // If it's negative, then an
                                             // error has occurred. Use
                                             // grapherrormsg to print an
                                             // appropriate error message.
  printf("Graphics initialization error: ");
  printf("%s \n", grapherrormsg(gerror));
  exit(1);                                   // Since error, quit program
}

// If no graphics error has occurred, then print a greeting
outtext("Hello graphics world!      Press any key to exit ...");

// Use getch to wait for the user to strike a key, otherwise the
// program will immediately execute closegraph and the screen will
// be cleared and switched to text mode.
getch();
closegraph();                                // Exit graphics mode
return 0;                                     // Return no error value to DOS
}
```

This program does a comprehensive job of error checking. If everything is okay, the message "Hello graphics world!   Press any key to exit ..." is displayed. If a problem occurs, however, an appropriate error message is displayed and the program is terminated.

One new function in the program that we haven't seen yet is **outtext( )**. It writes a text string to the graphics mode screen. This is one of two specialized graphics text output routines provided with the BGI. The other function is **outtextxy( )**, which allows you to display a text string at a specified screen location. We'll look at both of these functions in much greater detail in Chapter 3 when we present the techniques for working with BGI fonts and text.

WORKING WITH COORDINATES

In graphics mode, everything is drawn by setting the colors of tiny dots on the screen, called *pixels*. The pixels are arranged using a coordinate system similar to the way we access the rows and columns in a two-dimensional array data structure. This coordinate system is called the Cartesian coordinate system. Figure 1.1 illustrates how pixels are referenced with row and column coordinates. Quite often we'll overlay an (x,y) coordinate system, so that the positive x direction extends to the right of the screen and positive y points toward the bottom of the screen.

The extent of your system's coordinates is dependent on the video adapter that you are using. Fortunately, there are some standard techniques for handling pixel coordinates that you can use for any of the BGI supported video adapters. First, all graphics modes on the PC start their coordinates at the top

Figure 1.1 This figure illustrates the row and column addressing for pixels.

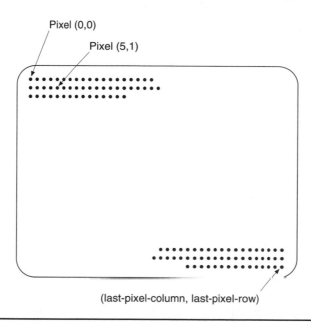

left of the screen with the coordinate (0,0). The highest pixel coordinate is at the bottom right of the screen. Its value is dependent on your graphics mode; however, Turbo C++ includes two functions, **getmaxx( )** and **getmaxy( )**, that you can call to get these values. They are typically used in statements such as:

```
max_x_coordinate = getmaxx();
max_y_coordinate = getmaxy();
```

It's good programming practice to exploit these function calls and create programs that can work equally well on several different graphics adapters and modes. Neither function requires an argument to be passed to them, and they return the index of the maximum pixel in the x direction and the index of the maximum pixel in the y direction, respectively. Therefore, the bottom-right coordinate is given by (**getmaxx( )**, **getmaxy( )**). With this information, we are now able to instruct the BGI where objects should be drawn on the screen. We'll now investigate some of the drawing functions.

DRAWING COMMANDS

Turbo C++ supports a wide variety of drawing commands that are amazingly simple to use. These extend from pixel level screen commands to high-level functions that draw three-dimensional bar graphs.

In the following sections, we'll explore a few of the more common BGI drawing functions. We'll begin with the lowest level drawing routines, the **putpixel()**/**getpixel()** functions, and then we'll work our way up to the higher level routines.

Getting Down to Pixels

Both **putpixel()** and **getpixel()** can access only one pixel on the screen at a time. The **putpixel()** function sets a pixel at a specified location (coordinate) to a particular color. The **getpixel()** function, in contrast, returns the current pixel color of a specific screen pixel. The prototypes for these functions are:

```
unsigned far getpixel(int x, int y);
void far putpixel(int x, int y, int color);
```

Note that **getpixel()** returns a value that corresponds to the pixel color at (x,y). A few sample calls for these functions are:

```
putpixel(100, 200, RED);
color = getpixel(20, 50);
```

To see how both of these functions are used in the context of an actual graphics program, let's write a program that randomly plots 1000 pixels on the screen using **putpixel()** and then relies on **getpixel()** to locate each pixel in order to thin them out. Here is the complete program:

```
// RANDPIXL.CPP: This program randomly plots 1000 pixels on the
// screen and then thins them out by erasing every other pixel.
#include <graphics.h>
#include <stdlib.h>
#include <conio.h>
#include <time.h>

main()
{
  int i, x, y, color, gmode, gdriver = DETECT;
  int maxx, maxy;          // Maximum coordinates of the screen
  int maxcolor;            // This mode's maximum color value

  initgraph(&gdriver, &gmode, "\\tcpp\\bgi");
  randomize();             // Initialize the random number generator
  // Get the maximum x and y screen coordinates and the largest valid
  // color for this mode
  maxx = getmaxx();
  maxy = getmaxy();
  maxcolor = getmaxcolor();
  for (i=0; i<1000; i++) {
    x = random(maxx+1);                    // Use +1 for these since
    y = random(maxy+1);                    // random returns a value
    color = random(maxcolor+1);            // between 0 and num-1
```

```
    putpixel(x, y, color);              // Color the pixel
  }
  // Now scan through the screen and thin out the nonblack pixels.
  // This is done by using the getpixel command to locate the nonblack
  // pixels. Every other pixel that is found is reset to black.
  i = 0;
  for (y=0; y<=maxy; y++)
    for (x=0; x<=maxx; x++)
      if (getpixel(x,y) != BLACK) {
        if (i%2 == 0)                   // Only reset every
          putpixel(x, y, BLACK);        // other pixel
        i++;
      }

  outtextxy(0, 0, "Press Any Key to Continue ...");
  getch();
  closegraph();
  return 0;
}
```

The program starts by initializing the graphics mode using the BGI's autoconfiguration feature. After the graphics mode is set, the maximum x and y screen coordinates are determined by calls to **getmaxx()** and **gctmaxy()**. In addition, a similar call is made to **getmaxcolor()**, which retrieves the highest color value that the currently installed video adapter can produce. This function gives us the full range of valid color values for the active video mode, since all colors lie between 0 and this number, inclusive. The **getmaxcolor()** function works much like **getmaxx()** and **getmaxy(),** and is invaluable for writing device-independent programs. One final part of the initialization process involves a call to **randomize()**. This seeds the random number generator we'll be using later to randomly place the original set of pixels.

Note that no error checking is performed in this program. Although it's good practice to verify that the graphics system has successfully initialized itself, for the sake of brevity, we'll ignore this possibility for now.

The first **for** loop generates the randomly drawn pixels. They are plotted throughout the screen in random locations and colors. The color values range from 0 (black) to the value returned in **getmaxcolor()** (usually white). After this loop, your screen will portray an impressive looking night sky filled with stars.

The next **for** loop travels through these stars and erases every other one by resetting them to black. To locate the randomly drawn stars, a search is made of the screen pixels. This is accomplished by calls to the **getpixel()** function. Every other time **getpixel()** encounters a pixel other than black, **putpixel()** is called to reset it to black. The thinning process is assured by the variable **i**, which allows **putpixel()** to plot its black pixels on every even occurrence of **i**. The indexing of the screen is limited by the variables **maxx** and **maxy**, which hold the maximum screen coordinates. These variables are set at the beginning of the program with calls to **getmaxx()** and **getmaxy()**.

DRAWING FIGURES

Now that we know how to plot and read pixels, let's move on and take a look at how to use some of the Turbo C++ BGI routines to draw figures. We'll start with the drawing functions that create outlines of figures and shapes. These are the **arc()**, **circle()**, **drawpoly()**, **ellipse()**, **line()**, and **rectangle()** routines. Each one of these six functions has its own unique features and peculiarities; rather than go into them now, we'll simply develop a program that will serve to introduce you to them briefly.

Each of these functions has a rather intuitive name and operates much as you might expect. For example, **arc()** draws an arc and **circle()** draws a circle. The **circle()** function requires three arguments: the x and y coordinates of its center and the radius of the circle. The other functions are similar. The only odd one is **drawpoly()**. This routine takes an array of x and y points and the number of points in the array and plots line segments connecting the points. If the first coordinate in the list of points matches with the last, then a closed polygon is drawn.

These six BGI drawing routines are pleasantly flexible. You can control the color that figures are drawn in, the type of line style used to make their perimeter, and the aspect ratio used (in the case of the **arc()** and **circle()** functions). In Chapter 2, we'll explore each of the drawing functions in much greater detail.

For now, let's write a program that illustrates these six drawing functions. The program is somewhat encumbered by the need to keep all of the indexes to the drawing functions device independent, but this is the cost of generality.

The screen is divided into six sections—one section for each type of figure. In addition, the program uses the **outtextxy()** text-display function to write labels for each of the figures. Here is the program:

```
// DRAW.CPP: This program shows you most of the simple drawing routines in
// the BGI. These do not include the fill routines or the various
// line styles that are available.
#include <graphics.h>
#include <conio.h>

main()
{
   int gmode, maxx, maxy, gdriver = DETECT;
   int points[10];

   initgraph(&gdriver, &gmode, "\\tcpp\\bgi");
   maxx = getmaxx();   maxy = getmaxy();
   // Draw an arc, circle, and polygon on the top portion of the screen,
   // and an ellipse, line, and rectangle on the lower portion of the screen
   arc(maxx/6, maxy/4, 0, 135, 50);
   outtextxy(maxx/6-textwidth("arc")/2, 0, "arc");
   circle(maxx/2, maxy/4, 60);
```

```
outtextxy(maxx/2-textwidth("circle")/2, 0, "circle");

points[0] = maxx*5/6-20;  points[1] = maxy/4-20;
points[2] = maxx*5/6-30;  points[3] = maxy/4+25;
points[4] = maxx*5/6+40;  points[5] = maxy/4+15;
points[6] = maxx*5/6+20;  points[7] = maxy/4-30;
points[8] = points[0];    points[9] = points[1];
drawpoly(5, points);
outtextxy(maxx*5/6-textwidth("drawpoly")/2, 0, "drawpoly");
ellipse(maxx/6,maxy*3/4, 0, 360, 75, 20);
outtextxy(maxx/6-textwidth("ellipse")/2, maxy-textheight("l"),
  "ellipse");
line(maxx/2-25, maxy*3/4-25, maxx/2+25, maxy*3/4+25);
outtextxy(maxx/2-textwidth("line")/2, maxy-textheight("l"), "line");
rectangle(maxx*5/6-30, maxy*3/4-20, maxx*5/6+30, maxy*3/4+20);
outtextxy(maxx*5/6-textwidth("rectangle")/2, maxy-textheight("l"),
  "rectangle");
getch();
closegraph();
return 0;
}
```

The display produced by this program is shown in Figure 1.2.

The following statements may help you better understand the parameters passed to the functions spotlighted in the program.

```
arc(x, y, st_angle, end_angle, radius);
circle(x, y, radius);
drawpoly(number_of_points, array_of_xy_points);
ellipse(x, y, st_angle, end_angle, xradius, yradius);
line(x1, y1, x2, y2);
rectangle(left, top, right, bottom);
```

Figure 1.2 DRAW.CPP produces this output.

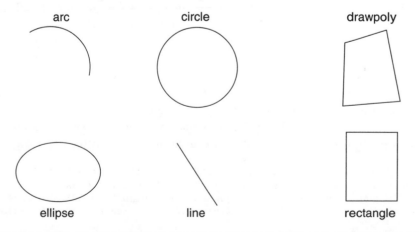

The different calculations and offsets included in the program illustrate the type of code typically needed to generate device-independent scenes in Turbo C++. In particular, note that we are using the **textheight( )** and **textwidth( )** functions to determine the size of the text strings that are displayed. We'll look at both of these functions in more detail in Chapter 3.

Keep in mind that we are only showing some of the powerful features of these drawing routines in our sample program. For example, several of the functions previously shown let you set their line styles, and they all let you control the color used to draw them. But we've avoided these for now so that we can show you their basic features in our quick tour.

FILLING FIGURES

In the previous section, we experimented with functions to draw outlines of objects. Turbo C++ also has a set of graphics functions that can draw and paint solid objects or objects filled with patterns. These functions are **bar( )**, **bar3d( )**, **fillpoly( )**, **fillellipse( )**, **pieslice( )**, and **sector( )**. Like the figure drawing routines, these functions are very flexible. Most support different fill patterns, colors, and even different line styles. These routines use the following prototypes:

```
void far bar(int left, int top, int right, int bottom);
void far bar3d(int left, int top, int right, int bottom,
 int depth, int top_flag);
void far fillpoly(int number_of_points, int far *array_of_xy_points);
void far fillellipse(int x, int y, int xradius, int yradius);
void far pieslice(int x,int y, int start_angle, int end_angle, int radius);
void far sector(int x, int y, int start_angle,
 int end_angle, int xradius, int yradius);
```

The functions **bar( )**, **bar3d( )**, **fillellipse( )**, **pieslice( )**, and **sector( )** are useful routines for creating impressive looking graphs and charts. In Chapter 4, we'll explore these and other functions in much greater detail when we develop several presentation graphics applications. The remaining function, **fillpoly( )**, works much like its companion routine **drawpoly( )**, except that it both draws and fills a polygon using the current drawing color and fill pattern.

Now let's write a program that uses each of these functions to draw some basic graphic objects. The program divides the screen into six regions and draws a different figure in each region. The display produced by the program is shown in Figure 1.3. The offset calculations make the code a bit cumbersome, but once again this is the cost of the generality. The complete program is:

```
// SHOWFILL.CPP: This program displays most of the functions
// that use the fill styles provided by the BGI. It draws a bar,
// a 3d bar, and a filled polygon on the top portion of the screen,
// and a pieslice, a filled ellipse, and a filled elliptical region
```

Figure 1.3 This display is created by the SHOWFILL.CPP program.

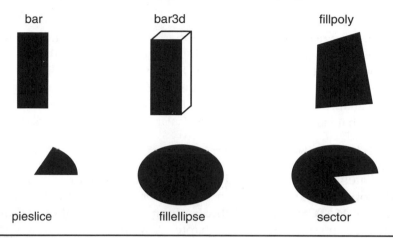

```
// on the bottom portion of the screen.
#include <graphics.h>
#include <conio.h>

main()
{
  int gdriver = DETECT, gmode;
  int maxx, maxy, points[10];

  initgraph(&gdriver, &gmode, "\\tcpp\\bgi");
  maxx = getmaxx();    maxy = getmaxy();
  bar(maxx/6-20, maxy/4-30, maxx/6+20, maxy/4+20);
  outtextxy(maxx/6-textwidth("bar")/2, 0, "bar");
  bar3d(maxx/2-20, maxy/4-30, maxx/2+20, maxy/4+20, 10, 1);
  outtextxy(maxx/2-textwidth("bar3d")/2, 0, "bar3d");
  points[0] = maxx*5/6-20;    points[1] = maxy/4-20;
  points[2] = maxx*5/6-30;    points[3] = maxy/4+25;
  points[4] = maxx*5/6+40;    points[5] = maxy/4+15;
  points[6] = maxx*5/6+20;    points[7] = maxy/4-30;
  points[8] = points[0];      points[9] = points[1];
  fillpoly(5, points);
  outtextxy(maxx*5/6-textwidth("fillpoly")/2, 0, "fillpoly");
  pieslice(maxx/6,maxy*3/4, 0, 45, 75);
  outtextxy(maxx/6-textwidth("pieslice")/2, maxy-textheight("l"),
    "pieslice");
  fillellipse(maxx/2, maxy*3/4, 75, 15);
  outtextxy(maxx/2-textwidth("fillellipse")/2,
    maxy-textheight("l"), "fillellipse");
  sector(maxx*5/6, maxy*3/4, 25, 295, 75, 10);
  outtextxy(maxx*5/6-textwidth("sector")/2, maxy-textheight("l"),
    "sector");
  getch();
```

```
    closegraph();
    return 0;
}
```

You may now be wondering, how do the fill commands know what type of fill pattern to use? Basically, each time you call one of the fill commands, it uses the current fill style and color. In our program, we did not explicitly set the fill style, so the program defaults to a solid fill painted in the maximum color available on the video adapter. Turbo C++ also provides the **setfillstyle( )** function that can change the fill style. As an example, if we added the statement

```
setfillstyle(HATCH_FILL, BLUE);
```

immediately after the call to **initgraph( )**, our program would have drawn all of the objects with a blue (on an EGA or VGA system) hatch pattern. The values for **HATCH_FILL** and **BLUE**, along with other colors and fill styles, are predefined in GRAPHICS.H. In Chapter 2, we'll show you how you can create your own fill patterns.

You may also be wondering whether Borland has provided enough fill commands in their BGI toolset. For example, there isn't a circle fill command; or is there? Actually, several of the Turbo C++ graphics commands serve dual roles. In the case of a circle, you can use the **pieslice( )** function to paint a filled circle. The trick is to call **pieslice( )** with a start and end angle that ranges a full 360 degrees. The **fillpoly( )** function is the real powerhouse, however. It has a tremendous amount of flexibility because you can use it to fill objects of any shape. Chapter 10 illustrates this technique.

TEXT AND FONTS

When it comes to text output and fonts, the BGI is quite impressive. Traditionally, text output in graphics mode on an IBM PC has been a bit of a disappointment. For example, in graphics mode the IBM PC only provides characters of a fixed size that are, in some cases, of poor quality. However, with the BGI tools, you can easily add high-quality text to your graphics displays. The BGI includes a font package that is well suited for drawing characters of various heights and widths. In addition, it is also capable of drawing vertical text.

Our next task is to write a program that displays a single line of text at varying scales and in both horizontal and vertical formats. The program uses the sans serif stroke font to display the message "Turbo C++" centered on your screen. The program also enables you to interactively rescale the size of the text, press the S key to shrink the text and the G key to make the text grow in size, press the spacebar to switch the text between a horizontal and a vertical format, and press the Q key to quit the program.

The following program takes a slight departure from the other sample programs we've presented because it uses a new component called a C++ *class*. This class, which is named **textobj**, houses a number of elements such as the variables **multx**, **divx**, **multy**, and the functions **initstyle( )**, **display( )**, and **erase( )**. What's unique about this C++ component is that it allows us to combine data and functions under one roof. In this case, we're using **textobj** to combine all of the data and functions required to display and process a text string. If you are unfamiliar with classes, you should read the sidebar *Creating Classes with Turbo C++* to help you get up to speed on these powerful structures.

Here's the complete program:

```
// SHOWTEXT.CPP: This program displays a line of text that you can
// scale as you please. The program allows the following user
// interaction
//            s     - shrink the text
//            g     - grow or enlarge the text
//            space - switch between horizontal and vertical text format
//            q     - quit the program
#include <graphics.h>
#include <conio.h>
#include <string.h>

const int INC = 10;
class textobj {
  int multx, divx, multy, divy;   // Data components
  int newdir, currentdir;
  int cx, cy, sw, sh;
  char *string;
public:                           // Functions
  textobj(void);
  void initstyle(void);
  void display(void);
  void erase(void);
  char updatesize(void);
};

main()
{
  int gdriver = DETECT, gmode;
  textobj text;
  char ch;

  initgraph(&gdriver, &gmode, "\\tcpp\\bgi");
  text.initstyle();
  do {
    text.display();
    ch = text.updatesize();
    text.erase();
  } while (ch != 'q');
```

```
      closegraph();
      return 0;
}

// Constructor function for textobj. It initializes the object.
textobj::textobj(void)
{
   multx = 100;           divx = 100;
   multy = 100;           divy = 100;
   currentdir = HORIZ_DIR;  newdir = HORIZ_DIR;
   string = "Turbo C++";
}

void textobj::initstyle(void)
{
   setfillstyle(SOLID_FILL, BLACK);
   cx = getmaxx() / 2;    cy = getmaxy() / 2;
   settextjustify(CENTER_TEXT, CENTER_TEXT);
}

// Erases the existing string. Uses a solid black bar to
// write over the text and erase it.
void textobj::erase(void)
{
   sw = textwidth(string) / 2;
   sh = textheight(string) *  3 / 2;
   if (currentdir == HORIZ_DIR) {
      if (sw > cx)  sw = cx + 1;
      if (sh > cy)  sh = cy + 1;
      bar(cx-sw, cy-sh, cx+sw, cy+sh);
   }
   else {
      if (sh > cx)  sh = cx + 1;
      if (sw > cy)  sw = cy + 1;
      bar(cx-sh, cy-sw, cx+sh, cy+sw);
   }
   currentdir = newdir;
}

// Resizes the text based on the character pressed
char textobj::updatesize(void)
{
   char ch;

   ch = getch();
   // Resize the text as long as the scale won't go to 0
   if (ch == 'g') {
      if (divx > INC) {
         divx -= INC;  multx += INC;
      }
      if (divy > INC) {
         divy -= INC;  multy += INC;
      }
```

```
  }
  else if (ch == 's') {
    if (multx > INC) {
      multx -= INC; divx += INC;
    }
    if (multy > INC) {
      multy -= INC; divy += INC;
    }
  }
  else if (ch == ' ')
    newdir = (newdir == HORIZ_DIR)? VERT_DIR : HORIZ_DIR;
  return ch;
}

// Displays the text with the new text specifications
void textobj::display(void)
{
  setusercharsize(multx, divx, multy, divy);
  settextstyle(SANS_SERIF_FONT, currentdir, USER_CHAR_SIZE);
  outtextxy(cx, cy, string);
}
```

This program might look a little different to you because of some of the new C++ features that we're using. Let's take a closer look. Note that the first function we've defined, **textobj**, has a rather unusual look:

```
textobj::textobj(void)
```

The first part, **textobj**, specifies the name of the class that the function is associated with; the actual function name follows the double colons. In this case, the function has the same name, **textobj**, as its associated class. Did we make a mistake? No, in C++ this type of function is called a *constructor* and it is used to initialize an object. When a C++ variable is declared using a class type, such as

```
textobj text;
```

the constructor function is automatically called. (A variable such as **text** is called an object because it is created using the **class** keyword.) Take a moment and look over the **textobj** constructor and you'll see that this routine sets each of the data components of the **textobj** object to an initial value.

The other functions that our sample program contains, **initstyle( )**, **display( )**, **erase( )**, and **updatesize( )**, operate more like traditional C functions. The only two things that are different about these functions are the way that they are called and the way that the function header is defined. For example, the new syntax used to call a C++ function is:

```
text.initstyle();
```

The first component, **text**, specifies the object name that requests the function. A period separates the object name from the function to invoke—in this case, **initstyle( )**.

Writing programs using C++ classes takes a major departure from traditional C programming because of its "object-oriented nature." That is, instead of writing programs that consist of function calls made by a main program or other functions, you can use objects to control the show. When an object calls a function, the object's data can be used by the function to perform computations. In one sense, you can think of an object as a miniature self-contained program.

Let's now look at how functions are declared differently in Turbo C++. As an example, take a second look at the declaration of **initstyle( )**:

```
void textobj::initstyle(void)
```

CREATING CLASSES WITH TURBO C++

Although classes are an extension of C structures, they are the main components that give C++ its object-oriented personality. When you first encounter classes, you may be wondering how they are different from traditional C structures. A class serves as a template for creating an object, whereas a C structure is used to create a data variable. The single factor that distinguishes an object from other variables is that an object consists of both data and code, whereas an ordinary C variable can only store data.

The two most important features that classes provide are encapsulation and inheritance. *Encapsulation* is the technique of packaging data in a class so that it can be hidden or at least packaged together. *Inheritance* is the technique of creating classes from existing classes. Inheritance is important in OOP because it allows us to easily re-use or share code.

Here is the basic syntax for declaring a class:

```
class <classname> {
private:
  // Private members go here
protected:
  // Protected members go here
public:
  // Public members go here
};
```

Each component in the class is called a class member, and a member can either be data or a function. As the general syntax shows, there are three types of members: private, protected, and public. A *private member* plays a

The difference between this declaration and a standard C function declaration is that the class name is included. This information tells the compiler which class the function is associated with. Note that the first component, **void**, specifies the function's return type, followed by the class name, and finally the function name with its argument list.

FRACTAL LANDSCAPES

Our tour of the BGI is almost over, but before we finish let's put together a program that uses many of the BGI features that we have been discussing. Of course, this program won't demonstrate everything that we have learned in this chapter, but it will show you the simplicity and the power of graphics programming with the BGI.

role similar to that of a local variable in a function. That is, it can be accessed only by other members (functions) of the class, much like a local variable is available only inside the function in which it is defined. Unless otherwise noted, all members of an object are private. *Public members* are accessible to any user of the class. These members should be used only if you aren't concerned about protecting a class' data from the outside world. We'll use the public designation throughout this book in order to keep the code simple and easy to modify. *Protected members* have a level of data hiding that's between private and public members.

Figure 1.4 summarizes the different components used in a typical class definition. Note that function members are listed just as they would be in the function prototype section of a C program. The code for a function can also be included inside a class. In such a case, the function is called an *inline* function. Normally, however, we'll place the functions outside of the classes. In particular, we'll define the classes in the header files and place the code for the functions in the corresponding .CPP source files.

Figure 1.4 This figure shows a typical class definition.

```
class string {
  char data[80];  ◄──────── Private data member
public:
  void copy(char *s)   { strcpy(data,s); }
  string(char *s="")   { copy(s); }
  . . .
};
```
Public member functions

The program uses the BGI tools to draw landscape scenes that are generated using fractal geometry. Each scene is designed with an ocean shoreline and a mountain skyline topped off with a glowing red sun. The contours of the mountains and the shoreline are both created with fractals. A sample scene created by the program is shown in Figure 1.5. We'll discuss fractals shortly, but first let's look at an important BGI function used in the program that we have not yet discussed.

The sky, the water, and the sun are all painted using a function called **floodfill( )**. This function simply fills a bounded region of any size or shape with the current fill settings and drawing color. The prototype for **floodfill( )** is:

```
void far floodfill(int x, int y, int border_color);
```

Here the arguments **x** and **y** specify what is called a *seed point*, and the argument **border_color** indicates the color of the border of the bounded region. The seed point should be a coordinate point that is somewhere inside the bounded region.

Now let's take a quick look at fractal geometry. Fractal technology was created by mathematical researchers who were attempting to model the complexity of nature efficiently. By using mathematical formulas, these researchers found it possible to create realistic, three-dimensional scenes of mountains complete with trees, lakes, bolts of lightning, and many other natural objects.

Figure 1.5 FRACTAL.CPP produces scenes like this mountain landscape.

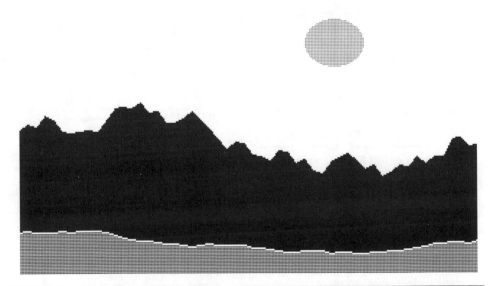

Our example program uses a fractal routine to generate a view of a coastal range against a shoreline. The contour lines of the mountains and the ocean actually begin as straight horizontal lines that extend across the screen. A function called **fractal( )** is invoked to contort these lines so that they take on the jaggedness of a mountain skyline or the meandering of a shoreline.

The **fractal( )** function calls the function **subdivide( )**, which actually performs the fractalization. This function takes a line segment, which is passed to it as two endpoints, calculates the midpoint for the line segment, and then uses the midpoint to bend the line up or down. The line is bent by a random amount. This adjusted midpoint, which will later correspond to the y value to be used when drawing the line at that point, is saved in a global array called **frctl**. The fractalization continues by taking the line segments to the left and right of the midpoint and bending them at their midpoints, too. Their segments are subdivided and bent in a similar fashion and the process is repeated until the segments become too small to subdivide. The resulting line is a connected series of small segments that vary in the y direction. Figure 1.6 shows the stages of the fractalization on a sample line segment. Note that the amount the line segment is bent decreases as the line segment is subdivided into smaller pieces.

The amount that the midpoint is bent, or perturbed, is randomly calculated. This gives the line a reasonably natural look. However, there are several variables that we'll be using to help control the way that the lines are generated. Let's start by examining the arguments used with the **fractal( )** function. Here is its function prototype:

```
void fractal(int y1, int y2, int maxlevel, double h, double scale);
```

Figure 1.6 The process of fractalizing a line continues until a line segment is too small to be subdivided.

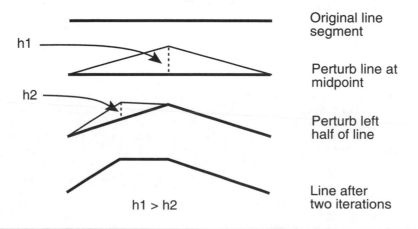

h1   Original line segment

Perturb line at midpoint

h2   Perturb left half of line

h1 > h2   Line after two iterations

The last argument in **fractal()**, called **scale**, partially defines the amount of the perturbation at each step in the fractalization. In addition, the preceding argument called **h** specifies a decay factor that is multiplied against the current perturbation value in **scale** at each subdivision of the line to reduce the size of **scale** with each smaller and smaller line segment. In other words, initially, line segments vary greatly, but as they get smaller, they are perturbed less and less. This scaling down creates a realistic roughness in many scenes. In fact, it is the combination of these two values, **scale** and **h**, that we'll use to control the outcome of the fractal line. For example, the mountain skyline is much rougher than the shoreline so its **h** decay factor is set to 0.5 (1 is the smoothest and close to 0 is the roughest). In addition, the mountains should be large, so scale is initially set to a rather large value of 50. However, the shoreline is supposed to be much smoother, so its **h** factor is 0.9, and **scale** is assigned a value of 30.0.

The key to fractal geometry is the randomness that is applied to the line, surface, or shape that is being fractalized. In our program the random function is intentionally kept very simple. In fact, it simply uses the Turbo C++ random function called **random( )** to determine how much to perturb the line segment. The **random( )** function returns a random value based on the clock in the PC. As a result, the scene generates different random values each time it is run. Therefore, our program generates a different landscape scene each time it is run. If you run the program more than once, you'll see what I mean. You may also want to try experimenting with the **h** and **scale** values passed to the fractal routine for the mountains and shoreline in order to see what effect these parameters have on the fractalized surface.

```
// FRACTAL.CPP: This program combines the BGI and a fractal routine
// to create a fractalized landscape scene. The scene generated is
// slightly different each time you run it. Press any key to quit the
// program after the scene is displayed.
#include <graphics.h>
#include <math.h>
#include <stdlib.h>
#include <conio.h>
#include <time.h>

const int MAXSIZE = 1000;    // The fractalized array has this room
const int MAXLEVEL = 6;      // Number of times line is cut in half
const int WATER = 1;         // Color of the water--on CGAC3 = blue
const int SUN = 2;           // Color of the sun -- on CGAC3 = red
const int SKY = 3;           // Color of the sky -- on CGAC3 = white

double frctl[MAXSIZE];       // Array used to hold fractalized lines

// This is the work-horse routine for the fractalization function. It
// computes the midpoint between the two points, p1 and p2, and then
// perturbs it by a random factor that is scaled by std. Then it
// calls itself to fractalize the line segments to the left and
```

```
// right of the midpoint. This process continues until no further
// divisions can be made.
void subdivide(int p1, int p2, double std, double ratio)
{
  int midpnt;
  double stdmid;
                                  // Break the line at the midpoint
  midpnt = (p1 + p2) / 2;         // of point 1 and point 2
  // If midpoint is unique from point 1 and point 2, then perturb it
  // randomly according to the equation shown
  if (midpnt != p1 && midpnt != p2) {
    frctl[midpnt] = (frctl[p1] + frctl[p2]) / 2 +
                    (double)((random(16) - 8)) / 8.0 * std;
    // Then fractalize the line segments to the left and right of the
    // midpoint by calling subdivide again. Note that the scale factor
    // used to perturb each fractalized point is decreased each call
    // by the amount in ratio.
    stdmid = std * ratio;
    subdivide(p1, midpnt, stdmid, ratio);  // Fractalize left segment
    subdivide(midpnt, p2, stdmid, ratio);  // Fractalize right segment
  }
}

// This is the main fractal routine. It fractalizes a line in one
// dimension only. In this case, the y dimension. The fractalized
// line is put into the global array frctl. The parameter maxlevel
// specifies how much to break up the line, and h is a number
// between 0 and 1 that specifies the roughness of the line (1 is
// smoothest), and scale is a scale factor that tells how much to
// perturb each line segment.
void fractal(int y1, int y2, int maxlevel, double h, double scale)
{
  int first, last;
  double ratio, std;

  first = 0;                                 // Determine bounds of
  last = (int)pow(2.0,(double)maxlevel);     // array to be used
  frctl[first] = y1;                         // Use y1 and y2 as end
  frctl[last] = y2;                          // points of line
  ratio = 1.0 / pow(2.0, h);                 // Defines fractalization
  std = scale * ratio;                       // decays at each level
  subdivide(first, last, std, ratio);        // Start fractalization
}

// This routine displays a fractalized line. The frctl array holds
// y values. The x values are equally spaced across the screen,
// depending on the number of levels calculated.
void draw_fractal(void)
{
  int i, x, xinc, l;

  l = (int)pow(2.0,(double)MAXLEVEL); // Number of points in frctl
  xinc = getmaxx() / l * 3 / 2;       // Calculate the x increment that
  moveto(0, 100);                     // is used to draw each line
```

```
    for (i=0, x=0; i<l; i++, x+=xinc)    // Draws one line at a time
      lineto(x, (int)frctl[i]);          // using y values in frctl
}

main()
{
    int gdriver = CGA;         // Sets the screen to CGAC3, which uses
    int gmode = CGAC3;         // Black=0, cyan=1, magenta=2, white=3

    initgraph(&gdriver, &gmode, "\\tcpp\\bgi");
    randomize();                              // Init random function
    rectangle(0, 0, getmaxx(), getmaxy());    // Draw a frame for picture
    setcolor(SKY);                            // Prepare to draw the sky
    fractal(100, 100, MAXLEVEL, 0.5, 50.0);   // Fractalize the mountain's
    draw_fractal();                           // line and then display it

    setfillstyle(SOLID_FILL, SKY);            // Use floodfill to paint
    floodfill(1, 1, SKY);                     // the sky
    setcolor(WHITE);                          // Use WHITE outline to draw
    fractal(170, 170, MAXLEVEL, 0.9, 30.0);   // a shoreline. Use smooth
    draw_fractal();                           // settings. Paint screen
    setfillstyle(SOLID_FILL, WATER);          // below the shoreline with
    floodfill(1, getmaxy()-1, WHITE);         // the color WATER.

    setfillstyle(SOLID_FILL, SUN);            // Draw a sun by using a
    setcolor(SUN);                            // circle floodfilled with
    circle(getmaxx()-100, 40, 20);            // the color SUN
    floodfill(getmaxx()-100, 50, SUN);
    getch();                                  // Hold scene until key
    closegraph();                             // press. Exit graphics mode.
    return 0;
}
```

2

BGI Drawing Functions

The heart of any graphics system is its drawing functions. As we saw in Chapter 1, the BGI provides a rich set of drawing routines that support several video adapters and modes. In this chapter, we're going to explore these basic drawing functions further and show you how to use them in your Turbo C++ programs.

We'll begin with the fundamental BGI drawing functions—the pixel-oriented routines. Then, we'll take a close look at how the BGI manages color on the screen. Next up, we'll explore routines to draw rectangles, circles, ellipses, polygons, and other shapes. We'll also briefly introduce the **getimage( )** and **putimage( )** functions, which are the core routines in most animation applications. Finally, we'll round out our discussion by experimenting with region-filling techniques and develop a program to help us design our own fill patterns.

PIXELS

The pixel is the basic building block for graphics programs. By grouping pixels, we can draw lines, figures, textures, and other graphics objects. Of course, if we were to construct all our graphics scenes by working only at the pixel level, we'd have a tremendous programming task before us. Nevertheless, pixels and the functions that manipulate them are an essential element of a graphics toolkit.

The BGI includes the two pixel functions, **putpixel( )** and **getpixel( )**, which were briefly introduced in Chapter 1. To refresh your memory, **putpixel( )** displays one pixel at a specified screen location and **getpixel( )** retrieves the current color of any pixel on the screen. In the following section, we'll use both of these functions to show how pixels are accessed and displayed.

25

Using Viewports

In Chapter 1, we briefly explained how pixels are addressed on the screen. By default, the top-left corner of the screen is the coordinate (0,0) and the bottom-right corner is the maximum column and row. You can reposition this coordinate system, however. For instance, if you were to display a pop-up window in the middle of the screen, it makes sense to address all the graphics routines to the top-left of the window and not the top-left of the screen. This new coordinate system is called a *viewport*. You can define your own viewport using the function **setviewport( )**:

```
void far setviewport(int left, int top, int right, int bottom, int clip);
```

The first four arguments of this function are the pixel boundaries of the new viewport. Unlike other graphics operations, these coordinates are *always* relative to the top-left corner of the screen. If the last parameter is non-zero, the BGI *clips* or cuts all subsequent drawing operations to the boundaries of the new viewport. Nothing will extend beyond the perimeter of the viewport. If you set **clip** to 0, however, the BGI doesn't perform any clipping.

The following statement, for example, defines a viewport that covers the bottom half of the screen:

```
setviewport(0, getmaxy() / 2, getmaxx(), getmaxy());
```

In a sense, a viewport defines your window to the screen. Once you've set the viewport, all subsequent graphics routines are relative to the top-left corner of the viewport rather than the screen. For instance, if we were to follow the previous statement with

```
line(0, 0, 100, 100);
```

a diagonal line would appear in the bottom portion of the screen.

You can retrieve the current viewport settings by calling the **getviewsettings( )** function. This function's sole parameter is a pointer to a structure of type **viewsettingstype**, which is defined in GRAPHICS.H as

```
struct viewsetttingstype {
  int left, top, right, bottom;
  int clip;
};
```

Plotting a Single Pixel

The **putpixel( )** function displays a single pixel of a specific color at a specified x and y coordinate. The function prototype for **putpixel( )** is:

```
void far putpixel(int x, int y, int pixelcolor);
```

The location where the pixel is displayed is relative to the origin of the current viewport. Initially the full screen is used, therefore the functions **getmaxx( )** and **getmaxy( )** return the maximum extents of x and y, respectively.

The **pixelcolor** argument specifies the pixel's color. Actually, the **pixelcolor** argument specifies an index location into a color palette (we'll discuss this in the next section). The **pixelcolor** argument, like the x and y coordinates, has a restricted range of values for each video mode. This range extends from 0 to the maximum color value returned by the **getmaxcolor( )** function.

WORKING WITH COLORS

Most of the BGI's drawing functions draw their figures using the *current drawing color*. By default, this color is usually white. The background color, which fills a blank screen, is usually black. You can manage the background and foreground drawing colors using the functions listed in Table 2.1. These functions, however, are only part of the story.

To use the BGI's color drawing and filling capabilities, you'll need to know how colors are displayed on your PC's screen. The available colors are stored in a *color palette*. Essentially, the color palette serves as a table for grouping sets of colors.

When your computer displays a pixel, it uses the currently selected drawing color as an *index* into a color palette, as shown in Figure 2.1. The palette stores the value actually painted on the screen. Realize that only the colors listed in the active palette can be displayed. The first entry in the palette table, (0), usually has a special meaning. It serves as the background color for the screen. To allow you to access the color palette, the BGI provides the seven functions listed in Table 2.2. The number of colors that can be displayed at the same time is restricted to the size of the current color palette. Its size depends on the graphics mode being used. For example, the color palette for the default VGA graphics mode contains 16 colors. Because each adapter works a little differently, we'll consider each one separately. If you need to review how the different adapters and modes work, you should read the sidebar *Working with the Graphics Hardware* later in this chapter.

Table 2.1 The Main Color Functions

Function	Description
getbkcolor()	Returns the active background color
getcolor()	Returns the active drawing color
getmaxcolor()	Returns the highest index in the color palette
setbkcolor()	Sets the active background color
setcolor()	Sets the active foreground or drawing color

Figure 2.1 Your computer uses this color indexing system when drawing pixels.

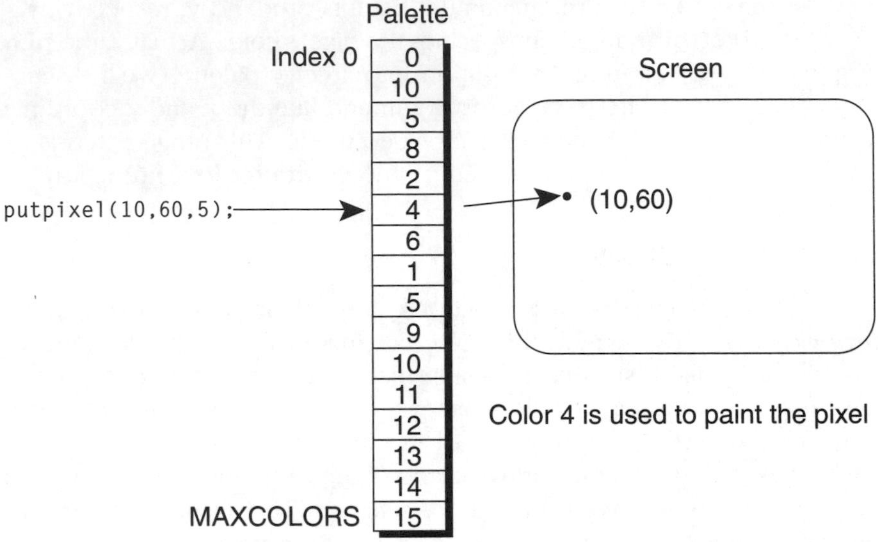

Table 2.2 Functions for Manipulating the Color Palette

Function	Description
getdefaultpalette()	Returns the default palette for the current mode
getpalette()	Returns the colors in the current palette
getpalettesize()	Returns the number of entries in the current palette
setallpalette()	Changes all palette colors
setpalette()	Changes a palette color
setrgbcolor()	Changes a color in the palette for RGB-type displays
setrgbpalette()	Updates a palette for an RGB-type display

CGA Colors

The CGA supports a low-resolution and high-resolution mode. The low-resolution mode can simultaneously display one of the four sets of colors listed in Table 2.3 (modes 0 to 3). The high-resolution mode (mode 4), can display only two simultaneous colors, and the background color must always be black. The foreground color can be set to any of the colors in Table 2.4.

Table 2.3 CGA Colors (Low-Resolution Mode)

Mode	Background Color (0)	Foreground Colors (1,2,3)
0	User selectable	Light green, light red, yellow
1	User selectable	Light cyan, light magenta, white
2	User selectable	Green, red, brown
3	User selectable	Cyan, magenta, light gray

Further, in the low-resolution mode, the foreground colors are predefined. For example, if you choose mode 2, the foreground colors are green, red, and brown. You can, however, choose your own background color by using any of the colors listed in Table 2.4. If you are using the high-resolution mode, however, you must set the foreground color using the **setbkcolor( )** function. This might not seem correct; however, in the high-resolution mode, the foreground color is treated as the background color.

Table 2.4 Standard EGA and VGA Palette Colors

Index	Symbolic Name
0	BLACK
1	BLUE
2	GREEN
3	CYAN
4	RED
5	MAGENTA
6	LIGHTGRAY
7	DARKGRAY
8	DARKGRAY
9	LIGHTBLUE
10	LIGHTGREEN
11	LIGHTCYAN
12	LIGHTRED
13	LIGHTMAGENTA
14	YELLOW
15	WHITE

EGA and VGA Colors

The EGA and VGA are much more powerful than the CGA when it comes to color. Both adapters provide a color palette that can be changed at any time. The standard color palette contains 16 entries that are set to the colors listed in Table 2.4 by default. You can change these colors to any of 64 colors. The functions listed in Table 2.2 are used with the EGA and VGA either to change one or more of colors stored in the active palette or determine which colors are currently stored.

The functions **setallpalette( )**, **getpalette( )**, and **getdefaultpalette( )** use the **palettetype** structure to represent the palette of the installed graphics adapter:

```
struct palettetype {
  unsigned char size;
  unsigned char colors[MAXCOLORS+1];
};
```

The **size** field gives the number of colors in the palette, and the **colors** field contains the actual color value for each entry in the palette.

Super VGA and 24-Bit Color

The BGI does not directly support Super VGA and 24-bit graphics adapters. However, several independent software developers have written BGI drivers to support these boards. A few of these drivers are available on CompuServe in Borland's programming forum. The shareware SVGA256.BGI driver, for instance, supports several 256-color modes on various graphics cards. This forum also contains the Borland driver, VGA256.BGI, which supports the VGA's standard 256-color, 320 x 200 video mode. In Chapter 14, we'll use this driver to gain access to 256 simultaneous colors.

To use one of these third-party drivers, you must call the BGI's **installuserdriver( )** function as follows:

```
installuserdriver("vga256", DetectVGA256);
```

The first parameter is the name of the driver, without the .BGI extension. The second parameter is a pointer to a function that you must also define. The **DetectVGA256** function returns a code that tells the driver what mode to switch into. For the VGA256 driver, we must define a function that returns 0:

```
int huge DetectVGA256(void)
{
  return 0;   // Selects VGA's 256-color, 320 x 200 mode
}
```

Note that the declaration of this routine is very important. You *must* include the **huge** keyword before the function name.

After calling **installuserdriver( )**, you can call **initgraph( )** to actually initialize the graphics system:

```
initgraph(&gdriver, &gmode, "");  // Initialize the graphics system
```

When using a 256-color palette, the first 16 entries are set to the default colors shown in Table 2.4. The remaining colors are undefined and vary from driver to driver. You can set them (and the first 16 colors) using the function **setrgbpalette( )**. To change a palette entry, you must specify the color index to update and the red, green, and blue color components to use. These three values are combined to create the final color. Each color component can range from 0 to 63, where 0 is fully off and 63 is fully on. Therefore, if you use the statement

```
setrgbpalette(0, 0, 0, 0);
```

palette entry 0 is set to black. Similarly, the following statement sets palette entry 0 to white:

```
setrgbpalette(0, 63, 63, 63);
```

To set the first 64 color entries to 64 shades of gray, you could use the following loop:

```
for (int i=0; i<64; i++)
  setrgbpalette(i, i, i, i);
```

What about 24-bit color? Unfortunately, the BGI is not a good match for 24-bit graphics adapters. The main problem is that all of the BGI's color routines use integer values to specify the colors, whereas colors on 24-bit color cards require three bytes each. Nonetheless, some BGI drivers have over-loaded the color functions to get around this. Because there's no agreed upon standard here yet, we won't be directly supporting 24-bit cards in this book.

DRAWING LINES

Although a line is always the shortest distance between two points, Turbo C++ provides three different ways of drawing one. The line-drawing and related positioning functions are shown in Table 2.5. No matter which technique is used, lines are always drawn using the current drawing color and line style when drawing a line.

Table 2.5 Line Drawing and Positioning Functions

Function	Description
line()	Draws a line from (x1,y1) to (x2,y2)
linerel()	Draws a line from the current position in the relative direction (dx,dy)
lineto()	Draws a line from the current position to the point (x,y)
moverel()	Moves the current position by the relative amount specified by (dx,dy)
moveto()	Moves the current position to the point (x,y)

Drawing Lines with Absolute Coordinates

The **line()** function takes two x,y coordinate pairs that specify the endpoints of the line to be drawn. A typical call to **line()** is:

```
line(5, 30, 200, 180);
```

WORKING WITH THE GRAPHICS HARDWARE

Although the BGI supports a variety of graphics adapters and modes, the basic concepts for working with each of these adapters and modes is the same. In each mode, the screen is divided into rows of pixels and each pixel is represented as an addressable memory location. The number of pixel rows and columns available is called the *resolution* of the screen. The upper-left corner of the screen is referenced as (0,0) and the lower-right corner as (last-pixel-column,last-pixel-row).

Each graphics adapter supported by the BGI provides a set of selectable modes. The mode determines the resolution of the screen and the number of colors available. In addition, some of the modes provide multiple pages of memory so that you can switch between different screens. The following table lists the adapters and modes that the BGI supports. The more popular adapters, such as CGA, EGA, and VGA, are listed first. Note that multiple drivers are provided for the EGA. The label component is the symbolic name of the mode that the BGI supports. These names are used with the functions, such as **initgraph()**, **detectgraph()**, **getmodename()**, **getmoderange()**, and so on, to initialize the graphics system. They are defined in the header GRAPHICS.H.

Adapter	Mode	Resolution	Colors	Pages	Mode Label
CGA	0–3	320 × 200	4	1	CGAC0, CGAC1, CGAC2, CGAC3
	4	640 × 200	2	1	CGAHI

This statement, if executed, will draw a line from point (5, 30) to point (200, 180). Similarly, the following code sequence will draw a triangle with the vertices (x1, y1), (x2, y2), and (x3, y3):

```
line(x1, y1, x2, y2);
line(x2, y2, x3, y3);
line(x3, y3, x1, y1);
```

An alternative technique for drawing lines is to use the **lineto()** and **moveto()** functions that allow you to draw lines by moving in discrete steps. Both of these functions take one coordinate pair as an argument, and neither returns a value. The **lineto()** function is used to draw a line from the *current position* to the coordinate specified by the function. The current position is a global pixel location that the BGI draws its figures relative to. When you initialize the graphics system or define a new viewport, the current position is set to the coordinate (0,0). The current position, however, is updated by various graphics operations. After a call to **lineto()**, the current position is

Adapter	Mode	Resolution	Colors	Pages	Mode Label
EGA	0	640 × 200	16	4	EGALO
	1	640 × 350	16	2	EGAHI
EGA64	0	640 × 200	16	1	EGA64LO
	1	640 × 350	4	1	EGA64HI
EGAMONO	0	640 × 350	2	1	EGAMONOHI
VGA	0	640 × 200	16	2	VGALO
	1	640 × 350	16	2	VGAMED
	2	640 × 480	16	2	VGAHI
MCGA	0–3	320 × 200	4	1	MCGAC0, MCGAC1, MCGAC2, MCGAC3
	4	640 × 200	2	1	MCGAMED
	5	640 × 480	2	1	MCGAHI
HERC	0	720 × 348	2	2	HERCMONOHI
ATT400	0–3	320 × 200	4	1	ATT400C0, ATT400C1, ATT400C2, ATT400C3
	4	640 × 200	2	1	ATT400MED
	5	640 × 400	2	1	ATT400HI
PC3270	0	720 × 350	2	1	PC3270HI
IBM8514	0	640 × 480	256	1	IBM8514LO
	1	1024 × 780	256	1	IBM8514HI

moved to the coordinate specified by the function. The **moveto( )** function also repositions the current position.

To draw the same triangle that was presented in our previous example using **moveto( )** and **lineto( )**, you would use:

```
moveto(x1, y1);
lineto(x2, y2);
lineto(x3, y3);
lineto(x1, y1);
```

In some cases, **lineto( )** provides a more convenient way of drawing line figures. For instance, if you are calculating points for a figure while you are drawing it but are not saving them as you go, the **moveto( )** and **lineto( )** pair may be an ideal way of drawing the lines.

Drawing Lines with Relative Coordinates

In some of your applications, you may need to draw lines using relative coordinates; for example, you may want to draw lines relative to other points or lines. The BGI provides the **linerel( )** and **moverel( )** functions for this reason.

For example, our triangle can be drawn using this code sequence:

```
moveto(x1, y1);
linerel(x2-x1, y2-y1);
linerel(x3-x2, y3-y2);
linerel(x1-x3, y1-y3);
```

Of course, this example is rather poor, because it leads to a lot of extra operations, so clearly it's not the best solution for this case. However, if we were calculating our way along a curved surface, the **linerel( )** and **moverel( )** routines might be the best choice.

Setting a Line Style

The BGI enables you to specify the color of a line, its thickness, and its style. By default, all lines are drawn as solid lines, one pixel wide using the current drawing color. However, we can change each of these drawing parameters.

For instance, in Chapter 1, you learned how to change the current drawing color with the **setcolor( )** function. In addition, the BGI supports four pre-defined line patterns as well as user-defined line styles. In the next section, we'll look at how we can change the line style and its thickness.

Predefined Line Patterns

The BGI provides the **setlinestyle( )** function to alter the line type and width of all lines drawn. Its function prototype is:

```
void far setlinestyle(int linestyle, unsigned pattern, int thickness);
```

The **linestyle** argument, which can be set to one of the five values listed in Table 2.6, specifies the line type that is used when a line is drawn. The first four constants specify predefined line patterns and are shown in Figure 2.2. These enable us to draw solid lines, dotted lines, and dashed lines. We can also create our own line style by using the **USERBIT_LINE** constant.

The second argument in the **setlinestyle( )** function, **pattern**, is used when a user-defined line pattern is desired. For now let's just assume we'll be using one of the predefined line-styles. In this case, the **pattern** argument is set to a value of 0. The last argument, **thickness**, specifies the thickness that all lines are to be drawn. The two possibilities are shown in Table 2.7.

Table 2.6 The Line Style Constants

Constant	Value
SOLID_LINE	0
DOTTED_LINE	1
CENTER_LINE	2
DASHED_LINE	3
USERBIT_LINE	4

Figure 2.2 Use the four predefined line styles to create solid, dotted, and dashed line styles.

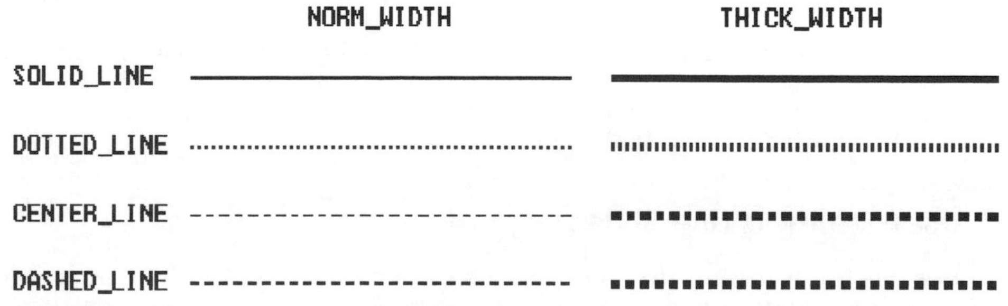

Table 2.7 Line Thickness Constants

Constant	Value	Pixel Width
NORM_WIDTH	1	1 pixel thick
THICK_WIDTH	3	3 pixels thick

Putting this together, let's draw a series of dashed, thick lines using the current drawing color. To do this, we must make the following call to **setlinestyle()**:

```
setlinestyle(DASHED_LINE, 0, THICK_WIDTH);
```

Once this is done, all lines that are drawn will use these line settings.

Determining the Current Line Style

The **getlinesettings()** function retrieves the current line style settings. Its sole parameter is a **linesettingstype** structure that is defined in GRAPHICS.H as:

```
struct linesettingstype {
  int linestyle;
  unsigned upattern;
  int thickness;
};
```

The function prototype for **getlinesettings()** is:

```
void far getlinesettings(struct linesettingstype far *lineinfo);
```

Therefore, to retrieve the current line settings, you can use the following pair of statements:

```
linesettingstype savedlineinfo;        // Declare line structure
getlinesettings(&savedlineinfo);        // Save line settings
```

Later, to restore the line settings, you can use the **setlinestyle()** function:

```
setlinestyle(savedlineinfo.linestyle, savedlineinfo.upattern,
  savedlineinfo.thickness);
```

User-Defined Line Styles

Besides the four predefined line styles shown in Figure 2.2, the BGI enables us to use the **setlinestyle()** function to define our own line styles. To specify a custom line style, the first argument for **setlinestyle()** must be set to **USERBIT_LINE** or a value of 4. The second argument defines the line pattern.

Figure 2.3 This figure illustrates several user-defined line patterns.

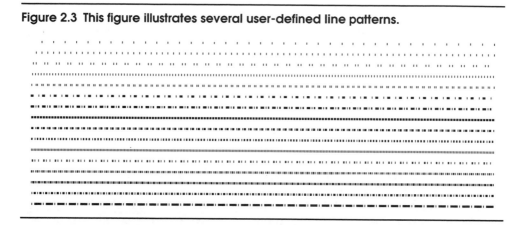

It is a 16-bit binary pattern that encodes the way that lines are to be drawn. Each bit in the pattern is equivalent to one pixel along a 16-pixel stretch of a line. If the bit is on (1), all pixels in its corresponding position on the line are displayed with the current drawing color. If the bit is off (0), its corresponding pixels are not painted or changed. Therefore, a user-defined line pattern that defines a solid line can be created by the function call:

```
setlinestyle(USERBIT_LINE, 0xFFFF, NORM_WIDTH);
```

The hex value 0xFFFF will turn all pixels on and will effectively create solid lines. Similarly, to draw a dashed line where every other pixel is on, you merely need to use a bit pattern with every other bit set to a 1. This can be accomplished with the line:

```
setlinestyle(USERBIT_LINE, 0xAAAA, NORM_WIDTH);
```

Figure 2.3 shows several line patterns that can be generated by varying the user-defined line pattern.

DRAWING RECTANGLES

The **rectangle( )** function is a one step routine for drawing rectangles. Its function prototype as given in GRAPHICS.H is:

```
void far rectangle(int left, int top, int right, int bottom);
```

The four arguments specify the pixel coordinates of the top-left and bottom-right corners of the rectangle. When using **rectangle( )**, keep in mind that it draws only the perimeter of a rectangle. In later sections of this chapter, we'll see how to use the **bar( )** and **bar3d( )** functions to draw filled rectangles. Like most of the functions we'll cover from here on, **rectangle( )** uses the current drawing color and line-style settings, and is drawn relative to the current viewport. It does not use or alter the current position.

WORKING WITH POLYGONS

The BGI also includes a generic routine to draw polygons, appropriately called **drawpoly()**. It takes an array of points and draws line segments between the points using the current line style and drawing color. In effect, **drawpoly()** is comparable to making a series of calls to a line routine. Its function prototype is:

```
void far drawpoly(int numpoints, int far *polypoints);
```

The first argument specifies the number of coordinates that are sent to **drawpoly()**. The second argument points to an array of alternating x and y coordinates that are joined by line segments.

Therefore, if we want to draw an open, three-sided figure, **numpoints** should be set to a value of three and the array of coordinate points should contain six integer numbers that correspond to the three line endpoints. The first array location will hold the first x coordinate, followed by its matching y coordinate and two more x and y coordinate pairs. Let's say that the three points are (10, 30), (300, 30), and (100, 90). The following lines of code would draw this figure for us:

```
int points[6] = {10,30, 300,30, 100,90};
drawpoly(3, points);
```

As I hinted to earlier, the **drawpoly()** function does not automatically close off the polygon. If you want a closed polygon, the last point in the polygon must be the same as the first. Therefore, to close the polygon presented in this example, we must use:

```
int points[8] = {10,30, 300,30, 100,90, 10,30};
drawpoly(4, points);
```

Note that the first and last coordinate pairs in the points array are the same and that the **numpoints** argument has been increased by 1 to accommodate this.

ARCS, CIRCLES, AND ELLIPSES

By now you're probably wondering if the BGI can do more than draw lines. Yes, it can. The BGI provides the functions **arc()**, **circle()**, **ellipse()**, **pieslice()**, **fillellipse()**, and **sector()** that can each draw curved figures. We'll begin by looking at the first three. We'll cover the **pieslice()**, **fillellipse()**, and **sector()** functions when we discuss filled regions later in this chapter.

Each of the curve drawing functions uses the current drawing color. They do not, however, use the current line style setting. Specifically, the perimeters of the objects are always drawn solid, yet they do use the current setting of the line thickness. In addition, like all the functions thus far, the coordinates of these functions are taken relative to the current viewport.

Drawing Arcs

The **arc()** function draws a portion of a circle or a complete circle. Its prototype is:

```
void far arc(int x, int y, int stangle, int endangle, int radius);
```

The first two arguments specify a screen coordinate for the center point of the arc. The **stangle** and **endangle** arguments are angles that specify the sweep of the arc, as illustrated in Figure 2.4. These values are in degrees and are measured counterclockwise starting from the 3 o'clock position. The last argument dictates the radius of the circle. This value is measured in pixels from the center of the arc along the current row until it intersects the arc or the location on the screen where it would intersect the arc if it were swept to its 0 angle. This description is important when you consider that the aspect ratio of a given screen mode may cause the radius to actually be a different number of pixels in length for different angles in the circle.

For example, suppose we want to draw an arc that extends 15 degrees from the horizon. For the sake of this example, let's center the arc at (200, 100) and give it a radius of 100. The line of code that will produce this arc is:

```
arc(200, 100, 0, 15, 100);
```

If you count the pixels along the radius of this arc, you'll be able to verify that the radius is 100 pixels along its horizon.

Figure 2.4 The parameters of the arc() function specifiy the coordinates and sweep of an arc.

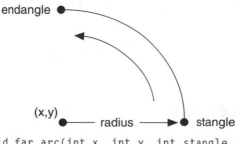

```
void far arc(int x, int y, int stangle,
int endangle, int radius);
```

Arc Endpoints

Often, it is useful to be able to tell where the endpoints of an arc have been drawn. For example, there are times when we may want to connect a line with the endpoints of an arc or link a series of arcs together. To accomplish this, the BGI provides the function **getarccoords( )**. Its function prototype is:

```
void far getarccoords(struct arccoordstype far *arccoords);
```

The only argument of **getarccoords( )** is a structure of type **arccoordstype**. This structure stores the endpoints of the last arc drawn and its center location. It is defined in GRAPHICS.H as:

```
struct arccoordstype {
  int x, y;
  int xstart, ystart;
  int xend, yend;
};
```

For example, suppose we want to draw the perimeter of a hemisphere. To do this we can use a combination of the **arc( )** and **line( )** functions. To properly connect the arc with the line segment, we'll use **getarccoords( )** to determine exactly where the endpoints of the arc are and consequently where the line should be drawn. The following program demonstrates this process by drawing a hemisphere at the center of the screen with a radius one fourth its width.

```
// HEMI.CPP: Draws a hemisphere at the center of the screen.
#include <graphics.h>
#include <conio.h>

main()
{
  int gmode, gdriver = DETECT;
  struct arccoordstype arccoords;

  initgraph(&gdriver, &gmode, "\\tcpp\\bgi");
  arc(getmaxx()/2, getmaxy()/2, 0, 180, getmaxx()/4);
  getarccoords(&arccoords);
  line(arccoords.xstart, arccoords.ystart, arccoords.xend,
    arccoords.yend);
  getch();
  closegraph();
  return 0;
}
```

Circles and Ellipses

You could use the **arc( )** function to draw a complete circle (by specifying a start angle of 0 degrees and an ending angle of 360 degrees); however, a better method would be to call the BGI's **circle( )** function. Its prototype is:

Figure 2.5 Experiment with the arguments of the ellipse() function to create a wide variety of ellipses.

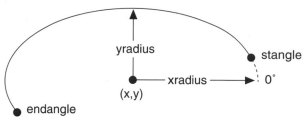

```
void far ellipse(int x, int y, int stangle,
int endangle, int xradius, int yradius);
```

```
void far circle(int x, int y, int radius);
```

The **x** and **y** arguments specify the center of the circle, and the last argument specifies its radius. As is the case with **arc( )**, the radius of the circle refers to the number of pixels from the center of the circle along its horizontal axis to its perimeter.

Note that **circle( )** only draws the perimeter of a circle. To draw a filled circle, you must use **pieslice( )** or, alternatively, flood fill the circle's interior as we'll see later.

You can also draw ellipses with the BGI using the **ellipse( )** function. This routine operates much like **arc( )**, because it can be used to draw all or part of an ellipse. The function prototype for **ellipse( )** is:

```
void far ellipse(int x, int y, int stangle, int endangle,
  int xradius, int yradius);
```

Figure 2.5 illustrates how each of **ellipse( )**'s arguments are used. Most of these arguments function the same as they have with the two previous routines. However, to achieve a wide variety of elliptic shapes, this function allows you to specify the radius in the y direction as well as in the x direction. The **ellipse( )** function does not affect the interior of each ellipse that it draws; rather, we need to use the **sector( )** and **fillellipse( )** functions to draw filled elliptic regions. We'll discuss each of these functions later in this chapter.

FUNDAMENTALS OF ANIMATION

Let's take a break from the drawing commands so that we can focus on the **getimage( )** and **putimage( )** functions. We'll be using these functions in the next section to develop an interactive program to create our own fill patterns.

Most often, **getimage( )** and **putimage( )** are used to manipulate rectangular regions of the graphics screen. Using these functions, we can easily cut, paste, move, or change regions of the screen without having to worry about screen memory addresses. We can, therefore, concentrate on using **getimage( )** and **putimage( )** for tasks such as animation effects, supporting pop-up windows, or allowing graphics objects to be easily edited and moved.

The function prototype for **getimage( )** is:

```
void far getimage(int left, int top, int right, int bottom,
  void far *bitmap);
```

The first four arguments of **getimage( )** specify the top-left and bottom-right pixel boundaries of a rectangular region on the screen that is to be copied. This copied image is saved in an array pointed to by its last argument, **bitmap**. The size of the **bitmap** array is dependent on the size of the screen image being saved and the current graphics mode. Remember that each mode supports a different screen resolution that requires different amounts of memory. To determine the size of a screen image, the BGI provides the **imagesize( )** function. This function takes the same pixel boundaries as **getimage( )**. Based on these boundaries, the function returns the number of bytes that should be allocated for the **bitmap** array. For example, suppose we want to copy the region of the screen bounded by (10,10) and (100,100). First, we need to declare and allocate space for the bitmap:

```
void *screenimage;
screenimage = malloc(imagesize(10, 10, 100, 100));
```

Next, the image can be copied into the **screenimage** array by a call to **getimage( )**:

```
getimage(10, 10, 100, 100, screenimage);
```

Now that we have a copy of the screen image in our **bitmap** array, we can copy it to a different screen location with the **putimage( )** function. The function prototype for **putimage( )** is:

```
void far putimage(int left, int top, void far *bitmap, int op);
```

The first two arguments specify the top-left location where the image passed to the function is supposed to be aligned. Note that the function does not require the bottom-right boundaries—this information is implied within the **bitmap** array encoding itself. The last argument of **putimage( )**, called **op**, specifies how the **bitmap** array is supposed to be copied to the screen. Table 2.8 shows the values **op** can take on.

Therefore in our example, if we want to copy the bitmap image to the location (110, 10) on the screen, we could use the statement:

```
putimage(110, 10, screenimage, COPY_PUT);
```

Figure 2.6 The effects created using getimage().

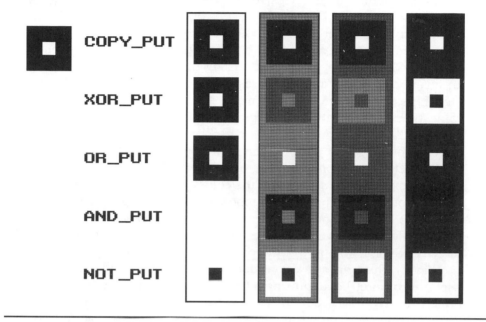

Similarly, if we want to invert the portion of the image that we saved earlier, we could use the statement:

```
putimage(10, 10, screenimage, NOT_PUT);
```

This technique can be useful in highlighting portions of a screen. Figure 2.6 shows the effects produced by each of the image-copying options listed in Table 2.8.

Table 2.8 Bitmap Operations

Constant	Value	Description
COPY_PUT	0	Copy bitmap image to screen as is
XOR_PUT	1	Exclusive-OR bitmap image and screen
OR_PUT	2	Inclusive-OR bitmap image and screen
AND_PUT	3	AND bitmap image and screen
NOT_PUT	4	Copy inverse of bitmap image to screen

Another extremely useful possibility with **putimage( )** is to use the **XOR_PUT** operation. It exclusive-ORs the bitmap image with the screen image. At a binary level the exclusive-OR operation sets all bits in the screen memory to a 1 if either—but not both—corresponding bits in the bitmap image and screen image are a 1. If both bits are 0 or 1, then the corresponding bit in the screen image is set to a 0. What makes this feature so useful is that copying an image over itself, in many cases, will erase any objects in the region and then repeating the process will make it reappear. This can be valuable for some types of animation. In a program later in this chapter, we'll use the **XOR_PUT** option to help move a cursor across the screen without having to worry about modifying the screen as it is moved. Note that the results of a **putimage( )** operation using the exclusive-OR function will depend on the current colors on the screen and the colors in the **bitmap** array.

The other two operations supported by **putimage( )** are the **AND_PUT** and **OR_PUT** selections. You can use these operations to achieve various special effects and even combine them to produce other types of results not directly possible with any of the predefined operations.

Finally, there are a few considerations that you should keep in mind while using **getimage( )** and **putimage( )**: First, although these functions are positioned relative to the current viewport coordinates, they are not affected by viewport clipping. However, if any portion of the bitmap image extends beyond the screen boundaries, the whole image will be clipped. Either situation may cause problems when moving objects about a region; however, most of the time this behavior is exactly what you want.

Another area that may lead to a restriction when using **getimage( )** and **putimage( )** is related to the maximum size allowed for any **bitmap** array. These functions are designed to accept images that are 64k in size or smaller. This may seem like more than enough memory for any situation; however, when dealing with graphics screens, this memory restriction can quickly become a problem. For example, in many of the 640 x 200 modes, we would be unable to save the entire screen at once, since it would require more than 64k for the **bitmap** array.

FILLING REGIONS

Thus far we have looked only at the graphics functions that draw the outlines of objects. Turbo C++ also provides several functions that can draw figures filled with either one of several predefined patterns or a user-defined pattern.

Before we proceed, let's take a quick look at these functions, which are listed in Table 2.9. (Refer to the program SHOWFILL.CPP in Chapter 1 for a demonstration of how these functions work.) The **bar( )** and **bar3d( )** functions are quite similar. There are two key differences, however. The **bar3d( )** function draws a three-dimensional bar while the **bar( )** function simply draws

Table 2.9 BGI's Drawing Routines That Draw Filled Figures

Function	Description
bar()	Draws a filled bar without an outline
bar3d()	Draws a three-dimensional, filled bar with an outline
fillpoly()	Draws a filled polygon
fillellipse()	Draws a filled elliptical region
pieslice()	Draws a pie slice
sector()	Draws a filled, elliptical pie slice

a filled rectangular region. We'll explore these routines more in Chapter 4. Actually, **bar3d()** can also be used to draw a two-dimensional bar by setting its depth to 0. However—and here is the other major difference—**bar3d()** draws an outline to its region in the current drawing color while **bar()** does not have any outline. This distinction will become important many times throughout this book. You should also be aware that **bar3d()** has an additional argument called **topflag**. If this argument contains a non-zero value, the function shades the top of the bar. Drawing a three-dimensional bar without a top can be useful if you want to stack several bars on top of one another.

The function **fillpoly()** is also much like its counterpart **drawpoly()**. Both are used the same way. The only difference is that **fillpoly()** draws the polygon passed to it, as well as filling its interior.

Finally, **pieslice()** and **sector()** can draw filled pie slices and filled elliptical shapes, respectively. Each has arguments to specify where the pie slice or sector is supposed to start and end. Both angles begin at the 3 o'clock position relative to the center point (x, y) of the figures.

A final note on **pieslice()**, **fillellipse()**, and **sector()** is in order. Although the BGI does not directly include a function that can draw a filled circle, we've suggested that you can use the **pieslice()** and **sector()** functions. The idea is to use a start angle of 0 degrees and an end angle of 360 degrees to draw a completely filled circle. However, the thing to note here is that both of these functions draw a perimeter in the current drawing color that will surround the shape as well as extend into its center. If the interior and border are different colors, you will see a line extending from the center of the circle to the 3 o'clock position on the border of the circle. The only way to avoid this is to make the border and the fill pattern the same color. The other approach is to use the **floodfill()** function, which we will discuss later in this chapter.

Now let's get back to the fill patterns. The BGI supplies 12 predefined fill patterns that the functions listed in Table 2.9 can use. They are enumerated in GRAPHICS.H and are listed in Table 2.10. Figure 2.7 displays each of these fill patterns in a rectangle. Besides the predefined fill patterns, you can use

Table 2.10 Predefined Fill Patterns

Constant	Value	Description
EMPTY_FILL	0	Fill with background color
SOLID_FILL	1	Fill with current fill color
LINE_FILL	2	Fill with horizontal lines
LTSLASH_FILL	3	Fill with thin left to right slash
SLASH_FILL	4	Fill with thick left to right slashes
BKSLASH_FILL	5	Fill with thick right to left slashes
LTBKSLASH_FILL	6	Fill with thin right to left slashes
HATCH_FILL	7	Fill with light hatch pattern
XHATCH_FILL	8	Fill with a heavy cross hatch
INTERLEAVE_FILL	9	Fill with interleaving lines
WIDE_DOT_FILL	10	Fill with widely spaced dots
CLOSE_DOT_FILL	11	Fill with closely spaced dots

USER_FILL to add your own fill pattern. (We'll take a look at this process soon.) By default, all fill operations use **SOLID_FILL** and paint the interior regions with the color returned by **getmaxcolor( )**—most often this will be white.

Figure 2.7 Use one of these BGI predefined fill patterns; or create your own.

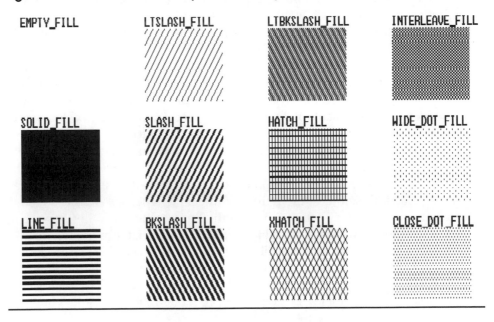

Setting the Fill Pattern

You select the fill pattern with the **setfillstyle( )** function. The function prototype for this routine is:

```
void far setfillstyle(int pattern, int color);
```

The pattern argument is one of the fill styles listed in Table 2.10. The color argument is the color for drawing the interior. All parts of the interior that are not part of the pattern are painted with the background color. One quirk that you may run across here is that in CGA high-resolution mode, all black patterns are drawn the same as white patterns.

User-Defined Fill Patterns

Defining a user-defined fill pattern is not done through **setfillstyle( )**. Instead, the function **setfillpattern( )** is used. The **setfillpattern( )** function is passed an 8 x 8 binary pattern representing the fill pattern to use and the color that it is to be drawn as. Its function prototype is:

```
void far setfillpattern(char far *upattern, int color);
```

The first argument, **upattern**, is a character array that specifies the pattern to use in the fill operation. It should be 8 bytes long, where each byte represents one row of eight pixels in the pattern. For example, a solid fill pattern could be defined as:

```
char fillpattern[8] = {0xFF, 0xFF, 0xFF, 0xFF, 0xFF, 0xFF, 0xFF, 0xFF};
```

Similarly, a checker pattern of alternating on and off pixels can be declared as:

```
char fillpattern[8] = {0xAA, 0x55, 0xAA, 0x55, 0xAA, 0x55, 0xAA, 0x55};
```

To set the current fill pattern to one of these user-defined patterns, you can use a statement such as:

```
setfillpattern(fillpattern, getmaxcolor());
```

Getting the Fill Pattern

As is the case with line styles, sometimes it is useful to be able to retrieve and save the current fill settings. This ability is often invaluable when you want to alter the fill settings temporarily. The function to access the current fill settings is:

```
void far getfillsettings(struct fillsettingstype far *fillinfo);
```

As you can see, **getfillsettings( )** uses a structure of type **fillsettingstype** to return the fill settings. This structure is defined in GRAPHICS.H as:

```
struct fillsettingstype {
  int pattern;
  int color;
};
```

Retrieving the fill settings is somewhat complicated by the user-defined fill patterns. If you are not using user-defined fill patterns all you need to do is call **getfillsettings( )** and it will return the pattern style and the fill color. However, if the current fill style is a user-defined fill pattern, the pattern component in the structure will be set to **USER_FILL**. Clearly, this can be used to tell that a user-defined pattern is being used, but it doesn't tell what the pattern is. Thus, whenever you want to save a user-defined pattern you must make an additional call to the **getfillpattern( )** function to retrieve the user-defined fill pattern.

The function prototype for **getfillpattern( )** is:

```
void far getfillpattern(char far *upattern);
```

This function copies the user-defined fill pattern that is currently being used into the array **upattern**, which is passed to it. Be sure to declare enough space for this array.

Putting all this together, let's say that we want to save the current fill settings, no matter what they are, perform some operations, and then restore the settings. To accomplish this, the following excerpted lines of code can be used:

```
char saveuserpattern[8];                    // Declare space for the user-
                                            // defined pattern and the
struct fillsettingstype savefill;           // fill settings

getfillsettings(&savefill);                 // Retrieve fill settings

if (savefill.pattern == USER_FILL)          // If user-defined fill
  getfillpattern(saveuserpattern);          // pattern, save it too

// ... code that can change fill settings ...

if (savefill.pattern == USER_FILL)          // Restore fill settings
  setfillpattern(saveuserpattern, savefill.color);
else
  setfillstyle(savefill.pattern, savefill.color);
```

Experimenting with User-Defined Fill Patterns

There are many possible user-defined fill patterns. Visualizing these patterns is a rather complicated thing to do; so instead, we'll develop a stand-alone

Figure 2.8 The USERFILL program enables you to create your own fill patterns.

Press Esc to quit

User Fill Pattern

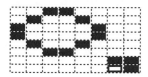

Test Polygon

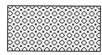

```
unsigned char fill[8] =
            {0x30, 0x48, 0x84, 0x84, 0x48, 0x30, 0x03, 0x03};
```

program that will enable us to explore different fill patterns interactively. The program, USERFILL.CPP, is shown at the end of this section.

The USERFILL program has three main components, as shown in Figure 2.8. At the top-left of the screen is an exploded view of a fill pattern that you can modify. To its right is a small rectangle that shows the same fill pattern at its actual size. In addition, along the lower portion of the screen you will see a valid C++ declaration that you can use in a program to declare the pattern you see on the screen. You won't have to figure out the bit patterns by hand!

You'll define your own fill patterns in the exploded 8 x 8 view of the fill pattern. Using the Arrow keys on the PC keypad, you'll be able to move the cursor through this pattern and select pixels in the fill pattern to change. When you want to toggle one of the pixels on or off, you simply press the Spacebar when the cursor is over it. This will automatically change the current fill pattern shown in the rectangle at the right of the screen and the C++ code that generates the fill pattern.

The Arrow Keys

The USERFILL.CPP program relies on the keyboard for user input. More specifically, the Arrow keys on the keypad are used to move the cursor around the enlarged fill pattern. These keys require special handling because each of the Arrow keys generates a two-byte sequence rather than the single character that you might expect. Consequently, it takes two calls to **getch( )** to acquire the full-key code for the Arrow keys. The question then becomes, how can we tell if we have an extended key code where we must make two calls to **getch( )** or a normal character in the keyboard buffer? Luckily, for the keys that we are interested in, this is not much of a problem. It turns out that the first byte of each of the Arrow keys is always a 0 and that none of the other regular keys on the keyboard generates a single character equal to 0. Consequently, when our

Table 2.11 Extended Key Codes for Arrow Keys

Arrow Key	First Byte	Second Byte
Home	0x00	0x47
Up	0x00	0x48
PgUp	0x00	0x49
Left	0x00	0x4b
Right	0x00	0x4d
End	0x00	0x4f
Down	0x00	0x50
PgDn	0x00	0x51

program reads a 0 character, it knows that an extended key code is in the buffer and that it must read another byte from the keyboard buffer. This second byte can be used to decipher which Arrow key was pressed. A list of these values is shown in Table 2.11.

In **main( )** of USERFILL.CPP the switch statement tests for the extended key codes by checking for a 0 value in the character that is read by the **getch( )** at the beginning of the **while** loop. If this value is 0, USERFILL.CPP recognizes that an Arrow key was pressed, and reads another character from the keyboard buffer. It is this value, shown in column three of Table 2.11, that is actually used in the switch statement to decide which Arrow key was pressed and which action to take.

```
// USERFILL.CPP: This program enables the user to interactively
// experiment with various user-defined fill patterns. The user
// manipulates an 8 x 8 enlarged version of the pattern that is
// drawn on the left side of the screen. On the right side of the
// screen is a rectangle filled with the current fill pattern. At
// the bottom of the screen is the C++ code for an array declaration
// that could be used to generate the current fill pattern. The user
// interaction allowed is:
//     arrow keys on keypad - moves cursor in enlarged fill pattern
//     space bar            - toggles the current pixel under the cursor
//     Esc                  - terminates the program
#include <graphics.h>
#include <stdarg.h>
#include <alloc.h>
#include <string.h>
#include <stdio.h>
#include <conio.h>

#define PLEFT 20            // Left column of the big pattern
#define PTOP  50            // Top row of the big pattern
#define BIGPIXEL 8          // The big pixels are 8 x 8 in size
```

```
// Contains the fill pattern. Initially, it is all set off.
unsigned char fill[8] = {0x00, 0x00, 0x00, 0x00, 0x00, 0x00, 0x00, 0x00};
void *bigpixel;               // Image used to hold a big pixel
void *cursor;                                 // The cursor image
char bigpatterntitle[] = "User Fill Pattern";    // A few titles
char polytitle[] = "Test Polygon";

// This routine draws a rectangular region on the right-hand side
// of the screen using the current user-defined fill pattern.
// Before it displays the pattern it erases the existing rectangle
// on the screen by drawing a BLACK rectangle.
void draw_test_polygon(void)
{
  setlinestyle(SOLID_LINE, 0, NORM_WIDTH);      // Erase the old filled
  setfillstyle(SOLID_FILL, BLACK);              // rectangle
  bar3d(400, PTOP, 500, PTOP+50, 0, 0);
  setfillpattern((char *)fill, getmaxcolor()); // Set to the new
  bar3d(400, PTOP, 500, PTOP+50, 0, 0);         // fill pattern and show it
}

// Show C++ code that can be used to declare the fill pattern shown
void show_pattern_code(void)
{
  int x=20, y=150;
  char buffer[80];

  // Erase the old text on the screen by drawing a filled rectangle with
  // BLACK. The rectangle extends across the screen and is eight pixels
  // high, since the default font is used.
  setcolor(BLACK);
  setlinestyle(SOLID_LINE, 0, NORM_WIDTH);
  setfillstyle(SOLID_FILL, BLACK);
  bar3d(x, y, getmaxx(), y+8, 0, 0);
  setcolor(WHITE);               // Restore the drawing color to WHITE
  outtextxy(x, y-textheight("T"), "unsigned char fill[8] = ");
  // Convert the values to a string that can be printed out by outtextxy
  sprintf(buffer,"              {0x%02x, 0x%02x, 0x%02x, "
    "0x%02x, 0x%02x, 0x%02x, 0x%02x, 0x%02x};        ",
    (unsigned)fill[0], fill[1], fill[2], fill[3], fill[4],
    fill[5], fill[6], fill[7], fill[8]);
  outtextxy(x, y, buffer);     // Write out the C++ code of the pattern
}

// This initialization routine is called once to create the images
// that are used for the big pixel and the cursor.
void init_images(void)
{
  int px, py, i, j;

  // Create the image of a big pixel. Do this at the top-left corner of
  // the big pattern. Once it is created, erase it by exclusive-ORing
  // its own image with itself.
  px = PLEFT;  py = PTOP;
  for (j=py+1; j<=py+BIGPIXEL; j++) {
```

```
      for (i=px+1; i<=px+2*BIGPIXEL; i++) {
        putpixel(i, j, getmaxcolor());
      }
    }
    bigpixel = malloc(imagesize(px+1, py+1, px+2*BIGPIXEL, py+BIGPIXEL));
    getimage(px+1, py+1, px+2*BIGPIXEL, py+BIGPIXEL, bigpixel);
    putimage(px+1, py+1, bigpixel, XOR_PUT);     // Erase the big pixel

    // Next, create a small cursor image where the big pixel just was
    px += 3;  py += 3;
    for (j=py; j<=py+BIGPIXEL-5; j++) {
      for (i=px; i<=px+2*BIGPIXEL-5; i++) {
        putpixel(i, j, getmaxcolor());
      }
    }
    cursor = malloc(imagesize(px, py, px+BIGPIXEL*2-5, py+BIGPIXEL-5));
    getimage(px, py, px+2*BIGPIXEL-5, py+BIGPIXEL-5, cursor);
}

// Using a series of dotted horizontal and vertical lines, draw an outline
// for the 8 x 8 large pattern on the left side of the screen. When done,
// call init_images() to create the big pixel and cursor images.
void draw_enlarged_pattern(void)
{
  setlinestyle(DOTTED_LINE, 0, NORM_WIDTH);
  int right = 2 * (PLEFT + (BIGPIXEL-1) * (BIGPIXEL + NORM_WIDTH)) - 1;
  int bottom = PTOP + 8 * (BIGPIXEL + NORM_WIDTH);

  for (int i=0; i<=8; i++) { // Draw outline of big pixels
    line(PLEFT, PTOP+i*(BIGPIXEL+NORM_WIDTH), right,
      PTOP+i*(BIGPIXEL+NORM_WIDTH));
    line(PLEFT+2*(i*(BIGPIXEL+NORM_WIDTH)), PTOP,
      PLEFT+2*(i*(BIGPIXEL+NORM_WIDTH)), bottom);
  }
  init_images();                 // Initialize the big pixel and cursor
}

// Toggle the value for the indicated pixel in the user-defined pattern
void toggle_pixel(int x, int y)
{
  unsigned char mask = 0x01;
  mask = mask << (8-(x+1));
  fill[y] ^= mask;
}

// This routine is called each time a pixel in the user-defined
// pattern is toggled. It toggles the current big pixel by
// exclusive-ORing the current cell with the big-pixel image. It then
// calls toggle_pixel() to toggle the pixel in the pattern array.
void toggle_bigpixel(int x, int y)
{
  int px = PLEFT + x * 2 * (BIGPIXEL + NORM_WIDTH) + 1;
  int py = PTOP + y * (BIGPIXEL + NORM_WIDTH) + 1;
```

```
    putimage(px, py, bigpixel, XOR_PUT);
    toggle_pixel(x, y);
}

// Toggle the cursor image on the screen by using the exclusive-OR
// feature of the putimage command
void toggle_cursor(int x, int y)
{
  int px, py;

  px = PLEFT + x * 2 * (BIGPIXEL + NORM_WIDTH) + 3; // Calculate location
  py = PTOP + y * (BIGPIXEL + NORM_WIDTH) + 3;      // of cursor
  putimage(px, py, cursor, XOR_PUT);                // Toggle cursor
}

main()
{
  char ch;
  int x=0, y=0, gdriver = DETECT, gmode;

  initgraph(&gdriver, &gmode, "\\tcpp\\bgi");
  outtextxy(PLEFT, PTOP-20, bigpatterntitle);    // Write the titles
  outtextxy(400, PTOP-20, polytitle);
  outtextxy(PLEFT, 0, "Press Esc to quit");
  draw_enlarged_pattern();                 // Create the enlarged pattern
  draw_test_polygon();                     // Draw the test-filled polygon
  show_pattern_code();                     // Show the code for the pattern

  while ((ch=getch()) != 0x1b) {           // While person doesn't press Esc
    if (ch == ' ') {                       // If it is a space, then toggle
      toggle_bigpixel(x, y);               // the big pixel and update the
      draw_test_polygon();                 // polygon and code that shows
      show_pattern_code();                 // the pattern
    }
    else if (ch == 0) {                    // If character was a 0, then it
      ch = getch();                        // may be an extended code for
      toggle_cursor(x, y);                 // an Arrow key, get next ch
                                           // and erase cursor from the screen
    // Move the cursor through the big pixel pattern according to the
    // arrow key that is pressed
    switch (ch) {
      case 0x4b : if (x > 0) x--;     break;      // Left arrow
      case 0x4d : if (x < BIGPIXEL-1) x++; break; // Right arrow
      case 0x48 : if (y > 0) y--;     break;      // Up arrow
      case 0x50 : if (y < BIGPIXEL-1) y++; break; // Down arrow
      case 0x47 : if (x > 0) x--;                 // Home key
                  if (y > 0) y--;
                  break;
      case 0x49 : if (x < BIGPIXEL-1) x++;        // PgUp key
                  if (y > 0) y--;
                  break;
      case 0x51 : if (x < BIGPIXEL-1) x++;        // PgDn key
                  if (y < BIGPIXEL-1) y++;
                  break;
```

```
        case 0x4f : if (x > 0) x--;                    // End key
                    if (y < BIGPIXEL-1) y++;
                    break;
        }
        toggle_cursor(x, y);                    // Restore cursor to the screen
    }
}
closegraph();                                   // Exit graphics mode
return 0;
}
```

FLOOD FILLS

So far all the fill operations that we have discussed have been oriented around various shapes. Sometimes, you may want to fill a region with a particular fill pattern that is bounded by a set of lines or objects. To accomplish this, you can use an operation called a flood fill where you specify a location to begin filling and then the filling process floods an area until the border of the object has been reached.

The function prototype for the BGI flood-fill operation is:

```
void far floodfill(int x, int y, int border);
```

Here, the values of **x** and **y** specify the starting location of the fill operation, commonly called the *seed point*. The border argument indicates the color that **floodfill( )** uses to determine when it has reached the boundary of the region it is filling. The function uses the current fill settings when filling the region.

One place where the flood fill operation may come in handy is when you want to draw a filled circle. This can be done using **pieslice( )**, **fillellipse( )**, or **sector( )**; however, we can also draw a filled circle by first drawing a circle and then filling it with a call to **floodfill( )**. The following code performs this sequence of operations.

```
setcolor(WHITE);            // Use WHITE for the circle
circle(100, 100, 50);       // Draw a circle
floodfill(100, 100, WHITE); // Fill the circle starting from its center
```

Note that the color of the circle must be the same as the border color specified in **floodfill( )** in order for this process to work correctly. Otherwise, the fill pattern will spread beyond the perimeter of the circle.

3

BGI Fonts and Text

This chapter continues our in-depth examination of the BGI with a closer inspection of its text manipulation functions. We'll begin by outlining the two forms of character generation that the BGI supports: bitmapped characters and stroke fonts. Then, we'll walk through the built-in routines that enable you to set the style, dimensions, and alignment of text. Finally, we'll construct a useful collection of text manipulation tools that can perform such tasks as automatically enclosing text within a border, sizing text to fit in an existing window, and entering text in graphics mode.

TEXT IN GRAPHICS MODE

The BGI provides its own fonts and special-purpose text display routines. We won't be able to use the standard C/C++ text output functions in our graphics programs. Instead, we'll select from one of two methods the BGI includes for writing characters to the screen in graphics mode. The default text scheme uses fast, bitmapped characters. An optional, more flexible approach uses *stroked* fonts. The method that you should choose for an application depends on the size of the text you want to write, the quality of text you need, and the font style you desire. In the following sections, we'll look at both methods for displaying text.

The Bitmapped Font

A bitmapped font is built into every program that you write under the BGI. By default, bitmapped characters are displayed whenever you write to the screen with one of the BGI text functions.

Figure 3.1 An exploded view of a bitmapped character.

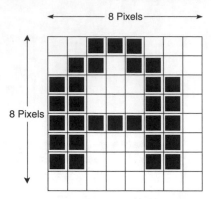

Bitmap characters are built from 8 x 8 bit patterns, where by default, each bit in the pattern corresponds to a screen pixel. If a bit in the pattern is a 1, a corresponding pixel is displayed on the screen in the current drawing color. If the same bit is a 0, however, the pixel is set to the background color. Larger characters are constructed by duplicating the pattern over several pixels. Since all characters are defined as an 8 x 8 pattern, the bitmapped characters are easy to work with and can be displayed quickly. The problem with bitmapped characters is that they appear to have jagged edges in low-resolution graphics modes or when characters are drawn in large font sizes. Figure 3.1 presents an exploded view of a bitmapped character *A*.

The Stroke Fonts

Although bitmapped characters are adequate for many applications, the BGI also provides several stroke fonts that are invaluable for displaying high-quality text output in graphics mode. Stroke fonts are not stored as bit patterns; instead, each character is defined as a series of line segments or *strokes*. The size of a character's description depends on its complexity. For example, the character M requires more strokes than the character T. Therefore, characters with curves or numerous segments may take dozens of strokes to be properly defined. Figure 3.2 displays an enlarged view of the strokes that make up the character *A*.

The major advantage of using a stroke font over a bitmapped font is that the BGI can readily scale stroke fonts without losing any quality. Depending on the compiler, the BGI stocks up to ten different stroke font styles. A sample of these fonts is shown in Figure 3.3. Borland has also made available a custom stroke font editor so that you can create and edit your own fonts. We'll take a closer look at this utility and how stroke fonts are structured a little later in this chapter.

Figure 3.2 A stroke font character requires a more complex description than a bitmapped character.

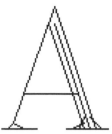

Figure 3.3 The letter A in several of the BGI stroke fonts.

The BGI Text Functions

The BGI furnishes the nine functions listed in Table 3.1 for working with both bitmapped and stroke font styles. You can´use most of these routines with either bitmapped or stroke fonts, however, the functions **setusercharsize( )** and **registerbgifont( )** work only with stroke fonts.

Table 3.1 The BGI Text-Related Functions

Function	Description
gettextsettings( )	Retrieves the current font, direction, size, and justification of the text
outtext( )	Displays a string of text at the current position
outtextxy( )	Displays a string of text at the location (x,y)
registerbgifont( )	Links a font file into a program's executable file

continued

Table 3.1 The BGI Text-Related Functions (Continued)

Function	Description
settextjustify()	Defines the justification style used by outtext() and outtextxy()
settextstyle()	Sets the font style, direction, and character magnification
setusercharsize()	Sets the magnification factor used by stroked fonts
textheight()	Returns the height in pixels of a string
textwidth()	Returns the width in pixels of a string

WRITING TEXT TO THE SCREEN

Because the BGI supports several different video modes, multiple font styles, and variable-sized text, it provides its own text functions to display screen output. The two primary functions for displaying text are **outtext()** and **outtextxy()**. You should avoid the Turbo C++ functions such as **cprintf()**, **printf()**, and **putch()** in graphics mode because these functions are not designed to write to the screen in graphics mode.

The function **outtext()** displays an ASCII string at the current screen position in the current viewport. Its function prototype is defined in GRAPHICS.H as:

```
void far outtext(char far *textstring);
```

The parameter **textstring** is the character string that is displayed. By default, the BGI writes the text horizontally and left justified with respect to the current position using the built-in bitmapped fonts. When the default settings are used, a call to **outtext()** updates the current position to the right-most side of the text. Therefore, the next call to **outtext()** places its string immediately to the right of the previously displayed string.

You'll see later that if you switch between fonts or use a text arrangement other than the default, then **outtext()** will not automatically update the current position after each call and you must keep track of its position yourself. We'll describe this process in the section *Determining Character Dimensions* later in this chapter.

Writing Text to a Pixel Location

A companion text output function of **outtext()** is **outtextxy()**. Like **outtext()**, it displays a string of text to the screen; however, with **outtextxy()**, the text is displayed with respect to a pixel coordinate that you specify. The function prototype for **outtextxy()** is:

```
void far outtextxy(int x, int y, char far *textstring);
```

The first two arguments specify the pixel coordinate about which the function justifies the **textstring**. Unlike **outtext()**, **outtextxy()** does not change the current drawing position after it displays a text string.

An Example of Text Display

The following program, TEXTTEST.CPP, demonstrates how to display text using the **outtext()** and **outtextxy()** functions. The program generates the screen shown in Figure 3.4. It begins by initializing the graphics mode using Turbo C++'s autodetect feature. As long as the initialization succeeds, the program displays several strings using the default settings. Consequently, the program displays bitmapped characters left justified and written horizontally. Here is the complete TEXTTEST program:

```
// TEXTTEST.CPP: Demonstrates the outtext() and outtextxy()
// functions in the BGI.
#include <graphics.h>
#include <stdio.h>
#include <stdlib.h>
#include <conio.h>

main()
{
  int gmode, gdriver = DETECT;

  initgraph(&gdriver, &gmode, "\\tcpp\\bgi");
  if (gdriver < 0) {
    printf("Graphics initialization failure.\n");
    exit(1);
  }
  // Display text
  outtext("This sentence is printed using outtext ");
  outtext("in the default font. ");
  outtextxy(getmaxx()/2, getmaxy()/2, "outtextxy printed this.");
  outtext("This sentence is also printed using outtext.");
  outtextxy(0, getmaxy()-20, "Press Any Key to Continue ...");
  // Wait for keypress
  getch();
  closegraph();
  return 0;
}
```

The first two calls to **outtext()** display two separate strings that form the top-left sentence on the screen. Since TEXTTEST uses the default justification setting, **outtext()** updates the current position after each call. As a result, the two strings are displayed next to each other.

The next statement calls **outtextxy()** to display a string originating at the middle of the screen. The **getmaxx()** and **getmaxy()** functions retrieve the

---

Figure 3.4 This is the output of the TEXTTEST program.

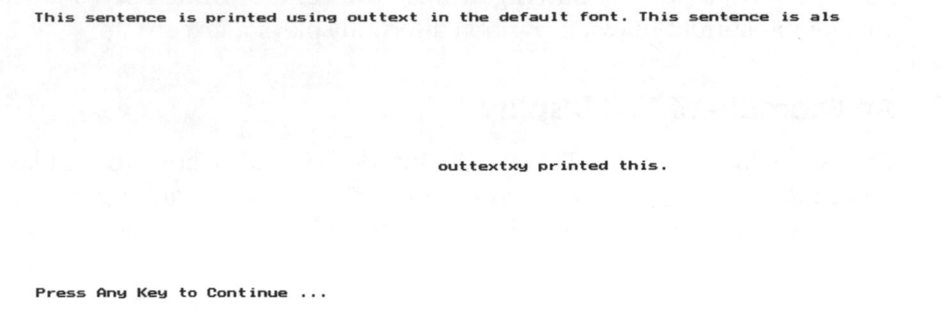

```
This sentence is printed using outtext in the default font. This sentence is als




                            outtextxy printed this.




   Press Any Key to Continue ...
```

---

width of the screen and are used to calculate the screen midpoint. Following this is a call to **outtext( )**. Since **outtextxy( )** does not update the current drawing position, note that its string is displayed after the last string printed by **outtext( )** and not after the string printed by **outtextxy( )**. Finally, the program calls **outtextxy( )** to display a status line at the bottom-left corner of the screen, telling you to press any key to continue.

How Turbo C++ Accesses Fonts

Unlike the default bitmapped characters, the stroke fonts are not built into every graphics program. In addition, only one of the stroke fonts is normally available in memory at one time while your program is running. Turbo C++ does this to avoid excessive use of memory, but it has several implications.

First, each stroke font is stored in a separate font file. These files, listed in Table 3.2, are included with your Turbo C++ disks and end with a .CHR extension. The font files include the strokes required to draw each letter for the various font styles. The stroke sequences for the triplex font, for instance, are in the file TRIP.CHR.

Table 3.2 The BGI Stroke Font Files

Filename	Description
BOLD.CHR	Characters are shown as outlines
EURO.CHR	A European-style font
GOTH.CHR	A stroked gothic font
LCOMP.CHR	A more complex appearing font
LITT.CHR	A stroked font of small characters
SANS.CHR	A stroked sans serif font

continued

Table 3.2 The BGI Stroke Font Files (Continued)

Filename	Description
SCRI.CHR	A script font
SIMP.CHR	A font with simple stroke patterns
TRIP.CHR	A stroked triplex font
TSCR.CHR	An italics version of the triplex font

If you plan to use the stroke fonts, the stroke font files must be accessible to your program at runtime. If they are not accessible, an error will occur. In addition, if you use more than one stroke font, the program must have access to the stroke files each time a different font style is selected. Alternatively, you can link the font file directly into your program's executable file as outlined in the sidebar *Loading Fonts and Drivers Using the Linking Method*.

Selecting and Loading a Font

To use one of the stroke fonts, you must explicitly select one of the font styles by calling the **settextstyle( )** function. Its function prototype is:

```
void far settextstyle(int font, int direction, int charsize);
```

The **font** argument is a numeric value that specifies the font type to be loaded. Table 3.3 shows the enumerated values used in GRAPHICS.H to represent the codes for the font files.

Table 3.3 BGI Stroke Font Codes

Constant	Value
DEFAULT_FONT	0
TRIPLEX_FONT	1
SMALL_FONT	2
SANS_SERIF_FONT	3
GOTHIC_FONT	4
SCRIPT_FONT	5
SIMPLEX_FONT	6
TRIPLEX_SCR_FONT	7
COMPLEX_FONT	8
EUROPEAN_FONT	9
BOLD_FONT	10

The second argument, **direction**, specifies whether the text should be written horizontally or vertically. Table 3.4 shows the valid values defined in GRAPHICS.H that can be used for **direction**.

The last argument, **charsize**, specifies the character magnification factor that **outtext( )** or **outtextxy( )** should use when displaying text. You can set

Table 3.4 Font Orientation Constants

Constant	Value
HORIZ_DIR	0
VERT_DIR	1

LOADING FONTS AND DRIVERS USING THE LINKING METHOD

In this chapter, we mentioned that calls to **settextstyle()** cause a font file to be loaded that corresponds to the font selected. Similarly, in Chapter 1, we explained that a graphics hardware driver is loaded in response to **initgraph()**. In both cases, when the appropriate driver is loaded, memory is allocated for the driver, and the appropriate .BGI or .CHR file is loaded from the disk. Unfortunately, this process has two disadvantages: it slows down the execution of a graphics program and, if the program is designed to run on other systems, you must ensure that the appropriate driver files are available on the new system. Fortunately, there's a trick you can use to get around this problem: link the graphics drivers and font drivers into your executable program. Turbo C++ provides the BGIOBJ utility for converting driver files into .OBJ files so that you can link them into a program. To convert a file, you simply call BGIOBJ using the following syntax:

```
bgiobj <driver filename>
```

Once the object files are created, you can add them to the list of files in your project file. For example, to link the EGAVGA.BGI driver into your program, you would first create an object version of the driver

```
bgiobj egavga
```

and then add the file it creates, EGAVGA.OBJ, to your project file using the Project | Add item menu options within Turbo C++'s integrated environment.

The final step is to register the drivers in your graphics program using the **registerbgidriver( )** and **registerbgifont( )** functions. Note that these functions require that you pass them a symbolic name that corresponds to

this argument to any integer value from 0 to 10. The effects of these various values in **charsize** will be discussed shortly.

Let's look at a few examples of how **settextstyle( )** is called. The following sample statement loads the gothic stroke font file, defines the direction flag so that all text is written horizontally, and sets the character magnification to a factor of 4:

```
settextstyle(GOTHIC_FONT, HORIZ_DIR, 4);
```

This next function call selects the triplex font, forces all text to be displayed vertically, and sets the character size to its largest value, 10:

```
settextstyle(TRIPLEX_FONT, VERT_DIR, 10);
```

the driver or font file being loaded (EGAVGA_driver for the EGAVGA.BGI, small_font for LITT.CHR, and so on). The BGIOBJ utility will display the symbolic name to use for the standard Borland .BGI files. A list of these symbolic names is also included in GRAPHICS.H. You can use the following program to try linking the EGAVGA.BGI graphics driver and the small font in LITT.CHR to an application.

```
// TESTREG.CPP: Shows how to register graphics drivers and font files.
#include <stdlib.h>
#include <conio.h>
#include <graphics.h>
main()
{
  int graphmode, graphdriver = DETECT;

  if (registerbgidriver(EGAVGA_driver) < 0) exit(1);  // Register
  if (registerbgifont(small_font) < 0) exit(1);        // drivers first
  initgraph(&graphdriver, &graphmode, "");
  settextstyle(SMALL_FONT, HORIZ_DIR, 4); // Select the registered font
  outtextxy(100, 100, "Text is displayed using the small font");
  getch();
  closegraph();
  return 0;
}
```

To build this example, you must first use the BIGOBJ utility to convert EGAVGA.BGI and LITT.CHR as outlined earlier. Then, you must compile and link the code using a project file that lists the three files—TESTREG.CPP, EGAVGA.OBJ, and LITT.OBJ. Once the program is built you can run it on any EGA- or VGA-supporting machine without worrying about copying over the proper BGI driver or the small font file.

Errors in Loading a Font

If a requested font file cannot be found or loaded, the BGI sets an internal error flag. You can call **graphresult( )** to determine what the status of this error flag is. The possible error conditions are listed in Table 3.5.

You can use the following function to change the currently selected font, as well as trap for any errors if they occur. If there is a problem, the routine calls **grapherrormsg( )** to print out the reason for the error and the program terminates. The **graphresult( )** function returns a value of **grOk** if no error occurs in **settextstyle( )**. The **grOk** constant is an enumerated value defined in GRAPHICS.H as 0.

```
void changetextstyle(int font, int direction, int charsize)
{
  int errornum;

  settextstyle(font, direction, charsize);
  if ((errornum=graphresult()) != grOk) {
    closegraph();
    printf("Graphics Error: %s\n", grapherrormsg(errornum));
    exit(1);
  }
}
```

CREATING CUSTOM FONTS

Now that we've covered the basics of how to use the built-in stroke fonts, let's take a slight detour and examine how we can create our own custom stroke fonts. Creating a new font is a lot easier than you might first think, especially because Borland has developed a special stroke font editor called FE.EXE. Although this utility does not come with Turbo C++, you can obtain it by downloading it from a network, such as CompuServe. (The font editor is

Table 3.5 Possible Errors when Loading a Font File

Constant	Return Value	Description
grFontNotFound	-8	Font file not found
grNoFontMem	-9	Not enough memory to load font
grError	-11	General error condition
grIOError	-12	Graphics input/output error
grInvalidFont	-13	Invalid font file
grInvalidFontNum	-14	Invalid font number

stored in the file BGI.ARC, which is in the Lib0 section of the Borland forum BPROGB. To get to this forum, type GO BPROGB.) We are also including this utility with our code disks, which you can obtain by using the order form in the back of this book.

The font editor allows you to interactively edit and create .CHR font files. You can also preview characters on the screen and send your output to a plotter such as an HP 7470. To run this utility, you'll need to be sure that you have a mouse installed and that your system is equipped with EGA or VGA display hardware. After you call up the font editor by typing in the filename FE, the screen shown in Figure 3.5 is displayed. Here, you must type in the name of an existing stroke font file, such as SANS.CHR, or the name of a new file. After the filename is entered, the screen will change to the one shown in Figure 3.6. Note that the editor is divided into three main sections: a main menu bar that provides the basic editing and file management commands, a font-drawing grid, and a character selection table that you use to select the active character for editing.

To edit or create a character, you simply select the desired character from the table, and then use the mouse with the drawing grid to edit or create the character. To draw a character, you must use straight-line segments, which the editor calls strokes. The editor does not support arcs or circles. When drawing strokes in the grid, remember that your strokes are shown in a magnified format. The character that you are drawing is shown at its actual size directly below the character selection table.

Figure 3.5 This figure shows the font editor's opening screen.

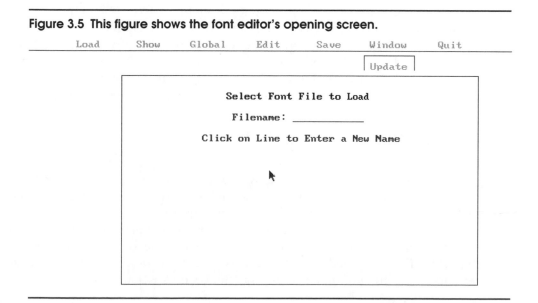

Figure 3.6 Use this screen to edit a font.

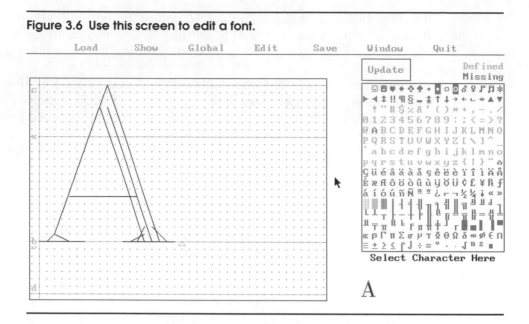

Working with the Font Editor's Menu Options

You can select each of the main menu options—Load, Show, Global, Edit, Save, Window, and Quit—by positioning the mouse cursor on the option name and clicking the right mouse button. Some of the options, such as Load, perform a simple action, and other options will bring up a submenu containing a new set of menu options. For example, when you select the Edit option, the menu bar changes and the options CopyChar, Flip, Shift, ShowAlso, ClipBoard, and Exit, are displayed. (Note that whenever you are working with a submenu, you can select the Exit option to take you back to the main menu.) Table 3.6 summarizes the basic commands performed by the main menu options.

Working with the Drawing Grid

The trickiest part about creating characters is learning how to use the drawing grid. With the drawing grid, you can add and delete strokes, and copy, flip, and move characters. Before we get into the techniques of drawing characters, we'll explore the components of the drawing grid.

Figure 3.7 shows the grid with its key components labeled. Note that the grid contains four horizontal lines that represent the different heights of a character. The line used as the origin is called the *base height*. This height defaults to a setting of 0 and represents the base of a character.

Table 3.6 The Font Editor's Menu Options

Command	Description
Load	Loads in a new or existing stroke font file
Show	Displays all the characters that have been created with the font editor; you can also use this option to plot your characters
Global	Allows you to set the left, right, and baseline spacings for the entire character set; an option is also included for copying characters from a different font file
Edit	Provides a number of editing options, including copying, flipping, and shifting
Save	Saves the work created in the editor to a .CHR stroke font file
Window	Provides a set of options for controlling the character editing window
Quit	Terminates the editor

Some characters, such as the lowercase letter *p*, contain a *descender*. In the case of the letter *p*, the descender is the stem that extends below the circle. On the drawing grid, the horizontal line labeled with the letter *d* represents the *descender height*. The line that is directly above the base height is the *lowercase height*. This line, which is labeled with an *x*, represents the height of each lowercase letter in a character set. Finally, the last line, which is labeled with a *c*, is the *capital height* because it represents the height of a capital letter.

When you draw characters, you should use the horizontal height markers as your guidelines. For example, if you want all the capital letters in a set to

Figure 3.7 Use the character drawing grid in the font editor to create your own stroke font characters.

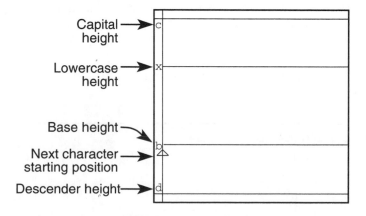

look uniform, make sure you start them at the base height and use the capital height as the top point of each character. The small triangle that intersects the base height serves as a marker to indicate where the next character will start. After you draw a character, you should make sure that you move the triangle by clicking it and dragging it to the right so that a space will be placed after the character you are drawing and the next character in the alphabet.

The four horizontal dimensions we've just discussed are assigned a default setting when you start the font editor (base height = 0, descender height = -7, lowercase height = 20, capital height = 40). Because these dimensions are determined using the base dimensions of the characters M, q, and x, you can change their settings by calling up the font editor, drawing these characters, and saving them. The next time the font is loaded, these new character dimensions will be used.

Once your dimensions are set, you can draw the strokes for each character by clicking and dragging the mouse. The editor uses a "rubber banding" technique for drawing lines. To erase a line, you simply draw over a line. If you start to draw a line and then you don't like how it looks, move the mouse cursor outside the drawing grid and the line will go away.

WORKING WITH TEXT JUSTIFICATION

The BGI provides a handful of text justification settings that you can use to format your graphics text output. The **outtext( )** and **outtextxy( )** functions use these settings to determine where to locate their text relative to the current drawing position. By default, text is left justified and displayed below the current position. You can modify these settings by calling the **settextjustify( )** function. Its function prototype is:

```
void far settextjustify(int horiz, int vert);
```

The first argument, **horiz**, sets the horizontal justification style. You can set it to one of the values listed in Table 3.7.

Similarly, the **vert** argument specifies the vertical justification. Its range of values is shown in Table 3.8.

Figures 3.8 and 3.9 display a set of strings using a combination of the BGI's justification settings.

Table 3.7 Horizontal Justification Values

Constant	Value
LEFT_TEXT	0
CENTER_TEXT	1
RIGHT_TEXT	2

Table 3.8 Vertical Justification Values

Constant	Value
BOTTOM_TEXT	0
CENTER_TEXT	1
TOP_TEXT	2

Figure 3.8 These are examples of horizontal text justifications.

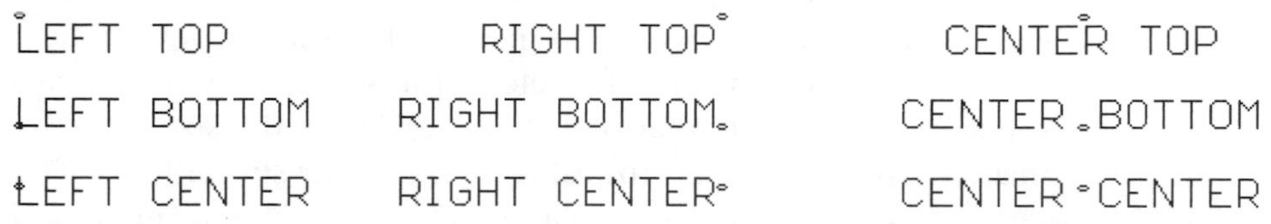

Figure 3.9 These are examples of vertical text justifications.

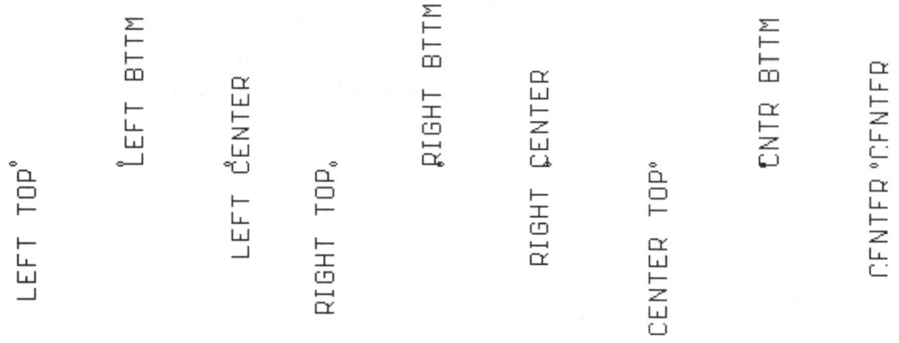

Determining the Current Text Settings

Turbo C++ provides the function **gettextsettings( )** to retrieve the current text settings. This function is particularly useful when you need to temporarily change the text style and later restore it. The function prototype for **gettextsettings( )** is:

```
void far gettextsettings(struct textsettingstype far *textinfo);
```

The function passes its information back to the caller in a special data structure named **textsettingstype**. You'll find this structure defined in the file GRAPHICS.H as:

```
struct textsettingstype {
  int font;
  int direction;
  int charsize;
  int horiz;
  int vert;
};
```

The component **font** contains the numeric code for the active font style. The second component, **direction**, indicates whether the current text is displayed in a horizontal or vertical direction. Moving down the list, the **charsize** component stores the magnification factor used to scale any text that is displayed.

The scale factor will be covered in greater detail later; but briefly, it can range from 0 to 10 where a value of 1 selects the standard size for bitmapped characters (8 x 8), 2 dictates bitmapped characters twice the size (16 x 16), and so on. Similarly, larger values of **charsize** create larger stroke font characters. A **charsize** of 0 is reserved for stroke fonts only and is used to select a secondary form of character magnification that we'll also discuss later. Finally, the last two components, **horiz** and **vert**, define the justification attributes used for displaying text in the horizontal and vertical directions.

Recapping, a call to **gettextsettings( )** will retrieve the font style, the direction flag, the character magnification, and the text justification settings and store this information in the **textsettingstype** structure. The following lines of code, for example, save the text settings, change them, and then restore the text specifications.

```
// Declare a structure to save the settings in
struct textsettingstype oldtext;

// Previous code ...
gettextsettings(&oldtext);

// Change the text settings here
settextstyle(oldtext.font, oldtext.direction, oldtext.charsize);
settextjustify(oldtext.horiz, oldtext.vert);

// Rest of the code ...
```

Determining Character Dimensions

Because the BGI allows you to magnify characters, it is necessary to be able to determine the actual pixel sizes of any text written to the screen. This is particularly important when you are trying to align text or enclose a text string within a window. The BGI provides two functions to determine the text dimensions of a string. These functions are:

```
int far textheight(char far *string);
int far textwidth(char far *string);
```

Figure 3.10 This figure shows the increasing magnification of a bitmapped character.

Individually, these functions return the height and width in pixels of the character string when it is displayed on the screen.

The values returned by these functions are always determined with respect to the orientation of the characters and not the screen axes. In other words, the **textheight()** and **textwidth()** functions return the same values whether the text is displayed horizontally or vertically.

A bitmapped character (remember that they are derived from an 8 x 8 bit pattern) with the default character magnification of 1, has a text width of 8 pixels. Similarly, its height is also 8 pixels. To understand the effects that magnification has on the dimensions of a bitmapped character refer to Figure 3.10. This figure shows the dimensions of the letter *A* with magnifications of 1 through 10 times the default size.

A Note about Vertical Character Dimensions

Although **textheight()** and **textwidth()** operate similarly whether text is written horizontally or vertically, they may confuse you when you are writing code. The thing to remember is that these functions return pixel dimensions that are oriented with respect to the character strings. For example, when a string is displayed horizontally, **textwidth()** returns the number of pixel columns that the text spans. However, when the text is displayed vertically, **textwidth()** returns the number of pixel rows that the text stretches across. You will need to be careful with **textwidth()** and **textheight()** when writing functions that are designed to handle horizontal and vertical text equally.

MAGNIFYING CHARACTERS

The BGI provides two methods for altering the size of text output. The approach to use depends on whether you are displaying bitmapped or stroke fonts.

The simplest way to customize the size of text is by altering the **charsize** field in the **textsettingstype** structure introduced earlier. You can set the **charsize** component by calling the **settextstyle( )** function. Remember, it defines the scale factor that the BGI applies to all text displayed by **outtext( )** and **outtextxy( )** and can range from 0 to 10. If the **charsize** value is between 1 and 10, it will affect both the default bitmapped characters and the stroke fonts. In the case of bitmapped characters, a **charsize** of 1 produces characters the default size of 8 x 8. Bitmapped text written with a **charsize** of 2 are twice as big as the default size (16 x 16), and so on up to a **charsize** of 10, which produces characters 80 x 80 in size.

The larger values of **charsize** also serve to magnify the stroke fonts, although they do not always generate characters of the same size as the bitmapped characters. Figure 3.11 shows each of the stroke fonts and the default font using the **charsize**s of 1, 2, 3, and 4.

The one remaining value of **charsize**, 0, is reserved exclusively for stroke fonts. If you set **charsize** to 0, you need to call **setusercharsize( )** and set a second group of scale factors. These additional parameters allow finer control over the stroke fonts so that you can adjust the height and width of the text independently. For instance, you can use the scale factors in **setusercharsize( )** to precisely fit a text string to a rectangular window.

The GRAPHICS.H header file prototypes **setusercharsize( )** as

```
void far setusercharsize(int multx, int divx, int multy, int divy);
```

where the four arguments represent the scale factors to be applied to the default size of the text displayed (which is a **charsize** of 4 for the stroke fonts).

Figure 3.11 Several BGI fonts using the charsize of 1, 2, 3, and 4.

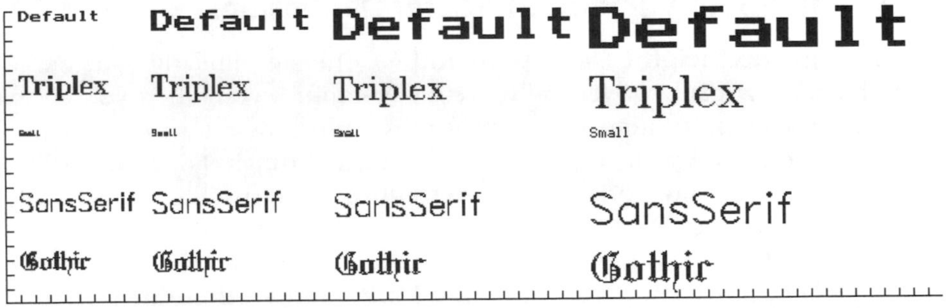

Figure 3.12 Scale factors influence stroke fonts.

The first two arguments indicate the amount that the text is to be stretched or compressed in the horizontal direction. These arguments work as a pair. It is the ratio of these values that define the scale factor that is applied. For example, to double the width of all text, **multx** can be set to 2 and **divx** to 1. Similarly, to reduce the height of all text to one third its default height, we can set **multy** to 1 and **divy** to 3. These numbers can take on any ratio of integers up to the screen width of the graphics mode you are using. Therefore, in the VGA high-resolution mode (640 x 480), the ratio **multx/divx** cannot exceed 639, and, similarly, the ratio **multy/divy** cannot be larger than 479. Figure 3.12 shows how the scale factor ratios influence the proportions of a stroke font character.

You should be aware that when using vertical text, the four arguments of **setusercharsize( )** are relative to the text displayed and not the screen. Therefore, changing **multx** and **divx** when the text is vertical will change the number of rows that the text stretches across.

Fitting Text inside a Box

Let's now see how we can scale a stroke font text string so that it fits into a rectangular region. The program presented in this section, AUTOSCAL.CPP, automatically scales a string within several different sized rectangles, as shown in Figure 3.13. This program is worth looking over because of its use of the **setusercharsize( )** function.

The program includes two functions, **scaletext( )** and **scaleverttext( )**. The first function scales the text so that it fits horizontally into the window specified in its arguments. The latter function operates in the same manner with the exception that it places the text vertically in the window.

In each function, the arguments **left**, **top**, **right**, and **bottom** specify the bounds of the region in which the text is to be displayed. The **string** array contains the text to display.

Figure 3.13 Scaling text strings to fit inside a rectangle—output of AUTOSCAL.CPP.

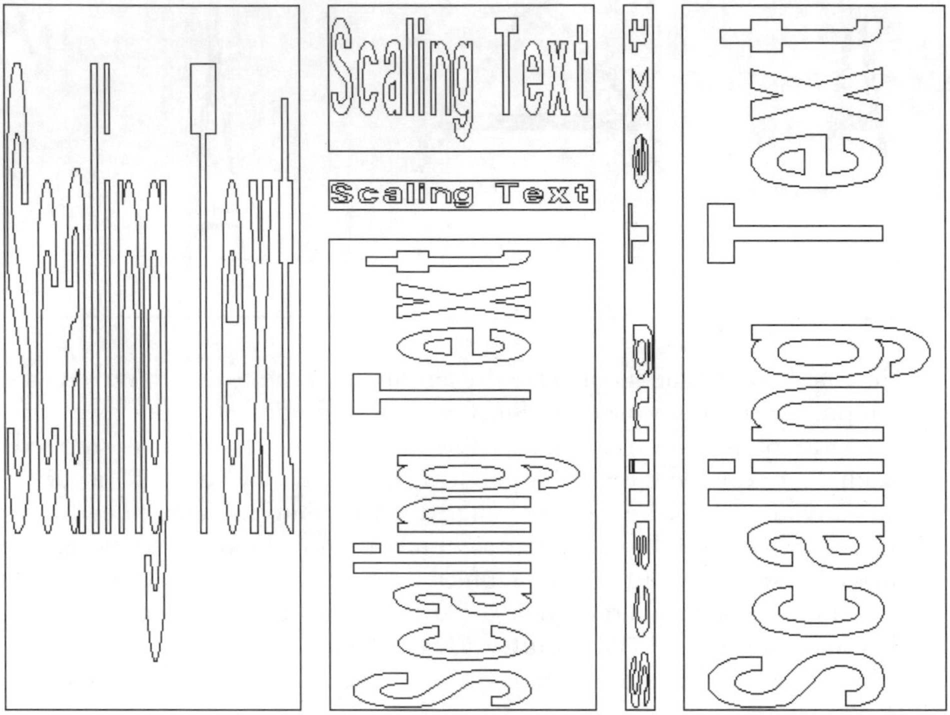

The following statements call **setusercharsize( )** to scale the text string so that it fits inside the specified window:

```
setusercharsize(1, 1, 1, 1);
settextstyle(font, HORIZ_DIR, USER_CHAR_SIZE);
// Note the order of the box coordinates. Compare them with the
// ordering for vertical text.
setusercharsize(right-left, textwidth(string),
  bottom-top, textheight(string));
```

Why are there two calls to **setusercharsize( )** here? Let's start with the second one. As mentioned before, the ratios of the arguments in **setusercharsize( )** define the scale factors applied to the text string. Since we want the text to stretch across the window, we can set **multx** to **right-left** and **divx** to the length of the string. Actually, we need to ensure the length of the string is calculated using the default text magnification, not the current settings, so this explains the earlier use of:

```
setusercharsize(1, 1, 1, 1);
```

Both of the functions center the text in both the horizontal and vertical directions using the statement:

```
settextjustify(CENTER_TEXT, CENTER_TEXT);
```

Here is the complete program:

```
// AUTOSCAL.CPP: Given a box of a particular size, this program
// scales a text string to fit within it. The scaling routines
// guarantee that the text string will fit in the box, but they
// don't guarantee that the text will look good or that it will be
// readable, which can happen if the box is too small for the text.
#include <graphics.h>
#include <conio.h>

// Scales horizontal text to fit in a rectangular region
void scaletext(int left, int top, int right, int bottom,
  int font, char *string)
{
  // Reset usercharsize to all 1s, so that the textwidth, textheight
  // functions will return the number of pixels on the screen that the
  // default font size uses, not the current size, whatever it may be.
  setusercharsize(1, 1, 1, 1);
  settextstyle(font, HORIZ_DIR, USER_CHAR_SIZE);

  // Note the order of the box coordinates. Compare with the ordering
  // for vertical text.
  setusercharsize(right-left, textwidth(string),
    bottom-top, textheight(string));
  settextjustify(CENTER_TEXT, CENTER_TEXT);

  // Clear screen and draw a box where text is to be displayed
  setfillstyle(SOLID_FILL, getbkcolor());
  bar3d(left, top, right, bottom, 0, 0);

  // Write text string centered in the box
  outtextxy((right+left)/2+1, (bottom+top)/2-textheight(string)/4, string);
}

// Scales vertical text to fit in a box
void scaleverttext(int left, int top, int right, int bottom,
  int font, char *string)
{
  // Reset usercharsize to all 1s, so that the textwidth, textheight
  // functions will return the number of pixels on the screen that the
  // default font size uses, not the current size, whatever it may be.
  setusercharsize(1, 1, 1, 1);
  settextstyle(font, VERT_DIR, USER_CHAR_SIZE);
  setusercharsize(bottom-top, textwidth(string),
    right-left, textheight(string));
  settextjustify(CENTER_TEXT, CENTER_TEXT);
```

```
  // Clear screen and draw a box where text is to be displayed
  setfillstyle(SOLID_FILL, getbkcolor());
  bar3d(left, top, right, bottom, 0, 0);
  // Write string centered in the box
  outtextxy((right+left)/2-textheight(string)/4, (bottom+top)/2-1, string);
}

main()
{
  int gmode, gdriver = DETECT;
  char string[] = "Scaling Text";

  initgraph(&gdriver, &gmode, "\\tcpp\\bgi");
  scaletext(0, 0, 200, getmaxy(), BOLD_FONT, string);
  scaletext(220, 0, 400, 100, BOLD_FONT, string);
  scaletext(220, 120, 400, 140, BOLD_FONT, string);
  scaleverttext(220, 160, 400, getmaxy(), BOLD_FONT, string);
  scaleverttext(420, 0, 440, getmaxy(), BOLD_FONT, string);
  scaleverttext(460, 0, getmaxx(), getmaxy(), BOLD_FONT, string);
  getch();
  closegraph();
  return 0;
}
```

A Note on Clipping Text

Although the BGI supports clipping for both bitmapped and stroke fonts, the two are handled slightly differently. If clipping is set for the current viewport, a bitmapped character will be completely clipped if any portion of it extends beyond the borders of the viewport. However, a stroke font character will have only that portion of the character that extends beyond the viewport. Figure 3.14 shows two text strings that are clipped to the viewport outlined by a rectangle. The top string is a bitmapped text string and the bottom one is a stroke font. Notice how the two strings are clipped differently.

Figure 3.14 Bitmapped and stroke fonts are clipped differently.

ROTATING TEXT

The BGI only provides a limited set of text rotation capabilities. You can display the text horizontally or vertically. However, there are many graphics applications where you need the ability to display text at any angle. This section describes a simple, albeit non-standard, way of rotating stroke font text. The idea is to read a stroke font file directly and display the strokes manually. As we draw the strokes on the screen, we'll rotate them to a desired angle. The program ROTTEXT.CPP, listed at the end of this section, does just this. It displays the string "Hello" in four different orientations, as shown in Figure 3.15. The program is hard-coded to use the SANS.CHR font; however, with minor modifications you could use the same technique with any of the stroke fonts.

Of course, in order to use this technique we have to be able to read and process the stroke font files. It turns out that this isn't too diffucult to do. We won't go into the intricate details of the font files here, but it is necessary to understand how the files are organized in order to be able to follow the ROTTEXT.CPP program. (You can find additional imformation on the format of font files in Borland's programming forums The ROTTEXT.CPP program, in fact, is based on a font dump utiltity, DUMP.C, available on CompuServe.)

For our purposes, it's important to realize that a font file consists of several blocks of information. At the beginning of the file is a header containing information about the number of characters in the file, where the stroke sequences begin, and so on. Toward the end of the file is the actual stroke font information, which is divided into two pieces. First, there is the stroke information itself. The strokes are encoded in a small four opcode command set. The commands tell the font display routine whether it should move the current position, draw a new line, and so on. We'll process these commands ourselves in order to rotate and display the stroke lines. The other part of the font data is a lookup table that specifies where each character's stroke sequence begins.

Figure 3.15 The ROTTEXT.CPP program shows how to rotate stroke font text.

The **main( )** function reads these two blocks of information into the **Font** and **Offset** data structures, respectively.

The **rotateouttext( )** function is a high-level routine that ROTTEXT provides to display a rotated text string. It calls **drawtext( )** to draw each character to the screen. This is where you'll find the code that actually rotates and displays the text. In Chapter 5, we'll explain the math behind the equations we're using here.

There are no special steps to compile the ROTTEXT.CPP program. You will, however, need to copy the SANS.CHR stroke font file into the same directory as the executable in order to run the program. Here's the complete ROTTEXT.CPP program:

```
// ROTTEXT.CPP: Demonstrates a technique for rotating stroke fonts.
// This program reads a font file directly and draws the rotated
// strokes for each character manually. This program is based on
// the DFONT.C program (DUMP FONT utility) available in Borland's
// CompuServe forum. The SANS.CHR font is used. The font file is
// assumed to be in the current directory.
#include <stdio.h>
#include <stdlib.h>
#include <conio.h>
#include <graphics.h>
#include <math.h>
#include <dos.h>

#define Prefix_Size 0x80    // The size of the prefix header
#define Major_Version 1     // The font file's version
#define Minor_Version 0
#define ID '+'              // Identifying character in a font file

enum OPCODES {              // The four encoded commands that are
    END_OF_CHAR = 0,        // used in a stroke font file to tell
    DO_SCAN =  1,           // how to draw a character
    MOVE = 2,
    DRAW = 3
    };

typedef struct {            // The header of a stroke font file
    char id;                // Identifying byte in a file
    int nchrs;              // Number of characters in file
    char undefined;         // Undefined
    char first;             // First character in file
    int cdefs;              // Offset to chararacter definitions
    char scan_flag;         // 1 if set is scanable
    char org_to_cap;        // Height from origin to top of capitol
    char org_to_base;       // Height from origin to baseline
    char org_to_dec;        // Height from origin to bottom of decender
    char fntname[4];        // Four character name of font
    char unused;            // Not used
} HEADER;
```

```
typedef struct {
  char opcode;              // Stroke opcode command
  int x;                    // Relative offset in x direction
  int y;                    // Relative offset in y direction
} STROKE;

typedef struct {
  unsigned int header_size;            // Version 2.0 header format
  unsigned char font_name[4];          // Internal font
  unsigned int font_size;              // Size of file (in bytes)
  unsigned char font_major, font_minor; // Driver version
  unsigned char min_major, min_minor;   // BGI version
} FHEADER;

const NUMROTINC = 4; // Sweep the text this many increments in 360 degrees

FILE *fp;                 // Font file
char *Font;               // Pointer to font storage
char Prefix[Prefix_Size]; // File prefix
HEADER Header;            // File header
int Offset[256];          // Font data offsets
int px, py;               // Text pivot point
double rot=0;             // The amount to rotate text--in radians
double costheta, sintheta; // Precomputed cos & sin values for rotation
                          // This helps to speed things up
// Decodes a single word in file to a stroke record
int decode(unsigned int *iptr, int& x, int& y)
{
  struct DECODE {
    int xoff : 7;
    unsigned int flag1 : 1;
    int yoff : 7;
    unsigned int flag2 : 1;
  } cword;

  cword = *(DECODE *)iptr;

  x = cword.xoff;
  y = cword.yoff;

  return (cword.flag1 << 1) + cword.flag2;
}


// Reads the stroke commands for the specified letter and displays
// that character on the screen. Note: You'll probably want to adjust
// for the aspect ratio of the screen. The variables are:
//    buf is a buffer that holds the font file data
//    index is the location in the buffer where the information
//      about the character to display is stored
//    x, y is the updated current position
void drawtext(char *buf, int index, int& x, int& y)
{
  unsigned int *pb;
  int num_ops = 0;
```

```
  int jx, jy, opcode;
  int cx=0, cy = 0;
  int xr, yr;

  pb = (unsigned int *)(buf + index); // Reset pointer to buffer

  while(1) {                          // For each byte in buffer
    num_ops += 1;                     // Count the operation
    opcode = decode(pb++, jx, jy);    // Decode the data record
    switch(opcode) {
      case END_OF_CHAR:               // End of character's strokes
        x = cx*costheta - cy*sintheta;
        y = -(cx*sintheta + cy*costheta);
        return;
      case DO_SCAN:                   // Just skip this
        break;
      case MOVE:                      // Move to this point
        cx = jx;    cy = jy;
        xr = jx*costheta - jy*sintheta;
        yr = jx*sintheta + jy*costheta;
        moveto(xr+px, py-yr);
        break;
      case DRAW:                      // Draw to this point
        cx = jx;    cy = jy;
        xr = jx*costheta - jy*sintheta;
        yr = jx*sintheta + jy*costheta;
        lineto(px+xr, py-yr);
        break;
    }
  }
}

// Main routine to display rotated text. Call settextrotation() to
// set the angle to display the text string.
void rotateouttext(char *str)
{
  int i, x, y;

  for (i=0; *(str+i) != '\0'; i++) {
    drawtext(Font, Offset[*(str+i)], x, y);
    px += x;  py += y;
  }
}

// Call this function to set the rotation angle. "angle" should
// be given in radians. The function saves the cos and sin of the
// angle so that these values don't have to be recomputed
// each time rotateouttext() is called. Zero degrees is at the
// 3 o'clock position and the angles increase counterclockwise.
void settextrotation(double angle)
{
  costheta = cos(angle);
  sintheta = sin(angle);
  rot = angle;
```

```
      }

      int main()
      {
        long length, current;                    // Font file locations
        int i, gmode, gdriver = DETECT;

        if ((fp=fopen("SANS.CHR", "rb")) == NULL) {  // Open the font file
          printf("Can't open SANS.CHR font file\n");
          exit(1);
        }

        initgraph(&gdriver, &gmode, "\\tcpp\\bgi"); // Initialize graphics

        fread(Prefix, Prefix_Size, 1, fp);       // Read the file prefix record
        fread(&Header, sizeof(HEADER), 1, fp);   // Read the header
        // Read the character offsets into the Offset array
        fread(&Offset[Header.first], Header.nchrs, sizeof(int), fp);
        // Skip past the character width table
        fseek(fp, Header.nchrs, SEEK_CUR);

        current = ftell(fp);        // Determine the size of
        fseek(fp, 0, SEEK_END);     // the stroke information, which
        length = ftell(fp);         // extends to the end of the file.
        fseek(fp, current, SEEK_SET); // Return to the start of the stroke data

        Font = (char *)malloc((int)length); // Allocate memory for the font data
        if (NULL == Font) {
          closegraph();
          printf("Not enough memory to load font\n");
          exit(1);
        }

        fread(Font, (int)length, 1, fp); // Read the stroke sequences

        circle(200, 100, 3);             // Rotate the text about this point
        for (i=0; i<NUMROTINC; i++) {
          // Set the angle of the text. Offset it by 45 degrees.
          settextrotation((M_PI * 2) / NUMROTINC * i + M_PI / 4);
          px = 200;  py = 100;
          rotateouttext("Hello");
          px = 200;  py = 100;
        }

        getch();
        closegraph();
        return 0;
      }
```

DISPLAYING CHARACTERS AND NUMBERS

Thus far we have only talked about writing text strings to a graphics screen. You may be wondering how you can display numeric values and the like in graphics mode. After all, **outtext()** and **outtextxy()** can only display text strings. The trick is to convert all values you want to display into ASCII strings and then display these strings through calls to **outtext()** and **outtextxy()**.

There are several ways to convert a numeric value to a character string, but probably the best way is through the C++ library function, **sprintf()**. Briefly, this function works much like **printf()**, except that the text is not written to the screen, but instead is copied to its first argument, which is a string. For example, the following section of code converts the value stored in the integer variable **x** to a character string and prints the result.

```
int x;
char buffer[80];
// ... other code ...
x = 10;
sprintf(buffer, "The value of x is %d", x);
printf("%s", buffer);
// ... other code ...
```

If you were to execute this excerpt of code, you'd see the string "The value of x is 10" on the screen. Of course, sprinkling your code with **sprintf()** statements every time you want to display a numeric value can become cumbersome. A better approach is to develop a **printf()** function that will work in graphics mode. This is exactly what we'll do in the next section.

EXTENDED TEXT MANIPULATION ROUTINES

Although the BGI text manipulation routines have great power, they lack several capabilities that need to be added in order to simplify our graphics programming tasks. For example, we need text output routines in graphics mode that have the versatility of the **printf()** function and input routines that operate like their counterparts in text mode.

In the next several sections, we'll develop a set of enhanced text routines that we'll be using throughout the rest of this book. These routines are packaged in the files GTEXT.H and GTEXT.CPP, which are listed at the end of this chapter. A list of the functions included in GTEXT.CPP is shown in Table 3.9.

A Graphics Version of printf()

At first glance, both **outtext()** and **outtextxy()** seem adequate for applications that manipulate text in graphics mode, but their limitations become apparent when we compare them to the versatile **printf()**. In this section, we'll develop a custom **printf()** function that works in graphics mode and is able to support the various features of the BGI. This function is called **gprintf()** and is included in GTEXT.CPP.

Table 3.9 Functions in GTEXT.CPP

Function	Description
gprintf()	Graphics text display routine that mimics printf()
gprintfxy()	Graphics printf() function that displays text at the location (x,y)
ggetche()	Gets a character and echoes it to the screen
ggets()	Allows user to enter a string while in graphics mode
gputch()	Puts a character on the graphics screen
gscanf()	Mimics scanf() function for graphics mode
gscanfxy()	Accepts user input at location (x,y)
readstring()	A text entry routine that supports the cursor and editing keys
settextbkcolor()	Sets the background color to be used with the text
settextcolor()	Sets the color of the text

The greatest difficulty in creating a function that mimics **printf()** comes from the fact that the routine will have to be able to process a variable number of arguments. Fortunately, Turbo C++ provides useful tools for such a situation. These tools include several library functions that are able to automatically process a format string like the one in **printf()** in conjunction with a variable number of arguments. Because you may not be an expert in using the variable length argument processing functions provided with Turbo C++, we'll go through our new graphics **printf()** in more detail.

Programming for variable length arguments is a must when you do not know how many arguments are going to be passed to a function. The function **printf()** encounters and handles this problem. Since our function **gprintf()** is mimicking **printf()**, we must incorporate this feature too. In writing our custom **printf()** routine, the first thing we must do is tell the compiler that the routine will be expecting a variable number of arguments. This is accomplished with the three dot notation in our **gprintf()** formal parameter list:

```
int gprintf(char *fmt, ...);
```

More specifically, this line tells the compiler to expect a format string followed by zero or more arguments. Of course, each of these additional arguments will correspond to a variable specified in the format string. The Turbo C++ compiler has built-in code to match up the variable number of arguments with the format string. We'll encounter these in a moment.

To extract the arguments from the function call at runtime, Turbo C++ provides the functions **va_start()** and **va_end()**. Both functions are prototyped in the header file STDARG.H and are used to initiate and terminate the extraction of the arguments from the stack. The function **va_start( )** returns a pointer to the first variable argument that appears on the stack. It returns a pointer to this location in **argptr**. With these routines, we can extract the format string and locate the beginning of the argument list.

If we knew the numbers of arguments at compile-time, we could write code with **sprintf( )**, as we did earlier, to match any variable with the format string. However, since we don't know how many parameters there are and what type they are, we cannot use **sprintf( )**. Fortunately, Turbo C++ provides a variant of the **sprintf( )** function that accepts a pointer to a format string, such as **sprintf( )**, as well as a pointer to a list of a variable number of arguments. We can extract both pieces of information by using the variable argument routines mentioned earlier. Therefore, **vsprintf( )** is used to combine the variable number of arguments with the format string, **fmt**, into an ASCII string. It returns the count of the number of arguments successfully formatted. Finally, **va_end( )** is used to terminate the variable argument **access**. Here's the code that processes the variable arguments:

```
int gprintf(char *fmt, ... )
{
  va_list argptr;                          // Pointer to argument list
  char str[BUFSIZE];                       // Buffer to build string into
  int cnt;                                 // Result of sprintf() conversion
  struct fillsettingstype oldfill;         // Current fill setting
  char userfillpattern[8];                 // Current user-fill pattern
  int xloc, yloc;                          // Current position

  va_start(argptr, fmt);                   // Initialize va_ functions
  cnt = vsprintf(str, fmt, argptr);        // Prints string to buffer
  if (str[0] == NULL) return(0);
```

After the arguments are formatted and placed in the character array **str**, **gprintf( )** calls **outtext( )** to display the string. Therefore, the text will be displayed and justified relative to the current position. If left justification and horizontal text styles are in force, then the current position will automatically be updated after a call to **gprintf( )**.

Clearing the Way for Stroke Fonts

An annoying thing about the BGI stroke fonts is that they make a mess when they overwrite graphics already displayed on the screen. The reason for this is that stroke fonts only draw a series of line segments, they do not erase the space below the character as each stroke character is displayed. There is a way around this problem: clear the screen where each character is to appear before it is displayed. You can easily accomplish this task by drawing a filled rectangular region the size of each character with the background color prior to writing the character.

We've extended our **gprintf( )** function so that it clears the portion of the screen where the character string is drawn. This is the version of **gprintf( )** that is included in the GTEXT.CPP source file. If you examine the code, you'll see that the **bar( )** function is used in conjunction with **SOLID_FILL** to set the background color (specified in **grtextbkcolor**) to clear the screen underneath the string that is displayed.

You can set the color of the text using the GTEXT function **settextcolor( )**. Similarly, to set the background color you can call **settextbkcolor( )**.

The gprintfxy() Function

The GTEXT.CPP source file also contains the function **gprintfxy( )**, which is similar to **gprintf( )**. The main difference is that **gprintfxy( )** writes a character string at an (x, y) coordinate position. Like the BGI **outtextxy( )**, **gprintfxy( )** does not update the current position. Because the routine is similar to **gprintf( )** we will not cover it in any detail.

WORKING WITH TEXT INPUT

Another area that the BGI does not directly support is text input. One important input routine to have is a character input function that echoes the input to the graphics screen. The next function we'll present is **ggetche( )**, which is a graphics-based version of the C++ library routine **getche( )**. The **ggetche( )** routine updates the current position as long as the text is left justified and being drawn horizontally. The complete function is:

```
int ggetche(void)
{
  char ch;

  ch = getch();              // Get character with no echo
  gprintf("%c", ch);         // Output character
  return ch;
}
```

The code is rather straightforward. The call to **getch( )** gets a single character input from the user without echoing the input. Once the character is retrieved, it is displayed by a call to our custom library routine **gprintf( )**. Remember, this routine will update the current position.

You may want to write a comparable routine that gets a single character input at a specified location. This routine might be called **ggetchexy( )** and could invoke the **gprintfxy( )** function instead of **gprintf( )**.

Entering Character Strings

Although this last function solves the problem of single character input in graphics mode, there is still the issue of entering sequences of characters. The **ggets( )** and **readstring( )** routines enable you to enter text in graphics mode.

One extremely important point to realize is that in graphics mode backspace characters and several of the other control characters do not maintain their functionality. You read these characters with **getch( )**, but they will not perform any action. For example, to delete a character, you actually have to handle the backspace operation yourself. In addition, there is no cursor in graphics mode.

These problems are solved in **ggets( )** and **readstring( )**. Both functions accept a buffer that holds all text typed until a carriage return is pressed. The **readstring( )** function also allows you to specify a default string. While the text is being typed, the function will provide an underbar as a cursor and will support the Backspace character. The function returns a character pointer to the buffer upon exiting. When using these functions, you must make sure that there is enough room in the character buffer passed to **ggets( )** to accept the entire typed-in string.

The **ggets( )** function has two main elements. The first is a **while** loop that continually accepts any text typed by the user until a carriage return is pressed. Every character that is typed is entered into the buffer passed to the function. Actually, the Backspace character is not entered into the buffer. Instead, it causes the last character typed to be rewritten in the background color, which effectively erases it. After this, the current position is moved left.

The **readstring( )** function is similar but much more complicated because it also enables the user to use the Arrow keys to move through in the text. Because of its flexibility, **readstring( )** is the routine you'll want to use in most cases.

As you look through the code you may see references to several **#ifdef**s. The GTEXT.CPP toolkit is defined so that it will eventually support the mouse toolkit that we'll build in Chapter 7. These blocks of code are compiled along with GTEXT.CPP when the MOUSE compiler constant is defined. In Chapter 7, we'll explain how to do this. If MOUSE is not defined, the code within the **#ifdef-#endif** pairs is not compiled and the GTEXT toolkit will work fine without the mouse.

Entering Numeric Values

Just as displaying numeric values in graphics mode is a problem, so is entering numeric values. The GTEXT.CPP source file also includes two functions called **gscanf( )** and **gscanfxy( )** that provide graphics-based emulation of the C++ **scanf( )** function. Both routines use **ggets( )**, described earlier, combined with Turbo C++'s variable argument string **scanf( )** function, **vsscanf( )**, to support user input while in graphics mode. Although these functions handle user input, in many ways they are similar to the **gprintf()** and **gprintfxy()** functions, so we will not go into greater detail looking at them.

• GTEXT.H

```
// GTEXT.H: Header file for GTEXT.CPP.
const TEXTSIZE = 8;         // The default font is 8 by 8 pixels in size
const int BUFSIZE = 140;
const char CR = 13;                     // Carriage return
const char BS = 8;                      // Backspace
const char ESC = 27;                    // Esc key
const char TAB = 0x09;                  // Tab key
#define INS 0x5200                      // Insert key
#define DEL 0x5300                      // Delete key
#define UP          0x4800              // The following is a list
#define DOWN        0x5000              // of various extended key codes
#define LEFT        0x4B00
#define RIGHT       0x4D00
#define PGUP        0x4900
#define HOME        0x4700
#define END         0x4f00
#define PGDN        0x5100
#define CTRL_LEFT   0x7300
#define CTRL_RIGHT  0x7400
#define CTRL_HOME   0x7700

#define  F1             0x3b00
#define  F2             0x3c00
#define  F3             0x3d00
#define  F4             0x3e00
#define  F5             0x3f00
#define  F6             0x4000
#define  F7             0x4100
#define  F8             0x4200
#define  F9             0x4300
#define  F10            0x4400

#define  SHIFT_F1       0x5400
#define  SHIFT_F2       0x5500
#define  SHIFT_F3       0x5600
#define  SHIFT_F4       0x5700
#define  SHIFT_F5       0x5800
#define  SHIFT_F6       0x5900
#define  SHIFT_F7       0x5a00
#define  SHIFT_F8       0x5b00
#define  SHIFT_F9       0x5c00
#define  SHIFT_F10      0x5d00

#define  CTRL_F9        0x6600
#define  CTRL_F10       0x6700
```

```
#define    CTRL_I              0x1709

#define    ALT_F1              0x6800
#define    ALT_F2              0x6900
#define    ALT_F3              0x6a00
#define    ALT_F4              0x6b00
#define    ALT_F5              0x6c00
#define    ALT_F6              0x6d00
#define    ALT_F7              0x6e00
#define    ALT_F8              0x6f00
#define    ALT_F9              0x7000
#define    ALT_F10             0x7100
#define    ALT_C               0x2e00
#define    ALT_D               0x2000
#define    ALT_B               0x3000
#define    ALT_E               0x1200
#define    ALT_F               0x2100
#define    ALT_I               0x1700
#define    ALT_K               0x2500
#define    ALT_M               0x3200
#define    ALT_O               0x1800
#define    ALT_P               0x1900
#define    ALT_Q               0x1000
#define    ALT_S               0x1f00
#define    ALT_V               0x2f00
#define    ALT_W               0x1100
#define    ALT_X               0x2d00
#define    ALT_Z               0x2c00
#define    ALT_1               0x7800
#define    ALT_2               0x7900

extern int grtextbkcolor;
extern int grtextcolor;

int settextbkcolor(int color);
int settextcolor(int color);
int gprintf(char *fmt, ... );
int gprintfxy(int xloc, int yloc, char *fmt, ... );
int ggetche(void);
int gputch(int c);
char *ggets(char *buffer);
int gscanfxy(int locx, int locy, char *fmt, ... );
int gscanf(char *fmt, ... );
char *readstring(int x, int y, char *def, char *outstr,
   int dlen, int maxstr, int *lastkey, int erase);
```

• GTEXT.CPP

```
// GTEXT.CPP: A set of text input and output routines for graphics mode.
#include <graphics.h>
#include <stdarg.h>
#include <stdio.h>
#include <string.h>
```

```
#include <math.h>
#include <conio.h>
#include <bios.h>
#include <ctype.h>
#include "gtext.h"

#ifdef MOUSE                // Define the MOUSE compilation switch
#include "kbdmouse.h"       // when you want to use the mouse with
extern kbdmouseobj mouse;   // this toolkit
#endif

int grtextbkcolor=0;     // The background color used with the text
int grtextcolor=15;      // Use white text

// Sets the color used in the toolkit to write the text. The
// function returns the previous setting of the text color.
int settextcolor(int color)
{
  int oldcolor = grtextcolor;

  grtextcolor = color;
  return oldcolor;
}


// Sets the color used for the background of the text. The
// function returns the previous setting of the background color.
int settextbkcolor(int color)
{
  int oldcolor=grtextbkcolor;

  grtextbkcolor = color;
  return oldcolor;
}

// A graphics-based printf() function. It will print the output
// at location xloc, yloc. It does not affect the current position.
// Assumes LEFT_TEXT and HORIZ_DIR justification.
int gprintfxy(int xloc, int yloc, char *fmt, ... )
{
  va_list argptr;                    // Pointer to argument list
  char str[BUFSIZE];                 // Buffer to build string into
  int cnt;                           // Result of sprintf() conversion
  struct fillsettingstype oldfill;   // Current fill setting
  char userfillpattern[8];           // Current user-fill pattern

  va_start(argptr, fmt);             // Initialize va_ functions
  cnt = vsprintf(str, fmt, argptr);  // Prints string to buffer
  if (str[0] == NULL) return 0;

  // Clear the space where the text is to be printed
  getfillsettings(&oldfill);
  if (oldfill.pattern == USER_FILL)
    getfillpattern(userfillpattern);
  setfillstyle(SOLID_FILL, grtextbkcolor);
```

```
    setcolor(grtextcolor);
#ifdef MOUSE
    mouse.hide();        // Hide the mouse before writing to the screen
#endif
    bar(xloc, yloc, xloc+textwidth(str), yloc+textheight("H")*5/4);
    if (oldfill.pattern == USER_FILL)
      setfillpattern(userfillpattern, oldfill.color);
    else
      setfillstyle(oldfill.pattern, oldfill.color);
    outtextxy(xloc, yloc, str);           // Write string to screen
#ifdef MOUSE
    mouse.show();
#endif
    va_end(argptr);                       // Terminate va_ functions
    return cnt;                           // Return the conversion count
}

// A graphics-based printf() function. It will update the current
// position. Assumes LEFT_TEXT and HORIZ_DIR justification.
int gprintf(char *fmt, ... )
{
    va_list argptr;                       // Pointer to argument list
    char str[BUFSIZE];                    // Buffer to build string into
    int cnt;                              // Result of sprintf() conversion
    struct fillsettingstype oldfill;      // Current fill setting
    char userfillpattern[8];              // Current user-fill pattern
    int xloc, yloc;                       // Current position

    va_start(argptr, fmt);                // Initialize va_ functions
    cnt = vsprintf(str, fmt, argptr);     // Prints string to buffer
    if (str[0] == NULL) return(0);
    // Clear the space where the text is to be printed
    xloc = getx();  yloc = gety();
    getfillsettings(&oldfill);
    if (oldfill.pattern == USER_FILL)
      getfillpattern(userfillpattern);
    setfillstyle(SOLID_FILL, grtextbkcolor);
    setcolor(grtextcolor);
#ifdef MOUSE
    mouse.hide();  // Hide the mouse before writing to the screen
#endif
    bar(xloc, yloc, xloc+textwidth(str), yloc+textheight("H")*5/4);
    if (oldfill.pattern == USER_FILL)
      setfillpattern(userfillpattern, oldfill.color);
    else
      setfillstyle(oldfill.pattern, oldfill.color);
    outtext(str);                         // Write string to screen
#ifdef MOUSE
    mouse.show();
#endif
    va_end(argptr);                       // Terminate va_ functions
    return cnt;                           // Return the conversion count
}
```

```
//  Graphics-based getche() function
int ggetche(void)
{
  char ch;

  ch = getch();                       // Get character with no echo
  gprintf("%c", ch);                  // Output character
  return ch;
}

// Graphics-based putch() function
int gputch(int c)
{
  char buffer[2];

  sprintf(buffer, "%c", c);
  gprintf(buffer);
  return c;
}

// A graphics-based text input routine. Returns the string entered.
// Echoes text as it is entered. It supports the Backspace character.
char *ggets(char *buffer)
{
  int currloc, maxchars, oldcolor, ch;
  struct viewporttype view;
  char charbuff[3];

  buffer[0] = '\0';
  currloc = 0;
  getviewsettings(&view);
  maxchars = (view.right - getx()) / textwidth("M") - 1;
  if (maxchars <= 0) return(NULL);
  gprintfxy(getx(),gety(),"_");
  while ((ch=getch()) != CR && ch != ESC) {
    if (ch == BS) {
      if (currloc > 0) {
        currloc--;
        if (currloc <= maxchars) {
          // Temporarily set the text color to the background color
          // in order to erase the last character and the underscore
          oldcolor = settextcolor(grtextbkcolor);
          sprintf(charbuff, "%c", buffer[currloc]);
          gprintfxy(getx()-textwidth(charbuff), gety(),
            "%c_", buffer[currloc]);
          settextcolor(oldcolor);
          moveto(getx()-textwidth(charbuff), gety());
        }
      }
    }
    else {
      if (currloc < maxchars) {
        oldcolor = settextcolor(grtextbkcolor);
```

```
            gprintfxy(getx(), gety(),"_");
            settextcolor(oldcolor);
            buffer[currloc] = ch;
            gputch(ch);
            currloc++;
        }
      else
        putch(0x07);
    }
    if (currloc < maxchars)
      gprintfxy(getx(), gety(), "_");
  }
  if (currloc <= maxchars) {
    oldcolor = settextcolor(grtextbkcolor);
    gprintfxy(getx(), gety(), "_");
    settextcolor(oldcolor);
  }
  if (ch == ESC) buffer[0] = '\0'; // Pressing Esc aborts the user input
    else buffer[currloc] = '\0';
  return buffer;
}

// A graphics-based scanf() function. It updates the current position.
// Assumes LEFT_TEXT and HORIZ_DIR justification.
int gscanf(char *fmt, ... )
{
  va_list argptr;                   // Argument list pointer
  char str[BUFSIZE];                // Buffer to accept user input
  int cnt;                          // Number of fields converted

  va_start(argptr, fmt);            // Initialize va_ functions
  ggets(str);                       // Get the user input
  cnt = vsscanf(str, fmt, argptr);  // Convert the input according
                                    // to the format string
  va_end(argptr);                   // Terminate the va_ functions
  return cnt;                       // Return the # of successful
                                    // input conversions

}

// A graphics-based scanf(). It does not affect the current
// position and will echo input as it is entered at (xloc, yloc).
// Assumes LEFT_TEXT and HORIZ_DIR justification.
int gscanfxy(int xloc, int yloc, char *fmt, ... )
{
  va_list argptr;                   // Pointer to argument list
  char str[BUFSIZE];                // Buffer to accept user input
  int cnt;                          // Number of conversions made
  int oldx, oldy;                   // Original current position

  oldx = xloc;                      // Save current position so that
  oldy = yloc;                      // it can later be restored
  moveto(xloc, yloc);               // Move to the new current position
  va_start(argptr, fmt);            // Initialize the va_ functions
  ggets(str);                       // Get the user's input
```

```
    cnt = vsscanf(str, fmt, argptr); // Convert input string
    va_end(argptr);                  // Terminate va_ function
    moveto(oldx, oldy);              // Restore current position
    return cnt;                      // Return conversion count
}


// Draws a cursor by exclusive-ORing a line below the text
// location (locx,locy). The code assumes that the line style
// is correct. Note: When erase is 1, locx, locy do not matter.
void drawcurs(int locx, int locy, unsigned char erase)
{
    static int lastx=0, lasty=0;

#ifdef MOUSE
    mouse.hide();
#endif
    if (erase) {
        setcolor(grtextbkcolor);
        moveto(lastx*TEXTSIZE, (lasty+1)*TEXTSIZE+1);
        lineto(lastx*TEXTSIZE+7, (lasty+1)*TEXTSIZE+1);
    }
    else {
        setcolor(grtextcolor);
        moveto(locx*TEXTSIZE, (locy+1)*TEXTSIZE+1);
        lineto(locx*TEXTSIZE+7, (locy+1)*TEXTSIZE+1);
        lastx = locx;  lasty = locy;
    }
#ifdef MOUSE
    mouse.show();
#endif
}


// Displays dlen characters of the string str at (locx,locy) --
// starting at the offset soffs into the string
void displaystr(int locx, int locy, int dlen, char str[])
{
    for (int i=0; i<dlen && str[i] != '\0'; i++)
        gprintfxy((locx+i)*TEXTSIZE, locy*TEXTSIZE, "%c", str[i]);
    // Blank out the rest of the line
    for (; i<dlen; i++)
        gprintfxy((locx+i)*TEXTSIZE, locy*TEXTSIZE, " ");
}


// This function provides a graphics-mode text input routine.
// It supports full editing of text input using the cursor keys.
// It also supports left and right text scrolling so that the
// text entered can be smaller than the "window" provided.
// The code assumes that the default font is used, which has a
// fixed size.
char *readstring(int x, int y, char *def, char *outstr,
    int dlen, int maxstr, int *lastkey, int erase=0)
{
    char ch;
    int key, cursor=0, cpy, soffs=0, cursoff=0;
```

```
linesettingstype oline;
getlinesettings(&oline);
setlinestyle(SOLID_LINE, 0, NORM_WIDTH);
moveto(x*TEXTSIZE, y*TEXTSIZE);
strcpy(outstr, def);
if (def[0] == '\0') {                       // No default value
  for (cursor=0; cursor<dlen; cursor++)     // Clear input line
    gprintf(" ");
  drawcurs(x, y, 0);                         // Draw cursor
  cursor = 0;
  outstr[0] = 0;
}
else {                                      // Show default string
  for (cursor=0; def[cursor] != '\0'; cursor++)
    outstr[cursor] = def[cursor];
  outstr[cursor] = '\0';
  soffs = 0;
  if (cursor >= dlen) {
    cursoff = 0;
    cursor = 0;
  }
  else
    cursoff = cursor;
  displaystr(x, y, dlen, &outstr[soffs]);
  drawcurs(x+cursoff, y, 0);
}
key = bioskey(0);
ch = (char)(key&0x00ff);
if (isalnum(ch) || ch == ' ' || ch == '\\' || ch == '*') {
  // The default string should not be used; erase it
  displaystr(x, y, dlen, "");
  drawcurs(0, 0, 1);
  drawcurs(x, y, 0);
  moveto(x*TEXTSIZE, y*TEXTSIZE);
  outstr[0] = '\0';      // Set to NULL string. The character
  cursor = 0;            // just typed will be inserted below.
  outstr[1] = '\0';
  cursoff = cursor;
  soffs = 0;
}
do {
  if (ch == ESC) {                   // Abort user input
    if (erase) { // ClearInputLine(); You'll need to supply this }
    drawcurs(0, 0, 1);
    *lastkey = key;
    setlinestyle(oline.linestyle, oline.upattern, oline.thickness);
    return "";
  }
  else if (ch == CR || ch == TAB) break;
  else if ((key&0x00ff) == 0) {
    // Determine which of the cursor keys was pressed, if any
    // Move the cursor as needed
    if (key == UP || key == DOWN) goto acceptval;
    else if (key == LEFT) {
```

```
        if (cursor > 0) {
          cursor--;
          if (soffs > 0) {
            soffs--;
            displaystr(x, y, dlen, &outstr[soffs]);
          }
          else if (cursoff > 0) {
            cursoff--;
          }
          // The "else" shouldn't occur here
        }
      }
      else if (key == RIGHT) {
        if (cursor < strlen(outstr)) {
          cursor++;
          if (cursoff >= dlen-1)
            soffs++;
          else
            cursoff++;
          displaystr(x, y, dlen, &outstr[soffs]);
        }
      }
      else if (key == HOME) {
        soffs = 0;
        cursoff = 0;
        cursor = 0;
        displaystr(x, y, dlen, &outstr[soffs]);
      }
      else if (key == END) {
        // Move the cursor to the end of the string
        cursor = strlen(outstr);
        if (cursor-soffs >= dlen) {
          cursoff = dlen - 1;
          soffs = cursor - dlen + 1;
        }
        else
          cursoff = cursor-soffs;
        displaystr(x, y, dlen, &outstr[soffs]);
      }
      else if (key == DEL) {
        if (cursor >= 0 && cursor < strlen(outstr)) {
          if ((cpy=strlen(outstr)-cursor) >= 0)
            memmove(&outstr[cursor], &outstr[cursor+1], cpy+1);
          displaystr(x+cursoff, y, dlen-cursoff, &outstr[cursor]);
        }
      }
    }
    else if (ch == BS) {    // Handle the backspace character
      if (cursor > 0) {
        if (soffs > 0) {
          cursor--;   soffs--;
          if ((cpy=strlen(outstr)-cursor) >= 0)
            memmove(&outstr[cursor], &outstr[cursor+1],cpy+1);
          displaystr(x, y, dlen, &outstr[soffs]);
```

```
        }
        else if (cursoff > 0) {
          cursoff--;  cursor--;
          if ((cpy=strlen(outstr)-cursor) >= 0)
            memmove(&outstr[cursor], &outstr[cursor+1], cpy+1);
          displaystr(x+cursoff, y, dlen-cursoff, &outstr[cursor]);
        }
        else {
          cursor--;   soffs--;
          if ((cpy=strlen(outstr)-cursor) >= 0)
            memmove(&outstr[cursor], &outstr[cursor+1], cpy+1);
          displaystr(x, y, dlen, &outstr[cursor]);
        }
      }
    }
    else {                       // Add the character entered
      if (cursor < maxstr) {     // The string is not full
        if (cursoff == dlen-1) {
          // Cursor at right of text field
          // Update whole string in text field
          if ((cpy=strlen(outstr)-cursor) >= 0)
            memmove(&outstr[cursor+1], &outstr[cursor], cpy+1);
          outstr[cursor] = (char)(key&0x00ff);
          soffs++;  cursor++;
          displaystr(x, y, dlen, &outstr[soffs]);
        }
        else {             // cursoff < dlen
          if ((cpy=strlen(outstr)-cursor) >= 0)
            memmove(&outstr[cursor+1], &outstr[cursor], cpy+1);
          outstr[cursor] = (char)(key&0x00ff);
          displaystr(x+cursoff, y, dlen-cursoff, &outstr[cursor]);
          cursor++;
          cursoff++;
        }
      }
    }
    if (cursor-soffs < dlen) {
      // Update location of cursor
      drawcurs(0, 0, 1);
      drawcurs(x+cursor-soffs, y, 0);
    }
    key = bioskey(0);
    ch = (char)(key&0x00ff);
  } while (key != CR);
  acceptval: drawcurs(0, 0, 1);
  if (erase) { // ClearInputLine(); You'll need to supply this }
  *lastkey = key;
  setlinestyle(oline.linestyle, oline.upattern, oline.thickness);
  return outstr;
}
```

Presentation Graphics

It has been said that a picture is worth a thousand words, and if you have ever experienced a good art gallery, you'll probably agree. Of course, when it comes to communication, pictures not only have a place in the art world but in the fast-moving business world as well. And with today's fast PCs equipped with high-resolution video systems, the field of *presentation graphics* has emerged. By presentation graphics we mean the technology of using the computer to represent complex information in the form of charts, graphs, and pictures.

In this chapter, we'll show you how to use Turbo C++'s graphics capabilities to produce high-quality business and scientific charts and graphs. In particular, we'll explore techniques for drawing pie charts, bar graphs, and coin graphs. We will not be able to cover all of the types of graphs and charts that can be generated with the BGI tools, but by the end of this chapter, you'll know enough to be able to customize your own C++ applications with presentation graphics.

THE BASIC GRAPH TYPES

The BGI provides three specialized functions for generating graphs and charts: a pie-chart routine, a bar-graph routine, and a three-dimensional bar-graph function. With these high-level functions, we can create professional looking charts and graphs with a minimum of effort. We'll explore each of these functions in detail in this chapter as well as use several of the other tools in the BGI to generate other types of charts and graphs, such as coin graphs.

GETTING STARTED

If you're looking for hard and fast rules for developing charts and graphs, you won't find them here. After all, a picture doesn't always tell the same story to all people. Our major goal is to display information in a consistent and meaningful manner. However, meaningful does not mean boring. In fact, a good graph or chart is one that is visually pleasing. Therefore, along the way, you may want to experiment with various colors, backdrops, and the layout of the graphs. This chapter will provide you with a few sample programs that will help you get started; however, feel free to experiment with your own ideas.

PIE CHARTS

If you pick up almost any magazine or newspaper, you're bound to see pie charts. In fact, you'll also find them in popular software applications such as Borland's Quattro Pro. In this section, we'll develop a utility that can automatically create a complete pie chart. All we need to do is provide the program with the data and titles for the pie slices. The program sizes the pie chart to fit on the screen, creates a legend, and writes a title. The program, PIE.CPP, is designed around Turbo C++'s **pieslice( )** function and a set of our own custom routines.

Drawing a Slice

In Chapter 2, we introduced the **pieslice( )** function. We will use it here to draw each pie slice in our pie charts. Our task then is to determine how to relate a set of data to the various slices in the pie chart. Typically, each slice represents the proportion of a particular group of data in relation to the whole chart. In other words, each slice represents a percentage of the whole pie.

For our program, we'll assume that a series of percentage values are available for us to use. Each percentage value corresponds to one pie slice and all the slices total to 100 percent. In some applications, a set of raw data is used from which the program must calculate appropriate percentage values. To keep our program simple, we'll assume that these percentages are already available.

Our enhanced version of the **pieslice( )** function is called **pieceofpie( )**. We'll invoke this custom function for each pie slice of the chart that we need to draw. The code for a simplified version of this function is:

```
void pieceofpie(int x, int y, int radius, double slicepercentage,
  int color, int fill)
{
  int startangle, endangle;
  static double startpercentage = 0.0;

  setfillstyle(fill, color);
  startangle = startpercentage / 100.0 * 360.0;
```

```
    endangle = (startpercentage+slicepercentage) / 100.0 * 360.0;
    pieslice(x, y, startangle, endangle, radius);
    startpercentage += slicepercentage;
}
```

The first three arguments to **pieceofpie( )** define the center point and radius of the pie slice to be drawn. From the code, you can see that these values are simply passed along to the Turbo C++ **pieslice( )** function. However, we still need to determine the overall size of the pie slice, which is dependent on the value in **slicepercentage**. But first, let's see how we determine the starting angle to begin drawing the current pie slice. This is the purpose of **static double startpercentage**. It keeps a running total of the percentage of the circle that has already been displayed. The declaration initializes it to 0:

```
static double startpercentage = 0.0;
```

Each time **pieceofpie( )** is called, **slicepercentage** is added to the running total. The next pie slice is then drawn starting at this location. Therefore, **startpercentage** specifies the starting angle for drawing the pie slice and **slicepercentage** instructs the routine on how big to make the slice. Actually, these percentage values must be converted before they can be used. The Turbo C++ **pieslice( )** function is expecting angles to be passed to it, not percentages. Therefore, we must convert these values to angles. This conversion is accomplished by the following two statements:

```
startangle = startpercentage / 100.0 * 360.0;
endangle = (startpercentage+slicepercentage) / 100.0 * 360.0;
```

The statements are similar; each is based on the following ratio:

$$\frac{\text{Angle desired}}{\text{360 degrees}} = \frac{\text{Percentage}}{\text{100 percent}}$$

The only other thing to note in the function is that it sets the current fill style and color to the values specified with the last two arguments that are passed to it. These drawing parameters are set so that each pie slice can be drawn differently.

As it stands, our function, **pieceofpie( )**, is ready to be called to create a pie chart. However, let's modify it slightly so that it will add labels for the percentage values alongside each pie slice.

Labeling Pie Slices

There are many different ways you can add labels to a pie chart. We'll write the percentage value of each pie slice off to the slice's side, which will make it easy for the viewer to determine the sizes of the pie slices. Some other possibilities are to write titles next to the pie slices or even write the titles or percentage values over the pie slices themselves. The PIE.CPP source file, listed later in this chapter, includes the updated routine as well as the rest of the code for our pie chart program.

When looking at the **pieceofpie( )** function the first thing to note is that it contains a new variable called **lradius**. This variable is used to determine the distance from the center of the pie chart to where the labels are written. For our application, the **lradius** is set to be 1.2 times the radius of the pie chart by the statement:

```
lradius = (double)radius * 1.2;  // Varies with character size
```

This calculation depends on how much room you have on the screen for the labels and the size of the text that you are using. You can derive a general equation for this, but to keep things simple, we'll just use the multiplication constant 1.2.

By convention, each label is placed at the center of a pie slice. Its angle is stored in **labelangle** and is halfway between the start angle of the pie slice and its ending angle. This value is converted into radians by the inline function **torad( )**.

```
labelangle = (startangle + endangle) / 2;
labelloc = torad(labelangle);
```

Next, the x and y coordinates of where the label is to be written are calculated by the following lines of code. (Note: the **y** value must be adjusted for the aspect ratio of the screen.)

```
x += cos(labelloc) * lradius;
y -= sin(labelloc) * lradius * aspectratio;
```

The following statements set the text parameters. First, the font style is set to the triplex stroke font. Next, you'll find a series of nested **if-else** statements that determine which type of text justification to use. For instance, if the label is to be printed to the right of the pie slice, then its justification is set to **LEFT_TEXT** and **CENTER_TEXT**. However, if the text is to be written on the left side of the pie chart, its justification is set to **RIGHT_TEXT** and **CENTER_TEXT**. Finally, the text is formatted using **sprintf( )** and written to the screen using **outtextxy( )**.

```
settextstyle(TRIPLEX_FONT, HORIZ_DIR, 1);
if (labelangle >= 300 || labelangle < 60)
  settextjustify(LEFT_TEXT, CENTER_TEXT);
else if (labelangle >= 60 && labelangle < 120)
  settextjustify(CENTER_TEXT, BOTTOM_TEXT);
```

```
else if (labelangle >= 120 && labelangle < 240)
  settextjustify(RIGHT_TEXT, CENTER_TEXT);
else
  settextjustify(CENTER_TEXT, TOP_TEXT);
sprintf(buffer, "%3.1lf%%", showpercentage);
outtextxy(x, y, buffer);
```

We've now seen how to draw each slice in a pie chart. To draw a complete pie chart we merely need to call the **pieceofpie( )** function repetitively with the appropriate values.

Making Each Slice Different

One thing that you will probably want to do is draw each pie slice a different color or at least fill it with a different fill pattern. To accomplish this we'll sequence through the colors supported by the current graphics mode and 11 of the fill patterns. (We won't use the empty fill pattern, since it doesn't generate a unique fill pattern in CGA high-resolution mode.)

The program in Listing 4.1 uses the function **nextcolorandfill( )** to sequence through each of the fill patterns and color combinations. It uses static variables that initially set the fill pattern at 1 and the fill color at 0. If all combinations of fill patterns and colors are used up, the function is written so that the program will exit. You may want to change this so that it cycles through the values again.

Creating a Legend

At the end of **pieceofpie( )**, the **showkey( )** function is called to write out an entry in a color key on the left side of the screen. This legend shows each color and fill pattern used in the pie chart along with its corresponding label. The function **showkey( )** draws one rectangle for each pie slice starting from the top left of the screen and working down. The **bar3d( )** function is used with a depth of 0 to draw the filled region. The boxes are 16 pixels in width and 16 pixels in height times the aspect ratio. This correction is made in order to make the region square. The location of the square is maintained by the static variables **x** and **y**. The **x** value is always equal to 3. However, the **y** location is incremented by 18 pixels each time the function is called.

A Pie Chart Program

Figure 4.1 presents the screen that PIE.CPP generates. Note that the program displays all of the objects that are typically found in a pie chart including a title, a legend, and labels for the chart. The main program performs the work of initializing the BGI and drawing the basic components of the pie chart. The

Figure 4.1 PIE.CPP creates this pie chart.

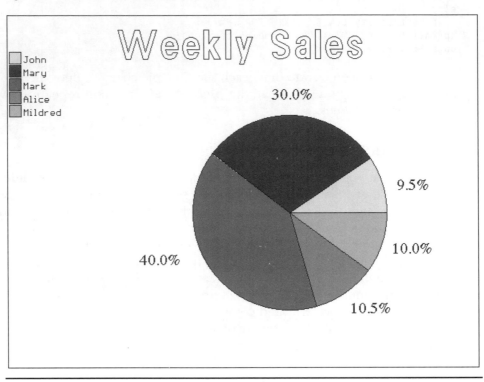

real work-horse function is **pieceofpie( )**, which is responsible for drawing each pie slice.

Although PIE.CPP is one of the most complex programs we've written up until now, you'll find that the program is not that difficult to follow. We are, however, introducing two new C++ features: *inline functions* and *passing variables by reference.* Since we'll explain the basic techniques of inline functions in the sidebar *Working with Inline Functions,* let's investigate the parameter issue now.

If you take a close look at the definition of **nextcolorandfill( )** you'll notice that the arguments **color** and **fill** are declared using the **&** symbol:

```
void nextcolorandfill(int& color, int& fill);
```

This technique tells the compiler that the variables are being passed by reference instead of as a pointer or by value. If this code were written in Turbo C instead of C++ we would have to define the function with the syntax

```
void nextcolorandfill(int *color, int *fill);
```

and the parameters would have to be passed as :

```
nextcolorandfill(&color, &fill);
```

The problem with this method is that it is easy to forget the address operator **(&)** or to forget to dereference the pointer variable using the * symbol when the variable's value is accessed. Either omission can really make your code run amuk. For example, take another look at the code in PIE.CPP and you'll see that **nextcolorandfill( )** is called with

```
nextcolorandfill(color, fill);
```

and the arguments **color** and **fill** are assigned values inside the body of the function using the simple syntax:

```
fill = ffill;
color = fcolor;
```

• PIE.CPP

```cpp
// PIE.CPP: Demonstrates the pie chart capabilities of the BGI.
#include <graphics.h>
#include <conio.h>
#include <stdio.h>
#include <stdlib.h>
#include <math.h>

double percentvalues[] = {9.5, 30, 40, 10.5, 10};
char *labels[] = {"John", "Mary", "Mark", "Alice", "Mildred"};
char title[] = "Weekly Sales";
int numvalues = 5;
double aspectratio;

// Inline function to convert degrees to radians
inline double torad(int d)
{
   return(( (double)(d) * M_PI) / 180.0);
}

// Shows a single label used in the pie chart
void showkey(int color, int fill, char *label)
{
   static int x = 3;
   static int y = 50;

   setfillstyle(fill, color);
   bar3d(x, y, x+16, y+16*aspectratio, 0, 0);
   settextjustify(LEFT_TEXT, CENTER_TEXT);
   settextstyle(SMALL_FONT, HORIZ_DIR, 5);
   outtextxy(x+20, y+8*aspectratio, label);
   y += 18;
}
```

```
// Displays one of the pie slices in the pie chart
void pieceofpie(int x, int y, int radius, double showpercentage,
  int color, int fill, char *label)
{
  int startangle, endangle, labelangle;
  double labelloc, lradius;
  static double startpercentage = 0.0;
  char buffer[40];

  // Offset label radius by a factor of 1.2. This value
  // is dependent on the size of characters you are using.
  lradius = (double)radius * 1.2;
  setfillstyle(fill, color);
  startangle = startpercentage / 100.0 * 360.0;
  endangle = (startpercentage + showpercentage) / 100.0 * 360.0;
  labelangle = (startangle + endangle) / 2;
  labelloc = torad(labelangle);
  pieslice(x, y, startangle, endangle, radius);
  x += cos(labelloc) * lradius;
  y -= sin(labelloc) * lradius * aspectratio;
  settextstyle(TRIPLEX_FONT, HORIZ_DIR,1);

  // Set text justification depending upon location of pieslice
  if (labelangle >= 300 || labelangle < 60)
    settextjustify(LEFT_TEXT, CENTER_TEXT);
  else if (labelangle >= 60 && labelangle < 120)
    settextjustify(CENTER_TEXT, BOTTOM_TEXT);
  else if (labelangle >= 120 && labelangle < 240)
    settextjustify(RIGHT_TEXT, CENTER_TEXT);
  else
    settextjustify(CENTER_TEXT, TOP_TEXT);
  sprintf(buffer, "%3.1lf%%", showpercentage);
  outtextxy(x, y, buffer);
  startpercentage += showpercentage;
  showkey(color, fill, label);
}

// Returns the next unique color and fill pattern to use in
// the pie chart
void nextcolorandfill(int& color, int& fill)
{
  static int ffill = 1;
  static int fcolor = 0;

  fcolor++;
  if (fcolor > getmaxcolor()) {
    fcolor = 1;
    ffill++;
    if (ffill > 11) {
      closegraph();
      printf("Too many calls to nextcolor ...");
      exit(1);
    }
  }
```

```
   fill = ffill;
   color = fcolor;
}

int main()
{
   int gdriver = DETECT, gmode;
   int i, x, y, radius, color, fill, xasp, yasp;

   initgraph(&gdriver, &gmode, "\\tcpp\\bgi");
   rectangle(0, 0, getmaxx(), getmaxy());
   // Write a header to the graph
   settextjustify(LEFT_TEXT, TOP_TEXT);
   settextstyle(BOLD_FONT, HORIZ_DIR, 4);
   outtextxy((getmaxx()-textwidth(title))/2, 0, title);
   x = getmaxx() / 2;        y = getmaxy() / 2;
   getaspectratio(&xasp, &yasp);
   aspectratio = (double)xasp / (double)yasp;
   radius = (double)y * 5.0 / 9.0 / aspectratio;
   y += textheight(title) / 2;
   x *= 6.0 / 5.0;
   nextcolorandfill(color, fill);
   for (i=0; i<numvalues; i++) {
      pieceofpic(x, y, radius, percentvalues[i], color, fill, labels[i]);
      nextcolorandfill(color, fill);
   }
   getch();
   closegraph();
   return 0;
}
```

Emphasizing a Slice

In some of your pie chart presentations, you might need to emphasize one or more pie slices. There are several ways to accomplish this. One approach is to offset the pie slice from the rest of the pie chart by a small amount, as shown in Figure 4.2. Although we won't add this feature to our previous example, we'll develop a function to implement it.

To offset the pie slice, we'll need to move it from the rest of the pie chart by extending it out along the radius of the circle. For instance, let's offset the pie slice by a multiple of its radius. This offset must be added to the x and y coordinates that mark the "center" of the pie slice and its label. The amount that must be added to the x versus the y location depends on where the pie slice is to be drawn. Also, we need to take into account the aspect ratio of the screen. Figure 4.3 shows the scaling and offset calculations for a moved pie slice.

The function **pieceofpie2()**, shown here, generates an offset pie slice. This function is similar to **pieceofpie()**—our previous routine. The key difference is that **pieceofpie2()** contains an additional argument, **offsetflag**. When

Figure 4.2 A pie slice can be offset for emphasis.

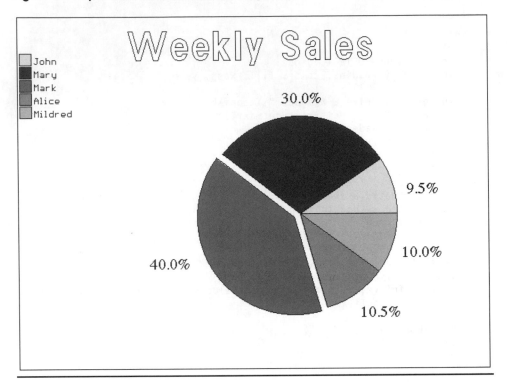

Figure 4.3 These are the calculations you'll need for offsetting a pie slice.

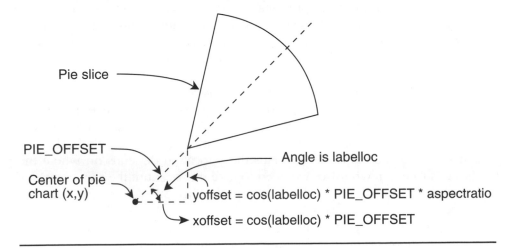

WORKING WITH INLINE FUNCTIONS

Turbo C++ supports a new type of function called, *inline functions*, that simplify the work of creating short, special-purpose routines. In one sense, you can think of an inline function as performing the type of task that a macro would be used for. Like macros, inline functions eliminate the overhead of a function call. Whenever an inline function is used, the code that makes up the function is usually inserted *inline*. Unlike macros, however, inline functions use the same scoping rules and argument passing conventions as other functions. Of course, this makes them much more flexible and reliable than macros. In fact, you can pass an inline function as an argument to other functions and the compiler will perform typechecking on the arguments used in the inline function. This feature is not available with macros.

There are two ways to declare inline functions. One way is to include the complete function definition in a class declaration. Here is a simple example:

```
class string {
  char data[40];
public:
  void copy(char *s) { strcpy(data, s); }    // Inline function
};
```

In this example, the **copy()** member function is implemented as an inline routine; therefore, all calls to **copy()** are replaced by:

```
strcpy(data, s);
```

Inline functions can also be declared explicitly using the **inline** keyword. We used this technique to declare the function **torad()** in the PIE.CPP program:

```
// Inline function to convert degrees to radians
inline double torad(int d)
{
  return(( (double)(d) * M_PI) / 180.0);
}
```

An equivalent C macro would be:

```
#define torad(d)  ( (double) (d) * M_PI / 180.0 )
```

As you can see, inline functions do not have to be class members. Any function can be used. However, because an inline function is physically copied whenever it is used, you should keep it as short as possible.

this argument is set to a non-zero value, the function draws a pie slice offset from the rest of the pie chart, as shown by the following statements. First, the amount of the offset is calculated by

```
xoffset = cos(labelloc) * PIE_OFFSET;
yoffset = sin(labelloc) * PIE_OFFSET * aspectratio;
```

where **PIE_OFFSET** is a constant set to a value of 10. Note that these statements are similar to the ones used to calculate the location of the label. Next, the call to **pieslice( )** must be changed to reflect this offset:

```
pieslice(x+xoffset, y-yoffset, startangle, endangle, radius);
```

In addition, the call to **outtextxy( )** to write the text label must be changed to use the offset values as:

```
outtextxy(x+xoffset, y-yoffset, buffer);
```

The full function follows. You can use the function like the last routine, except that when you want to offset a particular pie slice all you need to do is set the offset flag to a non-zero value. Otherwise, the pie slice is drawn normally.

```
const double PIE_OFFSET = 10.0;  // Amount of offset

void pieceofpie2(int x, int y, int radius, double showpercentage,
  int color, int fill, char *label, int offsetflag)
{
  int startangle, endangle, labelangle;
  double labelloc, lradius;
  char buffer[40];
  int xoffset, yoffset;
  static double startpercentage = 0.0;

  lradius = (double)radius * 1.2;     // Dependent on size of chars
  setfillstyle(fill, color);
  startangle = startpercentage / 100.0 * 360.0;
  endangle = (startpercentage + showpercentage) / 100.0 * 360.0;
  labelangle = (startangle + endangle) / 2;
  labelloc = torad(labelangle);
  if (offsetflag) {
    xoffset = cos(labelloc) * PIE_OFFSET;
    yoffset = sin(labelloc) * PIE_OFFSET * aspectratio;
    pieslice(x+xoffset, y-yoffset, startangle, endangle, radius);
  }
  else
    pieslice(x, y, startangle, endangle, radius);
  x += cos(labelloc) * lradius;
  y -= sin(labelloc) * lradius * aspectratio;
  settextstyle(TRIPLEX_FONT, HORIZ_DIR, 1);
  // Set text justification depending upon location of pieslice
  if (labelangle >= 300 || labelangle < 60)
```

```
    settextjustify(LEFT_TEXT, CENTER_TEXT);
  else if (labelangle >= 60 && labelangle < 120)
    settextjustify(CENTER_TEXT, BOTTOM_TEXT);
  else if (labelangle >= 120 && labelangle < 240)
    settextjustify(RIGHT_TEXT, CENTER_TEXT);
  else
    settextjustify(CENTER_TEXT, TOP_TEXT);
  sprintf(buffer, "%3.1lf%%", showpercentage);
  if (offsetflag)
    outtextxy(x+xoffset, y-yoffset, buffer);
  else
    outtextxy(x, y, buffer);
  startpercentage += showpercentage;
  showkey(color,fill,label);
}
```

Creating Bar Graphs

The BGI provides two specialized functions for drawing bar charts: **bar( )** and **bar3d( )**. We briefly visited these two functions in Chapter 2 and now we'll take a closer look at how we can actually use them to create presentation bar charts.

Creating a bar chart is in itself quite simple. The complexity arises, however, when we try to add in various embellishments to make a professional looking bar chart or to automate the chart-generation process. This section presents a bar chart program, called BARUTIL.CPP, that automatically generates a bar chart from a set of data, but it sacrifices some generality for the sake of brevity. More specifically, the program uses the BGI **bar( )** function to create bar charts like those in Figure 4.4. The data that is displayed is contained in the following three variables:

```
int yvalues[] = {5, 4, 7, 6};
char *xstrings[] = {"Jan", "Feb", "March", "April"};
char title[] = " Sales (in thousands) ";
```

In this example, the bar chart depicts four months of sales for a business. The title of the chart is stored in the character array called **title**. The data for the bars is placed in the **yvalues** array. For simplicity, these values are restricted to integers. The labels for these bars are listed in the array of characters stored in the **xstrings** array. These labels will appear below each bar on the horizontal axis. Finally, since there are four bars to be drawn, the **NUM_BARS** constant is set to 4.

The first step in drawing the chart consists of calling the **display_chart( )** function provided in BARUTIL.CPP. As you can see, this function is passed the various values and titles that are to be displayed, as well as a value called **numrules**. This integer value specifies the number of horizontal divisions that are to be used in the chart. In our example, we'll use four horizontal rules. You may want to experiment with this value to produce different charts.

Figure 4.4 Run BARUTIL.CPP to create this bar graph.

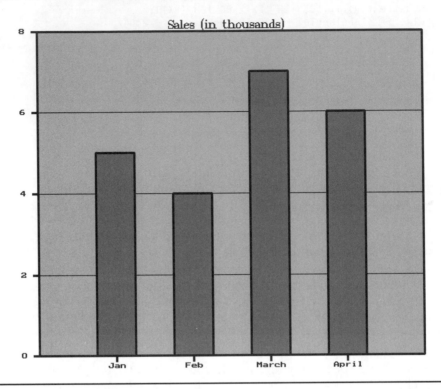

Essentially, **display_chart( )** is responsible for performing four important tasks. First, it calculates the bounds of the chart based on the size of the screen and the pixel boundaries defined by **SCREEN_BORDER_X** and **SCREEN_BORDER_Y**. Next, the title is written across the screen. To accommodate titles of varying lengths, a modified version of the **scaletext( )** function that we developed in Chapter 3 is used to automatically adjust the text to fit across the top of the chart. This version of **scaletext( )** is designed to stretch the text the same amount in the x and y directions to aid in readability.

The third part of **display_chart( )** consists of a call to the **getmax( )** function and a **while** loop, which determines the maximum value for the y (vertical) axis. The **getmax( )** function returns the maximum value in the array of values contained in **yvalues**. This value is saved in **maxyvalue**. The **while** loop increments **maxyvalue** until it reaches a number that is a multiple of the number of horizontal rules defined in the call to **display_chart( )**. The **while** loop ensures that the program selects a maximum value for the chart that will produce whole numbers that can be labeled on the y axis at each horizontal rule on the chart.

Finally, **drawchart()** is called. This function actually draws out a back-drop for the bar graph as well as the labels for the horizontal and vertical axes and the bars themselves. The backdrop is created by a call to **bar3d()**. Note that we are using this function instead of **fillpoly()** because its arguments are easier to specify. Alternatively, we could use the function **bar()**, but it would not draw a border to the backdrop like **bar3d()** does.

Within **drawchart()**, the four lines following the call to **bar3d()** and the **for** loop are used to draw the horizontal rules across the backdrop and create thick hash marks and labels on the y axis. The distance between the hash marks is calculated and stored in the variable **offset,** which is used within the **for** loop to place the rules across the chart. The two statements immediately following this **for** loop are used to write the label for the 0 value that corresponds to the horizontal axis.

Next, a scale factor is calculated that will later be used to determine exactly how high each bar should be drawn. The statement that performs this calculation is:

```
scale = (double)(bottom - top) / (double)maxyvalue;
```

As shown, the scale factor is dependent on the overall height of the chart and the maximum value that was determined in **display_chart()**. Figure 4.5 shows the scale factor calculation for a bar.

The lines of code following this statement are similar to those discussed previously to create the vertical labels. However, this code now marks out the divisions and labels on the horizontal axis. The **for** loop uses the strings in the **xstrings** array as the labels. Also within the **for** loop is a call to **bar3d()**. This statement actually creates each of the bars. Note that these calls to **bar3d()** use a depth of 0 so that the bars are drawn without a depth. As with the backdrop, **bar3d()** is used instead of the simpler **bar()** function because it provides borders around each of the bars.

Figure 4.5 Use these statements when calculating the height of a bar.

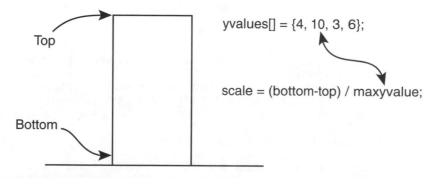

To adapt this chart program to your data, you will need to provide your own values in **xvalues**, **yvalues**, and **title**, as well as change the number represented by **NUM_BARS** to correspond to the number of unique data points you have. Finally, you can choose a value for **NUM_RULES** that will affect the number of horizontal rules drawn by the program and consequently the number of labels on the vertical axis.

Some additional things you might try adding are titles for the vertical and horizontal axes. You might also want to change the program so that it accepts float values along the vertical axes rather than just integers. Of course, there are a great many other alterations you might want to try also.

• BARUTIL.CPP

```
// BARUTIL.CPP: This is a utility program that generates a professional
// looking bar graph. It supports several options.
#include <stdio.h>
#include <graphics.h>
#include <conio.h>

const int SCREEN_BORDER_Y = 20; // Put a 10 pixel border at top and bottom
const int SCREEN_BORDER_X = 20; // Make a 10 pixel border on each side
const int NUM_RULES = 4;        // Use four rules on the backdrop
const int HASH_WIDTH = 8;       // Make hash marks on rules this long
const int NUM_BARS = 4;         // Four strings on x axis
int maxx, maxy;                 // Dimensions of graphics screen

// Scales the text so it fits into the specified rectangle. This
// routine is a modification of the scaletext() function in Chapter 3.
// It uses setusercharsize() to try to scale the text so that it
// looks good. Uses Triplex font.
void scaletext(int left, int top, int right, int bottom, char *string)
{
  int height;

  settextjustify(CENTER_TEXT, TOP_TEXT);
  setusercharsize(1, 1, 1, 1);
  settextstyle(TRIPLEX_FONT, HORIZ_DIR, USER_CHAR_SIZE);
  // In height calculation make room for letters extending below line
  // by multiplying textheight() by 5/4
  height = textheight(string) * 5 / 4;
  if (height > bottom-top) {        // Text is too tall
    // Try scaling down x and y by same amount in order to keep
    // text well proportioned
    setusercharsize(bottom-top, height, bottom-top, height);
    settextstyle(TRIPLEX_FONT, HORIZ_DIR, USER_CHAR_SIZE);
    // Enough room so write it
    if (textwidth(string) <= right - left)
      outtextxy((right+left)/2, top, string);
    else {
      // Doesn't fit with equal scaling, so squash it in!
```

```
        setusercharsize(1, 1, 1, 1);
        settextstyle(TRIPLEX_FONT, HORIZ_DIR, USER_CHAR_SIZE);
        setusercharsize(right-left, textwidth(string), bottom-top, height);
        settextstyle(TRIPLEX_FONT, HORIZ_DIR, USER_CHAR_SIZE);
        outtextxy((right+left)/2, top, string);
      }
  }
  // String is too long--try scaling equally
  else if (textwidth(string) > right-left) {
    setusercharsize(right-left, textwidth(string),
      right-left, textwidth(string));
    settextstyle(TRIPLEX_FONT, HORIZ_DIR, USER_CHAR_SIZE);
    // Enough room so write it
    if (textheight(string)*5/4 <= bottom-top)
      outtextxy((right+left)/2, top, string);
    else { // Doesn't fit with equal scaling, so squash it in!
      setusercharsize(1, 1, 1, 1);
      settextstyle(TRIPLEX_FONT, HORIZ_DIR, USER_CHAR_SIZE);
      setusercharsize(right-left, textwidth(string), bottom-top, height);
      settextstyle(TRIPLEX_FONT, HORIZ_DIR, USER_CHAR_SIZE);
      outtextxy((right+left)/2, top, string);
    }
  }
  else              // Just write out text--enough room
    outtextxy((right+left)/2, top, string);
}

// Finds and returns the largest value in the array of values
int getmax(int values[])
{
  int i=0, largest=1;

  for (i=0; i < 4; i++)
    if (values[i] > largest)
      largest = values[i];
  return largest;
}

// Draws the chart
void drawchart(int left, int top, int right, int bottom, int numrules,
  int maxyvalue, char *xstrings[], int yvalues[])
{
  int i, height, inc;
  double scale;
  char buffer[10];
  int offset;      // Draw horizontal rules this many pixels apart

  // Make a thick border
  setlinestyle(SOLID_LINE, 0, THICK_WIDTH);
  setfillstyle(CLOSE_DOT_FILL, BLUE);
  // Use bar3d() with a depth of 0 to draw a bar with a border
  bar3d(left, top, right, bottom, 0, 0);
  offset = (bottom - top) / numrules + 1;
  inc = maxyvalue / numrules;
```

```
      settextjustify(RIGHT_TEXT, CENTER_TEXT);
      settextstyle(DEFAULT_FONT, HORIZ_DIR, 1);
      for (i=0; i<numrules; i++) {
        // Draw rule as thin line
        setlinestyle(SOLID_LINE, 0, NORM_WIDTH);
        line(left, top+i*offset, right, top+i*offset);
        // Show thick hash mark
        setlinestyle(SOLID_LINE, 0, THICK_WIDTH);
        line(left-HASH_WIDTH, top+i*offset, left, top+i*offset);
        sprintf(buffer,"%d",inc * (numrules - i));
        outtextxy(left-HASH_WIDTH-textwidth(buffer), top+i*offset, buffer);
      }
      line(left-HASH_WIDTH, bottom, left, bottom); // Draw bottom hash mark
      outtextxy(left-HASH_WIDTH-textwidth(buffer), bottom, "0");
      // Now write out the values for the horizontal axis
      // Figure the amount to scale all bars
      scale = (double)(bottom - top) / (double)maxyvalue;
      setfillstyle(HATCH_FILL, BLUE);        // Make all bars HATCH_FILL
      offset = (right - left) / (NUM_BARS + 1);
      settextjustify(CENTER_TEXT, TOP_TEXT);
      settextstyle(DEFAULT_FONT, HORIZ_DIR, 1);
      for (i=1; i<=NUM_BARS; i++) {
        // Show thick hash mark
        setlinestyle(SOLID_LINE, 0, THICK_WIDTH);
        line(left+i*offset, bottom, left+i*offset, bottom+HASH_WIDTH);
        outtextxy(left+i*offset, bottom+HASH_WIDTH+2, xstrings[i-1]);
        // Draw the bars for the values. Make the total width of one of the
        // bars equal to half the distance between two of the hash marks on
        // the horizontal bar.
        height = yvalues[i-1] * scale;
        bar3d(left+i*offset-offset/4,bottom-height,
          left+i*offset+offset/4, bottom, 0, 0);
      }
    }

// High-level routine that displays the chart
void display_chart(char *title,char *xstrings[],int yvalues[],int numrules)
{
    int maxyvalue, left, top, right, bottom;

    if (numrules < 0) numrules = 1;   // Make sure the number of rules
                                      // is non-negative
    // Determine border points of backdrop
    left = SCREEN_BORDER_X + maxx / 8;
    top = SCREEN_BORDER_Y;
    right = maxx - SCREEN_BORDER_X;
    bottom = maxy - SCREEN_BORDER_Y;
    // Display the title at the top. Scale it to fit.
    scaletext(left, 0, right, top, title);
    // Determine a maximum value for the chart scale. It should be at least
    // as large as the largest list of values and a multiple of the number
    // of rules that the user desires. The number of rules should not be
    // greater than maxyvalue.
    maxyvalue = getmax(yvalues);        // Get the largest y value
```

```
    while ((maxyvalue % numrules) != 0)
      maxyvalue++;
    drawchart(left, top, right, bottom, numrules, maxyvalue,
      xstrings, yvalues);
}

int main()
{
  int gmode, gdriver = DETECT;
  int yvalues[] = {5,4,7,6};
  char *xstrings[] = {"Jan","Feb","March","April"};
  char title[] = " Sales (in thousands) ";

  initgraph(&gdriver, &gmode, "\\tcpp\\bgi");
  maxx = getmaxx();    maxy = getmaxy();
  display_chart(title, xstrings, yvalues, NUM_RULES);
  getch();
  closegraph();
  return 0;
}
```

Creating Three-Dimensional Bar Graphs

In the last section, we learned how to develop a bar graph utility that can create two-dimensional bar graphs. Next, we'll show you how to modify the program so that it can draw three-dimensional bar graphs. In fact, since **bar3d()** is already used to draw the bars, all we really have to do is change the depth argument passed to **bar3d()** in **drawchart()** to get a three-dimensional bar chart.

Generally, if you set the depth of the bar chart to one half the width of the bars you will get very pleasing results. With that in mind, here is an updated statement for **bar3d()**:

```
bar3d(left+i*offset-offset/4, bottom-height, left+i*offset+offset/4,
  bottom, offset/4, 1);
```

You can easily change the depth of the bars by altering the second to the last argument in **bar3d()**. If the depth is too large, however, the bars may begin to merge. If this happens, you will have to increase the spacing between the bars or use a smaller value for the depth of the bars. Figure 4.6 shows a version of BARUTIL.CPP that uses the BGI's three-dimensional bars.

Coin Graphs

Another modification you might try making to the BARUTIL.CPP program is to alter it so that it can create coin graphs like the one shown in Figure 4.7. This coin graph represents the sales of computer monitors for four computer sales-

---

Figure 4.6 This version of BARUTIL.CPP produces three-dimensional bars.

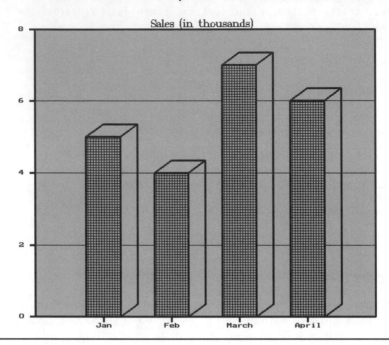

people. In order to make the chart interesting, small pictures of the monitors are stacked on top of each other like coins in order to represent the sales totals.

Probably the most challenging task of making a good coin graph is coming up with the right picture to use. You may need to experiment with various sequences of BGI functions before you come up with a design that satisfies you.

In order to create a coin chart, the basic idea is to draw a small picture, capture its image with **getimage( )**, and then redraw it as necessary using **putimage( )**. The coin chart in Figure 4.7 was created from the BARUTIL.CPP program with only a few minor modifications. Rather than show the entire code again and risk the possibility of obscuring these changes, we'll simply outline them one at a time.

First, we'll need to declare a few new variables. We'll use two constants to define the pixel dimensions of one of the monitors—the image for the coin chart. In addition, we'll need an array to hold the image of the monitor. Therefore, the following lines must be added to the top of BARUTIL.CPP:

```
const int PICT_HEIGHT = 24;      // Pixel height of each picture element
const int PICT_WIDTH = 32;       // Pixel width of each picture element
void *picture;                   // Pointer to picture element image
```

Figure 4.7 You can easily modify BARUTIL.CPP to create a coin graph.

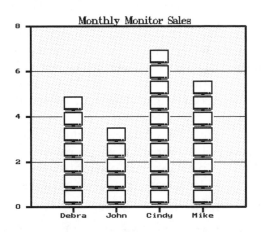

In addition, the program needs to be modified to use the following values and titles in generating the chart:

```
int yvalues[] = {5,4,7,6};
char *xstrings[] = {"Debra", "John", "Cindy", "Mike"};
char title[] = " Monthly Monitor Sales ";
```

The next change to make involves creating an image of the monitor. The monitor image used in Figure 4.7 was created from the following statements that were added to **main( )** immediately after the graphics initialization.

```
// The following lines create the picture of the monitor
bar(2, 2, PICT_WIDTH-2, PICT_HEIGHT-2);
setfillstyle(SOLID_FILL, BLACK);
bar(4, 4, PICT_WIDTH-4, PICT_HEIGHT-5);
setcolor(BLACK);
line(PICT_WIDTH-4, PICT_HEIGHT-3, PICT_WIDTH-5, PICT_HEIGHT-5);
line(PICT_WIDTH-8, PICT_HEIGHT-3, PICT_WIDTH-9, PICT_HEIGHT-5);
setcolor(getmaxcolor());
setfillstyle(SOLID_FILL, getmaxcolor());
bar(PICT_WIDTH/2-2, PICT_HEIGHT-2, PICT_WIDTH/2+2, PICT_HEIGHT);
line(4, PICT_HEIGHT, PICT_WIDTH-4, PICT_HEIGHT);
```

Once the picture of the object is drawn, its image is copied and saved into the array **picture** that we declared earlier. Here are the statements for this task:

```
picture = malloc(imagesize(0, 0, PICT_WIDTH, PICT_HEIGHT));
if (picture == NULL) {      // Couldn't allocate memory
  closegraph();
  printf("Failed to allocate picture image space.\n");
```

```
   exit(1);
}
getimage(0, 0, PICT_WIDTH, PICT_HEIGHT, picture);
putimage(0, 0, picture, XOR_PUT);
```

Note that we must erase the original picture on the screen before we go on. This is accomplished by using the **XOR_PUT** option as discussed in Chapter 2. Now that we have an image to work with, we are ready to call the chart program to create our coin graph. Note that since **malloc( )** is used, you must also include the header file ALLOC.H.

This leads us to our next change. Within the **drawchart( )** function, we need to replace the call to **bar3d( )**, which draws the bars, with the code to draw a stack of the coin images. Simply replace the call to **bar3d( )** with the following **for** loop, which stacks images of **picture** according to the height that represents the chart value:

```
for (j=PICT_HEIGHT; j<=height; j += PICT_HEIGHT)
  putimage(left+i*offset-PICT_WIDTH/2, bottom-j-4,picture, COPY_PUT);
```

You'll also need to declare an integer variable called **j** for this **for** loop. Note that this statement draws only whole copies of the coin image. It does not draw fractional images. If you need this additional capability you might try overwriting the percentage of the image you don't need by the background or backdrop color.

Two-Dimensional Graphics Techniques

In this chapter, we'll lay the foundation for developing two-dimensional graphics programs. We'll begin by exploring the relationship between screen coordinates and world coordinates, and we'll present techniques for mapping between these coordinates. In addition, we'll introduce the concept of transformations, which we'll use to describe how graphics objects can be manipulated in two dimensions. As part of our exploration, we'll develop a package called MAXTRIX.CPP that applies many of the concepts presented.

SCREEN COORDINATES

The BGI supports several different video adapters and modes, each with its own range of colors, resolution, and number of memory pages. Unfortunately, this flexibility introduces compatibility problems for the graphics programs that we develop. After all, how can we write a program so that it works equally well under the various graphics modes? One problem that we have already encountered is the issue of screen resolution. Not only must the resolutions of the various modes be considered, but we must also adjust for the *aspect ratio* of a screen in the various modes.

Working with Aspect Ratios

Each graphics mode has an aspect ratio associated with it. The aspect ratio is based on the ratio between the width and height of each pixel. This ratio is critical when we try to draw a figure of a particular size and shape on the screen. For instance, if we use the CGA 320 x 200 mode, each pixel is

Figure 5.1 To create a perfect square in CGA 320 x 200 mode, you must adjust for the screen's aspect ratio.

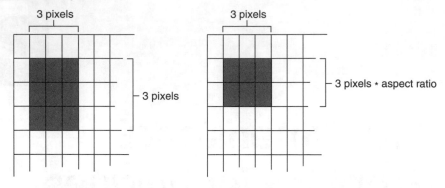

approximately twice as high as it is wide. Therefore, if we draw a 3 x 3 block of pixels we won't get a square on the screen. To actually draw a square we must adjust for the aspect ratio of the mode, as shown in Figure 5.1.

Fortunately, the BGI provides the **getaspectratio( )** function that we can use to determine the aspect ratio of the current mode. Its function prototype is declared in GRAPHICS.H as:

```
void far getaspectratio(int far *xasp, int far *yasp);
```

The arguments **xasp** and **yasp** can be divided to calculate the aspect ratio of the screen. In most modes, the pixels are taller than they are wide, therefore the BGI normalizes the **yasp** value to 10,000 and returns some value less than 10,000 in **xasp**. The aspect ratio of the screen, therefore, can be calculated as:

```
aspectratio = (double)xasp / (double)yasp;
```

This value can then be multiplied against each y dimension in order to draw an object correctly proportioned and positioned. For instance, in Figure 5.1, the height of the square shown becomes:

```
screen_height = y * aspectratio
```

Since **xasp** is generally smaller than **yasp**, **aspectratio** is set to some fractional value and **screen_height** is calculated as a value less than four. This produces the correctly proportioned square in Figure 5.1.

SCREEN AND WORLD COORDINATES

In the last section, we learned how to adjust for the difference between the x and y dimensions that exist in most of the graphics modes. Similarly, we must make adjustments to graphics objects so they retain their size when displayed in graphics modes with different screen resolutions. To achieve this, we'll use a standard coordinate system called *world coordinates*, which refers to measurements such as inches, feet, and meters. These world coordinates are then mapped to screen coordinates so that objects are properly sized and positioned.

Until now, we have only been working with screen coordinates. This approach can lead to problems when we work with graphics modes with different resolutions. For instance, a 10 x 10 square in a 320 x 200 mode appears quite different in a 640 x 200 mode. In addition, if we define an object to be located at (500, 150), it would not even appear in the 320 x 200 mode. We need the ability to map objects so that they are displayed proportionally and correctly positioned. We'll do this by expressing objects in world coordinates and then mapping them to screen coordinates so that they fit properly on the screen before they are drawn.

Mapping between Coordinate Systems

In general, we want to be able to map between world coordinates and screen coordinates, as shown in Figure 5.2. To do this we can use the relations shown in Figure 5.3. The equations

```
x' = a * x + b
y' = c * y + d
```

define how a point (x, y) in world coordinates can be mapped to a screen coordinate (x', y'). The values **L1**, **T1**, **R1**, and **B1** represent the range of values that we are considering in the world coordinates; similarly, **L2**, **T2**, **R2**, and **B2** define the size of the screen area that the object is to be mapped into. Now

---

Figure 5.2 You must map objects from world to screen coordinates.

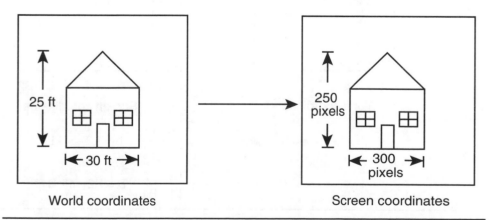

World coordinates   Screen coordinates

let's put these equations into our package MAXTRIX.CPP. The code for this file and its header, MATRIX.H, is shown near the end of this chapter.

First, we need two functions that can set the ranges of the world coordinates and screen coordinates. These functions are called **set_window()** and **set_viewport()**. Each is called with the left, top, right, and bottom bounds of its region, and internally sets an appropriate group of global variables within MAXTRIX.CPP to these ranges. In addition, **set_viewport()** calculates the ratios shown in Figure 5.3. For example, the two function calls

```
set_window(0.0, 0.0, 3.0, 3.0);
set_viewport(0, 0, getmaxx(), getmaxy());
```

set the range of values in the world and screen coordinates so that all objects between (0.0, 0.0) and (3.0, 3.0) in world coordinates are mapped to the full screen. Objects outside this range are clipped and not displayed.

As another example, you could use the same world coordinate settings but define the viewport on the screen to be:

```
set_viewport(0, 0, getmaxx()/2, getmaxy()/2);
```

In this case, the same objects would appear, but now they would appear in only the top-left half of the screen. Similarly, you can effectively zoom in on the objects displayed by decreasing the size of the region passed to **set_window()**.

Figure 5.3 Use these equations for mapping from world to screen coordinates.

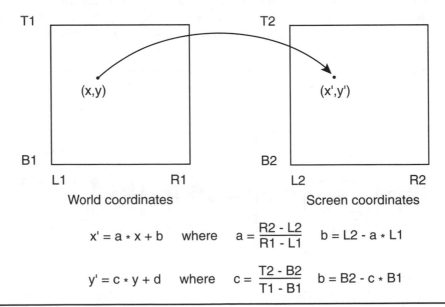

$$x' = a * x + b \quad \text{where} \quad a = \frac{R2 - L2}{R1 - L1} \quad b = L2 - a * L1$$

$$y' = c * y + d \quad \text{where} \quad c = \frac{T2 - B2}{T1 - B1} \quad b = B2 - c * B1$$

Note that, as written, you must match each call to **set_window( )** with a succeeding call to **set_viewport( )** in order to make changes take effect.

The functions in MAXTRIX.CPP that actually map between the coordinate systems are called **WORLDtoPC( )** and **PCtoWORLD( )**. Each function maps one point from one of the coordinate systems to the other. For example, the **WORLDtoPC( )** function maps a world coordinate to a screen coordinate by using the code:

```
void WORLDtoPC(double xw, double yw, int &xpc, int &ypc)
{
  xpc = (int)(a * xw + b);
  ypc = (int)(c * yw + d);
}
```

The arguments **xw** and **yw** are the world coordinates to be mapped to the screen coordinates **xpc** and **ypc**. You should compare these statements to the equations shown in Figure 5.3. Similarly, **PCtoWORLD( )** maps a screen coordinate to world coordinates by the statements:

```
void PCtoWORLD(int xpc, int ypc, double &xw, double &yw)
{
  xw = (xpc - b) / a;
  yw = (ypc - d) / c;
}
```

We'll be using these functions in the CAD program that we develop in Chapter 12 to define how and where objects are displayed.

TRANSFORMATIONS

In the last section, we learned how to map objects represented in world coordinates to the screen. Now let's explore ways to manipulate these objects so that they can be drawn at different locations, orientations, and scales. We'll use *transformations* to produce these effects.

Transformations are a basic mathematical operation in graphics programming. Literally, a transformation is a function (or equation) that defines how one set of data is to be changed or transformed into another. For example, let's say that we have a picture of a wheel on the screen that we want to rotate. We can use a rotation transformation to determine how the wheel is supposed to be affected as it is moved.

The most common transformations are translation, rotation, and scaling. In this section, we'll explore each of these transformations in detail and add functions to MAXTRIX.CPP to perform these operations. A list of the transformation functions that we will add to MAXTRIX.CPP is shown in Table 5.1.

The CAD program that we'll develop in Chapter 12 uses the MAXTRIX.CPP toolkit to translate and rotate objects. When we explore three-dimensional

Table 5.1 Two-Dimensional Transformations in MATRIX.CPP

Function	Description
PCpolytoWORLD	Converts a PC-based polygon array to world coordinates
PCrotatepoly()	Rotates a polygon in screen coordinates
PCscalepoly()	Scales a polygon in screen coordinates
PCshearpoly()	Shears a polygon in screen coordinates
PCtoWORLD	Converts a PC coordinate into an equivalent world coordinate
PCtranslatepoly()	Translates a polygon in screen coordinates
WORLDpolytoPCpoly	Converts a world-based polygon array to PC coordinates
WORLDrotatepoly()	Rotates a polygon in world coordinates
WORLDscalepoly()	Scales a polygon in world coordinates
WORLDtoPC	Converts a world coordinate into an equivalent PC coordinate
WORLDtranslatepoly()	Translates a polygon in world coordinates

graphics in Chapter 13, we'll rely on transformations to generate perspective views of three-dimensional objects. For now, however, we will only be concerned with objects in two dimensions.

Translation

One of the simplest transformations produces a *translation*. Essentially, a translation defines how a point is supposed to be moved from one location in space to another. For example, if we have a box drawn on the left side of the screen and we want to move it to the right, we can use a translation transformation to specify how each point must be moved.

You can translate a pixel on the screen with the following statement, which adds an appropriate value—the amount that the point is to be moved—to each of the x and y coordinates: .

```
new_x = x + translate_x;
new_y = y + translate_y;
```

The values **translate_x** and **translate_y** can be either positive or negative, and define how much the point (**x**, **y**) should be translated in the x and y directions, respectively.

Translating an object, such as a polygon, is only a matter of translating each of the points that make up the polygon, as illustrated in Figure 5.4. A function in MAXTRIX.CPP that does this is called **PCtranslatepoly()** and is written as:

Figure 5.4 When you translate an object, each point is translated individually.

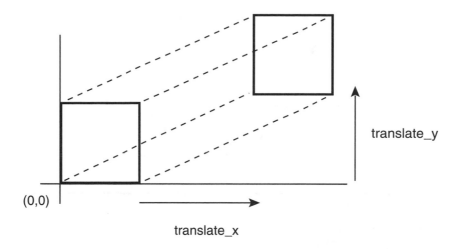

```
void PCtranslatepoly(int numpoints, int *poly, int tx, int ty)
{
  for (int i=0; i<numpoints*2; i+=2) {
    poly[i] += tx;
    poly[i+1] += ty;
  }
}
```

It is designed to work in screen coordinates, since the translation amounts are specified as integers. A similar function, **WORLDtranslatepoly( )**, is included in MAXTRIX.CPP, which is designed to translate a polygon specified in world coordinates. Because of this, **tx**, **ty**, and the array **poly** are defined as doubles.

As you review this function, note that we are using a shorthand method to declare the variable **i**. That is, the declaration for this variable is placed in the first line of the **for** statement. Although this type of declaration is not allowed in C, it is supported in Turbo C++. We'll be using it in many of our examples because it simplifies the task of declaring local variables.

Scaling a Two-Dimensional Polygon

Scaling a two-dimensional polygon can be accomplished by multiplying each of the coordinates of the original polygon by a scale factor. For example, assume we want to scale the box shown in Figure 5.5 by 2 in the x direction and by 1/2 in the y direction. Simply apply the following equations to each of the coordinates of the box:

Figure 5.5 This box is scaled by 2 in the x direction and 1/2 in the y direction.

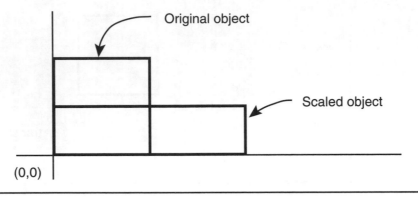

```
scaledx = x * scalex;
scaledy = y * scaley;
```

The following function, **PCscalepoly()**, in MAXTRIX.CPP, performs this operation for a polygon in screen coordinates:

```
void PCscalepoly(int numpoints, int *poly, double sx, double sy)
{
  for (int i=0; i<numpoints*2; i+=2) {
    poly[i] *= sx;
    poly[i+1] *= sy;
  }
}
```

A similar function—**WORLDscalepoly()**—exists for polygons specified in world coordinates.

Merely calling **PCscalepoly()** to scale an object does not always produce the results expected, however. Because each coordinate in the object is multiplied by a scale factor, the object may be moved, as well as scaled, as shown in Figure 5.6. You can prevent these side effects from occurring by setting one of the coordinates to (0, 0). This coordinate will always stay the same. Therefore, if you want to scale an object, yet keep one of its points stationary so that the object doesn't move, two additional steps must be taken. First, the object must be translated so that the point you want to scale about (keep fixed) moves to the origin. Second, after applying the scaling transformation, the object must be translated back by the amount that it was earlier translated. The net effect is that the object is scaled, but the point that is translated to the origin and back remains stationary. This scaling sequence, illustrated in Figure 5.7, is actually more useful than the first.

Figure 5.6 When you scale an object that is not at the origin, the size and location will both be affected.

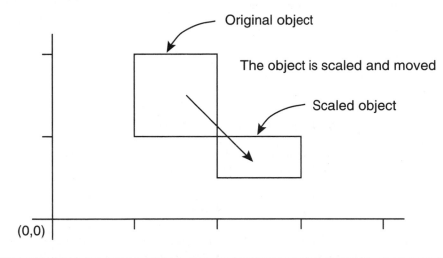

Figure 5.7 Follow this process to properly scale an object that is not at the origin.

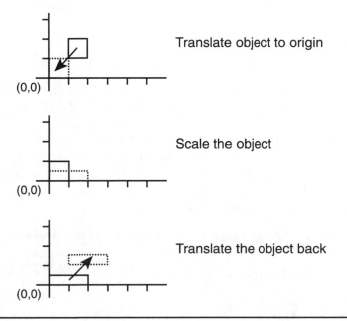

For example, the following code doubles the size of the polygon in the array **poly** by translating it so that its first point is at the origin, scaling it, and then translating the polygon back.

```
px = poly[0];
py = poly[1];
PCtranslatepoly(numpoints, poly, -px, -py);
PCscalepoly(numpoints, poly, 2.0, 2.0);
PCtranslatepoly(numpoints, poly, px, py);
```

Rotating a Two-Dimensional Polygon

Another useful transformation rotates an object about a point. These are the equations you'll need to perform the rotation:

```
rotatedx = x * cos(angle) - y * sin(angle);
rotatedy = x * sin(angle) + y * cos(angle);
```

Rather than go into the geometry that derives these equations, let's look at them from a user's standpoint. The **x** and **y** variables on the right side of the equation represent the point being rotated, and the **angle** variable specifies the angle on which the point is to be rotated. In Turbo C++, this value needs to be expressed in radians. Since degrees are more natural for specifying angles, we'll use the inline function **torad( )** to convert angles in degrees to radians.

```
inline double torad(int d)
{
  return (double)(d) * M_PI / 180.0;
}
```

Recall from Chapter 4 that inline functions are similiar to macros; however, they support typechecking and they make use of the scoping rules that other functions abide by.

To successfully rotate an object, we need to pick a point about which the object is to be rotated, translate it to the origin, rotate the polygon, and then translate the object back. The following function, **PCrotatepoly( )**, in MAXTRIX.CPP, performs the rotation operation and can be used to rotate a polygon, as shown in Figure 5.8.

```
void PCrotatepoly(int numpoints, int *poly, double angle)
{
  int i, x, y;
  double, double costheta, sintheta;

  rad = toradians(angle);
  costheta = cos(rad);
  sintheta = sin(rad);
```

Figure 5.8 This figure illustrates the rotation of an object.

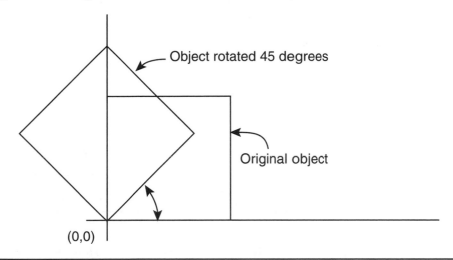

```
for (i=0; i<numpoints*2; i+=2) {
    x = poly[i];
    y = poly[i+1];
    poly[i] = x * costheta - y * sintheta / aspectratio;
    poly[i+1] = x * sintheta * aspectratio + y * costheta;
  }
}
```

Note that the **y** values in the equations are adjusted by **aspectratio**. This adjustment is required because this function is operating with screen coordinates. The function **WORLDrotatepoly( )** has a similar code, except that, since it is designed to work with world coordinates, it does not need these adjustments.

The Shear Transformation

Some transformations produce some rather interesting effects. One of the more common transformations that falls into this category shears the objects to which it is applied, as shown in Figure 5.9. This tansformation involves multiplying each of the coordinates of the object by a scale factor and then adding an offset. These are the pair of equations you need to produce the shear effect:

```
shearedx = x + c * y;
shearedy = d * x + y;
```

As with rotations, we want to shear the polygon about a point, thus we must translate the polygon to the origin, apply the shear transformation, and then translate the object back. In addition, if we transform pixels on the screen, we

---

Figure 5.9 There is even a transformation that allows you to shear an object.

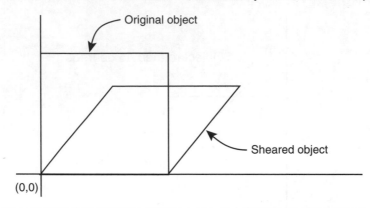

---

will need to compensate for the monitor's aspect ratio. Here is a routine that you can use to shear a polygon situated at the origin:

```
void PCshearpoly(int numpoints, int *poly, double c, double d)
{
  int i, x, y;

  for (i=0; i<numpoints*2; i+=2) {
    x = poly[i];
    y = poly[i+1];
    poly[i] = x + c * y / aspectratio;
    poly[i+1] = d * x * aspectratio + y;
  }
}
```

• MATRIX.H

```
// MATRIX.H: The following are a list of matrix operations that
// MATRIX.CPP supports.

void PCtranslatepoly(int numpoints, int *poly, int tx, int ty);
void PCscalepoly(int numpoints, int *poly, double sx, double sy);
void PCrotatepoly(int numpoints, int *poly, double angle);
void PCshearpoly(int numpoints, int *poly, double c, double d);
void copypoly(int numpoints, int *polyfrom, int *polyto);
void WORLDtranslatepoly(int numpoints, double *poly, double tx, double ty);
void WORLDscalepoly(int numpoints, double *poly, double sx, double sy);
void WORLDrotatepoly(int numpoints, double *poly, double angle);
void copyWORLDpoly(int numpoints, double *polyfrom, double *polyto);
void PCpolytoWORLDpoly(int numpoints, int *PCpoly, double *WORLDpoly);
void WORLDpolytoPCpoly(int numpoints, double *WORLDpoly, int *PCpoly);
void set_window(double xmin, double xmax, double ymin, double ymax);
```

```
void set_viewport(int xmin, int xmax, int ymin, int ymax);
void WORLDtoPC(double xw, double yw, int &xpc, int &ypc);
void PCtoWORLD(int xpc, int ypc, double &xw, double &yw);
```

• MATRIX.CPP

```cpp
// MATRIX.CPP: This file supports the matrix operations that will be
// used in the two- and three-dimensional graphics programs later in
// this book.
#include <graphics.h>
#include <math.h>
#include "matrix.h"

extern double aspectratio;       // Define the aspect ratio
static double a, b, c, d;         // Internal values set by
static int xvl, xvr, yvt, yvb;    // set_window()and set_viewport()
static double xwl, xwr, ywt, ywb; // to map to screen coordinates

// Inline function to convert degrees to radians
inline double torad(int d)
{
  return ((double)(d) * M_PI) / 180.0;
}


// Translates a two-dimensional polygon by tx and ty. The polygon
// should be in screen coordinates. Note the declaration style of i.
void PCtranslatepoly(int numpoints, int *poly, int tx, int ty)
{
  for (int i=0; i<numpoints*2; i+=2) {
    poly[i] += tx;    poly[i+1] += ty;
  }
}


// Scales a polygon by sx in the x dimension and sy in the y
// direction. The polygon should be in screen coordinates.
void PCscalepoly(int numpoints, int *poly, double sx, double sy)
{
  for (int i=0; i<numpoints*2; i+=2) {
    poly[i] *= sx;    poly[i+1] *= sy;
  }
}


// Rotates a polygon by the number of degrees specified in angle.
// The polygon should be in screen coordinates.
void PCrotatepoly(int numpoints, int *poly, double angle)
{
  int i, x, y;
  double rad, costheta, sintheta;

  rad = torad(angle);
  costheta = cos(rad);
  sintheta = sin(rad);
```

```
  for (i=0; i<numpoints*2; i+=2) {
    x = poly[i];        y = poly[i+1];
    poly[i] = x * costheta - y * sintheta / aspectratio;
    poly[i+1] = x * sintheta * aspectratio + y * costheta;
  }
}

// Shears a polygon by applying c to the x direction and d to
// the y dimension. The polygon should be in screen coordinates.
void PCshearpoly(int numpoints, int *poly, double c, double d)
{
  int i, x, y;

  for (i=0; i<numpoints*2; i+=2) {
    x = poly[i];        y = poly[i+1];
    poly[i] = x + c * y / aspectratio;
    poly[i+1] = d * x * aspectratio + y;
  }
}

// Copies from one integer polygon to another
void copypoly(int numpoints, int *polyfrom, int *polyto)
{
  for (int i=0; i<numpoints*2; i++)
    polyto[i] = polyfrom[i];
}

// Translates a polygon in world coordinates
void WORLDtranslatepoly(int numpoints, double *poly, double tx, double ty)
{
  for (int i=0; i<numpoints*2; i+=2) {
    poly[i] += tx;      poly[i+1] += ty;
  }
}

// Scales a polygon in world coordinates by sx and sy
void WORLDscalepoly(int numpoints, double *poly, double sx, double sy)
{
  for (int i=0; i<numpoints*2; i+=2) {
    poly[i] *= sx;      poly[i+1] *= sy;
  }
}

// Rotates a polygon in world coordinates
void WORLDrotatepoly(int numpoints, double *poly, double angle)
{
  double x, y, rad, costheta, sintheta;

  rad = torad(angle);
  costheta = cos(rad);
  sintheta = sin(rad);
  for (int i=0; i<numpoints*2; i+=2) {
    x = poly[i];        y = poly[i+1];
```

```
      poly[i] = x * costheta - y * sintheta;
      poly[i+1] = x * sintheta + y * costheta;
   }
}


// Copies one polygon in world coordinates to another
void copyWORLDpoly(int numpoints, double *polyfrom, double *polyto)
{
   for (int i=0; i<numpoints*2; i++)
      polyto[i] = polyfrom[i];
}


// Converts a world coordinate to a screen coordinate
void WORLDtoPC(double xw, double yw, int &xpc, int &ypc)
{
   xpc = (int)(a * xw + b+0.5);   ypc = (int)(c * yw + d+0.5);
}


// Converts a screen coordinate to a world coordinate
void PCtoWORLD(int xpc, int ypc, double &xw, double &yw)
{
   xw = (xpc - b) / a;  yw = (ypc - d) / c;
}


// Defines the window used in real world coordinates
void set_window(double xmin, double xmax, double ymin, double ymax)
{
   xwl = xmin;    xwr = xmax;
   ywb = ymin;    ywt = ymax;
}


// Defines the region on the screen in which world objects
// are mapped to
void set_viewport(int xmin, int xmax, int ymin, int ymax)
{
   xvl = xmin;    xvr = xmax;
   yvb = ymin;    yvt = ymax;
   a = (xvr - xvl) / (xwr - xwl);     b = xvl - a * xwl;
   c = (yvt - yvb) / (ywt - ywb);     d = yvb - c * ywb;
}


// Converts a list of polygon points from screen coordinates
// to world coordinates
void PCpolytoWORLDpoly(int numpoints, int *polypc, double *polyw)
{
   for (int i=0; i<numpoints; i++)
      PCtoWORLD(polypc[i*2], polypc[i*2+1], polyw[i*2], polyw[i*2+1]);
}


// Converts a list of polygon points from world coordinates to
// PC screen coordinates
void WORLDpolytoPCpoly(int numpoints, double *polyw, int *polypc)
{
```

```
  for (int i=0; i<numpoints; i++)
    WORLDtoPC(polyw[i*2], polyw[i*2+1], polypc[i*2], polypc[i*2+1]);
}
```

A Matrix Demo

The following program, MTXTEST.CPP, is a short program that you can use to test the matrix operations in MAXTRIX.CPP. It applies several of the transformations developed in MAXTRIX.CPP to the polygon in the array **points**. After displaying the result of each of the transforms, you must press a key to proceed to the next one.

To compile the program, you will need to link MAXTRIX.CPP with MTXTEST.CPP. If you are using your compiler's integrated environment, create a new project, and add the files MTXTEST.CPP and MAXTRIX.CPP to it. Now you're ready to compile, link, and run the program.

• MTXTEST.CPP

```
// MTXTEST.CPP: This program tests the transformations defined in MATRIX.CPP.
#include <graphics.h>
#include <conio.h>
#include <math.h>
#include "matrix.h"

int xasp, yasp;
double aspectratio;

main()
{
  int gmode, gdriver = DETECT;
  int points[] = {150,80, 400,80, 400,150, 150,150, 150,80};
  int px, py, numpoints = 5, polycopy[10];

  initgraph(&gdriver, &gmode, "\\tcpp\\bgi");
  getaspectratio(&xasp, &yasp);
  aspectratio = (double)xasp / (double)yasp;
  rectangle(0, 0, getmaxx(), getmaxy());
  // Tests translate polygon
  drawpoly(numpoints, points);
  copypoly(numpoints, points, polycopy);
  px = polycopy[0];
  py = polycopy[1];
  PCtranslatepoly(numpoints, polycopy, -px, -py);
  drawpoly(numpoints, polycopy);
  getch();

  // Scales the polygon about the point (px, py)
  copypoly(numpoints, points, polycopy);
  PCtranslatepoly(numpoints, polycopy, -px, -py);
```

```
    PCscalepoly(numpoints, polycopy, 1.5, 1.5);
    PCtranslatepoly(numpoints, polycopy, px, py);
    drawpoly(numpoints, polycopy);
    getch();

    // Rotates the object about the point (px, py)
    copypoly(numpoints, points, polycopy);
    PCtranslatepoly(numpoints, polycopy, -px, -py);
    PCrotatepoly(numpoints, polycopy, 45);
    PCtranslatepoly(numpoints, polycopy, px, py);
    drawpoly(numpoints, polycopy);
    getch();

    // Shears the object about the point (px, py)
    clearviewport();
    drawpoly(numpoints, points);
    copypoly(numpoints, points, polycopy);
    PCtranslatepoly(numpoints, polycopy, -px, -py);
    PCshearpoly(numpoints, polycopy, 0, 1);
    PCtranslatepoly(numpoints, polycopy, px, py);
    drawpoly(numpoints, polycopy);
    getch();
    closegraph();          // Exits graphics mode
    return 0;
}
```

6

Animation

Animation is an attractive graphics feature for several reasons. It can help draw attention to a portion of a display, demonstrate how something works, lay the foundation for interactive programs, or simply make a program more visually interesting. In this chapter, we'll explore some of the various animation techniques that you can experiment with in your own graphics programs. Some of the techniques presented include inbetweening, moving objects using **getimage( )** and **putimage( )**, animating objects by changing palette colors, and using multiple-screen pages to create motion.

INBETWEENING

Inbetweening is a simple technique. The basic idea is to define the start and stop coordinates of an object and then calculate and display the object as it progresses from its initial state to its final one. We'll now look at a simple example. Suppose we want to animate a single point by moving it from one location to another. All we need to know is where the point starts, stops, and the number of intermediate steps it should take. For example, if our point starts at (0, 0) and we want it to move to (150, 150) in 15 steps, we must move the point in 10-pixel increments.

The next step is to write a program that can calculate and plot the intermediate steps of our animated point. The calculation is merely a linear interpolation between the start and stop positions of the point. In our example, we want to plot the point 15 times, by moving it 10 pixels each time in the x and y directions. Therefore, the code that can perform this is:

```
number_of_steps = 15;
step_size = (stopx - startx) / number_of_steps;
for (j=0; j<number_of_steps; j++) {
  inc_amount = step_size * j;
  putpixel(startx + inc_amount, starty + inc_amount, WHITE);
  putpixel(startx + inc_amount, starty + inc_amount, BLACK);
}
putpixel(x + inc_amount, y + inc_amount, WHITE);
```

The variable **step_size** determines the distance the point should be moved between each state. It is dependent on the number of intermediate states that are desired (in this example, 15), and the total distance to travel. The **for** loop steps through each of the intermediate steps of the animation by calculating **inc_amount**, which determines where the pixel is moved to, plots the pixel by a call to **putpixel()**, and then erases it by another call to **putpixel()**. In this example, the x and y directions are incremented equally, but we can easily modify the code so that the x and y directions change by different amounts.

This example shows us how to move a point across the screen, but what about animating an object? The transition is simple. If we have an object that is drawn as a series of line segments, for instance, all we need to do is run our inbetweening algorithm on each of the endpoints of the line segments and draw the lines between the points at each step in the process. The next section looks at animating objects using this technique.

Animating a Line

Before we proceed with animating an object drawn from line segments, we need to re-examine the way we draw lines. In order to animate an object, we must draw the object, remove it from the screen, draw it in its new position, erase it, draw it at the next location, and so on. However, if we remove the line segments from the screen by overwriting them with the background color, it may quickly become a mess if there are other objects on it that the animated object crosses over. Clearly, this is not what we want.

In Chapter 3, we learned that an object could be moved *cleanly* by using the **XOR_PUT** option of the **putimage()** function. Although we won't use **putimage()** to animate a line segment, we can still use the same **XOR_PUT** option to *cleanly* move a line across the screen.

The BGI allows us to set the line-drawing functions so that they draw exclusive-OR lines. Because of the exclusive-ORing, we'll be able to remove any line from the screen by simply drawing it again. In order to turn the exclusive-OR capability of the line drawer on, we must use the **setwritemode()** function. Its function prototype is:

```
void far setwritemode(int mode);
```

The **mode** argument can be set to **COPY_PUT** or **XOR_PUT**. By default, the BGI uses **COPY_PUT**. This means that lines are drawn by setting each pixel along the line segment to the current drawing color. If the **XOR_PUT** option is used, each pixel in the line segment is exclusive-ORed with the screen image. Therefore, if a line routine is called twice with the same coordinates when the **XOR_PUT** option is used, the line will be drawn and then erased, without the original screen being affected.

Note that the **setwritemode( )** function works only with **line( )**, **linerel( )**, **lineto( )**, **rectangle( )**, and **drawpoly( )**.

Working with Inbetweening

Now let's apply **setwritemode( )** to inbetweening so that we can animate a set of line segments. The code shown next, for instance, will move a rectangle across the screen as shown in Figure 6.1.

The starting coordinates of the rectangle are defined in the integer array **startpoints**, where the array contains a series of x and y coordinates. The final location of the rectangle is stored in the array **stoppoints**. Since **drawpoly( )** is used to draw the lines, the arrays are declared so that their first and last coordinates are the same. An additional array, **points**, is also declared to be the same size as **startpoints** and **stoppoints** so that it can hold and display

---

Figure 6.1 This is the time-lapsed output of INBTWEEN.CPP.

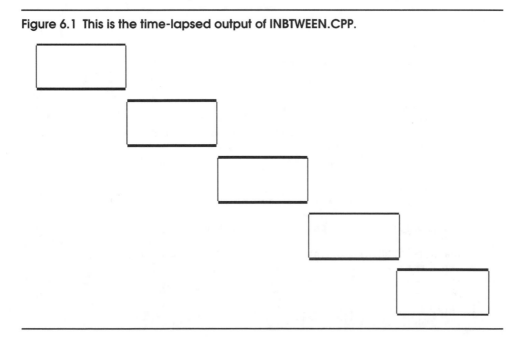

each intermediate state of the animated rectangle. The constant **NUM_STEPS** defines the number of intermediate steps used in the animation. In this example, **NUM_STEPS** is set to an integer value of 100. Other than the use of these variables, the inbetweening function is similar to the code presented earlier.

Here is the complete program:

```
// INBTWEEN.CPP: A simple program that demonstrates inbetweening.
#include <graphics.h>
#include <conio.h>
#include <dos.h>

const int NUM_STEPS = 100;   // Number of inbetweening steps
const int LENGTH = 5*2;      // Length of points array

int startpoints[LENGTH] = {0,0, 100,0, 100,20, 0,20, 0,0};
int stoppoints[LENGTH] = {400,100, 500,100, 500,120, 400,120, 400,100};
int points[LENGTH];          // Contains points to be drawn

// These statements will change a rectangle into a triangle. Uncomment
// these lines to generate Figure 6.2.
// int startpoints[LENGTH] =  {0,0, 639,0, 639,199, 0,199, 0,0};
// int stoppoints[LENGTH] = {210,120, 315,60, 420,120, 210,120, 210,120};

// This function does the inbetweening
void inbetween(void)
{
  float step_size, inc_amount;
  int i, j;

  step_size = 1.0 / (NUM_STEPS - 1);
  for (i=0; i<NUM_STEPS; i++) {
    inc_amount = i * step_size;
    for (j=0; j<LENGTH; j++) {
      points[j] = startpoints[j] + inc_amount *
                  (stoppoints[j] - startpoints[j]);
      points[j+1] = startpoints[j+1] + inc_amount *
                  (stoppoints[j+1] - startpoints[j+1]);
    }
    drawpoly(LENGTH/2, points);     // Draw lines
    delay(100);     // Wait before erasing to lessen flicker

    drawpoly(LENGTH/2, points);     // Erase lines
  }
  drawpoly(LENGTH/2, points);        // Redraw the final lines
}

main()
{
  int gmode, gdriver=DETECT;
```

```
initgraph(&gdriver, &gmode, "\\tcpp\\bgi");
setwritemode(XOR_PUT);
inbetween();
getch();
closegraph();
return 0;
}
```

An intriguing thing about inbetweening is that the first and last images of the object being animated do not have to be the same. Figure 6.2 shows the previous code modified so that the rectangle is turned into a triangle. The only restriction here is that the number of line segments in the start and final states must be the same. Actually, we can break this rule by adding various figures to the final version of the animated object to produce interesting results. As an exercise you might try turning a square into a face for instance. Of course, the difficulty here is coming up with the proper coordinates that can draw the shapes.

The following are two array declarations for **startpoints** and **stoppoints** that you can use to replace those shown in the previous example. The coordinates in these two arrays will produce a picture of a rectangle turning into a

Figure 6.2 You can use inbetweening to convert a rectangle into a triangle.

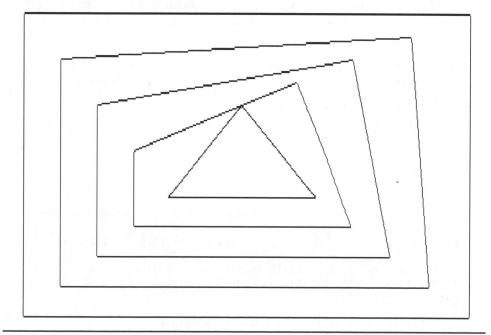

triangle as described earlier. Since the number of line segments must be the same in the start and stop states, but clearly the rectangle and triangle have different numbers of vertices, we have declared **stoppoints** so that the first and last coordinate is specified three times. In other words, one of the line segments in the rectangle shrinks to a line of zero length. Therefore, although there will be the same number of line segments declared in the arrays, it appears that the triangle has one less line.

```
int startpoints[LENGTH] = {0,0, 639,0, 639,199, 0,199, 0,0};
int stoppoints[LENGTH] = {210,120, 315,60, 420,120, 210,120, 210,120};
```

WORKING WITH GETIMAGE() AND PUTIMAGE()

One of the drawbacks to using inbetweening is that the animated object must be redrawn at each step along the way. For complex objects this process can be slow. An alternative method is to draw the image once and then move it across the screen using the **getimage()** and **putimage()** functions.

In Chapter 2, we introduced the **getimage()** and **putimage()** functions and described the various placement options that are available with **putimage()**. In this section, we'll focus on using them, rather than describing how they operate. (See Chapter 2 for more specific details on these routines and how they function.)

Our first animation example using **getimage()** and **putimage()** is to move a bicycle across the screen, as shown in Figure 6.3. The code for this example is:

```
// BIKE.CPP: This program demonstrates animation using the BGI's
// getimage() and putimage() functions. The program draws a bike on the
// screen and then copies the image of the bike across the screen using
// the XOR_PUT option of putimage().
#include <stdlib.h>
#include <stdio.h>
#include <graphics.h>
#include <alloc.h>
#include <conio.h>
#include <dos.h>

const int STEP = 5;          // Number of pixels to move bike each time

void *bike;                  // Points to the image of the bike

// Draw a bicycle using calls to circle() and line(). Then capture
// the image of the bicycle with getimage().
void drawbike(void)
{
  circle(50, 100, 25);       // Draw the wheels
  circle(150, 100, 25);
```

Figure 6.3 This is the time-lapsed output of BIKE.CPP.

```
    line(50, 100, 80, 85);    // Draw part of the frame
    line(80, 85, 134, 85);
    line(77, 82, 95, 100);
    line(130, 80, 150, 100);
    line(128, 80, 113, 82);   // Draw the Handlebars
    line(128, 80, 116, 78);
    line(72, 81, 89, 81);     // Draw the Seat
    line(73, 82, 90, 82);
    circle(95, 100, 5);       // Draw the pedals
    line(92, 105, 98, 95);
    line(91, 105, 93, 105);
    line(97, 95, 99, 95);
    line(95, 100, 136, 87);
    bike = malloc(imagesize(25, 75, 175, 125));  // Allocate image
    if (bike == NULL) {
      closegraph();
      printf("\nFailed to allocate memory for bike image.\n");
      exit(1);
    }
    getimage(25, 75, 175, 125, bike); // Capture image of bike
}

// Move bike across the screen in increments of STEP
void movebike(void)
{
  int i;

  for (i=0; i<getmaxx()-180; i+=STEP) {
    putimage(25+i, 75, bike, XOR_PUT);          // Erase bike
    putimage(25+STEP+i, 75, bike, XOR_PUT);     // Display bike
    delay(50);
  }
}

main()
{
  int gdriver = CGA;        // Use CGA high-resolution mode or
  int gmode = CGAHI;        // comparable 640 x 200 modes

  initgraph(&gdriver, &gmode, "\\tcpp\\bgi");
  drawbike();
```

```
    movebike();
    getch();
    closegraph();
    return 0;
}
```

The original image of the bicycle is created by a series of calls to **line( )** and **circle( )** in the function **drawbike( )**. Next, memory is allocated to the pointer **bike** by a call to **malloc( )** to hold the screen image of the bicycle. Note that a test is made of the pointer **bike** and the pointer returned from **malloc( )** is tested to see whether it is **NULL**. If so, the memory allocation fails and the program quits. Otherwise, the bike's image is retrieved by a call to **getimage( )**.

```
bike = malloc(imagesize(25, 75, 175, 125));  // Allocate image
if (bike == NULL) {
  closegraph();
  printf("\nFailed to allocate memory for bike image.\n");
  exit(1);
}
getimage(25, 75, 175, 125, bike);
```

Next, the function **movebike( )** is called to move the bicycle image in **bike** across the screen. In this example, the image is moved from the coordinate (25, 75) to (**getmaxx( )**–180, 75) in steps of 5 pixels. The movement is accomplished by the **for** loop in **movebike( )**, which is:

```
for (i=0; i<getmaxx()-180; i+=STEP) {
  putimage(25+i, 75, bike, XOR_PUT);          // Erase bike
  putimage(25+STEP+i, 75, bike, XOR_PUT);     // Display bike
  delay(50);
}
```

As you can see, the **for** loop calls **putimage( )** twice. The first one erases the current image of the bicycle by exclusive-ORing **bike** to the screen. The second one displays the bicycle image at its next location using the **XOR_PUT** option.

We can improve our example by rotating the bicycle's pedals as the bicycle moves. The basic idea is to create several images of the bike each with the pedals at different orientations and then sequence through them to make it look like the pedals are turning. There are two ways of accomplishing this. For instance, we could make several images of the whole bicycle with the pedals at different orientations and then sequence through them or we could have one complete image of the bicycle and a series of smaller images that show the pedals at various positions. With the second technique, the pedal images must overlay with the bike image to create the motion.

You may be wondering: why would we want to have two sets of images, one for the bicycle and the other for animating the pedals? One important reason, though not critical here, is that for large pictures we can speed up the animation process and save memory by swapping images only of the regions that must be changed. In addition, several images of the whole bicycle can consume a lot more memory than a single image of the bicycle and a companion set of smaller images—in high-resolution graphics modes, you will find it very easy to consume an excessive amount of memory.

Now let's get back to the task of animating the bicycle pedals. The next program we'll look at animates the bicycle by moving it across the screen, as well as rotating its pedals. The program accomplishes this by creating four different images of the bike, each with different pedal orientations, and sequencing through these images.

```cpp
// BIKE2.CPP: This program demonstrates animation using the BGI's
// getimage() and putimage(). The program creates four images of a
// bike--each with the pedals in a different orientation--so that
// when the images are played back it looks like the pedals are
// moving as the bicycle is moved across the screen.
#include <stdlib.h>
#include <stdio.h>
#include <graphics.h>
#include <alloc.h>
#include <conio.h>
#include <dos.h>

const int STEP = 5;          // Number of pixels to move bike each time

void *bike1, *bike2;         // Points to the image of the bike
void *bike3, *bike4;

// Draw a bicycle using calls to circle() and line(). Then capture
// the image of the bicycle with getimage().
void drawbike(void)
{
  void *pedals;

  circle(50, 100, 25);       // Draw the wheels
  circle(150, 100, 25);
  line(50, 100, 80, 85);     // Draw part of the frame
  line(80, 85, 134, 85);
  line(77, 82, 95, 100);
  line(130, 80, 150, 100);
  line(128, 80, 113, 82);    // Draw the handlebars
  line(128, 80, 116, 78);
  line(72, 81, 89, 81);      // Draw the seat
  line(73, 82, 90, 82);
  circle(50, 100, 25);       // Draw wheels
  circle(150, 100, 25);
  line(50, 100, 80, 85);     // Draw part of frame
  line(80, 85, 134, 85);
  line(77, 82, 95, 100);
  line(130, 80, 150, 100);
```

```
    line(128, 80, 113, 82);    // Draw the handlebars
    line(128, 80, 116, 78);
    line(72, 81, 89, 81);      // Draw the seat
    line(73, 82, 90, 82);
    bike1 = malloc(imagesize(25, 75, 175, 125));
    bike2 = malloc(imagesize(25, 75, 175, 125));
    bike3 = malloc(imagesize(25, 75, 175, 125));
    bike4 = malloc(imagesize(25, 75, 175, 125));
    pedals = malloc(imagesize(85, 90, 110, 110));
    if (bike1 == NULL || bike2 == NULL || bike3 == NULL ||
        bike4 == NULL || pedals == NULL) {
      closegraph();
      printf("\nFailed to allocate memory for bike images.\n");
      exit(1);
    }

    circle(95, 100, 5);                   // Draw base of pedals
    line(95, 100, 136, 87);
    getimage(85, 90, 110, 110, pedals);   // Save screen of pedals
    line(86, 100, 104, 100);              // Draw pedals in
    line(85, 100, 87, 100);               // first position
    line(103, 100, 105, 100);
    getimage(25, 75, 175, 125, bike1);
    putimage(85, 90, pedals, COPY_PUT);   // Restore pedal area
    line(88, 96, 102, 104);               // Draw pedals in second
    line(87, 96, 89, 96);                 // position
    line(101, 104, 103, 104);
    getimage(25, 75, 175, 125, bike2);

    putimage(85, 90, pedals, COPY_PUT);   // Restore pedal area
    line(95, 95, 95, 105);                // Draw pedals in third
    line(94, 95, 96, 95);                 // position
    line(94, 105, 96, 105);
    getimage(25, 75, 175, 125, bike3);

    putimage(85, 90, pedals, COPY_PUT);   // Restore pedal area
    line(102, 96, 88, 104);               // Draw pedals in fourth
    line(101, 96, 103, 96);               // position
    line(87, 104, 89, 104);
    getimage(25, 75, 175, 125, bike4);
    free(pedals);
}

// Sequences through the four images of the bicycle in order to move
// the bicycle across the screen.
void movebikeandpedals(void)
{
  int i, times;

  times = (getmaxx()-175) / STEP;
  for (i=0; i<times; i++) {
    switch(i%4) {
      case 0 : putimage(25+i*STEP, 75, bike4, XOR_PUT);
               putimage(25+(i+1)*STEP, 75, bike1, XOR_PUT);
```

```
                 break;
      case 1 : putimage(25+i*STEP, 75, bike1, XOR_PUT);
               putimage(25+(i+1)*STEP, 75, bike2, XOR_PUT);
               break;
      case 2 : putimage(25+i*STEP, 75, bike2, XOR_PUT);
               putimage(25+(i+1)*STEP, 75, bike3, XOR_PUT);
               break;
      case 3 : putimage(25+i*STEP, 75, bike3, XOR_PUT);
               putimage(25+(i+1)*STEP, 75, bike4, XOR_PUT);
               break;
    }
    delay(50);  // This delay controls the speed of the bicycle
  }
}

main()
{
  int gdriver = CGA;        // Use CGA high-resolution mode or
  int gmode = CGAHI;        // comparable 640 x 200 modes

  initgraph(&gdriver, &gmode, "\\tcpp\\bgi");
  drawbike();
  movebikeandpedals();
  getch();
  closegraph();
  return 0;
}
```

Animating Objects on a Backdrop

Thus far, we have used only **getimage( )** and **putimage( )** to move objects across a plain background. Unfortunately, this does not represent the typical situation. In most animation programs, you'll probably want to place several objects in the background to make the screen more interesting. For instance, we could use a country scene as the backdrop of our bicycle animation program. However, if we put objects on the screen that our bicycle must cross over, the bicycle might change its color as the two objects overlap. The reason for the possible color change is that the animated object and the screen are exclusive-ORed together. Therefore, wherever the image being animated contains a bit value of 1, copying the image to the screen will change its corresponding pixel color if the screen also has a bit value of 1 at that location. Fortunately, there is a way around this problem. The solution is to use two slightly different images for the animated object. These two special masks will be combined so that the animated object will not change color as it passes over the background.

The method uses one mask that is ANDed with the screen and a second mask that is XORed over the first mask. When these two masks are combined this way, the object will appear on the screen in its normal colors. To remove the object, we'll save the screen image underneath the region at which it is to

Table 6.1 Masks for Animating Objects

AND Mask Value	XOR Mask Value	Resulting Screen Bit
0	0	0
0	1	1
1	0	Unchanged
1	1	Inverted

be displayed, so that we can later restore the screen by copying the saved screen back to the display. Table 6.1 shows how the bits in the AND mask and the XOR mask can be combined to select particular colors on the screen. By choosing appropriate values in each mask, you can set each screen bit to 0 or 1, keep it the same value, or invert it.

Unfortunately, this technique of animation can be slow. And, since there are several screen images to deal with, this can be a problem. First, we must save the screen, then AND an image, followed by XORing an image, and later restoring the screen to its original state by copying back the saved screen image. This can take a great deal of time—especially when the size of the object being animated is large. In fact, even the bike image that we have been working with is too large to effectively animate with this approach.

Therefore, the next program we look at will only move a small ball across the screen that displays a backdrop, as shown in Figure 6.4. The ball is drawn to the screen using two masks as outlined earlier. Actually, the ball is made from two small circles filled with different colors, which should give you a good idea of how the dual-mask approach works.

The two masks that are combined to make up the ball are shown in Figure 6.5. In the program, these two masks are accessed through the pointers **andmask** and **xormask**. A third pointer, **covered**, is used to save the portion of the screen that is covered by the masks at any given time. Therefore, the process of moving the circle across the screen is encapsulated in the four lines of the function **moveball()**:

```
putimage(35+i, 85, covered, COPY_PUT);
getimage(35+STEP+i, 85, 65+STEP+i, 115, covered);
putimage(35+STEP+i, 85, andmask, AND_PUT);
putimage(35+STEP+i, 85, xormask, XOR_PUT);
```

The first statement overwrites the current position of the ball. The next line saves the screen where the ball will next appear. Finally, the last two statements write the two masks to the screen and draw the ball.

```
// BALL.CPP: This program demonstrates animation using an
// AND mask and an XOR mask.
```

Figure 6.4 This is the time-lapsed output of BALL.CPP.

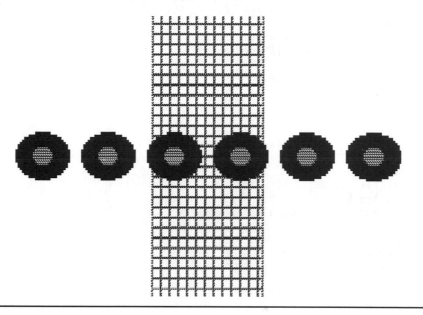

```
#include <graphics.h>
#include <conio.h>
#include <alloc.h>
#include <dos.h>
#include <stdlib.h>
#include <stdio.h>

const int STEP = 2;
const int DELAY = 50;

void *xormask, *andmask, *covered;
```

Figure 6.5 These are the masks used in BALL.CPP.

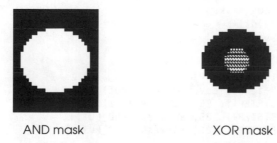

AND mask   XOR mask

```
void drawball(void)
{
  covered = malloc(imagesize(35, 85, 65, 115));
  xormask = malloc(imagesize(35, 85, 65, 115));
  andmask = malloc(imagesize(35, 85, 65, 115));
  if (covered == NULL || xormask == NULL || andmask == NULL) {
    closegraph();
    printf("Not enough memory\n");
    exit(1);
  }
  getimage(35,85,65,115,covered);
  // Create the AND mask first
  setfillstyle(SOLID_FILL, getmaxcolor());
  bar(35, 85, 65, 115);
  setcolor(0);
  setfillstyle(SOLID_FILL, 0);
  pieslice(50, 100, 0, 360, 12);
  getimage(35, 85, 65, 115, andmask);
  // Create the XOR mask
  putimage(35, 85, covered, COPY_PUT);
  setcolor(getmaxcolor());
  setfillstyle(SOLID_FILL, getmaxcolor());
  pieslice(50, 100, 0, 360, 12);
  setfillstyle(SOLID_FILL, 1);
  setcolor(1);
  circle(50, 100, 4);
  floodfill(50, 100, 1);
  getimage(35, 85, 65, 115, xormask);
  // Erase the ball and make the backdrop
  putimage(35, 85, covered, COPY_PUT);
  setfillstyle(HATCH_FILL, 2);
  bar3d(100, 10, 150, 199, 0, 0);

  // Redraw the ball on the screen by saving the screen area to
  // be overwritten, using the AND mask and then the XOR mask.
  getimage(35, 85, 65, 115, covered);
  putimage(35, 85, andmask, AND_PUT);
  putimage(35, 85, xormask, XOR_PUT);
}

// Move the ball across the screen by first overwriting the currently
// displayed ball and then moving it to the next location by using
// the AND and XOR masks.
void moveball(void)
{
  int i;

  for (i=0; i<150; i+=STEP) {
    putimage(35+i, 85, covered, COPY_PUT);
    getimage(35+STEP+i, 85, 65+STEP+i, 115, covered);
    putimage(35+STEP+i, 85, andmask, AND_PUT);
    putimage(35+STEP+i, 85, xormask, XOR_PUT);
    delay(DELAY);
```

```
  }
}

main()
{
  int gmode, gdriver = DETECT;

  initgraph(&gdriver, &gmode, "\\tcpp\\bgi");
  drawball();
  moveball();
  getch();
  closegraph();
  return 0;
}
```

Animating Multiple Objects

We can easily extend our program so that it will animate more than one object at a time. The major change that we need to make to the program is to supply more than one image or sequences of images to the screen to be moved. Then, by sequencing through the list of animated objects, as well as the images, we can easily create a scene with multiple moving objects.

Limitations of getimage() and putimage()

Using **getimage()** and **putimage()** to animate objects has several limitations that may restrict their usefulness. First, they can use up a lot of memory—particularly as the size of the image increases. In addition, as the image to save or write gets larger the speed at which **getimage()** and **putimage()** operate deteriorates.

However, when dealing with animation, one of the biggest drawbacks to using these two functions is that they do not allow for the bitmap image to be scaled or rotated. You could write functions to perform these operations yourself, but the bitmap patterns that the BGI uses are different for many of the modes. Therefore, you would have to write functions to handle each mode. This is a tedious task and one that we won't tackle here. Despite these issues, **getimage()** and **putimage()** provide a powerful, yet simple, way of moving objects around the graphics screen.

ANIMATION USING THE PALETTE

Typically, animation is created by drawing an object as it moves across the screen or copying the image of an object and moving it across the screen. However, an alternative method of animation that is sometimes quite dramatic and simple uses the palette. The basic idea is to draw objects on the screen using different colors. Then, you change the colors in the palette. Once this has occurred, all the objects on the screen immediately change their colors and it appears as if all the objects were redrawn to new locations. By ordering objects so that their colors reflect the series of color changes, you can create animation.

Unfortunately, not all graphics adapters support palette manipulation equally. In fact, EGA and VGA are the most powerful in terms of this feature. With either graphics adapter you can use the **setpalette( )** function to alter the colors in the palette. Only some graphics adapters allow you to change the palette.

A common example of animation using the color palette displays a mountain scene with flowing water. Actually, the water motion is induced by a series of changes to the palette. Since it would take a great deal of time and programming to create a good looking mountain scene, let's use a simpler programming example.

The program that we'll look at is FIREWORK.CPP, shown following this discussion. It continually displays a series of firework-like color bursts on the screen. Three images of random pixels are saved in memory and rapidly drawn to the screen using **putimage( )** to create an expanding explosion pattern. The trick in the program is to use changes in the palette in order to achieve a wide variety of burst colors, freeing us from the task of having to save many different burst patterns, each with a different color.

The program is written to operate on either an EGA or VGA system. The program won't work in a CGA mode because we'll be changing the palette, and this technique doesn't quite work the same way as it does on an EGA or VGA.

Now let's take a closer look at the code. The fireworks' burst pattern is generated by randomly plotting pixels on the screen. This is accomplished with the **for** loop

```
for (i=0; i<BLAST_SIZE*3/2; i++)
  putpixel(random(BLAST_SIZE),random(yrange), 1);
```

which plots some number of colored pixels in a region bounded by (0, 0) and (**BLAST_SIZE**, **yrange**). The bottom-right coordinate pair of this region is dependent on **BLAST_SIZE**. In this case it is 200 pixels wide. The variable **yrange** is simply **BLAST_SIZE**, which is scaled by the aspect ratio of the screen. After this **for** loop finishes, a square region on the top right of the screen will be filled with randomly placed pixels. Of course, we want a circular burst pattern,not a square one, so we'll use the following statements to extract a circle of pixels:

```
circle(BLAST_SIZE/2, yrange/2, BLAST_SIZE/2-10);
rectangle(0, 0, BLAST_SIZE, yrange);
floodfill(1, 1, getmaxcolor());
setfillstyle(SOLID_FILL, 0);
```

```
floodfill(1, 1, 0);
getimage(0, 0, BLAST_SIZE, yrange, blast3);  // Capture large burst pattern
```

These statements use the **floodfill( )** function to erase all the pixels between a circle (drawn to the size of the burst pattern desired) and a square encompassing the block of pixels. The first statement draws a circle that will define the burst pattern size. Next, the bounding rectangle is drawn by **rectangle( )**. Then **floodfill( )** is used to fill the region between the circle and rectangle with white. Note that black is not used because the background already contains it; therefore **floodfill( )** thinks that it has filled the region after encountering a few of the background pixels. Continuing to the next statement, the code refills the region between the circle and rectangle by another call to **floodfill( )**. This time, however, the region is filled with black. Now the only thing remaining on the screen is the circular burst pattern. The final step, therefore, is to call **getimage( )** to capture the image of the burst pattern, which is accomplished with the last statement shown. A similar process is performed in order to generate two smaller burst patterns, which are stored in **blast2** and **blast1**. Later, by sequencing through these images, it will appear that the burst pattern is expanding.

Of course, a good fireworks display would not be complete without a rocket to launch the fireworks from. The image for such a rocket is created by the next several lines in the code. The rocket is drawn using **bar( )**, **putpixel( )**, and two calls to **line( )**. The image of the rocket is saved to a pointer called **rocket**.

The **while** loop, which follows the code to create the rocket, is used to continually draw a series of fireworks explosions until a key is pressed. The location of the explosion is randomly calculated by the lines:

```
x = random(getmaxx()-BLAST_SIZE);
y = random(getmaxy()/3);
```

The (**x**, **y**) coordinate pair marks the top-left corner of the burst pattern images that will be used to create the fireworks effect. The **x** value is kept between 0 and **getmaxx( )–BLAST_SIZE** so that the burst images will not extend off the edge of the screen and be clipped. The **y** coordinate is restricted to one-third of the maximum y range, which you'll later see corresponds to the top portion of the screen.

The rocket is launched by the **for** loop after the two statements listed earlier. Its starting location and ending coordinates are calculated so that the rocket will steer to the middle of the burst pattern that is to be written to the screen. The call to **setpalette( )** before the **for** loop is to ensure that the rocket is drawn white.

The statements after the **for** loop display the burst patterns in **blast1**, **blast2**, and **blast3**. The burst images are displayed on the screen much like we have discussed in the past, so we will not look at them in detail. The unique part of the code, however, is the calls to the **setpalette( )** function. These calls are used to change the color of the fireworks. For instance, the line

```
setpalette(getmaxcolor(), random(15)+1);
```

randomly changes the last entry in the palette table to one of the sixteen possible colors in the current video mode (see Chapter 2 for a list of these). This is the color entry that is being used to color the fireworks. In order to provide a little variety, the color of the second burst pattern, **blast2**, is designed so that it may or may not be changed, depending on whether the **random( )** statement in the **if** statement that follows returns a 0 value (remember, **random( )** returns a value between 0 and n − 1):

```
if (!random(3))
  setpalette(getmaxcolor(), random(15)+1);
```

Similarly, the **if** statement surrounding the **putimage( )** function used to draw **blast3** is used to randomly restrict when it is drawn. By doing this, we tell the program to generate two different sized fireworks patterns.

You may have noticed a number of calls to the Turbo C++ **delay( )** function in FIREWORK.CPP. These statements are used to give the fireworks program an aesthetic appeal so the burst patterns don't flash by too quickly. Because, different machines may be able to display the burst patterns faster than others, you may need to adjust the delay based on which computer is being used.

The remaining part of the program involves the pointer called **covered**, which is used to save the screen before any of the burst patterns are generated or displayed. It is used to remove the fireworks from the screen and restore it to its original state.

```
// FIREWORK.CPP: This program simulates a fireworks display by using
// the getimage()/putimage() functions as well as palette animation.
#include <graphics.h>
#include <stdlib.h>
#include <dos.h>
#include <time.h>
#include <conio.h>
#include <stdio.h>

const int BLAST_SIZE = 200;        // Size of fireworks in pixels
const int ROCKET_HEIGHT = 7;       // Rocket is 7 pixels tall
const int ROCKET_WIDTH = 4;        // and 4 pixels wide
const int ROCKET_STEP = 2;         // Rocket moves 2 pixels at a time

main()
{
  int gdriver = EGA;               // Use EGA and EGALo or VGA and VGALo
```

```
int gmode = EGALO;                    // with this version of the fireworks
int x, y, i, xasp, yasp;              // program
int yrange, ry;
double aspectratio;
void *covered;                        // Holds screen under fire burst
void *blast1, *blast2, *blast3;       // Three burst patterns
void *rocket;                         // The fire rocket

initgraph(&gdriver, &gmode, "\\tcpp\\bgi");
if (gdriver != EGA && gdriver != VGA) {
  closegraph();
  printf("This program requires an EGA or VGA graphics adapter.\n");
  exit(1);
}
randomize();
getaspectratio(&xasp,&yasp);
aspectratio = (double)xasp / (double)yasp;
yrange = BLAST_SIZE * aspectratio;
blast1 = malloc(imagesize(0, 0, BLAST_SIZE, yrange));
blast2 = malloc(imagesize(0, 0, BLAST_SIZE, yrange));
blast3 = malloc(imagesize(0, 0, BLAST_SIZE, yrange));
covered = malloc(imagesize(0, 0, BLAST_SIZE, yrange));
if (covered == NULL || blast3 == NULL ||
    blast2 == NULL || blast1 == NULL) {
  closegraph();
  printf("Not enough memory\n");
  exit(1);
}
getimage(0, 0, BLAST_SIZE, yrange, covered);
// Make the burst pattern by randomly filling a square with pixels
for (i=0; i<BLAST_SIZE*3/2; i++)
  putpixel(random(BLAST_SIZE), random(yrange), getmaxcolor());

// Then convert the square pixel pattern into a circle by erasing
// all of the pixels outside of a circle. Use a floodfill to perform
// this operation. Repeat this process three times, each with a
// smaller circle capturing the circular burst
// pattern in burst1, burst2, or burst3 after each occurrence.

circle(BLAST_SIZE/2, yrange/2, BLAST_SIZE/2-10);
rectangle(0, 0, BLAST_SIZE, yrange);
floodfill(1, 1, getmaxcolor());
setfillstyle(SOLID_FILL, 0);
floodfill(1, 1, 0);
getimage(0, 0, BLAST_SIZE, yrange, blast3);  // Capture large
                                             // burst pattern
setfillstyle(SOLID_FILL, getmaxcolor());     // Make smaller pattern
circle(BLAST_SIZE/2, yrange/2, BLAST_SIZE/4+10);
rectangle(0, 0, BLAST_SIZE, yrange);
floodfill(1, 1, getmaxcolor());
setfillstyle(SOLID_FILL, 0);
floodfill(1, 1, 0);
getimage(0, 0, BLAST_SIZE, yrange, blast2);  // Capture middle
                                             // burst pattern
```

```c
      setfillstyle(SOLID_FILL, getmaxcolor());     // Make smallest burst
      circle(BLAST_SIZE/2, yrange/2, 20);
      rectangle(0, 0, BLAST_SIZE, yrange);
      floodfill(1, 1, getmaxcolor());
      setfillstyle(SOLID_FILL, 0);
      floodfill(1, 1, 0);
      getimage(0, 0, BLAST_SIZE, yrange, blast1);   // Get small burst
      putimage(0, 0, covered, COPY_PUT);            // Erase burst pattern

      // Create the rocket
      rocket = malloc(imagesize(0, 0, ROCKET_WIDTH, ROCKET_HEIGHT));
      setfillstyle(SOLID_FILL, getmaxcolor());
      bar(1, 2, ROCKET_WIDTH-1, ROCKET_HEIGHT-1);
      putpixel(2, 1, getmaxcolor());
      line(0, ROCKET_HEIGHT-2, 0, ROCKET_HEIGHT);
      line(ROCKET_WIDTH, ROCKET_HEIGHT-2, ROCKET_WIDTH, ROCKET_HEIGHT);
      getimage(0, 0, ROCKET_WIDTH, ROCKET_HEIGHT, rocket); // Rocket
      putimage(0, 0, rocket, XOR_PUT);              // Erase rocket image

      // Draw fireworks until a key is pressed
      while (!kbhit()) {
        // Randomly decide where the rocket should explode. Use the
        // upper half of the screen and avoid the edges of the screen.
        // (x, y) corresponds to the top-left corner of the blast images.
        x = random(getmaxx()-BLAST_SIZE);
        y = random(getmaxy()/3);
        setpalette(getmaxcolor(), 15);             // Make rocket white
        for (ry=getmaxy()-ROCKET_HEIGHT; ry>y+yrange/2;
            ry --= ROCKET_STEP) {
          putimage(x+BLAST_SIZE/2, ry, rocket, XOR_PUT);
          delay(20);
          putimage(x+BLAST_SIZE/2, ry, rocket, XOR_PUT);
        }
        setpalette(getmaxcolor(), random(15)+1); // Randomly select burst color
        getimage(x, y, x+BLAST_SIZE, y+yrange, covered); // Save screen
        putimage(x, y, blast1, COPY_PUT);          // Draw smallest burst
        delay(100);                                // Keep it on screen for awhile

        putimage(x, y, blast2, COPY_PUT);          // Show second burst
        if (!random(3))
          setpalette(getmaxcolor(), random(15)+1); // Maybe change color
        delay(100);

        if (random(2)) {                           // Randomly decide to
          putimage(x, y, blast3, COPY_PUT);        // show third burst
          if (!random(3)) setpalette(getmaxcolor(), random(15)+1);
        }
        delay(400+random(750));                    // Wait for a while
        putimage(x, y, covered, COPY_PUT);         // Erase burst
        delay(random(3000));                       // Wait for next rocket
      }
      closegraph();
      return 0;
    }
```

A slight variation on the palette animation is to make objects immediately appear on the screen. For instance, we can add a bolt of lightning to our fractal program in Chapter 1 that will immediately appear on the screen. The image is really there all the time, but the technique creates the image of an instant flash. The trick is to draw the lightning bolt the same color as the background color, using different palette index. Then to make the lightning appear for a short time, simply change the palette index color to the lightning color and then restore it to the background. Swapping the palette colors produces the effect that the lightning bolt is drawn to the screen, but since it is already there it saves the drawing time and makes for a very fast animation technique.

USING MULTIPLE SCREEN PAGES

Another animation technique that can produce fast animation effects uses multiple memory pages. This method takes advantage of the graphics hardware that provides several independent sections, or *pages*, of memory that you can draw in and display. However, like the palette trick, this approach is possible only on some graphics adapters—Hercules, EGA, and VGA. The basic idea is to have several partial or complete images of the screen ready to be displayed and then swap between them. By doing this, animation can be created. The number of pages available depends on the graphics mode being used. For a complete list of the graphics modes and the pages that they have, see Chapter 2.

The BGI function **setactivepage( )** is used to select where the graphics operations will be written. The function prototype for **setactivepage( )** is

```
void far setactivepage(int page);
```

where **page** is the page number to be used. Note that the active page does not have to be the page currently being displayed. In fact, the visual page is selected by the function **setvisualpage( )**. Its function prototype is:

```
void far setvisualpage(int page);
```

Another way to use multiple memory pages is as a scratch pad. Here the idea is to use one of the nonvisible pages as a working area to combine masks or create images of objects that can later be rapidly copied over to the visual page using **getimage( )** and **putimage( )**. This way, you can avoid having to display everything. For example, in the last program, we needed to create the pixel pattern for the fireworks. This was done on the screen, but if other memory pages had been available, we could have hidden these operations by doing them on a nonvisible page.

7

Creating Mouse Tools

One of the major benefits of using an object-oriented programming language (OOP) such as Turbo C++ is that you can build powerful collections of objects that can then be used to create other more powerful objects. And the more you work with objects, the more you'll discover that this "building block" approach to programming goes the extra mile in helping you create tools that can easily be re-used and extended.

In this chapter, we have two important goals. First, we'll develop a class called **mouseobj** that provides all the basic routines needed to interface a mouse to a graphics program. This package will be the first of a number of interactive graphics tools that we'll be developing in Chapters 7 through 10 and putting to use in several drawing applications in subsequent chapters. The second goal is to show you how to use OOP techniques, such as *inheritance*, to derive one class from another. In this case, we'll derive from **mouseobj** a class that allows you to use the keyboard to emulate the functions of a mouse. Inheritance is an important property that we'll be using throughout the remainder of this book so that we can build our programs in stages and later expand on what we've built.

STARTING WITH THE MOUSE

Although the keyboard is an invaluable input device, it's not always best suited for interactive graphics programs. Even with useful positioning features such as cursor keys, the keyboard lacks speed and the ability to randomly select locations on the screen. These operations are typically required in an interactive graphics environment. What is needed is an interactive pointing device such as a light pen, joystick, or a mouse. Because the mouse is more common on PCs than the other devices, we'll be selecting it as our primary input device. Although we'll try to support the keyboard as much as possible along the way, we'll design all our input routines around the mouse.

This chapter will show you how you can access a mouse from within your own graphics programs. Our mouse class, **mouseobj**, contains several member functions for performing such operations as initializing the mouse, determining the status and position of the mouse, and controlling its movement within a program. In addition, we'll be developing a class called **kbdmouseobj**, which will be used to support the keyboard if a mouse is not present. This class is derived from the mouse class and contains member functions for emulating the features of the mouse. These mouse and keyboard classes are implemented in the files MOUSE.H, MOUSE.CPP, KBDMOUSE.H, and KBDMOUSE.CPP, which are listed at the end of this chapter. Because of the object-oriented nature of our mouse tools, you'll see that we can easily emulate the mouse with the keyboard—a task that is usually hard and messy to program.

MOUSE OVERVIEW

Before we start coding up the mouse and keyboard classes, we'll need to cover the basics of how the mouse hardware and software work. If you have never written code to control the mouse, it might come as a surprise that the mouse is easy to support. In fact, only a few basic functions are required to initialize the mouse, obtain its cursor location, and move its cursor. As we work with the mouse, keep in mind that our code is designed to work with a Microsoft compatible mouse, which happens to be the most common mouse standard for the PC. If you are using a different type of mouse, you may want to consult the user's manual for your mouse hardware and make the necessary changes to the code that we present so that your mouse will operate properly.

A mouse system actually consists of two essential elements: the mouse mechanism and a memory resident program called a *mouse driver*. The mouse driver provides all of the low-level support needed to communicate with the mouse. In addition, it is responsible for automatically maintaining the mouse's cursor position and detecting any button presses.

Normally, the mouse driver is loaded into memory at power-up by a statement in your AUTOEXEC.BAT file. Once the driver is loaded, the mouse becomes available to any program that is subsequently executed.

A mouse is surprisingly simple to use in an application program. There are, however, some minor differences between text and graphics programs using the mouse, so consequently, we'll be focusing on the mouse in graphics mode only.

ACCESSING THE MOUSE DRIVER

We'll access the various features of the mouse and mouse driver through the PC software interrupt 33h. The mouse-driver services calls to this interrupt location by redirecting them to its built-in, low-level mouse functions. The specific function selected depends on the value in the AX register at the time of the interrupt. Three other registers, BX, CX, and DX, are used to pass parameters to the mouse routines. Similarly, the mouse functions use these four registers to return such things to the calling function as the mouse location and the status of the mouse buttons. Figure 7.1 shows how a program uses interrupt 33h to invoke a mouse function.

You invoke interrupt 33h with the special Turbo C++ function **int86( )**. This function provides direct access to the interrupt capabilities of the microprocessor and typically appears in the form

```
int86(interrupt_number, &inregs, &outregs);
```

where the first argument is the interrupt vector to be used and the second two arguments are pointers to a structure of register values. The declaration for this structure is defined in the BIOS.H header file.

The core mouse member function in the **mouseobj** class that we'll use to interact with the mouse driver is built around the **int86( )** function. The member function, **mouseintr( )**, simply loads the various registers with the arguments passed to it, calls the interrupt, and then copies the register values back into the arguments. The values contained in the arguments passed to

---

Figure 7.1 Your programs use this sequence to invoke a mouse function.

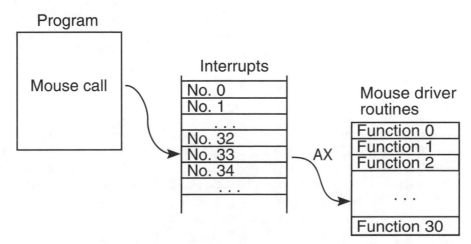

mouseintr( ) select the particular mouse function that is executed. Therefore, it is up to the caller of **mouseintr( )** to ensure that the correct argument values are provided. Throughout our program, we'll refer to the four mouse arguments as **m1**, **m2**, **m3**, and **m4**. They correspond to the registers AX, BX, CX, and DX, respectively. Here is the function **mouseintr( )**:

```
void mouseobj::mouseintr(unsigned int &m1, unsigned int &m2,
  unsigned int &m3, unsigned int &m4)
{
  union REGS inregs, outregs;

  inregs.x.ax = m1;    inregs.x.bx = m2;
  inregs.x.cx = m3;    inregs.x.dx = m4;
  int86(0x33, &inregs, &outregs);
  m1 = outregs.x.ax;   m2 = outregs.x.bx;
  m3 = outregs.x.cx;   m4 = outregs.x.dx;
}
```

By setting the arguments **m1**, **m2**, **m3**, and **m4** to different values, we can easily perform various operations such as initializing the mouse, reading the current position of the mouse, or determining the state of the mouse buttons. In the next section, we'll discuss several of these operations.

Note that this function is assigned to the class **mouseobj**, which serves as our base mouse class. We are careful to call this class the *base class* because it will be used to derive the keyboard class—**kbdmouseobj**.

Take a minute to examine MOUSE.H, you'll see that the technique of *encapsulation* is used to hide all of the data and coding details of the mouse-processing operations within the body of the class. Why was this done? After all, we could have coded the mouse support routines as a set of separate functions. By creating a mouse class, we are able to place all of the mouse-specific coding details under one roof and hide the low-level details of supporting the mouse hardware. Therefore, the application program that uses the mouse class doesn't have to know the intimate details of how the mouse works.

THE MOUSE FUNCTIONS

The mouse driver includes numerous mouse functions, several of which are listed in Table 7.1. We won't be using all these functions, but they are listed here for your reference. If you are interested in exploring the mouse further, you should refer to the *Microsoft Mouse Programmer's Reference Guide*.

Now let's take a step-by-step look at how the mouse is actually used so that we can begin to develop our custom class.

Table 7.1 The Mouse Driver Functions

Function Number	Description (placed in AX)
0	Resets the mouse and returns its status
1	Shows the mouse cursor on the screen
2	Removes the mouse cursor from the screen
3	Returns mouse location and state of the button
4	Moves the mouse cursor to virtual location (x,y)
5	Retrieves the number of times a button was pressed since the last call
6	Retrieves the number of times a button was released since the last call
7	Sets the horizontal limits of the cursor
8	Sets the vertical limits of the cursor
9	Defines the cursor used in graphics mode
10	Sets the cursor used in text mode
11	Reads the mouse movement counters
12	Sets up an interrupt routine
13	Turns light pen emulation on
14	Turns light pen emulation off
15	Sets ratio of the mouse movement to the cursor
16	Hides the mouse if it is within a region
19	Sets the parameters to allow faster mouse movement
20	Swaps interrupt vectors
21	Retrieves the mouse driver status
22	Saves the mouse driver status
23	Restores the mouse driver status
29	Sets the CRT page number used by the mouse cursor
30	Gets the CRT page number used by the mouse cursor

Mouse Initialization

Before being able to use the mouse, we must first initialize it by invoking mouse function **0** (see Table 7.1). After this function is called, the mouse driver is reset to various default values and returns a –1 in AX if the mouse hardware and driver are detected. Otherwise, it returns a 0. Therefore, by using the reset function, function **0**, we'll be able to tell whether a mouse is present or not. We can write our own mouse reset member function as:

```
int mouseobj::reset(void)
{
  unsigned int m1 = RESET_MOUSE, m2, m3, m4;

  mouseintr(m1, m2, m3, m4);
  return m1;
}
```

The **RESET_MOUSE** term is a constant for function **0** that we've put in a header file called MOUSE.H. We'll define similar constants for the other mouse functions that we'll be discussing in later sections. (The file, MOUSE.H, is listed near the end of the chapter along with MOUSE.CPP.)

Note that our reset routine does little more than load **m1** with the function number, make a call to **mouseintr( )**, and then return the status flag held in **m1**. The variables **m2**, **m3**, and **m4** are ignored in this case. Most other mouse routines will be similar in form.

Although **reset( )** provides the basic mouse reset function, we need a higher-level routine to handle the complete task of initializing the mouse. We'll call this member function **init( )**. Among other things, it calls **reset( )** and sets the **mouseobj** variable, **mouseexists**, to 1 if **reset( )** is successful. Otherwise, **mouseexists** is set to 0. Later, we'll see that the variable **mouseexists** is used in all our mouse member functions so that we can avoid making calls to the mouse driver if it hasn't been detected. In fact, when **mouseexists** is 0 we'll switch to the keyboard for input. We'll explore this feature later in this chapter.

Although we'll need to expand our **init( )** function, an intermediate form of it is shown next. The primary feature still missing is the one that processes the keyboard input when a mouse is not present. As previously mentioned, we will add this in a later section.

```
int mouseobj::init(void)
{
  int gmode;
  char far *memory = (char far *)0x00000449;

  mouseexists = 1;
  drawmouse = 0;
  oldx = 0;  oldy = 0;
  gmode = getgraphmode();
  if (gmode == HERCMONOHI) { // If Hercules card is used, patch BIOS
    *memory = 0x06;          // memory location 40h:49h with 6.
  }
  if (reset())              // If mouse reset okay, assume a mouse exists
```

```
    show();                   // Show the mouse
  else                        // No mouse found--emulate a
    mouseexists = 0;          // mouse using the keyboard
  return mouseexists;
}
```

The **init()** member function also sets the mouse location to the top-left corner of the screen by a call to the mouse function **move()** and switches the display of the mouse cursor on by a call to the member function **show()**. Both **move()** and **show()** are part of our mouse class and will be looked at shortly.

Note: One oddity of the **init()** function is the call to the BGI routine **getgraphmode()**. We use this routine to test whether your program is running on a Hercules card. If it is, you must write a value of 6 to memory location 40h:49h. This is a peculiarity of the Hercules board and is not needed for any other graphics adapter.

Additional Mouse Member Functions

Thus far, we have covered the mouse initialization and reset functions. Now we'll examine the routines that actually put the mouse to use. The complete list of mouse-specific member functions that we'll include in MOUSE.CPP is shown in Table 7.2. The last two functions, **getinput()** and **waitforinput()**, are designed to work with both the mouse and the keyboard. We'll examine these two routines when we discuss the keyboard class later in this chapter.

Table 7.2 Mouse Processing Member Functions in MOUSE.CPP

Function	Description
buttondown()	Returns non-zero if the specified mouse button is currently pressed
buttonpressed()	Tests whether a mouse button has been pressed since the last call
buttonreleased()	Tests whether a mouse button has been released since the last call
drawmousecursor()	Manages a manual crosshair cursor
getcoords()	Gets the coordinates of the mouse cursor
getinput()	Checks if a mouse button has been pressed and released or whether a key has been pressed
getinputpress()	Retrieves the user input from the keyboard or the mouse; unlike getinput(), it does not wait for a button release if a press occurs
hide()	Removes the mouse cursor from the screen
inbox()	Checks whether the mouse is in a screen region
init()	Initializes the mouse

continued

Table 7.2 Mouse Processing Member Functions in MOUSE.CPP (Continued)

Function	Description
move()	Moves the mouse to location (x,y)
mouseintr()	The interface for low-level mouse calls
reset()	Resets the mouse and return its status
sethorizlimits()	Sets the horizontal limits of the mouse's movement
setvertlimits()	Sets the vertical limits of the mouse's movement
show()	Displays the mouse cursor
showcursor()	Internal routine that manually draws a crosshair cursor
testbutton()	Internal routine to test the buttons
waitforinput()	Loops until a button key has been pressed

We'll begin by writing these functions assuming that a mouse is present. Later, we'll derive the **kbdmouseobj** class to support the keyboard when a mouse isn't detected. An interesting aspect about our approach is that we'll be able to use the member functions in **kbdmouseobj** to create the keyboard processing class.

The Mouse Cursor

The next member functions that we'll look at control the display of the mouse cursor. We saw in **init()** that there is a member function called **show()** that turns on the display of the mouse cursor. There is also a complementary function, **hide()**, that removes the mouse cursor from the screen. One important thing to note here is that both of these routines only affect the *display* of the mouse cursor. In other words, no matter what the display status of the mouse cursor is, the mouse driver will always update and maintain the cursor's position.

The **show()** and **hide()** functions use mouse functions **1** and **2**, respectively. They do not require any arguments or return any values. Both functions are straightforward and are included in the MOUSE.CPP source file.

It's easy to imagine that there are times when it is necessary to turn the mouse cursor on or off by using **show()** and **hide()**. However, their use is probably more important than first imagined. It turns out that whenever you *read or write anything* to the screen while using the mouse, you must always turn the mouse off first by a call to **hide()**. After you are done accessing the screen, you can restore the mouse display by calling **show()**. Why? Because the mouse-cursor image is actually combined into the screen image. Therefore, whenever you access the screen when the mouse cursor is on, you run the risk of accessing the mouse-cursor image or at least incorrectly modifying whatever is under the mouse cursor. Only by using **hide( )** and **show( )** before and after accessing the screen can you guarantee that the mouse will not interfere with what is on the screen.

One additional caution: You should not call **hide( )** if the mouse is not already displayed. If you violate this rule, you must accompany every subsequent call to **hide( )** with a companion call to **show( )**. This is required because of the way that the mouse driver internally determines when to display the mouse cursor.

The Default Mouse Cursor

In graphics mode, the default mouse cursor is displayed as an arrow symbol, as shown in Figure 7.2. Although it is possible to change the type of cursor displayed by calling function **9**, we won't take advantage of this feature in the mouse driver. (Refer to the *Microsoft Mouse Programmer's Reference Guide* if you would like to explore this further.)

THE MOUSE AND SUPER VGA

If you use third-party VGA BGI drivers, you may find that your mouse cursor does not appear. The problem is that many mouse drivers do not directly support Super VGA modes. There are so many modes possible that the mouse drivers don't bother. However, although you can't see the mouse cursor, the mouse is working. One way to solve the problem is to draw the mouse cursor ourselves. This is the approach that the MOUSE.CPP toolkit takes. If you find that your mouse cursor does not appear after your code has initialized the mouse, then set the **drawmouse** flag in **mouseobj** to 1. Then, as long as you call the high-level, user input functions in MOUSE.CPP, which we'll discuss in a bit, a mouse cursor will occur. The **drawmousecursor( )** and **showcursor( )** routines in **mouseobj** work together to draw a crosshair cursor. The crosshair is drawn using exlcusive-ORed lines. The functions are kept simple, so you may run into a little trouble if your programs frequently change the line style settings or call **setwritemode( )** while using the mouse.

In order to use the manual mouse, you'll also need to set the limits of the mouse's movement to the extents of the screen. You must call the two routines **sethorizlimits( )** and **setvertlimits( )** to set the horizontal and vertical limits

---

Figure 7.2 This is the default graphics mouse cursor.

of the mouse cursor. Assuming you are using a **mouseobj** object called **mouse**, you can set the manual mouse cursor's limits to the full screen using these two statements:

```
mouse.sethorizlimits(0, getmaxx());
mouse.setvertlimits(0, getmaxy());
```

Realize that the approach we've taken here to manually draw the mouse does not guarantee that the mouse cursor will always be displayed correctly. We've taken a deliberately simple approach in order to keep the code simple.

Mouse Position

In the previous sections, we learned how the mouse driver controls the display of the mouse cursor's image. Now let's see how we can access and control the position of the mouse cursor through the driver.

Part of the responsibility of the mouse driver is to maintain the position of the mouse cursor. In addition, we can query the mouse driver to return the coordinates of the mouse by calling function **3**. Our mouse class includes a member function called **getcoords( )** that performs this operation.

Function **3** does not expect any arguments to be passed to it, and it returns the x and y coordinates of the mouse in **m3** and **m4**. Actually, mouse function **3** does more than just return the mouse coordinates. It also returns the current status of the buttons in **m2**; however, we'll be ignoring this aspect of the function.

The coordinates that function **3** returns will, in most cases, correspond to the screen coordinates of the mouse. Note, however, that we say "in most cases." It turns out that the mouse driver refers to all mouse coordinates in a virtual coordinate system and not in screen coordinates. Usually these two coordinate systems are identical in graphics mode. However, whenever the screen is in a mode with 320 columns, the virtual coordinates in the x direction are not identical. Fortunately, the adjustment is fairly simple. In these situations, the real-screen coordinates are always one-half the virtual coordinates. Therefore, the coordinates to the mouse driver need only be divided by two whenever the current graphics mode has 320 columns. Figure 7.3 shows the relationship between the coordinate systems for a 320-column graphics mode. For now, our **getcoords( )** member function becomes:

```
void mouseobj::getcoords(int &x, int &y)
{
  unsigned int m1 = GET_MOUSE_STATUS, m2;

  mouseintr(m1, m2, (unsigned int)x, (unsigned int)y);
  if (getmaxx() == 319 && !drawmouse)
    x /= 2;  // Adjust for virtual coordinates of the mouse
}
```

Figure 7.3 This figure illustrates the mapping between mouse and CGA 320 x 200-mode coordinates.

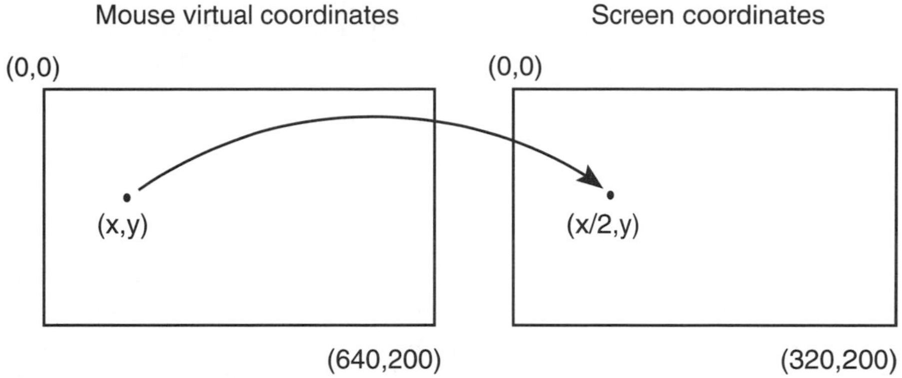

Mouse virtual coordinates   Screen coordinates

(0,0)   (0,0)

(x,y)   (x/2,y)

(640,200)   (320,200)

Mouse Buttons

The Microsoft mouse also provides two buttons that can be accessed through the mouse driver. Note that although other mice may have more buttons, usually these additional buttons can be handled as a superset of the Microsoft mouse.

There are three ways to test the mouse buttons. For each button you can check its current state—whether it has been pressed and whether it has been released. We'll use the last two member functions for testing buttons in our programs. This will allow us to avoid having to continually test the current status of the mouse buttons.

Mouse functions **5** and **6** are used to determine the number of times that one of the mouse buttons has been pressed or released since the last check or mouse initialization. Both functions can test either of the buttons. Which particular button is tested depends on the value in argument **m2** at the time of the function call. If **m2** is 0, then the left button is checked; if **m2** is 1, then the right button is tested. The number of button actions (that is, the number of button presses for function **5**) is returned in **m2**. In addition, these functions return the location of the last button action in **m3** and **m4** (**m3** is the x coordinate and **m4** is the y coordinate). Note that the left and right buttons status information is maintained separately.

Our mouse class uses functions **5** and **6** in the member functions **buttonpressed( )** and **buttonreleased( )** to test the status of the mouse buttons. Both are boolean functions that accept a single argument that specifies which button is to be tested. This argument can take on one of three values, which are defined in MOUSE.H as **LEFT_BUTTON**, **RIGHT_BUTTON**, and **EITHER_BUTTON**. In the case of **buttonpressed( )**, the function returns a non-zero value if the button indicated has been pressed since the last call to

buttonpressed( ). Otherwise, the function returns 0. Similarly, **buttonreleased( )** only returns a non-zero value if the button specified in its argument list has been released since the last time it was invoked.

Therefore, assuming we have declared a **mouseobj** called **mouse**, we can write the following loop that waits until either of the buttons is pressed:

```
while (!mouse.buttonpressed(EITHER_BUTTON)) ;
```

Actually, the low-level mouse functions do not allow us to ask whether either button has been pressed. We have to test the left and right buttons individually. However, this is easy to do.

Since there is a lot of similarity between the button pressed and button released functions, we have combined their code into a member function called **testbutton( )**. This function also returns a boolean value; however, it takes two arguments. They are the action to test for (whether it is a button press or release) and which button to check. The member function is:

```
int mouseobj::testbutton(int testtype, int whichbutton)
{
  unsigned int m1, m2, m3, m4;

  m1 = testtype;
  if (whichbutton == LEFT_BUTTON || whichbutton == EITHER_BUTTON) {
    m2 = LEFT_BUTTON;
    mouseintr(m1, m2, m3, m4);
    if (m2) return 1;          // Return 1 if the action occurred
  }
  if (whichbutton == RIGHT_BUTTON || whichbutton == EITHER_BUTTON) {
    m1 = testtype;
    m2 = RIGHT_BUTTON;
    mouseintr(m1, m2, m3, m4);
    if (m2) return 1;          // Return 1 if the action occurred
  }
  return 0;                    // Return 0 as a catchall
}
```

Note that the mouse function number, which is loaded into **m1**, is passed as the argument **testtype**. In addition, the mouse variable **m2** is loaded from the argument **whichbutton** in order to select between the left and right buttons. Remember, this variable can take on one of the values: **LEFT_BUTTON**, **RIGHT_BUTTON**, or **EITHER_BUTTON**. Note, however, that if the user specifies **EITHER_BUTTON**, both buttons must be individually checked.

After **testbutton( )** calls the mouse driver via **mouseintr( )**, **m2** contains the number of button actions for the button specified in **whichbutton**. Since we are only concerned with whether the button has been pressed or released, not how many times it has occurred, **testbutton( )** simply returns **TRUE** if **m2** indicates that there was one or more button presses. Otherwise, **testbutton( )** returns a value of 0.

The function **testbutton()** ignores two pieces of information that you may find valuable. First, it throws away the number of button actions that have taken place since the last test. You may find this useful; although in tight loops of code it is very rare that you'd be able to click fast enough to register more than one button press or release.

Also, both functions **5** and **6** return the coordinates of the last button action in **m3** and **m4**. We'll ignore these and use **getcoords()** instead to retrieve the location of the mouse after a button action; however, the delay between the button detection and the call to **getcoords()** can be significant. Therefore, you may want to try to integrate the coordinates returned in **m3** and **m4** to your code to avoid this situation.

Mouse in a Box

When using the mouse, we'll often want to test whether the mouse cursor is within a particular region on the screen. In order to accomplish this, a member function called **inbox()** is included in the mouse class. The function **inbox()** checks to see whether the mouse cursor coordinates given to it are within a rectangular region bounded by a pair of screen coordinates, as shown in Figure 7.4. The screen coordinates correspond to the upper-left and lower-right corners of the region being checked. If the mouse cursor is in the rectangle, **inbox()** will return 1; otherwise it will return 0. The function is:

```
int mouseobj::inbox(int left, int top, int right, int bottom, int x, int y)
{
  return((x >= left && x <= right && y >= top && y <= bottom) ? 1 : 0);
}
```

Figure 7.4 The inbox() function tests whether the mouse is within a rectangular region.

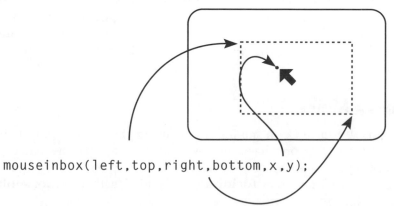

```
mouseinbox(left,top,right,bottom,x,y);
```

More Mouse Control

Our mouse control functions are rounded out by the **move( )** member function. This function uses mouse function **4** to move the mouse cursor to a particular (x, y) screen location. Note that in **move( )** the screen coordinates passed to it must be adjusted into virtual coordinates when the graphics adapter is in a 320-column mode (although you do not have to make this adjustment if the mouse cursor is being drawn manually). To make the adjustment, we've added this line to the toolkit:

```
if (getmaxx() == 319 && !drawmouse)
  x *= 2;                      // Adjust between virtual and actual coordinates
```

Adding Keyboard Input

Although the mouse is an excellent input device in the graphics world, sometimes it is useful to be able to use the keyboard. For instance, there are times when it's easier for the user to select a function by typing a quick key combination rather than using the mouse. Therefore, we're going to need some new routines for processing the keyboard.

If you take a close look at the **mouseobj** class, you'll see that we've included three member functions for processing the keyboard—**getinput( )**, **getinputpress( )**, and **waitforinput( )**. These functions are designed to work with the keyboard and the mouse. They are written so that they first check the keyboard buffer to see if any keys have been pressed. If so, these functions immediately return the first character in the keyboard buffer. Otherwise, the routines test the appropriate mouse buttons to see if they have been pressed or released. The **getinputpress( )** routine is similar to **getinput( )** except that it does not wait for the mouse button to be released if it detects a mouse press. Actually, **waitforinput( )** does nothing more than call **getinput( )** in a loop until a button has been pressed or the user has typed a character.

The keyboard buffer is checked by the Turbo C++ function **kbhit( )**. If it returns a 0, no key has been pressed, and **getinput( )** proceeds to test if the mouse buttons have been pressed. If they have been, then **getinput( )** returns a –1. Otherwise, if a key has been pressed, **getinput( )** returns the value of the keypress.

EMULATING A MOUSE

Thus far, we have been talking about using the mouse almost exclusively. However, not everyone has a mouse, and the reality of the situation is that a good program must accommodate nonmouse systems. Although you could use **getinput( )** and **waitforinput( )** provided with the **mouseobj** class to help support both the keyboard and the mouse, you would have to integrate the keyboard support into your application programs. This can get very messy.

We'll be able to provide a better solution by deriving the **kbdmouseobj** class. Because this class is derived from the **mouseobj** class, it inherits all of the mouse class' data and functions (see *Using Inheritance* later in this chapter for more information). To support the keyboard, we can then modify some of the inherited member functions, such as **init( )**, and add new ones that are specifically designed to work with the keyboard to control an emulated mouse. That is, we'll be able to use our new class whether or not there is actually a mouse connected. We'll use the cursor keys to move the emulated mouse cursor around the screen and the Ins and Del keys to simulate the mouse buttons. This approach allows us to take advantage of code that we have already written rather than having to start from scratch.

The new member functions introduced by **kbdmouseobj** are listed in Table 7.3. They are responsible for supporting the keyboard only. The other functions provided are designed to integrate both the mouse and the keyboard. If you examine the class definition in KBDMOUSE.H, you'll see that the member functions that support both devices are declared with the **virtual** keyword. For example, note that the declaration of the **init( )** function is:

```
virtual int init(void);
```

These functions are actually inherited from the **mouseobj** class, and they are declared as **virtual** because we will be overriding them so that they can perform different operations. To see how this technique is used, let's take a close look at the **init( )** member function.

Initializing a Keyboard Object

To support the keyboard, you'll need to create an object using the **kbdmouseobj** class. And before a keyboard object is used, you must remember to call the

Table 7.3 Keyboard Input Member Functions in kbdmouseobj

Member Function	Description
getkbinteraction()	Updates the location and status of the simulated mouse cursor when a key is pressed
getkb()	Reads the keyboard's extended key codes
initcursor()	Initializes the keyboard object so that it simulates a mouse
togglecursor()	Turns the simulated mouse cursor on and off
drawcursor()	Draws a simulated mouse cursor

init( ) member function. This function is slightly different than any other function we've written because it makes a call to another **init( )** member function—the one that is defined in the **mouseobj** class. To see how this works, let's examine the complete **init( )** function for **kbdmouseobj**:

```
int kbdmouseobj::init(void)
{
  if (!mouseobj::init()) {        // No mouse found--emulate the mouse
    cinc = 1; cminx = 0;          // The functionality is the
    cmaxx = getmaxx() - 1;        // same as the real thing
    cmaxy = getmaxy()-1;          // Therefore, set the emulated
    cminx = 0; cminy = 0;         // cursor to the top left of the
    cdeltax = cdeltay = 0;        // screen, set its bounds to the
    cx = cmaxx/2; cy = cmaxy/2;   // full screen and initialize its
    lbuttonpress = 0;             // mouse movement counters, and
    rbuttonpress = 0;             // initialize all button states
    numlpress = 0;                // to false
    numrpress = 0;                // Set simulated mouse button
    numlrelease = 0;              // press and release counters to
    numrrelease = 0;              // 0
    initcursor();                 // Create cursor image
```

Using Inheritance

How many times have you written a useful function, such as converting a character string, only to later realize that you would have to rewrite the function to use it in a different context? The problem with most structured languages is that they don't provide a mechanism for letting you use and extend code that you've previously written. However, because of Turbo C++'s object-oriented nature, it includes a feature called inheritance that allows you to derive new classes from existing ones. Such a derived class incorporates all the members (data and functions) of the existing class. That is, it *inherits* the members, and it can also add new members of its own.

To see how inheritance works, let's create a class and derive a new one from the original class. Our first class, which we'll call **cursor**, prints a simple message:

```
class cursor {
public:
  int x, y;
  virtual void init(int xi, int yi) {
    printf("Call initializer in base class\n");
    x = xi;    y = yi;
  }
};
```

```
      cursoron = 0;
      show();                        // Call show() to display it
      return 0;                      // return a "no mouse found" flag
   }
  else
    return 1;
}
```

The first code statement in the function gives away the secret for how this initialization works:

```
if (!mouseobj::init()) {
```

The code checks to see if a mouse is installed by calling the **init( )** routine associated with the **mouseobj** class. Because of inheritance, we can access any of the member functions in the **mouseobj** class from our keyboard object if the **mouseobj** class name is placed before the function call as shown. If a mouse is found, our new **init( )** keyboard member function skips over the necessary code to set up the mouse emulation.

Now suppose we wanted another class to display the message as well as the position of the cursor. Instead of changing the original class, we can derive a new one using the original:

```
class pos_cursor : public cursor {
public:
  virtual void init(int xi, int yi)
    { printf("The position is", xi, yi); }
};
```

The syntax **pos_cursor : public cursor** instructs the compiler that **pos_cursor** uses all of the members in the cursor class. If the **pos_cursor** class was used, it would display its message as well as the message from the **cursor** class and it would assign values to the variables **x** and **y**.

As you're looking over the definition of both of these classes, note that the keyword **virtual** is used to define each of the **init( )** functions. The function in **pos_cursor** is a special kind of member function because it is *overloaded*. Virtual functions are treated differently than other functions. When a function related to an object is called, it is usually linked up to the object at compile time. With virtual functions, this binding does not take place until runtime, called *late binding*.

To use virtual functions, they must be declared properly. For example, **init( )** is declared as virtual in both the **cursor** and (optionally) in the **pos_cursor** classes.

Note that emulating the mouse requires several new variables to be set and functions to be called. First, an emulated cursor must be created, and variables must be initialized to keep track of the location of the mouse cursor, as well as the status of its buttons. Because all of the data needed to process the keyboard is hidden in the **kbdmouseobj** class, you don't have to worry about keeping track of this information. Needless to say, the approach that we've taken greatly simplifies the work of adding the keyboard to an interactive graphics application. In fact, the only decision you have to make is whether or not you want to add the keyboard. If you want to use the mouse only, create an object such as:

```
mouseobj mouse1;
```

However, if you want to use the mouse if one is present, or the keyboard if a mouse is not available, use the **kbdmouseobj** class:

```
kbdmouseobj inpdev;
```

Whatever class you use, the initialization process is the same. Simply remember to call the **init( )** member function at the beginning of your program after the graphics adapter has been initialized.

The Emulated Mouse Cursor

We will now look at how we can emulate the mouse cursor. The basic idea is to use **getimage( )** and **putimage( )** to move the image of an emulated mouse cursor about the screen. We'll create the simulated cursor image in a new member function called **initcursor( )**. A pointer, private to the **kbdmouseobj** class, called **cursor** will point to the cursor image that we'll actually draw in the function **drawcursor( )**. The space for the cursor image is allocated in **initcursor( )** by a call to **malloc( )**. In addition, memory is allocated in **initcursor( )**, so that another private pointer, called **undercursor**, can be used to save the portion of the screen currently covered by the emulated mouse cursor. Moving the emulated cursor on the screen then becomes a three-step process:

1. Remove the current cursor image from the screen by overwriting it with the previously saved image in **undercursor**.
2. Use **getimage( )** to save the screen region in **undercursor** where the cursor is to appear next.
3. Use **putimage( )** to draw the cursor at its new location.

Creating the original cursor image in **initcursor( )** follows this same process. First, the screen area where the cursor image is to be created is saved in **undercursor**. Then an arrow-shaped cursor is drawn by **drawcursor( )**

using a series of calls to **line( )**. Next, the cursor image is saved in **cursor** by a call to **getimage( )** so that it can later be copied to the screen. Finally, the screen is restored to its original state by overwriting the cursor with the image in **undercursor**. This removes the cursor image and restores the screen to its original state.

If you'd like to experiment with the cursor we have used, you need only to modify **drawcursor( )**. The size of the cursor is specified by the constants **CURSHEIGHT** and **CURSWIDTH**, defined in KBDMOUSE.H to be 8 pixels high and 8 pixels wide.

Emulated Mouse Position

The position of the emulated mouse cursor is maintained in the variables **cx** and **cy**. Consequently, a call to **getcoords( )** does nothing more than return these values when the emulated cursor is used. The variables **cx** and **cy** are updated whenever an application program calls **getinput( )** and the user has pressed one of the Arrow keys on the keypad. This latter change involves an extensive portion of code in a new member function called **getkbinteraction( )**. Essentially, this routine checks to see if any keyboard action has taken place. If so, it calls **getkb( )** to retrieve the input (which may be an extended scan code). Next, the input is matched against a list of codes that correspond to various key combinations. If one of the Arrow keys was pressed, the function updates **cx** and **cy**. Note that the emulated cursor position is also clipped to the coordinates **cminx**, **cminy**, **cmaxx**, and **cmaxy**. These clipping parameters can be used to mimic mouse functions **7** and **8**, which restrict the movement of the mouse cursor to a rectangular region on the screen. Finally, note that **getkbinteraction( )** returns 0 whenever it adjusts the position of the emulated cursor. This response is equivalent to telling the calling function that no action need be taken; or, in other words, that no key was pressed or no emulated button was pressed.

Emulated Mouse Buttons

The mouse buttons are emulated by the Ins and Del keys on the keypad. The **switch** statement in **getkbinteraction( )** tests to see whether either of these keys has been pressed and sets either the flag **lbuttonpress** or **rbuttonpress** if one has been pressed. These flags equal 1 if the left and right buttons have been pressed, respectively. In addition, the two counters **numlpress** and **numrpress** are incremented each time there is a button press. These values are used by the routines **buttonpressed( )** and **buttonreleased( )** to detect any button presses and report the fact to the user.

Detecting button presses is easy using this technique. However, emulating button releases is another matter. To solve this problem, we'll count every other press of the Ins or Del keys as a button release. Therefore, whenever **lbuttonpress** or **rbuttonpress** is 1 and the Ins or Del key is pressed, it is considered to be a button release and the special counters **numlrelease** and **numrrelease** are incremented. As before, these values are used by the simulated button routines to detect any button releases and report the fact to the user.

• MOUSE.H

```
// MOUSE.H: Header file for MOUSE.CPP. The constants list the
// mouse functions supported in MOUSE.CPP.

#ifndef MOUSEH
#define MOUSEH
const int RESET_MOUSE = 0;
const int SHOW_MOUSE = 1;
const int HIDE_MOUSE = 2;
const int GET_MOUSE_STATUS = 3;
const int SET_MOUSE_COORD = 4;
const int CHECK_BUTTON_PRESS = 5;
const int CHECK_BUTTON_RELEASE = 6;
const int SET_HORIZ_LIMITS = 7;
const int SET_VERT_LIMITS = 8;
const int GET_MOUSE_MOVEMENT = 11;
const int LEFT_BUTTON = 0;      // Use left button
const int RIGHT_BUTTON = 1;     // Use right button
const int EITHER_BUTTON = 2;    // Use either button

int getkey(void);        // Helper function to get a key

class mouseobj {
public:
  int mouseexists;        // Internal variable set to 1 if a mouse driver is
                          // detected during initialization. This variable
                          // is used to select between the mouse code (if a
                          // mouse exists) and the keyboard emulated mouse.
  unsigned char drawmouse; // Equals 1 if toolkit should draw mouse cursor
  int oldx, oldy;         // Owner drawn mouse cursor location
  virtual void mouseintr(unsigned int &m1, unsigned int &m2,
    unsigned int &m3, unsigned int &m4);
  virtual int init(void);
  virtual int reset(void);
  virtual void hide(void);
  virtual void show(void);
  virtual void move(unsigned int x, unsigned int y);
  virtual void getcoords(int &x, int &y);
  virtual void sethorizlimits(int minx, int maxx);
  virtual void setvertlimits(int miny, int maxy);
  virtual unsigned char buttondown(unsigned int &button);
  virtual int buttonreleased(int whichbutton);
  virtual int buttonpressed(int whichbutton);
  int testbutton(int testtype, int whichbutton);
  int inbox(int left, int top, int right, int bottom, int x, int y);
```

```
    virtual int getinput(int whichbutton);
    int getinputpress(int whichbutton);
    int waitforinput(int whichbutton);
    void drawmousecursor(void);
    void showcursor(int x, int y);
};
#endif
```

• MOUSE.CPP

```
// MOUSE.CPP: Routines to support a Microsoft-compatible mouse.
// Mouse support is divided into two classes. The first,
// mouseobj, provides most of the functions you'll need to control
// the mouse. The other, kbdmouseobj, is a class derived from
// mouseobj that overrides the mouse functions so that they are
// emulated by the keyboard. This class is used when a mouse does
// not exist. Both classes assume they are running in graphics mode.
// To move the emulated cursor, use the Arrow keys on the keyboard
// and the Ins and Del keys as the left and right mouse buttons,
// respectively. The gray + and - keys can be used to change the
// amount the emulated mouse cursor is moved by.
#include <alloc.h>
#include <math.h>
#include <dos.h>
#include <graphics.h>
#include <process.h>
#include <stdio.h>
#include <conio.h>
#include "mouse.h"

// This routine provides the communication between the mouse driver and
// an application program. There are several predefined mouse functions
// supported by the Microsoft mouse--see accompanying text. Parameters
// are sent back and forth to the mouse driver through the AX, BX, CX,
// and DX registers.
void mouseobj::mouseintr(unsigned int &m1, unsigned int &m2,
  unsigned int &m3, unsigned int &m4)
{
  union REGS inregs, outregs;

  inregs.x.ax = m1;    inregs.x.bx = m2;
  inregs.x.cx = m3;    inregs.x.dx = m4;
  int86(0x33,&inregs,&outregs);
  m1 = outregs.x.ax;  m2 = outregs.x.bx;
  m3 = outregs.x.cx;  m4 = outregs.x.dx;
}

// Call this routine at the beginning of your program, but after the
// graphics adapter has been initialized. The routine will initialize the
// mouse and display the mouse cursor in the middle of the screen.
// Returns 0 if a mouse is not detected.
int mouseobj::init(void)
{
```

```
    int gmode;
    char far *memory = (char far *)0x00000449;

    mouseexists = 1;
    drawmouse = 0;
    oldx = 0;  oldy = 0;
    gmode = getgraphmode();
    if (gmode == HERCMONOHI) { // If Hercules card is used, patch BIOS
      *memory = 0x06;            // memory location 40h:49h with 6
    }
    if (reset())              // If mouse reset okay, assume a mouse exists
      show();                 // Show the mouse
    else                      // No mouse found--emulate a
      mouseexists = 0;        // mouse using the keyboard
    return mouseexists;
}

// Resets the mouse cursor to: screen center, mouse hidden, using arrow
// cursor, and with minimum and maximum ranges set to full virtual screen
// dimensions. If a mouse driver exists, this function returns a 1;
// otherwise, it returns a 0.
int mouseobj::reset(void)
{
    unsigned int m1 = RESET_MOUSE, m2, m3, m4;

    mouseintr(m1, m2, m3, m4);
    return m1;
}

// Moves the mouse to the location (x,y)
void mouseobj::move(unsigned int x, unsigned int y)
{
    unsigned int m1 = SET_MOUSE_COORD, m2;

    if (getmaxx() == 319 && !drawmouse)
      x *= 2;                        // Adjust between virtual and actual
    mouseintr(m1, m2, x, y);         // coordinates if necessary
}

// Removes the mouse cursor from the screen. Call this function before you
// write or draw anything to the screen. It is also a good idea to turn
// off the mouse at the end of a program. Use show() to restore the mouse
// on the screen. The mouse movement will be maintained while the mouse is
// not visible. Due to a peculiarity of the mouse driver, make sure you
// don't call hide() if the mouse is not already visible. See text
// discussion for more on this.
void mouseobj::hide(void)
{
    unsigned int m1 = HIDE_MOUSE, m2, m3, m4;

    mouseintr(m1, m2, m3, m4);
}
```

```
// Displays the mouse cursor. Normally, you should not call this
// function if the mouse is already visible. The keyboard mouse
// is clipped to the minimum and maximum ranges in this routine.
void mouseobj::show(void)
{
  unsigned int m1 = SHOW_MOUSE, m2, m3, m4;

  mouseintr(m1, m2, m3, m4);     // Display the mouse cursor
}

// Gets the current location of the mouse cursor
void mouseobj::getcoords(int &x, int &y)
{
  unsigned int m1 = GET_MOUSE_STATUS, m2;

  mouseintr(m1, m2, (unsigned int)x, (unsigned int)y);
  if (getmaxx() == 319 && !drawmouse)
    x /= 2;  // Adjust for virtual coordinates of the mouse
}

// Sets the horizontal extents of the mouse
void mouseobj::sethorizlimits(int minx, int maxx)
{
  unsigned int m1 = SET_HORIZ_LIMITS, m2;

  mouseintr(m1, m2, (unsigned int)minx, (unsigned int)maxx);
}

// Sets the vertical extents of the mouse
void mouseobj::setvertlimits(int miny, int maxy)
{
  unsigned int m1 = SET_VERT_LIMITS, m2;

  mouseintr(m1, m2, (unsigned int)miny, (unsigned int)maxy);
}

// Returns non-zero if the specified mouse button is currently down
unsigned char mouseobj::buttondown(unsigned int &button)
{
  unsigned int m1 = GET_MOUSE_STATUS, m2, m3, m4;

  mouseintr(m1, m2, m3, m4);
  return (button&m2) ? 1 : 0;
}

// Tests if a button has been released since the last call to this
// function. If so, return 1; otherwise, return 0.
int mouseobj::buttonreleased(int whichbutton)
{
  return testbutton(CHECK_BUTTON_RELEASE, whichbutton);
}

// Returns a 1 if the mouse button specified has been pressed since the
// last check with this function. If the button has not been pressed,
```

```
// return a 0.
int mouseobj::buttonpressed(int whichbutton)
{
  return testbutton(CHECK_BUTTON_PRESS, whichbutton);
}

// Retrieves a key from the keyboard if the user has pressed one.
// It returns the extended key codes that begin with zero.
int getkey(void)
{
  int c;

  if (kbhit()) {                     // Check if a key has been pressed
    if ((c=getch()) == 0)
      return getch()<<8;             // Return the character
    else
      return c;
  }
  return 0;
}

// Called by buttonpressed() and buttonreleased() to explicitly
// test the mouse button states. The function returns 1 if the
// specified mouse button (in whichbutton) performed the specified
// action (as indicated by testtype). Otherwise, the function returns
// 0, which means that the action tested for did not occur.
int mouseobj::testbutton(int testtype, int whichbutton)
{
  unsigned int m1, m2, m3, m4;

  m1 = testtype;
  if (whichbutton == LEFT_BUTTON || whichbutton == EITHER_BUTTON) {
    m2 = LEFT_BUTTON;
    mouseintr(m1, m2, m3, m4);
    if (m2) return 1;          // Return 1 if the action occurred
  }
  if (whichbutton == RIGHT_BUTTON || whichbutton == EITHER_BUTTON) {
    m1 = testtype;
    m2 = RIGHT_BUTTON;
    mouseintr(m1, m2, m3, m4);
    if (m2) return 1;          // Return 1 if the action occurred
  }
  return 0;                    // Return 0 as a catchall
}

// Test if the mouse cursor is within the box specified. Returns 1
// if the mouse is in the box; otherwise, the function returns 0.
int mouseobj::inbox(int left, int top, int right, int bottom, int x, int
y)
{
  return (x >= left && x <= right && y >= top && y <= bottom) ? 1 : 0;
}
```

```
// Returns a character if a key has been pressed, -1 if a mouse
// button has been pressed, or a 0 if none of the above. If a
// mouse exists, this routine favors any keyboard action.
int mouseobj::getinput(int whichbutton)
{
  int c = getkey();
  if (c)                            // Check if a key has been pressed
    return c;
  else {
    if (buttonpressed(whichbutton)) {
      while (!buttonreleased(whichbutton)) ;
      return -1;
    }
    else if (buttonreleased(whichbutton))
      return -1;
    return 0;
  }
}

// Similar to getinput(); however, if the mouse button is pressed the
// code does not wait for the button to be released before returning
int mouseobj::getinputpress(int whichbutton)
{
  if (drawmouse)                    // Manually draw the mouse cursor
    drawmousecursor();
  int c = getkey();                 // Check if a key has been pressed
  if (c)
    return c;
  else {
    if (buttonpressed(whichbutton))
      return -1;
    else if (buttonreleased(whichbutton))
      return -2;
    return 0;
  }
}

// Calls getinput() until a button or key has been pressed
int mouseobj::waitforinput(int whichbutton)
{
  int c;

  while ((c=getinput(whichbutton)) == 0) ;
  return c;
}

// Draws the crosshair cursor
void mouseobj::showcursor(int x, int y)
{
  const int curswd = 4;
  const int cursht = 4;

  line(x-curswd, y, x+curswd, y);
```

```
    line(x, y-cursht, x, y+cursht);
}

// Manually draw a crosshair cursor. This function is useful
// when your mouse driver does not support the graphics mode
// you're using.
void mouseobj::drawmousecursor(void)
{
    int x, y;
    int oldcolor;
    viewporttype vp;

    getcoords(x, y);
    if (x != oldx || y != oldy) {
        // Note: This code doesn't set the line style settings
        // or save the write mode
        oldcolor = getcolor();
        setcolor(15);
        getviewsettings(&vp);
        setviewport(0, 0, getmaxx(), getmaxy(), 0);
        setwritemode(XOR_PUT);
        showcursor(oldx, oldy);
        showcursor(x, y);
        oldx = x;   oldy = y;
        setwritemode(COPY_PUT);
        setcolor(oldcolor);
        setviewport(vp.left, vp.top, vp.right, vp.bottom, vp.clip);
    }
}
```

• KBDMOUSE.H

```
// KBDMOUSE.H: Derived mouseobj class that emulates the mouse
// with the keyboard.
#ifndef KBDMOUSEH
#define KBDMOUSEH
#include "mouse.h"

const int MAXINC = 32;  // Largest increment amount of emulated mouse cursor
const int CURSWIDTH = 8;     // The emulated cursor is 8
const int CURSHEIGHT = 8;    // pixels by 8 pixels

class kbdmouseobj : public mouseobj {
    int cx, cy;           // Internal variables used to maintain
                          // the cursor location when the mouse is not used
    int cinc;             // Internal variable used for the increment
                          // amount of the nonmouse cursor
    void *cursor;         // Points to image of the emulated mouse
    void *undercursor;    // Area saved under emulated mouse
    int cursoron;         // Equals 1 if the cursor is currently visible
    int cminx, cmaxx;     // Minimum, maximum x coordinates for
                          // internal cursor
```

```
       int cminy, cmaxy;      // Minimum, maximum y coordinates for internally
                              // maintained cursor
       int lbuttonpress;      // Equals 1 if simulated left or right
       int rbuttonpress;      // button is pressed
       int numlpress;         // Count the number of button presses
       int numrpress;
       int numlrelease;       // Count the number of button releases
       int numrrelease;
       int cdeltax, cdeltay; // Keeps track of emulated mouse's movements
public:
    virtual int init(void);
    virtual void hide(void);
    virtual void show(void);
    virtual void move(unsigned int x, unsigned int y);
    virtual void getcoords(int &x, int &y);
    virtual int buttonreleased(int whichbutton);
    virtual int buttonpressed(int whichbutton);
    virtual int getinput(int whichbutton);
    int getkbinteraction(int whichbutton);
    int getkb(void);
    void initcursor(void);
    void togglecursor(void);
    void drawcursor(int x, int y);
};
#endif
```

• KBDMOUSE.CPP

```
// KBDMOUSE.CPP: Routines to emulate a mouse with a keyboard.
// To move the emulated cursor, use the Arrow keys on the keyboard
// and the Ins and Del keys as the left and right mouse buttons,
// respectively. The gray + and - keys can be used to change the
// amount the emulated mouse cursor is moved. Note that the routines
// will call the mouseobj member functions if a mouse exists.
#include <alloc.h>
#include <math.h>
#include <dos.h>
#include <graphics.h>
#include <process.h>
#include <stdio.h>
#include <conio.h>
#include "mouse.h"
#include "kbdmouse.h"

// Call this function at the beginning of your program, after the graphics
// adapter has been initialized. It will initialize the mouse and display
// the mouse cursor in the middle of the screen. If a mouse is not
// present, it will cause the emulated mouse to appear and the keyboard
// will be used to move the "mouse" cursor.
int kbdmouseobj::init(void)
{
  if (!mouseobj::init()) {       // No mouse found--emulate the mouse
    cinc = 1; cminx = 0;         // The functionality is the
```

```
      cmaxx = getmaxx() - 1;        // same as the real thing
      cmaxy = getmaxy()-1;          // Therefore, set the emulated
      cminx = 0; cminy = 0;         // cursor to the top left of the
      cdeltax = cdeltay = 0;        // screen, set its bounds to the
      cx = cmaxx/2; cy = cmaxy/2;   // full screen and initialize its
      lbuttonpress = 0;             // mouse movement counters, and
      rbuttonpress = 0;             // initialize all button states
      numlpress = 0;                // to false
      numrpress = 0;                // Set simulated mouse button
      numlrelease = 0;              // press and release counters to
      numrrelease = 0;              // 0
      initcursor();                 // Create cursor image
      cursoron = 0;
      show();                       // Call show() to display it
      return 0;                     // Return a "no mouse found" flag
    }
  else
    return 1;
}

// Moves the mouse to the location (x,y)
void kbdmouseobj::move(unsigned int x, unsigned int y)
{
  if (mouseexists)
    mouseobj::move(x,y);
  else {
    hide();                         // Erase the current mouse cursor
    cx = x;   cy = y;               // Update the mouse cursor's location
    show();                         // Display mouse at the new location
    cdeltax = cdeltay = 0;          // Reset the mouse movement variables
    return;
  }
}

// Removes the mouse cursor from the screen. Call hide() before writing or
// drawing to the screen. It is also a good idea to turn off the mouse at
// the end of a program. Use show() to restore the mouse on the screen.
// The mouse movement will be maintained while the mouse is not visible.
// Due to a peculiarity of the mouse driver, make sure you don't call
// hide() if the mouse is not already visible. See text discussion for
// more on this.
void kbdmouseobj::hide(void)
{
  if (mouseexists)
    mouseobj::hide();
  else                              // Mouse doesn't exist, so turn
    togglecursor();                 // off the emulated cursor
}

// Display the mouse cursor. Normally, you should not call this
// function if the mouse is already visible. The keyboard mouse
// is clipped to the minimum and maximum ranges in this routine.
void kbdmouseobj::show(void)
```

```
{
  if (mouseexists)
    mouseobj::show();              // If the mouse doesn't exist,
  else
    togglecursor();                // turn on the emulated cursor
}

// Get the current location of the mouse cursor
void kbdmouseobj::getcoords(int &x, int &y)
{
  if (mouseexists)
    mouseobj::getcoords(x, y);
  else {
    x = cx; y = cy;                // The position of the emulated
  }                                // mouse is given by cx and cy
}

// Test if a button has been released since the last call to this
// function. If so, return 1, otherwise return 0. In the keyboard mode,
// button release is simulated by striking on the "button key" again.
int kbdmouseobj::buttonreleased(int whichbutton)
{
  if (mouseexists)
    return(mouseobj::buttonreleased(whichbutton));
  else {
    if ((whichbutton == LEFT_BUTTON || whichbutton == EITHER_BUTTON) &&
                          numlrelease) {
      numlrelease--;
      return 1;
    }
    else if ((whichbutton == RIGHT_BUTTON || whichbutton == EITHER_BUTTON)
                        && numrrelease) {
      numrrelease--;
      return 1;
    }
    // If there isn't already a button released, check and see if
    // the user just released one, and if so, repeat the tests above.
    else if (getkbinteraction(whichbutton) < 0) {
      if (whichbutton == LEFT_BUTTON || whichbutton == EITHER_BUTTON)
        return 1;
      else if (whichbutton == RIGHT_BUTTON || whichbutton ==
                EITHER_BUTTON)
        return 1;
    }
    return 0;      // Return a value that the button was not pressed
  }
}

// Return a 1 if the mouse button specified has been pressed since the
// last check with this function. If the button has not been pressed,
// return a 0.
int kbdmouseobj::buttonpressed(int whichbutton)
{
```

```
    if (mouseexists)
      return(mouseobj::testbutton(CHECK_BUTTON_PRESS,whichbutton));
    else {
      if ((whichbutton == LEFT_BUTTON || whichbutton == EITHER_BUTTON) &&
                    numlpress) {
        numlpress--;
        return 1;
      }
      else if ((whichbutton == RIGHT_BUTTON || whichbutton == EITHER_BUTTON)
                          && numrpress) {
        numrpress--;
        return 1;
      }
      // If there isn't already a button pressed, check and see if
      // the user just pressed one, and if so repeat the tests above.
      else if (getkbinteraction(whichbutton) < 0) {
        if (whichbutton == LEFT_BUTTON || whichbutton == EITHER_BUTTON)
          return 1;
        else if (whichbutton == RIGHT_BUTTON || whichbutton ==
                  EITHER_BUTTON)
          return 1;
      }
      return 0;       // Return a value that the button was not pressed
    }
}

// Returns a character if a key has been pressed, -1 if an emulated
// mouse button has been pressed, or a 0 if none of the above. If a
// mouse exists, this function calls the mouse routines.
int kbdmouseobj::getinput(int whichbutton)
{
  int c;

  if (mouseexists)
    return(mouseobj::getinput(whichbutton));
  else {
    c = getkbinteraction(whichbutton);
    return c;
  }
}

// This routine is used only if the mouse does not exist. It updates
// the location of the cursor whenever an Arrow key is pressed or
// will set the button pressed flags if a button keys is pressed. In
// addition, it will change the cursor increment amount if the plus or
// minus keys are pressed. If the "button" specified is pressed or was
// already pressed, the function returns -1. If an Arrow key is pressed,
// then a 0 is returned, which means that the caller does not have to
// perform any action. Finally, if some other key is pressed, then its
// value is returned.
int kbdmouseobj::getkbinteraction(int whichbutton)
{
  int c;
```

```
if (kbhit()) {
  c = getkb();
  hide();                       // Emulated mouse may be moved
  switch(c) {
  case 0x5200 :                 // Ins key emulates left mouse button press
    lbuttonpress = (lbuttonpress) ? 0 : 1;
    show();
    if (whichbutton == LEFT_BUTTON || whichbutton == EITHER_BUTTON)
      return -1;                // Return mouse button click signal
    if (lbuttonpress) numlpress++;
      else numlrelease++;
    return 0;                   // Wrong mouse "button" pressed
  case 0x5300 :                 // Del key emulates right mouse button
    show();
    rbuttonpress = (rbuttonpress) ? 0 : 1;
    if (whichbutton == RIGHT_BUTTON || whichbutton == EITHER_BUTTON)
      return -1;                // Return mouse button signal
    if (rbuttonpress) numrpress++;
      else numrelease++;
    return 0;                   // Wrong mouse "button" pressed
  case 0x002B :                 // '+' key: increase the mouse movement amount
    cinc = (cinc < MAXINC) ? cinc + 6 : MAXINC;
    break;
  case 0x002D :                 // '-' key: decrease the mouse movement amount
    cinc = (cinc > 1 + 6) ? cinc - 6 : 1;
    break;
  case 0x4800 :                 // Up Arrow key moves the cursor up by the
    if ((cy -= cinc) < cminy) cy = cminy;
    cdeltay -= cinc;            // increment amount and clip; also
    break;                      // decrement movement amount
  case 0x5000 :                 // Down Arrow key
    if ((cy += cinc) > cmaxy) cy = cmaxy;
    cdeltay += cinc;
    break;
  case 0x4B00 :                 // Left Arrow key
    if ((cx -= cinc) < cminx) cx = cminx;
    cdeltax -= cinc;
    break;
  case 0x4D00 :                 // Right Arrow key
    if ((cx += cinc) > cmaxx) cx = cmaxx;
    cdeltax += cinc;
    break;
  case 0x4700 :                 // Home key
    if ((cy -= cinc) < cminy) cy = cminy;
    if ((cx -= cinc) < cminx) cx = cminx;
    cdeltax -= cinc;   cdeltay -= cinc;
    break;
  case 0x4900 :                 // PgUp key
    if ((cy -= cinc) < cminy) cy = cminy;
    if ((cx += cinc) > cmaxx) cx = cmaxx;
    cdeltax += cinc;  cdeltay -= cinc;
    break;
  case 0x4F00 :                 // End key
```

```
      if ((cy += cinc) > cmaxy) cy = cmaxy;
      if ((cx -= cinc) < cminx) cx = cminx;
      cdeltax -= cinc;  cdeltay += cinc;
      break;
    case 0x5100 :                 // PgDn key
      if ((cy += cinc) > cmaxy) cy = cmaxy;
      if ((cx += cinc) > cmaxx) cx = cmaxx;
      cdeltax += cinc;  cdeltay += cinc;
      break;
    default : show(); return c;
    }
    show();                       // Restore mouse to possibly new position
  }
  return 0;                       // Tell caller not to take any action
}

// Low-level keyboard input that retrieves some of the extended
// codes produced by the Arrow keys and gray keys. This function does
// not support all of the extended key codes.
int kbdmouseobj::getkb(void)
{
  int ch1, ch2;

  ch1 = getch();
  if (ch1 == 0) {               // Arrow keys have two character sequences
    ch2 = getch();              // where the first character is a 0
    ch2 = ch2 << 8;             // Combine these two characters into one
    ch2 |= ch1;                 // and return the value
    return ch2;
  }
  else
    return ch1;
}

// Creates the image of the simulated mouse. It calls drawcursor(),
// which is a routine that you must supply to actually draw the cursor.
// Note: A drawcursor() routine, which draws an arrow, is provided below.
void kbdmouseobj::initcursor(void)
{
  // Allocate space for the emulated mouse cursor and for the space
  // below it. If not enough memory, quit the program.
  cursor = malloc(imagesize(0, 0, CURSWIDTH, CURSHEIGHT));
  undercursor = malloc(imagesize(0, 0, CURSWIDTH, CURSHEIGHT));
  if (cursor == NULL || undercursor == NULL) {
    closegraph();
    printf("Not enough memory for program.\n");
    exit(1);
  }
  // Save the image of the screen where the cursor image will be created.
  // Clear this space and call drawcursor() to draw the cursor.
  getimage(cx, cy, cx+CURSWIDTH, cy+CURSHEIGHT, undercursor);
  setlinestyle(SOLID_LINE, 0, 0);
  setfillstyle(SOLID_FILL, BLACK);
  bar(cx, cy, cx+CURSWIDTH, cy+CURSHEIGHT);
```

```
    drawcursor(cx, cy);
    // Save the image of the cursor and overwrite the screen area where the
    // cursor is with the original screen image.
    getimage(cx, cy, cx+CURSWIDTH, cy+CURSHEIGHT, cursor);
    putimage(cx, cy, undercursor, COPY_PUT);
}

// Used by the simulated mouse to turn the mouse cursor on and off.
// The viewport settings may have changed so temporarily reset them
// to the full screen while the cursor image is displayed or erased.
void kbdmouseobj::togglecursor(void)
{
    struct viewporttype vp;
    int oldx, oldy;

    getviewsettings(&vp);                       // Save view settings
    oldx = getx();   oldy = gety();             // and current position
    setviewport(0, 0, getmaxx(), getmaxy(), 1);
    if (cursoron) {                             // To erase the cursor,
        putimage(cx, cy, undercursor, COPY_PUT);// overwrite it with
        cursoron = 0;                           // the saved image of
    }                                           // the screen
    else {                                      // To draw the cursor,
        getimage(cx, cy, cx+CURSWIDTH, cy+CURSHEIGHT, undercursor);
        putimage(cx, cy, cursor, COPY_PUT);     // first save the area
        cursoron = 1;                           // where the cursor
    }                                           // will be and then
                                                // display the cursor
    // Reset the viewport settings and its current position
    setviewport(vp.left, vp.top, vp.right, vp.bottom, 1);
    moveto(oldx, oldy);
}

// This function draws a cursor if a mouse does not exist. It draws
// a small arrow. If you want a different cursor, just change this
// routine. CURSWIDTH and CURSHEIGHT define the dimensions of cursor.
void kbdmouseobj::drawcursor(int x, int y)
{
    setcolor(getmaxcolor());
    line(x+1, y+1, x+CURSWIDTH-1, y+CURSHEIGHT-1);
    line(x+2, y+1, x+CURSWIDTH-1, y+CURSHEIGHT-2);
    line(x+1, y+2, x+CURSWIDTH-2, y+CURSHEIGHT-1);
    line(x+2, y+1, x+2, y+5);
    line(x+1, y+1, x+1, y+5);
    line(x+1, y+1, x+5, y+1);
    line(x+1, y+2, x+5, y+2);
}
```

Putting Your Mouse to the Test

The MOUSETST.CPP program that follows will partially test your mouse code. The program does nothing more than set your system into graphics mode and then initialize the mouse. If a mouse is detected, it is displayed and you can move the mouse cursor around. The program will continue until you press one of the buttons on the mouse.

If a mouse is not detected, the emulated mouse will appear. You can move it around the screen by using the Arrow keys. Use the gray + and - keys to change the amount that the emulated mouse cursor is moved. The program will continue until you press either the Ins or Del keys (these are the emulated mouse buttons).

Note that an object called **mouse** is declared to be of type **kbdmouseobj**. This variable is then used to access all the features of the mouse toolkit. You'll need a similar statement in your applications.

MOUSETST.CPP uses the mouse toolkit, therefore to compile the program you must create a project file that includes the files MOUSETST.CPP, MOUSE.CPP, and KBDMOUSE.CPP.

Although, it's not necessary here, when using the mouse toolkit with some of the other tools in this book, you'll need to specify the **MOUSE** compiler constant in order for the tools to work with this mouse. The **MOUSE** constant is used in conjunction with **#ifdef** compilation switches to ensure that mouse-specific code is only compiled into the toolkits when the mouse is being used. If you use your compiler's integrated development environment (IDE), you can define the **MOUSE** compiler switch, by typing "MOUSE" in the *Defines* field of your IDE's compiler options dialog box.

```
// MOUSETST.CPP: This program tests the mouse packages MOUSE.CPP and
// KBDMOUSE.CPP. It displays a mouse cursor and allows you to move it
// around the screen until a mouse button is pressed. If no mouse is
// detected, the keyboard emulated mouse is used. Use the Arrow keys
// to move this mouse and the Ins or Del keys as the mouse buttons in
// order to quit the program.
#include <stdio.h>
#include <graphics.h>
#include "mouse.h"
#include "kbdmouse.h"                      // Keyboard mouse functions

main()
{
  int c, gmode, gdriver=DETECT;            // Use autodetect
  kbdmouseobj mouse;

  initgraph(&gdriver, &gmode, "\\tcpp\\bgi");  // Initialize the screen
  if (graphresult() != grOk) {
    printf("Failed to initialize graphics\n");
    return 1;
  }
  if (!mouse.init()) {
    mouse.hide();                          // Always turn the mouse cursor
    outtextxy(0, 0, "No mouse detected");  // off while writing to the
```

```
      mouse.show();                             // screen
    }
  mouse.hide();
  outtextxy(0, 10, "Press a mouse button to quit");
  outtextxy(0, 20, "or the INS or DEL key if a mouse isn't present");
  mouse.show();                             // Wait until the mouse routine
  do {                                      // returns a negative value.
    c = mouse.waitforinput(EITHER_BUTTON); // This indicates that a button
  } while (c >= 0);                         // was pressed.
  // It's a good idea to turn the mouse off when done
  mouse.hide();
  closegraph();                            // Exit graphics mode
  return 0;
}
```

8

Working with Icons

I f you've ever used a Microsoft Windows application, such as a painting program, you're probably aware of the benefits of icons. Icons are a great way of succinctly representing commands on the screen. To select a command, the user simply clicks on the icon with the mouse. In this chapter, we'll take a close look at icons and develop a standalone icon editor that we'll use to create, save, and edit icons. In addition, we'll present several sample icon patterns that you can use in the custom graphics programs we'll be developing in Chapters 11 through 14.

Why Icons?

Many graphics-based applications, such as CAD and paint programs, use icons in order to represent complex commands as symbols or pictures. As a result, extremely intuitive and easy to use graphics interfaces can be designed around them. Instead of having to type a command or select one from a list of often ambiguous menus, the mouse can be used to point and click on an icon to invoke the command. Placed in a toolbar, icons don't take up too much room so you can leave them on the display at all times, making the more common commands only one mouse click away.

Our goal here is to develop a program that allows us to create icons interactively. Although we could design our icons by hand, the interactive nature of this program simplifies the process of drawing and editing icons. The program, ICONED.CPP (shown at the end of this chapter), closely resembles the fill pattern editor that we created in Chapter 3. One difference is that we'll be using the mouse tools that we developed in Chapter 7 to improve the user interface.

195

USING ICON FILES

Icons can be represented in many different ways. Our primary concern here is to develop icons that look good when displayed with the different graphics modes supported by the BGI. An icon drawn in one mode may appear different if it is drawn in another because of the varying screen resolutions and aspect ratios that exist. In general, it is nearly impossible to create one icon pattern that looks the same in all graphics modes. For more on this issue, refer to *Writing Device-Independent Graphics Programs* below.

We'll standardize our icons so that they are either 16 x 16 or 32 x 32 pixels in size. Each icon will be stored in a separate file of hexadecimal numbers that specify the color of each pixel in the icon. The colors can range from 0 to 15

WRITING DEVICE-INDEPENDENT GRAPHICS PROGRAMS

One issue that comes up again and again in graphics programming is whether a particular program can run in different graphics modes. A program that can accomplish this is said to be *device independent*. Clearly, this is an admirable goal, because an application that is not tied to a particular graphics standard has a better chance of getting used by more people. However, there are so many different graphics "standards" that achieving a device-independent application can be a real challenge. Essentially, there are three issues that you must deal with:

• Screen resolution

• Aspect ratio

• Colors

The problems relating to screen resolution and aspect ratio are somewhat overlapping. Generally, you want to try to avoid writing statements that display graphics figures at specific screen coordinates. For example, a program that draws a square with the upper-left coordinate at (0,0) and the bottom-right coordinate at (240,240) will work in VGA's high-resolution mode but not in CGA, because CGA does not have 240 rows available. One way to get around this is to scale all of your calculations based on the dimensions of the screen—in this case, it would be better to use the coordinates (0,0) and (240,**getmaxy( )**/2).

Unfortunately, even if you follow this approach, your figures may still not display equally well in different modes. The reason is that different modes have different pixel aspect ratios. For instance, in 320 x 200 CGA mode, pixels are twice as tall as they are wide. However, in a VGA high-resolution mode, pixels are about the same in both dimensions. You can

and correspond to the standard colors on EGA and VGA graphics adapters. To simplify our application programs and make our icons easier to maintain, we'll store the icons in text format.

The format of the icon files we're creating consists of two major parts—a header and a body. The header is located at the top of the file and is a single line that specifies the icon's width and height. All of our icons are either 16 x 16 or 32 x 32 pixels, therefore, the first line will start with either of these two sets of numbers. The rest of the file contains the icon pattern, which is organized so that each row of the icon is on a separate line. Therefore, a 16 x 16 icon has 16 numbers per line where each pixel of the icon image is represented by a hexadecimal digit. Figure 8.1 shows a sample icon and the

adjust for the difference in the aspect ratio by scaling your figures using a ratio calculated from the values returned by the BGI function **getaspectratio( )**. You have two choices here: You can either, stretch the figure in the x direction to compensate for the screen resolution difference, or you can compress the y values. In trying to draw a good square, let's take the latter approach. For example, to improve the image, we must first calculate the screen's aspect ratio

```
getaspectratio(&xasp, &yasp);
aspectratio = (double)xasp / (double)yasp;
```

and then multiply each y dimension by **aspectratio**. Therefore, the square's top-left and bottom-right coordinates become (0,0) and (240,240***aspectratio**). Now the square will truly appear as a square. This example, still forces the size to a specific value, but with the scaling technique shown earlier in this sidebar, you can get around this.

Compensating for the various colors is another matter. Generally, if you only use the EGA or VGA standard palette, you shouldn't have a problem when going between these two graphics adapters. However, if you try to use the same program in a CGA mode or on a monochrome system, you'll only have a few "colors" available and the same display may not look the way you intended it to. Some of this can be avoided by planning ahead and making clever choices for colors and fill patterns. One technique you might try is to create a *logical palette* that all of your code accesses to select colors and which is assigned a set of colors from those available when your program runs. Of course, this doesn't add colors to modes where they don't exist, but it will help you to program with the color settings in mind and when you run across a mode where your program doesn't look good, it's a often a simple matter of changing the values in the logical palette for that particular mode.

Figure 8.1 The text file on the right defines the icon on the left.

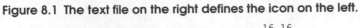

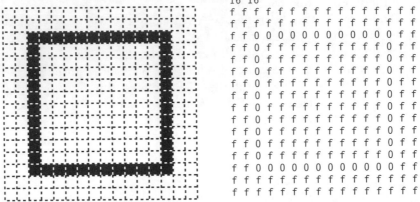

file that is used to store it. If you compare the two, you'll see that there is a one-to-one correspondence between each pixel set in the icon and each value of 1 in the file.

Because we'll be supporting color icons, we'll run into a bit of a problem: What colors are displayed if an icon specifies a color that is not supported by the current hardware? There are several approaches you can take to solve the problem. We could develop a translation algorithm that specifies what colors to use, or we could define several versions of the same icon where each one is intended for a different graphics mode.

THE INTERACTIVE EDITOR

Figure 8.2 shows the Icon Editor while it is being used to edit a 32 x 32 icon. There are four primary components of the icon editor's environment. On the top-left side of the screen is an enlarged representation of the icon being edited. You perform all editing tasks within this window. On the top-right side of the screen is the current state of the icon pattern shown in its actual size. Along the bottom of the screen is a palette of colors that you can use in the icon. Below the enlarged icon pattern is a rectangular box that shows the current color being used.

To edit the enlarged icon, simply click the left mouse button while over the desired cell you want to set to the current drawing color. If you want to paint consecutive cells, hold the mouse button down and drag the mouse to other cells. Each time one of the big pixels is updated, the actual-sized icon on the right side of the screen is updated. You can set the whole icon to the current drawing color by clicking on the rectangle below the enlarged icon. To

Figure 8.2 Use the Icon Editor program to modify your icons.

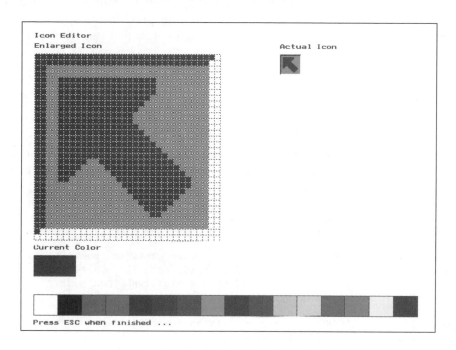

change the current drawing color, click the mouse on the desired color in the palette at the bottom of the screen.

By default, the Icon Editor is set up to edit 16 x 16 icons. You can however, force the editor to work with 32 x 32 icons by including the number 32 on the program's command line when you invoke it.

To exit the editing process, press the Esc key. The Icon Editor clears the screen and you are asked if you want to save the current icon pattern to a file of your choice. If so, you will be prompted to enter the filename. Once you have named the file, the program saves the icon pattern and terminates. Otherwise, the program simply ends.

REPRESENTING ICONS

Internally, our Icon Editor represents an icon pattern as a two-dimensional array of integers. Here's the declaration for this array:

```
const int ICONWIDTH = 16;      // An icon is a 16 x 16 pattern
const int ICONHEIGHT = 16;
int icon[ICONHEIGHT*2][ICONWIDTH*2];      // Allow up to 32 x 32 icons
```

The constants **ICONHEIGHT** and **ICONWIDTH** specify the default height and width of the icon, respectively, and are defined as the value 16. Consequently, each location in the icon array represents one pixel in the icon pattern. The **icon** array, however, doubles these dimensions so that the ICONED program can handle 32 x 32 icons.

Creating the Screen

The first several statements in the ICONED program initialize various aspects of the Icon Editor. The process begins by reading an icon file (if necessary), initializing the graphics mode, initializing the mouse, drawing the color palette, and displaying the initial state of the icon pattern. Here are the statements that execute these actions:

```
if (argc == 2 && *argv[1] == '3' && *(argv[1]+1) == '2') {
  iconwd = 32;  iconht = 32;
}
iconexists = readicon();        // If a user wants an icon file to
initgraphsys();                 // be read, read it; otherwise,
                                // show a big blank icon
rectangle(0, 0, getmaxx(), getmaxy());

drawpalette(BIGICONLEFT, getmaxy()-txtht*3-iconht,
  getmaxx()-BIGICONLEFT*2, iconht);
activecolor = 15;
displayactivecolor();
mouse.init();                   // Initialize the mouse
drawbigicon();                  // Draw the icon edit box
```

These statements must be called in this order. In particular, we want to keep the **readicon()** function in text mode (before graphics initialization), in order to simplify the user interaction. In addition, the mouse initialization must always come after the graphics initialization. The ordering of the other statements is probably a little more obvious. We'll look at these two routines later in this section.

The statements shown next print a series of banners to the screen by calling **outtextxy()**. Notice that a pair of **mouse.hide()** and **mouse.show()** function calls surround the screen output statements. They are needed to ensure that the mouse cursor is turned off while the screen is being updated with the displayed messages.

```
mouse.hide();                       // When using the mouse, first turn
                                    // it off before writing to screen
outtextxy(BIGICONLEFT, BIGICONTOP-txtht*4, "Icon Editor");
outtextxy(BIGICONLEFT, BIGICONTOP-txtht*2,"Enlarged Icon");
outtextxy(ICONLEFT, BIGICONTOP-txtht*2,"Actual Icon");
outtextxy(BIGICONLEFT, bigiconbottom+txtht, "Current Color");
```

```
outtextxy(BIGICONLEFT, getmaxy()-txtht*2,
  "Press ESC when finished ...");

mouse.show();                           // Redisplays the mouse to the screen
```

Finally, if there was an icon file read, it is displayed when the following statement is encountered:

```
if (iconexists) showicon();      // Draws the icon read from the file
```

Creating the Enlarged Icon

The function **drawbigicon( )** generates a grid on the left side of the screen in which the enlarged icon pattern is edited. The grid consists of a series of horizontal and vertical dotted lines that mark out the grid for the enlarged icon pattern. The number of lines drawn depends on whether the editor is editing a 16 x 16 or 32 x 32 icon. The dimensions of the icon are stored in global variables **iconwd** and **iconht**, as illustrated in Figure 8.3. These two variables are initialized when ICONED begins. The grid is drawn by the following two **for** loops:

```
mouse.hide();                      // Draw vertical and horizontal dashed
for (int i=0; i<=iconht; i++) // lines to make the big icon pattern
  line(BIGICONLEFT, BIGICONTOP+i*(BIGBITSIZE+NORM_WIDTH), right,
       BIGICONTOP+i*(BIGBITSIZE+NORM_WIDTH));
for (i=0; i<=iconwd; i++)
  line(BIGICONLEFT+aspect*(i*(BIGBITSIZE+NORM_WIDTH)), BIGICONTOP,
       BIGICONLEFT+aspect*(i*(BIGBITSIZE+NORM_WIDTH)), bigiconbottom);
mouse.show();
```

Figure 8.3 These are the dimensions of the editing grid used in ICONED.CPP.

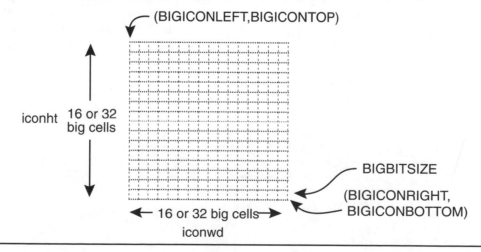

Table 8.1 Constants and Variables Used in Drawing the Enlarged Icon Pattern

Constant/Variable	Description
BIGBITSIZE	Size of the big pixels in the enlarged icon pattern
bigiconbottom	The bottom row of the enlarged icon
BIGICONLEFT	The column where the big icon pattern begins
BIGICONTOP	The top row of the big icon pattern
DOTTED_LINE	From GRAPHICS.H, specifies the line type
iconht	Height of an icon
iconwd	Width of an icon
NORM_WIDTH	From GRAPHICS.H, specifies the pixel width of lines
right	Right edge of the enlarged icon

Notice that before anything is written to the screen, the mouse is first turned off by a call to **mouse.hide( )** and later restored by a call to **mouse.show( )**.

You probably have noticed that **drawbigicon( )** relies on numerous constants and variables. A list of these constants along with a description of their meanings is shown in Table 8.1. You may want to refer to this table to help you understand how the function works.

Displaying the Original Icon

The **showicon( )** function displays the initial state of the icon pattern. This function consists of two nested **for** loops that sequence through the **icon** array. The color stored in each cell of the array is used in the corresponding locations in the enlarged icon and small icon patterns. The **drawbigbit( )** function displays each cell in the enlarged icon pattern and **seticonsbit( )** paints the corresponding pixel in the small icon pattern. The small icon is displayed at the column indicated by **ICONLEFT**. Its top row coincides with **BIGICONTOP**.

Here is the code section to illustrate these processes:

```
void showicon(void)
{
  for (int j=0; j<iconht; j++) {
    int line1 = BIGICONTOP+j*(BIGBITSIZE+NORM_WIDTH);
    for (int i=0; i<iconwd; i++) {
      int col1 = BIGICONLEFT+aspect*(i*(BIGBITSIZE+NORM_WIDTH));
      drawbigbit(col1, line1, icon[j][i]);
      seticonsbit(i, j, icon[j][i]);
    }
  }
}
```

CREATING A COLOR PALETTE

A color palette is painted at the bottom of the screen. In a standard EGA or VGA mode, the color palette contains 16 colors. The **drawpalette()** routine spreads the palette across the screen by dividing the screen width by the number of colors available. The code forces the maximum number of colors to 15. Of course, if you're using a monochrome mode, you'll only get two colors: black and white. Here's the complete **drawpalette()** function:

```
void drawpalette(int x, int y, int wd, int ht)
{
  int maxcolors = getmaxcolor();
  if (maxcolors > 15) maxcolors = 15;
  int colorwd = wd / (maxcolors + 1);
  palleft = x;   paltop = y;   palcolorwd = colorwd;   palht = ht;
  for (int i=0; i<=maxcolors; i++, x+=colorwd) {
    setfillstyle(SOLID_FILL, i);
    bar3d(x, y, x+colorwd, y+ht, 0, 0);
  }
}
```

We'll use a similar technique to create color palettes in the paint and CAD programs in Chapters 11 and 12.

User Interaction

After the screen is initialized, the Icon Editor is ready for business. You can use these four types of input while you are editing an icon:

• Press the left mouse button on a cell of the enlarged pattern to set that cell to the current drawing color

• Press Esc to exit the program

• Position the mouse over the active color rectangle and click to fill the icon with that color

• Click on one of the colors in the palette to reset the active color

The following **while** loop, located in the function **main()**, supports this user interaction:

```
while ((c=mouse.getinputpress(LEFT_BUTTON)) != ESC) {
  // Get input from mouse/keyboard. If input is Esc, quit program.
  if (c < 0) {                      // If input < 0, then a mouse button
    mouse.getcoords(x, y);          // has been pressed; get current
    if (!setbigbit(x, y)) {         // coordinates and set big bit color
      if (!setactivecolor(x, y))    // Change the active color
        floodcolor(x, y);           // Set big icon to the active color
    }
    else {  // Paint pixels while the left mouse button is down
      oldx = x;  oldy = y;
```

```
  while (!mouse.buttonreleased(LEFT_BUTTON)) {
    mouse.getcoords(x, y);
    if (x != oldx || y != oldy) {
      setbigbit(x, y);
      oldx = x;  oldy = y;
    }
  }
}
}
}                                   // Turn mouse off and then get out
```

The loop centers around the use of the **mouseobj** member function **getinputpress( )**, which we developed in Chapter 7. This function returns a negative value if the button specified, in this case the left mouse button, is pressed, or it returns the value of a key pressed. The **while** loop is written so that the program will continue until the user presses the Esc key. If the left mouse button is pressed, the routine will progress to the **if** statement. At this point, **getcoords( )** retrieves the current location of the mouse cursor and calls the routines **setbigbit( )**, **setactivecolor( )**, and possibily **floodcolor( )**. Each of these routines tests whether the mouse was pressed while over its valid screen region. If so, that function processes the mouse action and returns true. Otherwise, the routines return 0, and don't do anything.

Painting an Icon Pixel

When the user clicks the mouse while the mouse is positioned over one of the cells in the enlarged icon pattern, three operations take place:

• The pixel's value in the icon is set to the currently active color

• The big pixel image in the enlarged icon pattern is updated

• The icon's pixel in the small icon pattern is changed

Each of these actions is set in motion by a call to **setbigbit( )**. This function takes two arguments that correspond to the screen coordinates of the enlarged icon bit that is to be changed. This screen coordinate is determined from the location of the mouse cursor at the time of the button press. The mouse coordinates come from our **mouseobj** member function **getcoords( )**.

The bulk of **setbigbit( )**, shown next, is involved in determining which icon bit, if any, should be toggled.

```
for (int j=0; j<iconht; j++) {
  int line1 = BIGICONTOP+j*(BIGBITSIZE+NORM_WIDTH);
  int line2 = BIGICONTOP+(j+1)*(BIGBITSIZE+NORM_WIDTH);
  if (line1 <= y && y < line2) {
    for (int i=0; i<iconwd; i++) {
      int col1 = BIGICONLEFT+aspect*(i*(BIGBITSIZE+NORM_WIDTH));
      int col2 = BIGICONLEFT+aspect*((i+1)*(BIGBITSIZE+NORM_WIDTH));
```

```
    if (col1 <= x && x < col2) {
      drawbigbit(col1, line1, activecolor);
      seticonsbit(i, j, activecolor);    // Toggle the corresponding
      return 1;                          // pixel in the small icon
    }
   }
  }
}
```

The two **for** loops in the function are responsible for determining whether the bit should be toggled. They sequence through the locations of the big icon pattern and test whether the coordinates passed to **setbigbit( )** fall within any of the rows or columns in the big icon pattern. If so, the code calls **drawbigbit( )** to paint that icon location. Here's the **drawbigbit( )** function:

```
void drawbigbit(int x, int y, int color)
{
  mouse.hide();            // Hide the mouse before drawing to the screen
  for (int j=1; j<=BIGBITSIZE; j++) {      // Draw the big bit one
    for (int i=1; i<=aspect*BIGBITSIZE; i++)   // pixel at a time
      putpixel(x+i, y+j, color);
  }
  mouse.show();                            // Turn the mouse back on
}
```

Notice that this function compenstates for the aspect ratio of the screen so that the icon pattern will be square.

Now we need to change the corresponding bit in the small icon pattern. Fortunately, **setbigbit( )** is designed so that the line number and column number determined by the **for** loops correspond to the indices that can access the same bit in the **icon** array. These values, stored in the variables **i** and **j**, are passed to another function, **seticonsbbit( )** to actually change the **icon** array value and update the small icon on the screen.

SAVING AN ICON

The **saveicon( )** function writes an icon pattern to disk. To simplify the user input, **saveicon( )** assumes that it is called while the program is in text mode. First, the function prompts for the filename of the icon file. Then, it calls **fopen( )** to open this file. If the file cannot be opened or created, **fopen( )** returns NULL and the function immediately returns without performing any other actions. However, if **fopen( )** is able to open the file, **saveicon( )** writes the icon pattern stored in the array **icon** to the file using the following statements:

```
// Write the header to the file:
fprintf(iconfile, "%d %d\n", iconwd, iconht);
```

```
for (int j=0; j<iconht; j++) {          // Write the icon
  for (int i=0; i<iconwd; i++)          // pattern to a file,
    fprintf(iconfile, "%x ", icon[j][i]); // one row at a time
  fprintf(iconfile, "\n");
}
fclose(iconfile);
```

The first **fprintf( )** function in this code writes the header data containing the width and height of the icon to the file. The nested **for** loops that follow copy the icon pattern to the file by writing each row of the icon pattern on a separate line. After the icon pattern is completely written, the file is closed with a call to **fclose( )**.

READING AN ICON FILE

The **readicon( )** function reads an icon file into the **icon** array if an icon file is specified when the program starts. Like **saveicon( )**, this function is designed to run in text mode in order to simplify the text input.

The function begins by initializing an icon pattern so that it contains all zeros, as shown here:

```
for (j=0; j<ICONHEIGHT; j++) {   // Initialize the icon array
  for (i=0; i<ICONWIDTH; i++)    // to all zeros
    icon[j][i] = 0;
}
```

This technique ensures that the icon pattern starts as a completely black icon. The **readicon( )** function then continues by displaying a program banner and asking you if you wish to edit an existing icon file. If your response is *yes* (any character but the letter n), **readicon( )** assumes you want to edit an existing icon and asks you for the name of the file where the pattern is stored. Remember that during this process, the data entry operations are performed in text mode in order to simplify the code. You can, however, try to integrate the GTEXT.CPP text processing utilities developed in Chapter 3 into the function, in order to keep the whole program in graphics mode.

Once the filename is determined, **readicon( )** attempts to open it for reading. If this operation is successful, the first line of the file, which contains the header, is read. As long as this line consists of two values equivalent to **iconwd** and **iconht**, **readicon( )** continues. If any other numbers are found, then the file is invalid and **readicon( )** prints a message and returns to the function **main( )** immediately.

Two **for** loops, similar to those used in **saveicon( )**, read the icon's data into the **icon** array: The difference is that here the **fscanf( )** function is used to read the icon pattern from the file. Once the icon pattern has been read into the array **icon**, we can display it.

Exiting the Icon Editor

The **while** loop in **main()** terminates when the user presses the Esc key. Once this key is pressed, the mouse cursor is disabled, the screen is returned to text mode, and the user is prompted to save the icon currently in the Icon Editor. If you respond with anything other than the letter *n*, the program enters the **saveicon()** function and prompts for the filename in which to store the icon.

Compiling the Program

In order to compile the icon editor program, you'll need to create a project file with the files shown in Table 8.2.

Sample Icons

The icons in Figure 8.4 were all developed with the Icon Editor used in this chapter. Each icon is 16 x 16 in size, We will use similar 32 x 32, sculpted icons in Chapter 11 through 14. To minimize any confusion, we have provided specific filenames for these icons that you should also use. This should guarantee the greatest compatibility with any code we will be developing later.

• ICONED.CPP

```
// ICONED.CPP: This program enables you to interactively create,
// edit, and save icon patterns. Icons are saved to a file.
// Mouse interaction is supported. Icons must have the format
// discussed in Chapter 8. By default, the program works with 16
// x 16 icons. You can use this program to edit 32 x 32 icons
// by using the command-line argument "32." Alternatively, if you
// specify an icon file that is 32 x 32 in size, the program will
// automatically adjust to this larger size. To compile the program,
// you must link ICONED.CPP with MOUSE.CPP and KBDMOUSE.CPP.
#include <stdio.h>
#include <graphics.h>
#include <stdlib.h>
#include <conio.h>
#include "kbdmouse.h"
```

Table 8.2 Files to Compile the Icon Editor Program

Main File	Header File	Chapter
MOUSE.CPP	MOUSE.H	7
KBDMOUSE.CPP	KBDMOUSE.H	7
ICONED.CPP	None	8

```
const int BIGICONLEFT = 20;      // The left side of the big icon pattern
const int BIGICONTOP = 50;       // The top edge of the big icon pattern
const int BIGBITSIZE = 8;        // The big bits are 8 pixels in size
const int ICONWIDTH = 16;        // An icon is a 16 x 16 pattern
const int ICONHEIGHT = 16;
const int ICONLEFT = 400;        // The small icon pattern is located here
const int ESC = 27;              // The value of the Esc key
```

Figure 8.4 These sample icons were created with the Icon Editor.

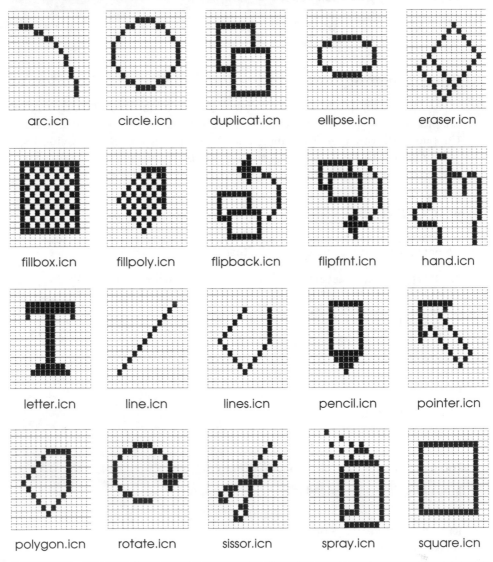

```
// The global variables
int icon[ICONHEIGHT*2][ICONWIDTH*2];    // Allow up to 32 x 32 icons
kbdmouseobj mouse;                       // The mouse object
int aspect;                              // Aspect ratio of screen
int activecolor;                         // Current color to use
int palleft, paltop, palcolorwd, palht;  // Dimensions of the palette
int bigiconbottom;                       // Bottom row of big icon
int txtht;                               // Pixel height of text
int iconwd=ICONWIDTH, iconht=ICONHEIGHT; // Icon dimensions

// This routine draws an enlarged view of the icon pattern. The
// left side of the icon is at BIGICONLEFT and the top is at BIGICONTOP.
void drawbigicon(void)
{
  setlinestyle(DOTTED_LINE, 0, NORM_WIDTH);
  int right = BIGICONLEFT+iconwd*aspect*(BIGBITSIZE+NORM_WIDTH);
  mouse.hide();                  // Draw vertical and horizontal dashed
  for (int i=0; i<=iconht; i++) // lines to make the big icon pattern
    line(BIGICONLEFT, BIGICONTOP+i*(BIGBITSIZE+NORM_WIDTH), right,
         BIGICONTOP+i*(BIGBITSIZE+NORM_WIDTH));
  for (i=0; i<=iconwd; i++)
    line(BIGICONLEFT+aspect*(i*(BIGBITSIZE+NORM_WIDTH)), BIGICONTOP,
         BIGICONLEFT+aspect*(i*(BIGBITSIZE+NORM_WIDTH)), bigiconbottom);
  mouse.show();
}


// Paints a single big bit in the large icon
void drawbigbit(int x, int y, int color)
{
  mouse.hide();          // Hide the mouse before drawing to the screen
  for (int j=1; j<=BIGBITSIZE; j++) {         // Draw the big bit one
    for (int i=1; i<=aspect*BIGBITSIZE; i++)   // pixel at a time
      putpixel(x+i, y+j, color);
  }
  mouse.show();          // Turn the mouse back on
}


// This routine updates one pixel in the icon pattern. The
// arguments x and y are between 0 and iconwd or iconht. The routine
// plots several pixels to adjust for the aspect ratio of the
// graphics screen. You may want to remove this. The array icon saves
// the icon pattern.
void seticonsbit(int x, int y, int color)
{
  int i;

  mouse.hide();
  // Set the color of the pixel
  for (i=0; i<aspect; i++)
    putpixel(aspect*x+i+ICONLEFT, BIGICONTOP+y, color);
  icon[y][x] = color;
  mouse.show();
}
```

```
// When the user clicks on the big icon pattern, set the
// appropriate big bit and the corresponding pixel in the icon
// pattern to the currently active color. This routine accepts screen
// coordinates that specify where the mouse button was pressed. The
// two for loops test to see which logical bit in the icon pattern
// must be updated. The routine calls seticonsbit() to set the
// appropriate pixel in icon pattern.
int setbigbit(int x, int y)
{
  for (int j=0; j<iconht; j++) {
    int line1 = BIGICONTOP+j*(BIGBITSIZE+NORM_WIDTH);
    int line2 = BIGICONTOP+(j+1)*(BIGBITSIZE+NORM_WIDTH);
    if (line1 <= y && y < line2) {
      for (int i=0; i<iconwd; i++) {
        int col1 = BIGICONLEFT+aspect*(i*(BIGBITSIZE+NORM_WIDTH));
        int col2 = BIGICONLEFT+aspect*((i+1)*(BIGBITSIZE+NORM_WIDTH));
        if (col1 <= x && x < col2) {
          drawbigbit(col1, line1, activecolor);
          seticonsbit(i, j, activecolor);   // Toggle the corresponding
          return 1;                         // pixel in the small icon
        }
      }
    }
  }
  return 0;
}

// This routine writes the icon pattern to a file. The user is
// prompted for the filename to write the file to. The format of
// the file is given in this chapter.
void saveicon(void)
{
  char filename[80];
  FILE *iconfile;

  printf("\nEnter the filename to store the icon in: ");
  scanf("%s", filename);
  if ((iconfile=fopen(filename,"w")) == NULL) {  // Open the file
    printf("Could not open file.\n");
    return;
  }
  // Write the header to the file:
  fprintf(iconfile, "%d %d\n", iconwd, iconht);
  for (int j=0; j<iconht; j++) {                 // Write the icon
    for (int i=0; i<iconwd; i++)                 // pattern to a file,
      fprintf(iconfile, "%x ", icon[j][i]);      // one row at a time
    fprintf(iconfile, "\n");
  }
  fclose(iconfile);
}

// This routine reads an icon file into the icon pattern array.
// The header of the file specifies the size of the icon. No error
// checking is done here. If the user does not want a file read in
```

```c
// or there is an error reading the icon file, the function returns
// with the icon pattern initialized to all black.
int readicon(void)
{
  char filename[80];
  FILE *iconfile;

  for (int j=0; j<iconht; j++)     // Initialize the icon array
    for (int i=0; i<iconwd; i++)   // to all zeros
      icon[j][i] = 0;

  printf("\n\n----------  ICON EDITOR ------------\n\n");
  printf("Do you want to edit an existing icon? (y) ");
  if (getch() == 'n') return 0;
  printf("\nEnter the name of the file to read the icon from: ");
  scanf("%s", filename);
  if ((iconfile=fopen(filename,"r")) == NULL) {
    printf("Cannot open file.  --  Press any key to continue...\n");
    getch();
    return 0;
  }
  // The first line of the icon file contains the icon's dimensions
  fscanf(iconfile, "%d %d", &iconwd, &iconht);
  for (j=0; j<iconht; j++)
    for (int i=0; i<iconwd; i++)
      fscanf(iconfile, "%x", &icon[j][i]);
  fclose(iconfile);
  return 1;
}


// Shows the icon pattern that is in the icon array
void showicon(void)
{
  for (int j=0; j<iconht; j++) {
    int line1 = BIGICONTOP+j*(BIGBITSIZE+NORM_WIDTH);
    for (int i=0; i<iconwd; i++) {
      int col1 = BIGICONLEFT+aspect*(i*(BIGBITSIZE+NORM_WIDTH));
      drawbigbit(col1, line1, icon[j][i]);
      seticonsbit(i, j, icon[j][i]);
    }
  }
}


// Displays the color currently being used in the icon
void displayactivecolor(void)
{
  setfillstyle(SOLID_FILL, activecolor);
  bar3d(BIGICONLEFT, bigiconbottom+txtht*3, BIGICONLEFT+iconwd*2,
    bigiconbottom+iconht+txtht*3, 0, 0);
}


// Determines whether the user has clicked on one of the colors
// in the palette. If so, the active color is set to the new selection.
int setactivecolor(int x, int y)
```

```
{
  int maxcolors = getmaxcolor();
  if (maxcolors > 15) maxcolors = 15;

  if (y >= paltop && y < paltop+palht) {
    for (int i=0, col=palleft; i<=maxcolors; i++, col+=palcolorwd) {
      if (col <= x && x < col+palcolorwd) {
        activecolor = i;
        displayactivecolor();
        return 1;
      }
    }
  }
  return 0;
}

// Paints the whole icon with the active color
void colorall(void)
{
  for (int j=0; j<iconht; j++) {
    int line1 = BIGICONTOP+j*(BIGBITSIZE+NORM_WIDTH);
    for (int i=0; i<iconwd; i++) {
      int col1 = BIGICONLEFT+aspect*(i*(BIGBITSIZE+NORM_WIDTH));
      drawbigbit(col1, line1, activecolor);
      seticonsbit(i, j, activecolor);
    }
  }
}

// Fills the whole icon with the currently active color if the
// mouse is pressed while positioned over the current color box
int floodcolor(int x, int y)
{
  setfillstyle(SOLID_FILL, activecolor);
  if ((x >= BIGICONLEFT && x < BIGICONLEFT+iconwd*2) &&
      (bigiconbottom+txtht*3 <= y &&
        y < bigiconbottom+iconht+txtht*3)) {
    colorall();
    return 1;
  }
  return 0;
}

// Draws a palette that contains up to 16 colors. The top left of
// the palette is the pixel location (x,y) and its width and height
// are wd and ht.
void drawpalette(int x, int y, int wd, int ht)
{
  int maxcolors = getmaxcolor();
  if (maxcolors > 15) maxcolors = 15;
  int colorwd = wd / (maxcolors + 1);
  palleft = x;  paltop = y;  palcolorwd = colorwd;  palht = ht;
  for (int i=0; i<=maxcolors; i++, x+=colorwd) {
    setfillstyle(SOLID_FILL, i);
```

```
      bar3d(x, y, x+colorwd, y+ht, 0, 0);
   }
}

// Initializes the graphics mode and sets several global variables
void initgraphsys(void)
{
   int xasp, yasp, gmode, gerror, gdriver = DETECT;

   initgraph(&gdriver, &gmode, "\\tcpp\\bgi");
   if ((gerror = graphresult()) < 0) {
      printf("\nFailed graphics initialization: gerror=%d\n", gerror);
      exit(1);
   }
   getaspectratio(&xasp, &yasp);
   aspect = yasp / xasp;
   txtht = textheight("T");
   // Calculate the bottom of the big icon
   bigiconbottom = BIGICONTOP+iconht*(BIGBITSIZE+NORM_WIDTH);
}

int main(int argc, char *argv[])
{
   int x, y, c, iconexists, oldx, oldy;

   if (argc == 2 && *argv[1] == '3' && *(argv[1]+1) == '2') {
      iconwd = 32;  iconht = 32;
   }
   iconexists = readicon();         // If a user wants an icon file to
   initgraphsys();                  // be read, read it; otherwise,
                                    // show a big blank icon
   rectangle(0, 0, getmaxx(), getmaxy());

   drawpalette(BIGICONLEFT, getmaxy()-txtht*3-iconht,
      getmaxx()-BIGICONLEFT*2, iconht);
   activecolor = 15;
   displayactivecolor();
   mouse.init();                    // Initialize the mouse
   drawbigicon();                   // Draw the icon edit box
   mouse.hide();                    // When using the mouse, first turn
                                    // it off before writing to screen
   outtextxy(BIGICONLEFT, BIGICONTOP-txtht*4, "Icon Editor");
   outtextxy(BIGICONLEFT, BIGICONTOP-txtht*2,"Enlarged Icon");
   outtextxy(ICONLEFT, BIGICONTOP-txtht*2,"Actual Icon");
   outtextxy(BIGICONLEFT, bigiconbottom+txtht, "Current Color");
   outtextxy(BIGICONLEFT, getmaxy()-txtht*2,
      "Press ESC when finished ...");

   mouse.show();                    // Redisplays the mouse to the screen
   if (iconexists) showicon();      // Draws the icon read from the file
   while ((c=mouse.getinputpress(LEFT_BUTTON)) != ESC) {
      // Get input from mouse/keyboard. If input is Esc, quit program.
      if (c < 0) {                  // If input < 0, then a mouse button
         mouse.getcoords(x, y);     // has been pressed; get current
```

```
        if (!setbigbit(x, y)) {        // coordinates and set big bit color
          if (!setactivecolor(x, y)) // Change the active color
            floodcolor(x, y);          // Set big icon to the active color
        }
        else {  // Paint pixels while the left mouse button is down
          oldx = x;  oldy = y;
          while (!mouse.buttonreleased(LEFT_BUTTON)) {
            mouse.getcoords(x, y);
            if (x != oldx || y != oldy) {
              setbigbit(x, y);
              oldx = x;  oldy = y;
            }
          }
        }
      }
    }                                   // Turn mouse off and then get out
  mouse.hide();                         // of graphics mode to make user
  closegraph();                         // input easier for filename
  printf("Do you want to save this icon to a file? (y) ");
  if (getch() != 'n') saveicon(); // Save the icon to a file
  return 0;
}
```

9

Pop-Up Windows in Graphics

T his chapter presents another useful feature often found in interactive graphics environments—pop-up windows. Our goal in this chapter is to develop a pop-up window package that we can use in any of the BGI's standard graphics modes. This window package, which we'll call GPOPUP.CPP, will enable us to pop-up and remove windows in graphics mode with two simple commands. The window tools that we develop here will form the foundation for the user interfaces in the programs in Chapters 11 through 14.

THE BASIC APPROACH

With the help of the low-level BGI screen tools, pop-up windows are easy to support in Turbo C++. In this section, we'll show you the steps involved in both creating and removing a pop-up window. The source files for the GPOPUP window package, GPOPUP.H and GPOPUP.CPP, are listed at the end of this chapter.

What's most unique about the window system that we'll be developing is that it is fully object-oriented. (For a discussion of how to divide an application into objects, refer to *How to Select an Object* later in this chapter.) The main building block of the system is the class **gwindows**. This class contains its own window stack for managing how windows are displayed and removed, a set of variables for storing the data needed to process graphics windows, and a set of special-purpose member functions for creating, displaying, and removing pop-up windows.

INTRODUCING THE GWINDOWS CLASS

Since the heart of our window system is the **gwindows** class, let's introduce it now:

```
class gwindows {
public:
  gwindows(void);
  int gpopup(int left, int top, int right, int bottom, int bordertype,
    int bordercolor, int backfill, int backcolor, int drawcolor);
  int  gunpop(void);
  void unpopallwindows(void);
  virtual void paintwindow(int left, int top, int right, int bottom,
    int bt, int bfc, int bft, int bc);
  int printfxy(int xloc, int yloc, char *fmt, ... );
private:
  GRAPHICSWINDOW *wstack[NUMWINDOWS]; // The window stack
  int wptr;                           // Points to next free stack location
  int savewindow(int left, int top, int right, int bottom);
};
```

The first member function, **gwindows( )**, is the constructor used to initialize a window object. It is responsible for performing one important task—setting the stack pointer, **wptr**, so that it points to the bottom of the stack. This is the state of an empty stack. The **gpopup( )** member function is the real work-

HOW TO SELECT AN OBJECT

One important issue that comes up when programming with Turbo C++ involves the process of determining which program components should be represented as objects. Although this process might at first seem like black magic, there are some general rules we can follow to help us design our object-oriented applications. The bottom line is that you want to design your code so that you can take advantage of the three key properties of OOP: *encapsulation, inheritance,* and *polymorphism.* Here are some guidelines that you can follow to help you get started:

• Most traditional dynamic data structures, such as linked lists, trees, queues, stacks, buffers, and so on, typically are good candidates for objects. Why? The object structure allows you to encapsulate the operations needed to process the data structure with the data stored in the structure itself. The advantage here is that the data structure (object) can more easily be managed since all its features are stored under one roof.

• User interface components, such as windows, menus, buttons, dialog boxes, and so on, are also good candidates for objects. These types of components can really benefit from the property of inheritance. For example, you can

horse of the system. It stores information about the pop-up window on the stack and ensures that the screen underneath the window is saved. The counterpart to **gpopup( )** is **gunpop( )** which de-allocates memory for a window and removes it from the screen. If you want to remove all of the windows that are currently displayed, you can call the **unpopallwindows( )** member function. The **paintwindow( )** member function actually draws the window. The **printfxy( )** routine displays a text string in the current pop-up window.

The private section of the **gwindows** class consists of two variables and a member function for supporting a window stack. We'll be exploring these components in much more detail when we examine how the window stack operates.

CREATING POP-UP WINDOWS

The process of creating a pop-up window is outlined in Figure 9.1. As shown in the figure, the basic idea is to save the region of the screen that is to be overlayed by the pop-up window as well as any screen and drawing parameters that might be changed so that later this information can be used to restore the screen to its state before the pop-up window was created. We'll save this information on a stack so that we can build up layers of pop-up windows. Unfortunately, the stack approach does limit access to the windows. That is,

define a window object to work in text mode and then use that object to derive a window that works in graphics mode. The base window object could also be used to derive a menu object or an interactive button object, and so on.

- Components that are used in your programs that model real-world objects or events, such as gauges, graphs, charts, people, countries, planets, and so on, should be considered as objects.

- Hardware components, such as the mouse, keyboard, and the screen, also make useful objects. When working with these types of objects, you might want to back up a level and define a general input and output device object and then use it to define more specific I/O objects to support the mouse, keyboard, and screen.

- There are situations where the code that is usually placed in your main program can itself be represented as an object.

- You might find it helpful to represent algorithms as objects. For example, you could create a search object to encapsulate different search algorithms or a compression object to encapsulate compression algorithms. You could even represent a general parser as an object and derive different parsers from the general parser object to handle different languages.

Figure 9.1 Follow these steps when you are creating a pop-up window.

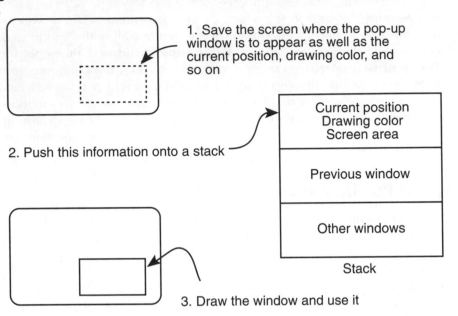

1. Save the screen where the pop-up window is to appear as well as the current position, drawing color, and so on

2. Push this information onto a stack

Current position
Drawing color
Screen area

Previous window

Other windows

Stack

3. Draw the window and use it

the windows will have to be removed in the reverse order that they were created. Therefore, we won't be able to arbitrarily bring a window that is covered by several other windows to the front of the screen. Actually, this feature can be added, but to keep the code simple, we have elected to leave it out.

Similarly, to remove a pop-up window from the screen, all we need to do is overwrite the pop-up window with the stored image of the screen by popping it from the stack and then restore the screen parameters that were saved on the stack. After this process is complete, the screen will appear as if the pop-up window never existed.

We'll save and restore the screen image using the **getimage()** and **putimage()** functions provided by the BGI. Since these functions work in all the graphics modes supported by the BGI, our pop-up windows will also. The screen parameters that we'll save include such attributes as the current drawing position and the drawing colors. We need to save these attributes because the pop-up windows may change them.

Working with a Stack

The main data structure that we'll be using to maintain the pop-up windows is a stack. In order to keep things simple, our stack is implemented as a single-

Figure 9.2 The window stack is an array of pointers to structures.

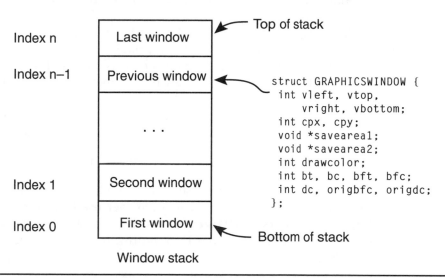

Window stack

dimensioned array, as shown in Figure 9.2, where each element in the array stores the information discussed earlier for a single pop-up window. Note that the stack pointer is essentially the index of the array and normally points to the next available location on the stack. It is incremented by 1 each time a new window is pushed on the stack. Therefore, if there are four items on the stack, the stack pointer will point to the fourth element (remember arrays in C++ start at 0).

Each element in the array is defined as a pointer to a structure of type **GRAPHICSWINDOW**. The structure is used to save the viewport settings, the current position, the drawing parameters, and the region of the screen that is underneath the window. This structure is defined in GPOPUP.CPP as:

```
struct GRAPHICSWINDOW {              // Structure to save graphics settings
  int vleft,vtop,vright,vbottom;     // Pixel boundaries of parent window
  int fleft,ftop,fright,fbottom;     // Frame pixel boundaries
  int cpx,cpy;                       // Cursor location in parent window
  void *savearea1;                   // Pointers used to save the area
  void *savearea2;                   // that is overwritten by the window
  int drawcolor;                     // Current drawing color
  int bt, bc, bft, bfc;              // Border type and color; background
                                     // type and color
  int dc;                            // Text and drawing color
  int origbfc, origdc;               // Restore colors when window is closed
};
```

The structure is used to save any of the things that might be changed when a window is popped up. These attributes are then used to restore the screen settings to their original states when the pop-up window is removed from the screen. Beginning at the top of the structure, **vleft**, **vtop**, **vright**, and **vbottom** save the current viewport boundaries at the time the pop-up window is created. Similarly, **cpx** and **cpy** save the coordinate of the current position. The **savearea1** and **savearea2** variables are pointers to the screen area to be saved. The memory storage for saving the screen is allocated just before the window is written. Finally, the various drawing parameters are saved in the last several fields of the structure.

Recall that our stack, which is an array of pointers to structures of type **GRAPHICSWINDOW**, is defined in the private section of the **gwindows** class as:

```
GRAPHICSWINDOW *wstack[NUMWINDOWS];  // The window stack
```

We'll wait to allocate space to these structures until we need them. In this manner, we won't be wasting memory that is never used. Also, note that we have declared 10 pointers (**NUMWINDOWS** is a constant set to 10). This means that we'll only be able to have 10 pop-up windows at a time. For most applications, this should be more than enough. If you develop an application program that needs more windows open at once, then you should increase this number appropriately.

The stack pointer, **wptr**, is an index into this array. It is also defined in the class **gwindows**. We'll show how this pointer is used in the following section. Figure 9.3 shows how the stack changes as a new window is added to the screen.

Figure 9.3 The stack changes when a window is added to the screen.

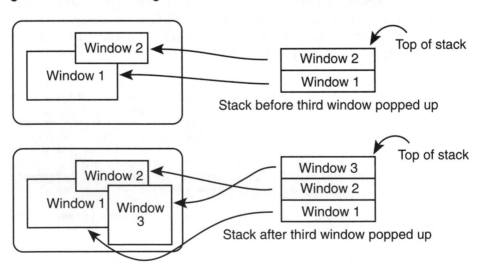

Stack before third window popped up

Stack after third window popped up

INITIALIZING THE WINDOWS PACKAGE

Like many of the other tools in this book, we need to call an initialization function before using any of the pop-up window routines. As we've seen, the window initialization function in GPOPUP.CPP is called **gwindows( )**. It is responsible for initializing the stack pointer to the first element of the stack array:

```
wptr = 0;
```

The Pop-Up Routine

Now let's take a look at the member function **gpopup( )**, which we'll use to pop-up a window. It is prototyped in the file GPOPUP.H as:

```
int gpopup(int left, int top, int right, int bottom, int bordertype,
  int bordercolor, int backfill, int backcolor, int drawcolor);
```

As you can see, **gpopup( )** takes a hefty nine arguments. The first four specify two opposing corners of the pop-up window and must be in full-screen coordinates, not the coordinates of the current window. The last five arguments, which define the graphics parameters to be used in the pop-up window, are shown in Table 9.1.

Lastly, **gpopup( )** returns a 1 if the window is successfully created; otherwise, it returns a 0 if it fails to create the window.

Now let's see how to pop up a window, using **gpopup( )**, that stretches from the top-left of the screen to its middle, and has a solid, white border and interior. Assuming we have declared a **gwindows** object called **winobj**, we can use the line:

```
winobj.gpopup(0, 0, getmaxx()/2, getmaxy()/2,
  SOLID_LINE, WHITE, SOLID_FILL, WHITE, BLACK);
```

Table 9.1 Window-style arguments used in gpopup()

Argument	Description
backcolor	Sets the color used in the fill pattern
backfill	Defines the fill pattern used to fill the pop-up window
bordertype	Defines the line style used to draw the border of the window
bordercolor	Sets the drawing color used to draw the border
drawcolor	Sets the drawing color used inside the window

A Closer Look at gpopup( )

Now that we have a functional description of the pop-up window routine, let's take a closer look at how it works. In this section, we'll be examining portions of the **gpopup( )** member function, but for a complete listing of the routine refer to the GPOPUP.CPP source code listed near the end of this chapter.

The first thing that needs to be done in **gpopup( )** is to test whether the stack is full. Since we are using an array to implement the stack, this is simply a matter of testing whether or not the stack pointer, **wptr**, has reached the end of the array **wstack**. If it has, then **gpopup( )** returns a 0 indicating that it cannot pop up the window. Remember that the stack pointer normally points to the next available location in the stack; therefore, the test for whether the stack is full is:

```
if (wptr >= NUMWINDOWS) return 0;
```

Once we know that there is enough room on the stack for another window, we must allocate space for one of the **GRAPHICSWINDOW** structures used to hold the current state of the screen. This is accomplished by the lines:

```
wstack[wptr] = new GRAPHICSWINDOW;
if (wstack[wptr] == 0) return 0;     // Not enough memory
```

Note that we must check the pointer that is returned from the call to **new** for a 0 value to make sure that the memory allocation has not failed. If there is a problem, then **gpopup( )** immediately returns with a value of 0 to its caller.

The next step in the process is to save the viewport and drawing parameters, because these may be changed when we pop up the window. This is done in the lines immediately following the allocation of the **GRAPHICSWINDOW** structure.

Next, we'll save the region of the screen that is to be overwritten by the pop-up window by calling the member function **savewindow( )**, which we'll discuss in the next section. However, first the viewport settings are set to the full screen since our pop-up window coordinates are given relative to the full screen and not the current viewport. This allows us to specify locations for pop-up windows anywhere on the screen, no matter what view settings are currently active. The **if** statement in **gpopup( )** makes the call to **savewindow( )**, which saves the region of the screen to be overwritten. If **savewindow( )** returns as 0, then the operation has failed and the pop-up window should not be created. If this is the case, the viewport settings must be restored (because they were changed before the call to **savewindow( )**) and the **GRAPHICSWINDOW** structure that was allocated must be freed. Once these tasks are done, the **gpopup( )** routine reports a failure by returning 0. The code that performs these operations is:

```
if (savewindow(left,top,right,bottom) == 0) {
  // Save screen failed. Restore viewport settings
  // and current position.
  setviewport(oldview.left, oldview.top, oldview.right,
    oldview.bottom, 1);
  moveto(oldx, oldy);
  delete(wstack[wptr]);
  return 0;                            // Return failure flag
}
```

Before continuing, let's take a closer look at the **savewindow( )** member function.

Saving the Screen

The **savewindow( )** member function is called to save the region of the screen that is to be overwritten by the pop-up window. We'll use **getimage( )** to capture a copy of this screen image. Actually, we'll divide the screen region to be copied into two equal sections and use *two* calls to **getimage( )**—one for each region. We do this because in some high-resolution modes, placing a single call to **getimage( )** may not allocate enough memory—only 64K—to save a screen image. Therefore, first we must allocate memory for the two screen image pointers, **savearea1** and **savearea2**. This is done with the calls to **malloc( )** using **imagesize( )** to determine the size of the memory.

```
halfpoint = (top + bottom) / 2;  // Divide the screen region
wstack[wptr]->savearea1 =        // to be saved into two parts
  malloc(imagesize(left,top,right,halfpoint));
wstack[wptr]->savearea2 =
  malloc(imagesize(left,halfpoint+1,right,bottom));
if (wstack[wptr]->savearea1 == NULL || wstack[wptr]->savearea2 == NULL)
  return 0;                      // Not enough memory to save screen
```

Once again, there is the possibility that the system might be out of memory and **malloc( )** will fail. If it does fail, either **savearea1** or **savearea2** may be NULL, which will cause **savewindow( )** to return immediately with a value of 0. Otherwise, the function continues and makes two calls to **getimage( )** to save the screen, and then returns a value of 1 indicating that **savewindow( )** was successful.

```
#ifdef MOUSE
  mouse.hide();
#endif
  // Save the screen image where the window is to appear
  getimage(left, top, right, halfpoint, wstack[wptr]->savearea1);
  getimage(left, halfpoint+1, right, bottom, wstack[wptr]->savearea2);
#ifdef MOUSE
  mouse.show();
```

```
#endif
  return 1;                              // Return a success flag
```

Keep in mind that when using the pop-up window function it will fail if you try to save a window that is too large. Your program may run out of memory. The maximum area that each pointer can handle is 64K in size. This allows us to store up to 128K of the screen. This may seem like a lot of memory, but the higher-resolution modes on the EGA and VGA can easily surpass this.

What are the **#ifdef** statements used for in this code? They selectively compile code compatible with the mouse toolkit that we developed in Chapter 7. If the **MOUSE** compiler switch is defined, GPOPUP will support the mouse. Primarily, the extra code hides and shows the mouse to prevent the mouse cursor from messing up the screen. Recall, this is the same technique we used in Chapter 3's GTEXT.CPP toolkit.

Creating the Pop-Up Window

Now let's return to our discussion of the **gpopup()** member function. We left it at the point where it had just made a call to **savewindow()** to save the screen image. Next, the drawing parameters that are used to draw the pop-up window are saved on the stack. Then, the pop-up window is drawn by a call to the **paintwindow()** member function. It in turn calls **bar3d()** to draw the window. The **bar3d()** function is used rather than **bar()** or **rectangle()** because it supports both line styles for its border as well as the full range of fill patterns. We use a depth of 0 for **bar3d()** so that it draws a rectangular region.

Note that **paintwindow()** is defined as a virtual member function. We did this because we wanted to make it easy for you to override it. Currently, this function supports two types of windows: those with simple borders and three-dimensional-looking windows. Figure 9.4 shows each of these window types. If you want to create your own style of windows, you can easily create your own version of **paintwindow()**.

Figure 9.4 The GPOPUP toolkit supports these two types of windows.

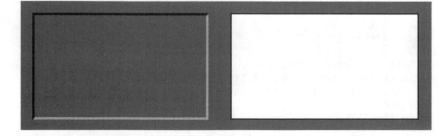

After a window is drawn, the current state of the drawing parameters that were previously temporarily saved are copied into the current **wstack** structure. In addition, the fill style, line style, and drawing color are restored to their values before the window was drawn. Then the stack pointer is incremented so that it points to the next location on the stack and **gpopup( )** returns 1 as a success flag.

Removing a Pop-Up Window

Removing a pop-up window from the screen is handled by the member function **gunpop( )**. It is this function that is responsible for restoring the original screen image that is overwritten by the pop-up window and for resetting the various screen parameters.

The **gunpop( )** member function does not take any arguments and normally returns a 1 when invoked. However, if the stack is empty, meaning that there aren't any windows left to remove, **gunpop( )** returns a value of 0 without doing anything else. This test is performed by checking whether the stack pointer, **wptr**, is less than or equal to 0. Actually, it really only needs to test if it is equal to 0, but clearly a negative stack pointer value here would indicate a problem.

The next step in the removal of the pop-up window is to decrement the stack pointer. Since it normally points to the next free location on the stack, decrementing the stack pointer forces it to the top-most window displayed. The pointer to the structure for this window is then copied into **w**, a temporary pointer that we'll use to refer to this structure.

Now we have access to the window structure that contains the state of the screen before the window was created. First, we'll restore the screen image by two calls to **putimage( )** using **COPY_PUT**. (Remember, we are saving the screen in *two* buffers, **savearea1** and **savearea2**):

```
putimage(0, 0, w->savearea1, COPY_PUT);
putimage(0, (currview.bottom-currview.top)/2+1, w->savearea2, COPY_PUT);
```

Note that the top-left coordinate of the current window is used as the location to place the **savearea1** image. The other screen image, **savearea2**, is placed halfway down the current window since it saved the lower portion of the screen where the pop-up window was placed.

The next several lines of **gunpop( )** reset the viewport, current position, and various drawing parameters to there state before the pop-up window was created.

Finally, the memory for the screen images and the window structure that were allocated in **savewindow( )** and **gpopup( )** are freed, and **gunpop( )** returns a 1 indicating that the removal of the pop-up window member function was successful.

Removing All Windows

Sometimes, it is handy to remove all of the pop-up windows at once. For this purpose, **gwindows** includes the **unpopallwindows()**. It contains the single line

```
while (gunpop()) ;
```

which will loop until **gunpop()** has removed all of the pop-up windows from the screen, at which time it will return a 0.

DISPLAYING TEXT IN A POP-UP WINDOW

To simplify the process of displaying text in a pop-up window, the gwindows class includes the **printfxy()** member function. It's similar to the **gprintfxy()** function we developed for GTEXT.CPP in Chapter 3. The difference, of course, is that **printfxy()** uses the drawing parameters and current position defined for the pop-up window. The following statement, for instance, will display the string "Hello" in a pop-up window:

```
win.printfxy(10, 10, "Hello");
```

The text is displayed in the drawing color defined for the program. Currently, only the default font style is supported. As with all figures drawn in a pop-up window, the text is clipped to the boundaries of the interior of the pop-up window.

• GPOPUP.H

```
// GPOPUP.H: Header file for GPOPUP.CPP.
#ifndef GPOPUPH                    // Prevents recompilation
#define GPOPUPH
const int NUMWINDOWS = 10;         // Allow for 10 pop-up windows
const int THREED = 10;             // Selects three-dimensional windows

struct GRAPHICSWINDOW {            // Structure to save graphics settings
  int vleft,vtop,vright,vbottom;   // Pixel boundaries of parent window
  int fleft,ftop,fright,fbottom;   // Frame pixel boundaries
  int cpx,cpy;                     // Cursor location in parent window
  void *savearea1;                 // Pointers used to save the area
  void *savearea2;                 // that is overwritten by the window
  int drawcolor;                   // Current drawing color
  int bt, bc, bft, bfc;            // Border type and color; background
                                   // type and color
  int dc;                          // Text and drawing color
  int origbfc, origdc;             // Restore colors when window is closed
  };
```

```
class gwindows {
public:
  gwindows(void);
  int gpopup(int left, int top, int right, int bottom, int bordertype,
    int bordercolor, int backfill, int backcolor, int drawcolor);
  int  gunpop(void);
  void unpopallwindows(void);
  virtual void paintwindow(int left, int top, int right, int bottom,
    int bt, int bfc, int bft, int bc);
  int printfxy(int xloc, int yloc, char *fmt, ... );
private:
  GRAPHICSWINDOW *wstack[NUMWINDOWS]; // The window stack
  int wptr;                           // Points to next free stack location
  int savewindow(int left, int top, int right, int bottom);
  };
#endif
```

● GPOPUP.CPP

```
// GPOPUP.CPP: Pop-up graphics window package. This is a set of
// utilities that provides pop-up windows in graphics mode. The
// routines use Turbo C++'s BGI tools to simplify the code. Most of
// the graphics settings are saved before a new window is opened,
// and they are restored when the window is closed. The window data
// is maintained in a stack that is part of the class gwindows.
// The stack is implemented as an array in order to keep things simple.
// Note that these functions allow you to pop up window regions larger
// than 64K by breaking them up into smaller regions. This is useful
// for saving large pop-up windows in high-resolution graphics modes.
// To use this package, you should declare a window object of type
// gwindows. Using this object, you can call gpopup() and gunpop()
// to pop up and unpop windows.
#include <graphics.h>
#include <alloc.h>
#include "gpopup.h"        // Header file for windows package
#include "gtext.h"

#ifdef MOUSE
#include "kbdmouse.h"
extern kbdmouseobj mouse;
#endif

// The constructor initializes the stack pointer
gwindows::gwindows(void)
{
  wptr = 0;
}


// Pushes the graphics window onto the window stack. This is an internal
// routine to save the area where the window is supposed to appear. This
// routine will return 1 if successful and 0 if not. The latter case
// may occur if there isn't enough memory to save the screen area or
```

```
// the stack is full. Note that the saved region is divided into two
// sections so that you can save large-screen regions in high-
// resolution modes.
int gwindows::savewindow(int left, int top, int right, int bottom)
{
  int halfpoint;

  halfpoint = (top + bottom) / 2;    // Divide the screen region
  wstack[wptr]->savearea1 =          // to be saved into two parts
    malloc(imagesize(left,top,right,halfpoint));
  wstack[wptr]->savearea2 =
    malloc(imagesize(left,halfpoint+1,right,bottom));
  if (wstack[wptr]->savearea1 == NULL || wstack[wptr]->savearea2 == NULL)
    return 0;                        // Not enough memory to save screen
#ifdef MOUSE
  mouse.hide();
#endif
  // Save the screen image where the window is to appear
  getimage(left, top, right, halfpoint, wstack[wptr]->savearea1);
  getimage(left, halfpoint+1, right, bottom, wstack[wptr]->savearea2);
#ifdef MOUSE
  mouse.show();
#endif
  return 1;                          // Return a success flag
}


// Call this function to pop up a window in graphics mode. It
// returns 1 if successful and 0 if not. It will fail if there
// is not enough memory.
int gwindows::gpopup(int left, int top, int right, int bottom,
  int bordertype, int bordercolor, int backfill, int fillcolor,
  int drawcolor)
{
  struct viewporttype oldview;
  int oldx, oldy, savecolor;
  struct linesettingstype saveline;
  struct fillsettingstype savefill;

  if (wptr >= NUMWINDOWS) return 0;  // Stack is full
  wstack[wptr] = new GRAPHICSWINDOW;
  if (wstack[wptr] == 0) return 0;   // Not enough memory
  // Save the view settings and current position so that we can
  // temporarily switch the viewport to the full-screen coordinates
  getviewsettings(&oldview);
  oldx = getx();
  oldy = gety();
  setviewport(0, 0, getmaxx(), getmaxy(), 1);
  // Save current drawing parameters before drawing window.
  // This does not support user-defined line styles or user-defined
  // fill patterns.
  getlinesettings(&saveline);
  savecolor = getcolor();
  getfillsettings(&savefill);
```

```
    if (savewindow(left,top,right,bottom) == 0) {
      // Save screen failed. Restore viewport settings
      // and current position.
      setviewport(oldview.left, oldview.top, oldview.right,
        oldview.bottom, 1);
      moveto(oldx, oldy);
      delete(wstack[wptr]);
      return 0;                               // Return failure flag
    }
    wstack[wptr]->bc = bordercolor;
    wstack[wptr]->bt = bordertype;            // Save window style
    wstack[wptr]->bft = backfill;
    wstack[wptr]->bfc = fillcolor;
    wstack[wptr]->dc = drawcolor;
    paintwindow(left, top, right, bottom, bordertype,
      fillcolor, backfill, bordercolor);
    // Set the viewport to the window, minus the window's border
    if (bordertype == THREED)
      setviewport(left+2, top+2, right-2, bottom-2, 1);
    else
      setviewport(left+1, top+1, right-1, bottom-1, 1);

    // Save the current state of all settings on the stack
    wstack[wptr]->fleft = left;
    wstack[wptr]->ftop = top;
    wstack[wptr]->fright = right;
    wstack[wptr]->fbottom = bottom;
    wstack[wptr]->vleft = oldview.left;
    wstack[wptr]->vtop = oldview.top;
    wstack[wptr]->vright = oldview.right;
    wstack[wptr]->vbottom = oldview.bottom;
    wstack[wptr]->cpx = oldx;
    wstack[wptr]->cpy = oldy;
    wstack[wptr]->drawcolor = savecolor;
    wstack[wptr]->origbfc = settextbkcolor(fillcolor);
    wstack[wptr]->origdc = settextcolor(drawcolor);
    // Restore drawing parameters
    setlinestyle(saveline.linestyle, saveline.upattern, saveline.thickness);
    setcolor(savecolor);
    setfillstyle(savefill.pattern, savefill.color);

    wptr++;                                   // Increment the stack pointer
    return 1;                                 // Return success flag
}

// Draw the window using the styles specified. This member function
// is made virtual so that you can override it to define your own
// window styles.
void gwindows::paintwindow(int left, int top, int right, int bottom,
  int bt, int bfc, int bft, int bc)
{
  int i;
```

```
#ifdef MOUSE
   mouse.hide();
#endif
   if (bt == THREED) {
     // Bottom and left edge are dark gray. Top and left sides
     // are drawn white. Use solid lines.
     setlinestyle(SOLID_LINE, 0, NORM_WIDTH);
     for (i=0; i<2; i++) {
       setcolor(DARKGRAY);
       line(right-i, top+i, right-i, bottom-i);
       line(left+i, bottom-i, right-i, bottom-i);
       // Left and top are white
       setcolor(WHITE);
       line(left+i, top+i, right-i, top+i);
       line(left+i, top+i, left+i, bottom-i);
     }
     setcolor(bfc);
     setlinestyle(SOLID_LINE, 0, NORM_WIDTH);
     // Fill in the window
     setfillstyle(bft, bfc);
     bar3d(left+2, top+2, right-2, bottom-2, 0, 0);
   }
   else {
     // Set the graphics parameters for the pop-up window to be displayed.
     // Then make the window. Use bar3d() so that there will be a border.
     setlinestyle(bt, 0, NORM_WIDTH);
     setcolor(bc);
     setfillstyle(bft, bfc);
     bar3d(left, top, right, bottom, 0, 0);
   }
#ifdef MOUSE
   mouse.show();
#endif
}

// Remove the current graphics window from the screen
int gwindows::gunpop(void)
{
   struct viewporttype currview;
   struct GRAPHICSWINDOW *w;

   if (wptr <= 0) return 0;          // If at bottom of stack, quit
   wptr--;
   w = wstack[wptr];                 // Get the top-most window
   // Restore the screen image
   setviewport(w->fleft, w->ftop, w->fright, w->fbottom, 1);
   getviewsettings(&currview);       // Get the window size
#ifdef MOUSE
   mouse.hide();
#endif
   // Set the viewport to the outer part of the window's frame
   putimage(0, 0, w->savearea1, COPY_PUT);
   putimage(0,(currview.bottom-currview.top)/2+1, w->savearea2,COPY_PUT);
```

```
#ifdef MOUSE
  mouse.show();
#endif
  // Restore the view settings to those values before the window
  // was created
  setviewport(w->vleft, w->vtop, w->vright, w->vbottom, 1);
  moveto(w->cpx, w->cpy);
  setcolor(w->drawcolor);

  settextbkcolor(w->origbfc);
  settextcolor(w->origdc);

  free(w->savearea1);               // Free stack structure and screen
  free(w->savearea2);
  delete(wstack[wptr]);
  return 1;                         // Return a success flag
}

// Remove all popped up windows that currently exist. This is a handy
// routine to clean up the screen in certain situations.
void gwindows::unpopallwindows(void)
{
  while (gunpop()) ;
}

int gwindows::printfxy(int xloc, int yloc, char *fmt, ... )
{
  int oldbc = settextbkcolor(wstack[wptr-1]->bfc);
  int olddc = settextcolor(wstack[wptr-1]->dc);

  int cnt = gprintfxy(xloc, yloc, fmt);

  settextbkcolor(oldbc);
  settextcolor(olddc);

  return cnt;                       // Return the conversion count
}
```

USING THE WINDOWS PACKAGE

Now that we have discussed all of the preliminaries, let's explore how you can use the windows package. It's actually a very simple process. First, you should include the GPOPUP.H header file in your application program. You'll also need to declare a window object of type **gwindows** in your application. Recall that its constructor initializes the window stack for you so the window object will be ready to use. Whenever you want to pop up a window, call **gpopup()** as discussed earlier in the chapter. Remember that the pop-up window coordinates are specified relative to the whole screen and not the current viewport. This gives you the greatest control over the placement of the pop-up window. To remove the window, make a call to **gunpop()**. You must use one call to **gunpop()** for every window that you create.

Figure 9.5 Each time you pop up a window, the location of the current position is reset.

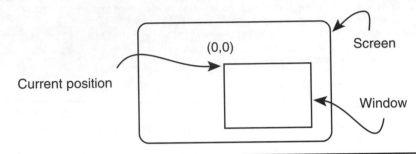

Also, keep in mind that the pop-up windows are maintained on a stack. Therefore, when you call **gunpop( )** the last window created will be the first one removed.

Once a pop-up window is created, the viewport settings will be changed to reflect the new window. As Figure 9.5 illustrates, the top-left corner of the new pop-up window will correspond to location (0,0), the current position will be set to this point, and clipping will be set on.

Test Program

Before we end this chapter, we'll present a test program that will put our graphics window package through its paces. It will also demonstrate how to put the pop-up window package to work. The test program, POPTEST.CPP, creates three pop-up windows, shown in Figure 9.6, and then removes them from the screen. After each window is displayed or removed, you must press a key in order to proceed with the program.

As written, POPTEST uses the default mode provided by your video adapter. If you want to try one of the other graphics modes, change the values assigned to **gdriver** and **gmode** in **main( )**. And finally, note how the program accesses the coordinates in each of the windows. For instance, in the first pop-up window, a circle is drawn at its center. In order to determine the center of the window, the code calls **getviewsettings( )** to retrieve the current viewport settings and calculates the center of the window using these values. This technique works because the window toolkit sets the viewport to the inside portion of the window.

```
getviewsettings(&view);
// Draw a circle in the window
circle((view.right-view.left)/2, (view.bottom-view.top)/2,
  (view.left+view.right)/4);
```

Figure 9.6 POPTEST.CPP produces these pop-up windows.

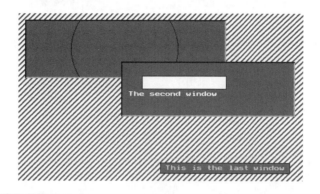

Table 9.2 Files Used to Compile and Link POPTEST.CPP

Main File	Header File	Chapter
GPOPUP.CPP	GPOPUP.H	9
GTEXT.CPP	GTEXT.H	3
POPTEST.CPP	None	9

To compile and link POPTEST.CPP you'll need to create a project file called POPTEST.PRJ that contains the three files POPTEST.CPP, GTEXT.CPP, and GPOPUP.CPP. Table 9.2 lists each of the files you'll need and where you can locate them.

• POPTEST.CPP

```
// POPTEST.CPP: Tests the graphics pop-up window routines. This
// program displays three overlapping pop-up windows on a patterned
// background. The windows are drawn one at a time and then removed one
// at a time. Press any key to step through the various phases of this
// demonstration. This routine demonstrates how the screen is saved and
// the use of the screen coordinates in a pop-up window. Use the large
// memory model when compiling this program because it may require
// a large amount of memory to save the windows--particularly if you
// use a high-resolution mode.
#include <graphics.h>
#include <conio.h>
#include "gpopup.h"                  // Header file for the graphics
                                     // pop-up window package

gwindows w;                          // Declare a window object
```

```
main()
{
  int gmode, gdriver = DETECT;          // Use a mode with several colors
  struct viewporttype view;
  char message[] = " This is the last window ";
  int halfwidth, height;

  initgraph(&gdriver, &gmode, "\\tcpp\\bgi");
  setfillstyle(SLASH_FILL, BLUE);        // Draw a backdrop that
  setlinestyle(DASHED_LINE, 0, WHITE);   // covers the whole screen
  bar(0, 0, getmaxx(), getmaxy());

  // Pop up a three-dimensional-style window in the top-left portion
  // of the screen
  w.gpopup(10, 10, getmaxx()/2, 100, THREED, getmaxcolor(),
    SOLID_FILL, LIGHTGRAY, BLACK);

  // The view settings are now equal to the pop-up window boundaries
  getviewsettings(&view);
  // Draw a circle in the window
  circle((view.right-view.left)/2, (view.bottom-view.top)/2,
    (view.left+view.right)/4);
  getch();                               // Wait until a key is pressed

  // Draw a second pop-up window with a three-dimensional border
  w.gpopup(getmaxx()/4, 75, getmaxx()*2/3, getmaxy()/3,
    THREED, getmaxcolor(), SOLID_FILL, LIGHTGRAY, BLACK);
  setfillstyle(WIDE_DOT_FILL, BLACK);
  bar3d(30, 20, getmaxx()/4, 40, 0, 0); // Draw a box in the window
  setcolor(getmaxcolor());
  w.printfxy(10, 44, "The second window");
  getch();                               // Wait for a key to be pressed

  // The last pop-up window displays a message at the center of the
  // screen. This type of pop-up window is good for displaying error
  // messages in graphics mode.
  halfwidth = textwidth(message)/ 2;   // Base the size of the window
  height = textheight(message);        // on the string it'll display
  w.gpopup(getmaxx()/2-halfwidth, getmaxy()/2-height,
    getmaxx()/2+halfwidth, getmaxy()/2+height, SOLID_LINE, WHITE,
    SOLID_FILL, LIGHTGRAY, RED);

  setcolor(0);
  settextjustify(CENTER_TEXT, CENTER_TEXT);    // Center message and
  getviewsettings(&view);                      // display it
  w.printfxy((view.right-view.left)/2, (view.bottom-view.top)/2, message);
  getch();                               // Wait for a key to be pressed
  w.gunpop();                            // Remove the last window
  getch();                               // Wait until a key is pressed
  w.gunpop();                            // Remove the middle window
  getch();                               // Wait until a key is pressed
  w.gunpop();                            // Remove the first window
  closegraph();                          // Exit graphics mode
  return 0;
}
```

10

Interactive Drawing Tools

I t's simple enough to draw figures using the BGI by placing drawing functions in a program. However, in a paint or CAD application we need to *interactively* draw figures using the mouse or keyboard. As you've seen, the BGI does not include interactive drawing routines, so we must create our own. Therefore, in this chapter we'll take the time to construct a set of classes that provide rubber-banding lines, a spray painting effect, polygon drawing, text entry, and more.

These classes will become the primary drawing tools we'll use in the paint and CAD programs in Chapters 11 and 12. However, you'll find that these interactive drawing tools are general enough to be useful in other interactive graphics applications that you create on your own.

We'll accomplish this flexibility by building the tools using the resources of object-oriented programming. In particular, each drawing tool will be implemented as a separate class. As the details of the various classes unfold, you'll see how OOP can be a powerful means of sharing code and a great way of leaving the door open for extending a toolkit—which is exactly what we'll be doing in the CAD program in Chapter 12 and the three-dimensional viewing packages in Chapters 13 and 14.

AN INTERACTIVE GRAPHICS PACKAGE

The interactive drawing package we'll develop includes 13 drawing tools, where each tool is implemented as a separate class, as indicated in Table 10.1. All of the tools share a common ancestor—the **drawingtool** class. The class hierarchy is shown in Figure 10.1.

Table 10.1 Interactive Drawing Classes Included in DRAWTOOL.CPP and DRAW.CPP

Class	Description
arctool	Draws arcs interactively
circletool	Draws circles interactively
clearwindowtool	Clears the drawing window
drawingtool	Base class for all interactive drawing classes
ellipsetool	Draws ellipses interactively
erasertool	Erases a portion of the screen
fillpolygontool	Allows the user to draw filled polygons
fillrectangletool	Draws filled rectangles interactively
linetool	Interactive line drawing class
penciltool	Supports freehand drawing
polygontool	Interactive polygon drawing class
spraycantool	Provides a spray painting effect
rectangletool	Draws rectangles interactively
texttool	Supports text entry

At first, the number of classes may seem a bit overwhelming. However, as you explore the code, you'll see that most of these classes are rather small and build upon others in simple, manageable steps.

The **drawingtool** class outlines the basic flow of the user interaction and provides a common programming interface for the drawing routines. Since all of the tools are built from the same *base* class, we'll be able to fully take advantage of the OOP technique called *polymorphism* in our application programs. We'll see this technique in action in the paint and CAD programs in Chapters 11 and 12. (Chapter 11 explains polymorphism further.)

The definition for the base **drawingtool** class is defined in the files DRAWTOOL.H and DRAWTOOL.CPP. Both of these files are listed at the end of this chapter. The DRAWTOOL files, however, only define the format of the drawing tool. We've derived a series of specific drawing tools from them. These are the drawing tools we'll actually use in our graphics programs. You can find them in the DRAW.H and DRAW.CPP source files, also listed at the end of this chapter.

Drawing Conventions

Each of the interactive drawing classes adheres to several conventions. First, the classes assume that the mouse class we developed in Chapter 7 is being

Figure 10.1 We will create this class hierarchy of drawing tools.

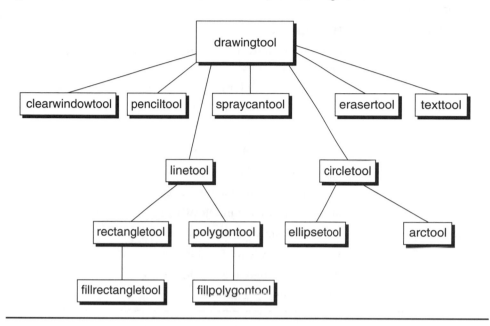

used. Since our mouse member functions support both the mouse and the keyboard, the drawing member functions will work with either input device. You'll find, however, that the mouse provides the best performance.

Second, there are a series of global variables that are used by the drawing tools. These variables, listed in Table 10.2, must be assigned appropriate values in your applications before you call any of the interactive drawing functions in DRAWTOOL.CPP and DRAW.CPP. These variables are defined in DRAWTOOL.CPP and control various color and drawing settings.

In particular, the drawing functions restrict their output to a predefined window. Therefore, whenever one of the drawing functions is called, the current viewport is set to the drawing window and clipping is enabled. When the drawing action ends, the viewport is restored to the full screen. The boundaries of the drawing window, therefore, must be initialized in the application program by setting the four global variables **wl**, **wt**, **wr**, and **wb** to the left, top, right, and bottom sides of the drawing window desired.

In addition, there are five global variables that must be set to initialize the drawing parameters that are used by the drawing member functions. These variables are listed at the top of Table 10.2. They should be set to the appropriate macro constants defined in GRAPHICS.H. For example, **globalfillstyle** can take on values of **SOLID_FILL**, **EMPTY_FILL**, or any of the other acceptable fill pattern values defined in GRAPHICS.H.

Table 10.2 Global Variables Defined in an Application Program Using DRAWTOOL and DRAW

Variable	Description
globaldrawcolor	Defines the drawing color to be used in any of the drawing member functions
globalfillcolor	Defines the fill color to use
globalfillstyle	Defines the fill style to use
globallinestyle	Defines the line style to use
globaltextstyle	Defines the text style to use
maxx	Right-most coordinate of screen
maxy	Bottom-most coordinate of screen
mouse	Mouse object used in DRAW.CPP
wb	Bottom of drawing window
wl	Left side of drawing window
wr	Right side of drawing window
wt	Top of drawing window

Lastly, the drawing package DRAW.CPP defines a **kbdmouseobj** object called **mouse** for your application. Recall, that the **kbdmouseobj** class is defined in the keyboard and mouse packages developed in Chapter 7 and uses the mouse if one is present or the keyboard if one isn't.

THE DRAWINGTOOL CLASS

Now we're ready to walk through the hierarchy of interactive drawing classes. We'll begin with the base class, **drawingtool**, supplied in DRAWTOOL.CPP. The **drawingtool** class, shown next, provides the basic shell that prescribes the programming interface we'll use with the drawing tools. Here's its definition:

```
class drawingtool {
public:
   int x, y, oldx, oldy;                // Current and last mouse position
   int left, top, right, bottom;        // Bounds of the figure
   int drawcolor;                       // Color to be used in the figure
   virtual void draw(void);             // High-level drawing function
   virtual void performdraw(void);      // Defines user interaction
   virtual void startdrawing(void);     // Sets up for drawing
   virtual void updatedrawing(void);    // Interactively draws figure
   virtual void finishdrawing(void);    // Finalizes drawing
   virtual void hide(void) {  }         // Removes figure from screen
```

```
virtual void show(void) {  }          // Displays or updates figure
virtual void setproperties(int code, int val); // Sets object values
// The following functions will be defined in the CAD program
virtual void display(void) {  }
virtual void getbounds(int &l, int &t, int &r, int &b) {  }
virtual void translate(double transx, double transy) {  }
virtual void rotate(double angle) {  }
virtual drawingtool *dup(void) { return this; }
virtual int read(FILE *fp) { return 0; } // Loads the object from a file
virtual int save(FILE *fp) { return 0; } // Saves the object to a file
};
```

The **drawingtool** class starts with the four instance variables **x**, **y**, **oldx**, and **oldy**, which keep track of the current and previous location of the mouse. These variables will be updated when events such as button presses occur.

The top-most member function, **draw()**, is the high-level function that we'll call when we want to interactively draw a figure. We'll assume that this is the member function called when a specific drawing function has been selected.

If you look at the code, however, you'll notice that **draw()** does very little. It merely sets the viewport coordinates and enables clipping to the size of the drawing window, calls **performdraw()**, and then restores the viewport coordinates to their previous settings. You might now be wondering if **performdraw()** does the actual drawing. Not quite. But it does give us a better clue as to how the user interaction is managed within the **drawingtool** class. Let's take a look.

The **performdraw()** function is built around an infinite while loop that waits for the user to press the left mouse button:

```
while (!mouse.buttonpressed(LEFT_BUTTON)) ;
```

Once the left button is pressed, the mouse coordinates are retrieved by a call to **mouse.getcoords()**. These coordinates, which are saved in the instance variables **x** and **y**, are checked against the drawing viewport to see if the user has clicked outside of the drawing window. If so, **performdraw()** exits via the return statement:

```
mouse.getcoords(x,y);
if (x < wl || y < wt || y > wb || y > wr) return;
startdrawing();
updatedrawing();
finishdrawing();
```

Otherwise, the member function continues by calling the trio of functions **startdrawing()**, **updatedrawing()**, and **finishdrawing()**. These latter three member functions are actually the ones where the drawing takes place.

Why is the drawing process split between three functions? Because we'll be deriving drawing tools from each other, we need our base class to be as flexible as possible so that we can override only those portions of the code that need to be modified. In this way, we'll be able to share the greatest amount of code and only have to modify small blocks of code in our derived classes.

Let's examine each of these three new functions. The first, **startdrawing()**, is responsible for setting up any variables for the drawing process. For example, when you draw a line, **startdrawing()** will move the current position to the location where the mouse was pressed.

In a similar fashion, **finishdrawing()**, performs any cleanup actions that need to be done after the figure has been drawn. For instance, it might fill the interior of a polygon after its exterior has been sketched out. The base class, however, leaves this function empty. Derived classes can override it as necessary.

The **updatedrawing()** function, if you haven't already guessed, is the work horse. It's where the real interaction takes place. Here's its code:

```
void drawingtool::updatedrawing(void)
{
  while (!mouse.buttonreleased(LEFT_BUTTON)) {  // Button must be pressed
    mouse.getcoords(x,y);                       // Get current location of mouse
    if (x != oldx || y != oldy) {               // Only update figure if the mouse
      hide();                                    // has moved. Remove part or all
      show();                                    // of the figure. Draw the figure.
      oldx = x;  oldy = y;                       // Update saved position of mouse
    }
  }
}
```

This function is also built around a **while** loop, but this time the loop continues as long as the left mouse button is pressed. (Recall that the drawing process began in **performdraw()** once the mouse button was initially pressed.) In other words, drawing a figure continues as long as the mouse button is pressed. However, to avoid unnecessary screen writing, **updatedrawing()** only proceeds with a drawing if the mouse's position has changed. This prevents the screen from flickering when nothing really needs to be updated. The mouse's position is regulated by the **if** statement that compares the mouse's most recent position with its last recorded location:

```
if (x != oldx || y != oldy) {    // Only update figure if the mouse
  hide();                         // has moved. Remove part or all
  show();                         // of the figure. Draw the figure.
  oldx = x;  oldy = y;            // Update saved position of mouse
}
```

The pieces are beginning to fall together.

But where is the drawing done? For this we need to turn to the **show()** and **hide()** member functions, which are called in **updatedrawing()**. These functions are used to draw and erase a figure from the drawing window.

The **show()** member function is probably self-explanatory, but what about **hide()**? Remember that in interactive drawing, the user can change the size of the figure. As a result, the **hide()** function is used to erase the old figure so that **show()** can come along and repaint the figure with its new dimensions. This is where the **if** statement, shown earlier, comes in. If the location of the mouse hasn't changed, then the figure's size hasn't changed, so we bypass **hide()** and **show()**. The member variables **oldx** and **oldy** keep track of the last location of the mouse, and hence the last position and size of the figure. The initial values of **oldx** and **oldy** are set in **startdrawing()**, and then are updated each time through the **while** loop in **updatedrawing()**.

The **setproperties()** member function is a special-purpose routine that enables the caller to set various fields of the object. For instance, you can use **setproperties()** to set the drawing color of an object. The first parameter of **setproperties()** is a special code that identifies the field to modify. The second parameter is the value to assign to this field. This scheme enables us to avoid having to make sure an object actually contains a specific field. The object simply ignores the call if it doesn't own the specified field. In contrast, DRAWTOOL.H defines the value **DRAWCOLORPROP**, which indicates that the drawing color is to be changed. Since all our drawing tools will have a drawing color, it's processed in **drawingtool**'s **setproperties()** function. Other drawing tools will override the **setproperties()** function if they need to set additional properties.

Drawing with a Pencil

Now that we've pulled apart the components of the **drawingtool** class, let's see how the class is used to derive a specific drawing tool. We'll begin with the **penciltool** class, which is used to draw freehand figures like those shown in Figure 10.2. The **penciltool** class and the other derived drawing tools are located in the source files DRAW.H and DRAW.CPP.

With **penciltool**, you can draw a continuous curve as long as the left mouse button is pressed. Whenever the mouse button is released, the drawing

Figure 10.2 You can draw freehand curves with the pencil tool.

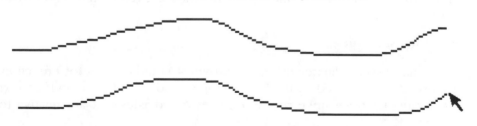

stops. To resume drawing, you simply hold down the left button again. To exit the function, you click the left mouse button outside the drawing window. Presumably, this will be to select another drawing function. We'll see how this technique works in Chapter 11 when we develop our paint program.

Deriving a tool, like **penciltool** from **drawingtool**, is a matter of overriding those member functions where we need to replace the inherited class' functions or supplement them. We'll start at the highest level and work our way down, adding as we go. The **penciltool** class definition, therefore, indicates which functions we have overridden to implement the pencil tool. Here's its definition:

```
class penciltool : public drawingtool {// A curve drawing class
public:
  virtual void draw(void);
  virtual void startdrawing(void);
  virtual void show(void);
};
```

The **draw()** function needs to be overridden first so that we can set the drawing color used in the pencil drawing operation. The drawing color is reset to the value in **globaldrawcolor** because it may have been changed by another function in the application program. We'll override **draw()** in the other classes for a similar reason. Once the drawing parameter is reset, the inherited **draw()** function from **drawingtool** is called to proceed with the drawing:

```
void penciltool::draw(void)
{
  setcolor(globaldrawcolor);     // Switch to the global drawing color
  drawingtool::draw();           // Draw with the pencil
}
```

Next, **startdrawing()** is overridden to initiate the drawing action. (Recall that this member function is invoked when the left mouse button has been pressed.) The freehand curves are created by drawing a line from the mouse's current location to its previous position. Therefore, as the mouse moves, the line grows. To start this process, then, **startdrawing()** calls **moveto()** to set the current position to the location of the mouse given by the class variables **x** and **y**

```
moveto(x-wl, y-wt);
```

Note that the coordinates passed to **moveto()** (and the **lineto()** function that follows it) are adjusted by the left and top boundaries of the drawing viewport. This must be done since **moveto()** uses coordinates that are relative to the current viewport (the drawing window) and the mouse coordinates, **x** and **y**, are always given in full-screen coordinates.

Finally, the **show()** function is overridden to complete the line drawing by making a call to **lineto()**:

```
void penciltool::show(void)
{
  mouse.hide();                         // Hide mouse before drawing
  lineto(x-wl, y-wt);                   // Draw a line from last position
  mouse.show();                         // Restore the mouse cursor
}
```

As this code illustrates, calls to **mouse.hide()** and **mouse.show()** surround **lineto()** in order to prevent the mouse cursor from interfering with the screen.

Erasing

Now that we've learned how to draw figures, let's see how we can erase them. For this, we'll introduce the class **erasertool**, which is designed to set a rectangular screen region below the mouse cursor to the background color. By holding down the left mouse button and moving the mouse around, you can erase any area of the drawing window that you'd like.

The **erasertool** class is similar to **penciltool**, except that it draws small bars filled with the background color to the screen rather than a series of lines. In order to generate these small erasing blocks, the fill style is set to **SOLID_FILL** and the fill and drawing colors are set to the background color. This is accomplished by overriding **draw()** as we did with **penciltool** and inserting the following statements before the inherited **draw()** function is called:

```
setcolor(getbkcolor());               // Use the background color
setfillstyle(SOLID_FILL, getbkcolor()); // to erase the screen
```

The function draws these small solid-filled bars wherever the mouse cursor is located while the mouse button is pressed. The pixel dimension of the eraser bar is specified by **ERASERSIZE**, which is a constant defined just before the **erasertool** class in DRAW.H to a size of 5:

```
const int ERASERSIZE = 5;      // Half the size of the eraser
```

You might try making the eraser size a variable so that the user can interactively change the size of the eraser.

The erasing action then occurs in **show()** by using the BGI's **bar()** function:

```
bar(x-wl, y-wt, x-wl+ERASERSIZE, y-wt+ERASERSIZE);  // Erase region
```

244 ▲ Chapter 10

Spray Painting Effect

The function **spraycantool** provides a simple spray painting effect by randomly setting pixels within a rectangular region to the current drawing color.

While the left mouse button is pressed, the spray painting action will occur, as shown in Figure 10.3. The longer you hold mouse in one position, the more that screen location will be filled in. To temporarily stop the spray painting, you release the left mouse button. To exit the spray painting function, you move the mouse outside the drawing viewport and click the left button.

Since the spray painting effect continually paints while the mouse button is pressed—even when the mouse is not being moved—we need to override **updatedrawing()**. Recall that the implementation of **drawingtool**'s **updatedrawing()** only calls **hide()** and **show()** if the mouse has been moved.

The spray painting effect is produced by two **for** loops in the overridden function **show()**:

```
for (i=0; i<8; i++)
  putpixel(x-random(SPRAYSIZE)+5-wl,
    y-random(SPRAYSIZE)+5-wt, globaldrawcolor);
for (i=0; i<8; i++)
  putpixel(x-random(SPRAYSIZE-2)+3-wl,
    y-random(SPRAYSIZE-2)+3-wt, globaldrawcolor);
```

Each of the **for** loops is responsible for plotting eight pixels in a rectangular region around the mouse cursor. The first **for** loop plots pixels away from the mouse cursor while the second **for** loop plots pixels closer. Note that the particular pixel that is painted by each iteration of the **for** loops is randomly selected using the Turbo C++ function **random()**. This distributes the pixels evenly. The size of the spray region is partly determined by the constant **SPRAYSIZE** declared in **spraycantool**. However, the other integer values in the two **for** loops affect the distribution and location of the spray painting as well. You may want to experiment with other spray patterns.

Figure 10.3 You can create a sprayed effect by using the spray can tool.

Drawing Lines

The **linetool** class is used to draw line segments. It lets you draw a single line by pointing to where the line is to begin, pressing and holding down the left mouse button, and then dragging the mouse to the desired end point. When the button is released, the line is frozen. However, while the button is pressed, **linetool** continues to draw the line from the initial location of the mouse, where the button was pressed, to the mouse's current position. Therefore, as the mouse is moved around the screen, the line will shrink and stretch as needed. This type of line, shown in Figure 10.4, is called a *rubber-banding* line because it appears to be flexible like a rubber-band. To draw more lines, you just repeat this simple process.

As you might expect, **linetool** is similar to the previously discussed functions. The first thing **linetool** does is override **draw()** in order to set the drawing color and line style:

```
setlinestyle(globallinestyle,0,NORM_WIDTH);
setcolor(globaldrawcolor);
```

Note that the line width is restricted to **NORM_WIDTH**. This is done to simplify the code. You may want to modify DRAW.CPP so that the line width is a variable like **globallinestyle** and **globaldrawcolor**.

An important aspect of **linctool** is the rubber-banding line effect. The technique uses the exclusive-ORing feature provided by the BGI **setwritemode()** function (discussed in Chapter 6) to allow us to draw and move a line around the screen without permanently affecting what it overwrites. Once the exclusive-OR mode is set, lines can be erased from the screen by writing over them with another line. The exclusive-OR feature is turned on in **startdrawing()** after the left button is pressed by the line:

```
setwritemode(XOR_PUT);
```

After this point, all lines are drawn by exclusive-ORing them to the screen. Sometimes you will see the effects of the exclusive-ORing as the line changes color when it crosses over other figures on the screen.

Figure 10.4 You can create lines by using the linetool object.

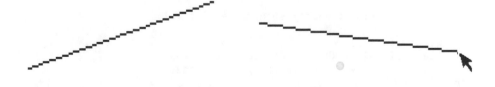

The line is restored to its normal mode in **finishdrawing()** by calling **setwritemode()** with the argument **COPY_PUT**.

When you press the left mouse button while inside the drawing window, the exclusive-ORing mode is set as described earlier and the first line is drawn, although at this time it is merely a point. While the mouse button is pressed, the code remains in the **while** loop in **updatedrawing()**.

Within this loop, you can see that the line drawing is performed by the calls to **hide()** and **show()**, which are almost identical. Notice that **hide()** calls **line()** using the fixed coordinate (**x1,y1**) and the last mouse location (**oldx,oldy**)

```
line(x1-wl, y1-wt, oldx-wl, oldy-wt);
```

whereas **show()** uses the same fixed point but the mouse's new location given by (**x,y**):

```
line(x1-wl,y1-wt,x-wl,y-wt);
```

Since the exclusive-ORing mode is on, the first time **line()** is called—by calling **hide()**—the old line is erased, and the second call to **line()**—by the member function **show()**—draws the line at the new position. Notice that the first coordinate pair in each call to **line()** corresponds to the position on the screen where the user first pressed the mouse button. This point does not change. The only end point of the line that does change is the one that is dragged around the screen with the mouse. These two lines create the rubber-banding effect.

When the left mouse button is released, the **finishdrawing()** member function is called. It has been overridden to redraw the line using the following statements:

```
setwritemode(COPY_PUT);
show();
```

The line is redrawn with **setwritemode()** taken out of the exclusive-OR mode, so that the line is drawn in its proper color. Remember that a figure exclusive-ORed with an object on the screen may change its color.

The **linetool** class also overrides **drawingtool**'s **setproperties()** function so that it can set the object's line style field. Here's the modified function:

```
void linetool::setproperties(int code, int val)
{
  switch (code) {
    case LINESTYLEPROP: linestyle = val; break;
    default: drawingtool::setproperties(code, val);
}
```

This function sets **linestyle** to the contents of **val** if **code** equals **LINESTYLEPROP**. The constant is defined in DRAW.H. Notice that if something other than **LINESTYLEPROP** is passed in, the function passes along its parameters to the inherited **setproperties()** function so that it can process it.

Drawing Polygons

There are two classes in our toolkit that allow you to draw polygons—**polygontool** and **fillpolygontool**. The first, **polygontool**, allows you to draw a series of lines connected at their end points. The second, **fillpolygontool**, is capable of drawing closed polygons using any of the predefined fill patterns.

In affect, **polygontool** is nothing more than a variation of **linetool**. As a result, **polygontool** is derived from **linetool**. Similarly, **fillpolygontool** operates just like **polygontool**, except it draws filled polygons; consequently, it is derived from **polygontool**. Now you can see where our class hierarchy is really paying off since we are able to share the code in the inherited member functions.

Both polygon classes operate in a similar manner, although the way they work is slightly different from the classes previously discussed. As before, they begin their drawing after the first click of the mouse's left button. Next, they draw a rubber-banding line as the mouse is moved around the screen, which defines one side of the polygon, until the left button is pressed again. The current line then becomes frozen and a new rubber-banding line is drawn starting from the current mouse location. This procedure, shown in Figure 10.5, can be repeated to create additional sides to the polygon. When you want to close off the polygon, however, simply press the right mouse button and the

Figure 10.5 You can draw a polygon with polygontool.

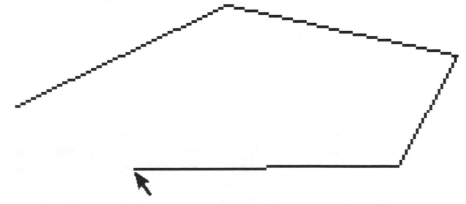

closing side of the polygon is drawn. If **fillpolygontool** is used, the interior of the polygon is filled.

Since the user interaction is different, we have overridden **updatedrawing()** so that we can replace the **while** loop we were using earlier with a **do** loop that waits for the closing signal—a right button press. To refresh your memory, the **while** loop was used to draw a figure as long as the left mouse button was pressed. In **polygontool**, the **do** loop is used to test for a right button press. In addition, inside the **do** loop, an **if** statement has been added that tests for the left button. If any left button presses occur, the mouse coordinates are saved, the current rubber-banding line is frozen, and a new rubber-banding line is started at the previous line's endpoint. If, on the other hand, the right button is pressed, the polygon is closed off by tying it back to the first coordinate in **finishdrawing()**.

Again, the exclusive-ORing technique is used to create the rubber-banding effect by a call to **setwritemode()** with **XOR_PUT**. So that the correct colors will be displayed, the complete polygon must then be redrawn with the write mode set to **COPY_PUT** after the user has closed off a polygon. For this reason, the polygon classes keep track of the screen coordinates that are used to draw the polygon. These coordinates are saved in the **poly** array included in the **polygontool** class. For simplicity, the size of the array is declared to be the size of **MAXPOLYSIZE**, a constant in **polygontool**, which is set to 40.

Drawing Rectangles

We'll now develop two companion classes to interactively draw a rectangle and a filled rectangle—**rectangletool** and **fillrectangletool**. These tools are built around the BGI's **rectangle()** and **bar3d()** commands, respectively.

Once again we'll use the BGI's exclusive-OR feature to create a rubber-banding effect. But how does this work with the filled rectangle version of the tool? Since **bar3d()** is not affected by the **setwritemode()** option, we'll use a dashed empty rectangle to size the rectangle and then fill it when the size is set by calling **bar3d()**. (Remember from Chapter 2 that **bar3d()** can draw a filled square if its depth is set to 0.) This suggests that **fillrectangletool** should be derived from **rectangletool**, and that's exactly what we'll do. In addition, we'll derive **rectangletool** from **linetool** so that we can take advantage of its user interaction and the code that sets the line styles appropriately. Because of this, the only functions we need to override in the **rectangletool** class are **show()** and **hide()**. They both call **rectangle()** to draw a rectangle, however, **hide()** uses the previous location of the mouse specified by (**oldx**,**oldy**) and **show()** uses the new mouse location (**x**,**y**). Remember we're using the exclusive-OR feature here to toggle between drawing the line and erasing it.

To draw filled rectangles we only need to add a little more code. First, **draw()** and **startdrawing()** are overridden in order to set the fill settings and the line style to dashed lines. (Remember, we're using a dashed rectangle until the rectangle is the desired size.) Second, we'll override **finishdrawing()** so that once the rectangle's size has been set—when the left mouse button is released—we'll paint over the outline rectangle with the filled rectangle. This is done using the call to **bar3d()**:

```
bar3d(x1-wl,y1-wt,x-wl,y-wt,0,0);   // Draw the filled rectangle
```

As before, drawing does not begin until the left button is pressed. In addition, the only way to exit the drawing member function is to click the mouse outside of the drawing window.

Drawing Circles

The next class in line to derive is the **circletool** class, which allows us to interactively draw a circle as shown in Figure 10.6. Drawing a circle with **circletool** begins by specifying the center point of the circle. This is done by moving the mouse to the desired location and pressing the left mouse button. Then, while holding down the left mouse button, you can drag the mouse to the left and right to change the size of the circle.

You may be wondering how we create a rubber-banding circle. After all, the **circle()** function is not affected by **setwritemode()**. There are a couple approaches we could take. For instance, we could write our own **circle()** function so that it does support exclusive-ORing. For an example of this, refer to *Creating Rubber-Banding Circles* later in this chapter. We won't take this approach, however.

Instead, we'll use **getimage()** and **putimage()** to help us create the rubber-banding effect needed to draw circles. This is done by saving the screen image where the circle is to be drawn, so that later we can remove it from the screen by copying the saved image back to the screen with **putimage()**.

Figure 10.6 You can draw circles by using the circletool.

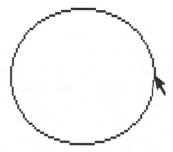

In effect, we are doing nothing more than popping-up a window with a circle figure inside it. Let's begin by taking a closer look at **circletool**.

The first thing you'll notice about **circletool** is that it is much longer and probably more intimidating than any of the prior classes. However, taken in pieces, the class is actually similar to those discussed earlier.

There are two basic reasons why the code in **circletool** is more complex than what we've seen before. First, as we just described, we'll be simulating the rubber-banding effect by using **getimage()** and **putimage()**. But because of this, we'll need to handle the clipping of these images ourselves. Secondly, using **getimage()** and **putimage()** is a challenge in higher-resolution modes. Because many of these modes require more than 64K to save the whole drawing window, we can't use a single call to **getimage()**. Instead, we'll split the drawing window into two regions and save each independently. The screen regions are saved into the two blocks of memory pointed to be **covered1** and **covered2**, which are new instance variables declared in **circletool**.

The **draw()** member function is overridden so that we can allocate and de-allocate the memory required to save the screen. Once the memory is allocated, the inherited **draw()** member function is called to perform the drawing operation. Then, after the drawing is finished, the memory claimed by **covered1** and **covered2** is freed.

If there isn't enough memory to save the screen image, the function **mallocerror()** is called. Currently, **mallocerror()** aborts the program. You might want to modify this error handler to make the program more user-friendly.

The drawing process begins in the **startdrawing()** member function. Note that it calls **getimage()** twice to save the screen located at the cursor. Although it is effectively saving only a point, this will begin our rubber-banding process.

Drawing a circle is regulated by the **updatedrawing()** member function. As the mouse is moved, the radius of the circle is continually calculated by taking the absolute value of the difference between the center x coordinate of the circle and the mouse's current position:

```
absradiusx = abs(centerx - x);
```

The **absradiusx** result is later used as the radius argument in the call to the BGI function **circle()** in the member function **show()**.

The rest of the complexity of **updatedrawing()** is due to clipping the bounds of the screen region used by **getimage()** and **putimage()**. Keep in mind that these two functions do not clip their images relative to the current viewport. We must perform the clipping ourselves. The clipping process is illustrated in Figure 10.7.

Figure 10.7 We must perform the clipping process for rubber-banding circles.

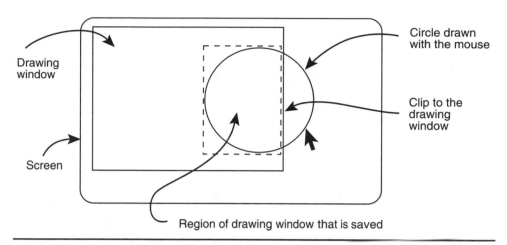

The clipping is accomplished with four **if-else** statements in **updatedrawing()** that check to see if the circle extends beyond the edge of the drawing window. Since the aspect ratio of the screen may be different in the x and y directions, this member function may wind up saving too much of the drawing window, particularly in the y direction. However, this is not much of a problem.

One other point to note about **circletool** is that it does not draw the circle if the radius is 0. This is needed because the BGI function **circle()** will draw a circle of radius 0 with a 1-pixel radius. Since this is not what we want, we avoid drawing such circles in **show()** by checking whether the **absradiusx** variable has a value of 0. We'll have to do the same type of tests for the **ellipse()** and **arc()** functions too.

Drawing Ellipses

Drawing an ellipse is accomplished by the **ellipsetool** class, which is very similar to **circletool**. The primary difference between the two is that **ellipsetool** allows you to change both the x and y radius of the ellipse. As with **circletool**, the x radius is changed by dragging the mouse left and right, but now the y radius can also be changed by dragging the mouse up and down.

Since **ellipsetool** is so similar to the **circletool** class, we've derived **ellipsetool** from it. This way we'll inherit the code from **circletool** that allocates and de-allocates the memory required to save the screen. However, we'll still need to override **updatedrawing()** so that we can keep track of the changes in the y coordinate of the ellipse. Similarly, **show()** is overridden so that we can draw the ellipse rather than a circle.

Drawing Arcs

The **arctool** class allows us to interactively draw a series of arcs. Unfortunately, the BGI **arc()** function is not well suited for an interactive arc drawing function. The main difficulty is that it is cumbersome to come up with a way to interactively specify all the parameters needed by the **arc()** function, such as

CREATING RUBBER-BANDING CIRCLES

One way to create a rubber-banding circle is to write your own circle routine. We could do this from scratch, but another approach is to draw a circle using a series of very small lines with the BGI's **line()** function. We have written a **circle()** function that does just this.

The arguments to the custom **circle()** function are the same as the BGI's, except that it accepts one additional argument, which specifies the number of line segments to be used to draw the circle. The larger this number, the smoother the circle, although there's really not much reason to make the number larger than about 100.

The **circle()** function works by rotating a line segment so that its end points fall on the perimeter of a circle. As long as the line segments are very short in relation to the size of the circle, you'll get a good approximation of a circle by drawing the rotated segments. The length of the line segment, and the smoothness of the circle, depends on the number of divisions you request in the variable **numsides**.

The **for** loop calculates the rotation for each line segment specified. The calculations in the **for** loop should look familiar. They're the same calculations introduced in Chapter 5 for rotating two-dimensional figures.

The **circle()** function also adjusts for the screen's aspect ratio in the call to **line()** by multiplying the y coordinate by the **aspectratio** value calculated in **main()**. This is very important to do, particularly in some modes. Otherwise, the circle drawn will look more like an ellipse.

If you're wondering, the same approach can be applied to drawing ellipses. All you need to do is multiply the radius in the x and y directions by some scale factor.

```
// CIRCLE.CPP: Draws a circle using a series of line segments.
#include <graphics.h>
```

the center point, the radius, and the sweep angle. We'll sidestep this problem and create an extremely simple member function to draw arcs.

Our class, **arctool**, always begins drawing arcs at the 3 o'clock position, but it allows you to change the sweep angle and the radius of the arc. The components used to draw an arc are shown in Figure 10.8. The center point of the arc is selected when the left mouse button is first pressed. Then by dragging the mouse right and left, with the left button pressed, the radius of the arc is increased and decreased, respectively. In addition, by moving the mouse down, the angle the arc sweeps is increased. Similarly, when the mouse

```c
#include <conio.h>
#include <math.h>

double aspectratio;

// Draws a circle as a series of line segments. The center of the
// circle is specified by (x,y). The variable numsides determines
// how many line segments the circle will be divided into.
void circle(int x, int y, int radius, int numsides)
{
  int i;
  double x0, y0, xi, yi;
  const double tinc = 3.141596 * 2 / numsides;
  const double ct = cos(tinc), st = sin(tinc);
  x0 = radius;  y0 = 0.0;
  for (i=0; i<numsides; i++) {
    xi = x0 * ct - y0 * st;
    yi = x0 * st + y0 * ct;
    line(x0+x, y0*aspectratio+y, xi+x, yi*aspectratio+y);
    x0 = xi;  y0 = yi;
  }
}

main()
{
  int gdriver=DETECT, gmode, xasp, yasp;

  initgraph(&gdriver, &gmode, "\\tcpp\\bgi");
  getaspectratio(&xasp,&yasp);
  aspectratio = (double)xasp / (double)yasp;
  // Draw a circle using the function below
  circle(100, 100, 50, 40);
  getch();
  closegraph();
  return 0;
}
```

Figure 10.8 These are the components of an arc.

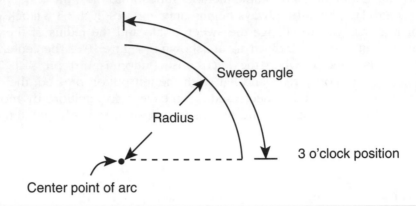

is moved up while the left button is pressed, the angle the arc sweeps is decreased. The procedure for drawing an arc is illustrated in Figure 10.9.

As with **circletool** and **ellipsetool**, we'll track the mouse movement by calculating the absolute value of the difference between the mouse's current position and the center point of the arc. In addition, **getimage( )** and **putimage( )** are used to produce the exclusive-OR rubber-banding effect that we used in some of the other drawing routines. The **arctool** class saves a rectangular region large enough to contain the full 360-degree arc. These features are available to **arctool** by deriving **arctool** from **circletool**.

Figure 10.9 You can draw an arc with the arctool class.

Miscellaneous Drawing Support

We've covered all of the drawing classes included in DRAW.CPP, but we're not finished yet. The toolkit includes two additional classes: the **texttool** and **clearwindowtool** classes.

The first class, **texttool**, allows you to enter text in the drawing window. To use **texttool**, you click the left mouse button where you want to begin entering text. Then a vertical bar will appear as the cursor. As you type in text, it will be displayed left-to-right, starting from the vertical bar. When you are finished entering a block of text, you must click the left mouse button again.

The vertical cursor is made by drawing an exclusive-ORed line the height of the text. The cursor is drawn, for instance, for the first time in **startdrawing()**, by the statements:

```
setwritemode(XOR_PUT);
mouse.hide();
line(x-wl,y-wt,x-wl,y+textheight("S")-wt);
mouse.show();
setwritemode(COPY_PUT);
```

For the most part, entering the text is handled by the **updatedrawing()** function. As characters are typed in, the text cursor position is updated and the character is added to **string**, a new variable added to **drawingtool**, so that the text can later be used by an application program.

The **texttool** class also allows you to enter a series of carriage returns by pressing the Enter key. The test for this feature can be found in the **while** loop in **updatedrawing()**. It tests for a carriage return value, CR, and then simulates the carriage return by the statements:

```
if (c == CR) {
  y += textheight("S") + 2;
  x = leftx;
  moveto(x-wl,y-wt);
  if (len < MAXSTRING-1) string[len++] = '\n';
}
```

If a carriage return is detected, the text cursor is moved down by the height of the text. The current position is then set to the original x location, **leftx**, and the new calculated height, given by **y**.

The **texttool** class does not support vertical text or control over the text justification. The Backspace key, however, is supported. The problem with deleting characters, though, is deciding what colors to use to erase the text. Currently, **texttool** erases characters using black. This may leave a mess on the screen, but if you have access to the objects in the drawing, you can refresh the screen to remove the holes left by the Delete key. We'll take this approach in Chapter 12's CAD program.

The **clearwindowtool** class is also a supplemental drawing tool. It is used to erase the whole drawing window by setting the viewport to the drawing window and then calling **clearviewport()**. Although we didn't need to encapsulate this operation in an object, we did so that it would have a consistent program interface with the other drawing functions. This will be important in our application programs.

• DRAWTOOL.H

```
// DRAWTOOL.H: Defines a generic class that we'll derive
// specific interactive drawing tools from.

#ifndef DRAWTOOLH
#define DRAWTOOLH
#include <stdio.h>
#include "kbdmouse.h"

const DRAWCOLORPROP=0;     // Every object has a drawing color property

// The base class that defines the basic format of the drawing tools
class drawingtool {
public:
  int x, y, oldx, oldy;               // Current and last mouse position
  int left, top, right, bottom;       // Bounds of the figure
  int drawcolor;                      // Color to be used in the figure
  virtual void draw(void);            // High-level drawing function
  virtual void performdraw(void);     // Defines user interaction
  virtual void startdrawing(void);    // Sets up for drawing
  virtual void updatedrawing(void);   // Interactively draws figure
  virtual void finishdrawing(void);   // Finalizes drawing
  virtual void hide(void) {  }        // Removes figure from screen
  virtual void show(void) {  }        // Displays or updates figure
  virtual void setproperties(int code, int val); // Sets object values
  // The following functions will be defined in the CAD program
  virtual void display(void) {  }
  virtual void getbounds(int &l, int &t, int &r, int &b) {  }
  virtual void translate(double transx, double transy) {  }
  virtual void rotate(double angle) {  }
  virtual drawingtool *dup(void) { return this; }
  virtual int read(FILE *fp) { return 0; } // Loads the object from a file
  virtual int save(FILE *fp) { return 0; } // Saves the object to a file
};

void mallocerror(void);  // Function called if memory allocation fails

// The fill parameters, drawing colors, and so forth are all kept as global
// variables. From time to time, the current drawing, fill, and line
// styles may be changed. So before using any drawing function, make sure
// the various drawing parameters are reset to these global values.
extern int globalfillstyle;  // Holds the fill style that should be used
extern int globalfillcolor;  // Holds the fill color that should be used
```

```
extern int globaldrawcolor;    // Holds the drawing color that should be used
extern int globallinestyle;    // Holds the line style that should be used
extern int globaltextstyle;    // Specifies the text font that should be used
extern int wl, wt, wr, wb;     // Boundaries of the drawing window
extern int maxx, maxy;         // Boundaries of the full screen
extern kbdmouseobj mouse;      // A mouse object is used for input


#endif
```

• DRAWTOOL.CPP

```
// DRAWTOOL.CPP: The base class definition of a drawing tool.
#include <graphics.h>
#include <stdlib.h>
#include "kbdmouse.h" // Emulated mouse utilities
#include "drawtool.h"


// The fill parameters, drawing colors, and so forth are all kept as global
// variables. From time to time, the current drawing, fill, and line
// styles may be changed. So before calling any drawing function, make
// sure the various drawing parameters are reset to these global values.
int globalfillstyle;       // Holds the fill style that should be used
int globalfillcolor;       // Holds the fill color that should be used
int globaldrawcolor;       // Holds the drawing color that should be used
int globallinestyle;       // Holds the line style that should be used
int globaltextstyle;       // Specifies the text font that should be used
int wl, wt, wr, wb;        // Window bounds where drawing is to be done
int maxx, maxy;            // Maximum dimensions of the screen
kbdmouseobj mouse;         // A keyboard mouse is used for interaction

// You can call this routine to set various properties
// of the object
void drawingtool::setproperties(int code, int val)
{
  switch (code) {  // The base object only allows you to change
    case DRAWCOLORPROP: drawcolor = val; break;  // the drawing color
  }
}


// The high-level method that is called to draw a figure. It sets
// the viewport to the drawing window, called performdraw(), to
// perform the drawing action, and then restores the viewport to
// the full screen.
void drawingtool::draw(void)
{
  struct viewporttype vu;

  getviewsettings(&vu);              // Save the viewport coordinates
  setviewport(wl, wt, wr, wb, 1);    // Set viewport to drawing window
  drawcolor = globaldrawcolor;       // Save the drawing color
  performdraw();                     // Draw the figure
  // Restore viewport coordinates to those saved earlier
```

```
    setviewport(vu.left, vu.top, vu.right, vu.bottom, vu.clip);
}


// Drawing begins when the left mouse button is pressed. Then the
// coordinates of the mouse are checked to see if the mouse was pressed
// outside of the drawing window. If so, the drawing routine ends.
// Otherwise, the drawing begins by calling startdrawing().
void drawingtool::performdraw(void)
{
  while (1) {
    while (!mouse.buttonpressed(LEFT_BUTTON)) ; // Wait for button press
    mouse.getcoords(x,y);          // Get location where button was pressed
    if (x < wl || y < wt || y > wb || y > wr) return;  // Exit drawing
    startdrawing();                // Setup for the drawing
    updatedrawing();               // Do the drawing
    finishdrawing();               // Clean up drawing as needed
  }
}


// Initializes the drawing style and various variables used by the
// drawing function. By default, it saves the last location of the mouse.
void drawingtool::startdrawing(void)
{
  oldx = x;  oldy = y;
}


// Completes the figure being drawn. Most of the derived classes will
// draw while the left mouse button is pressed. Note: The figure is not
// updated if the mouse has not been moved.
void drawingtool::updatedrawing(void)
{
  while (!mouse.buttonreleased(LEFT_BUTTON)) {  // Button must be pressed
    mouse.getcoords(x,y);                // Get current location of mouse
    if (x != oldx || y != oldy) {        // Only update figure if the mouse
      hide();                            // has moved. Remove part or all
      show();                            // of the figure. Draw the figure.
      oldx = x;  oldy = y;               // Update saved position of mouse
    }
  }
}


// Performs any final operations that must be made to finish the drawing.
// For instance, figures that are drawn with exclusive-OR lines must
// be redrawn with the exclusive-OR feature disabled so that the figure's
// color will come out correctly. By default, nothing is done here.
void drawingtool::finishdrawing(void) {  }
```

• DRAW.H

```
// DRAW.H: Header file for the interactive drawing utilities
// used in the paint and CAD programs.
#ifndef DRAWH
#define DRAWH
```

```
#include <stdio.h>
#include "drawtool.h"
#include "kbdmouse.h"

const LINESTYLEPROP=1;     // Properties that you can change
const FILLSTYLEPROP=2;     // for some of the graphics objects
const FILLCOLORPROP=3;     // defined in DRAW.CPP

class penciltool : public drawingtool {     // A curve drawing class
public:
  virtual void draw(void);
  virtual void startdrawing(void);
  virtual void show(void);
};

const int ERASERSIZE = 5;                    // Half the size of the eraser
class erasertool : public drawingtool {     // An eraser class
public:
  virtual void draw(void);
  virtual void startdrawing(void);
  virtual void show(void);
};

const int SPRAYSIZE = 15;                    // Size of the spray area
class spraycantool : public drawingtool {    // A spraycan class
public:
  virtual void draw(void);
  virtual void updatedrawing(void);
  virtual void show(void);
};

class linetool : public drawingtool {        // Draws single lines
public:
  int x1, y1, x2, y2;                        // End points of line drawn
  int linestyle;                             // Line style used for lines
  virtual void draw(void);
  virtual void startdrawing(void);
  virtual void finishdrawing(void);
  virtual void hide(void);
  virtual void show(void);
  virtual void setproperties(int code, int val); // Sets object values
};

class rectangletool : public linetool {// Draws a rectangle
public:
  virtual void hide(void);
  virtual void show(void);
};

class fillrectangletool : public rectangletool { // A filled rectangle
public:
  int fillstyle;                             // Fill pattern used in rectangle
  int fillcolor;                             // Color used in fill pattern
  virtual void draw(void);
```

```
     virtual void startdrawing(void);
     virtual void finishdrawing(void);
     virtual void setproperties(int code, int val); // Sets object values
};

const int MAXPOLYSIZE = 40;              // Can have this many edges
class polygontool : public linetool {    // Draws a polygon
public:
     int poly[MAXPOLYSIZE], numpts;      // Not used here, but will be later
     int fillstyle;                      // Fill pattern used
     int fillcolor;                      // Color used in fill pattern
     virtual void startdrawing(void);
     virtual void updatedrawing(void);
     virtual void finishdrawing(void);
     virtual void setproperties(int code, int val); // Sets object values
};

class fillpolygontool : public polygontool { // Draws filled polygon
public:
     virtual void startdrawing(void);
     virtual void finishdrawing(void);
};

class circletool : public drawingtool {  // Draws a circle
public:
     int halfx, oldright;                // These three variables are used to
     void *covered1, *covered2;          // save an image where circle is drawn
     int cleft, cright, cbottom, ctop;   // Clipped figure
      int centerx, centery, absradiusx, oldleft, oldtop; // Figure's dimensions
     virtual void draw(void);
     virtual void startdrawing(void);
     virtual void updatedrawing(void);
     virtual void hide(void);
     virtual void show(void);
};

class ellipsetool : public circletool {  // Draws an ellipse
public:
     int absradiusy;                     // The y radius of ellipse. The
     virtual void updatedrawing(void);   // x radius is inherited from
     virtual void show(void);            // the circletool class.
};

class arctool : public circletool {      // Draws an arc
public:
     int radius, angle;                  // Radius and sweep angle of arc
     virtual void updatedrawing(void);
     virtual void show(void);
};

const int MAXSTRING = 255;               // A string can be this long
class texttool : public drawingtool {    // Text entry class
public:
```

```
    int leftx, lefty;                    // Top left location of text
    char string[MAXSTRING];              // String entered
    int len;                             // Length of string
    int textstyle;                       // Font used
    void draw(void);
    void startdrawing(void);
    void updatedrawing(void);
    void finishdrawing(void);
};

class clearwindowtool : public drawingtool {
    virtual void draw(void);             // Erases drawing window
};

#endif

void mallocerror(void);  // Function called if memory allocation fails
```

• DRAW.CPP

```
// DRAW.CPP: Interactive drawing utilities used in the Paint and
// CAD programs.
#include <stdio.h>
#include <graphics.h>
#include <alloc.h>
#include <stdlib.h>
#include <string.h>
#include <time.h>
#include <conio.h>
#include "gtext.h"
#include "kbdmouse.h" // Emulated mouse utilities
#include "draw.h"      // Function prototypes for draw.cpp

// Sets the drawing color to the global drawing color
void penciltool::draw(void)
{
    setcolor(globaldrawcolor);           // Switch to the global drawing color
    drawingtool::draw();                 // Draw with the pencil
}

// Initializes drawing with a pencil by moving the current position to
// the current location of the mouse. Adjusts for the fact that the
// mouse coordinates are given with respect to the whole screen and
// the pencil tool's coordinates are relative to the drawing window.
void penciltool::startdrawing(void)
{
    drawingtool::startdrawing();         // Call drawingtool's startdrawing()
    moveto(x-wl, y-wt);                  // Set the current position
}

// Draws a line from the last position of the mouse to its current position
void penciltool::show(void)
{
```

```
  mouse.hide();                        // Hide mouse before drawing
  lineto(x-wl, y-wt);                  // Draw a line from last position
  mouse.show();                        // Restore the mouse cursor
}

// Uses a solid, background color to erase a region of the screen
void erasertool::draw(void)
{
  setcolor(getbkcolor());                   // Use the background color
  setfillstyle(SOLID_FILL, getbkcolor());   // to erase the screen
  drawingtool::draw();                      // Draw with the eraser
}

// Erases the spot pointed to when the left mouse button is pressed
void erasertool::startdrawing(void)
{
  drawingtool::startdrawing();
  show();
}

// Erases a rectangular region of the screen where the mouse is located
void erasertool::show(void)
{
  mouse.hide();                               // Remove the mouse from screen
  bar(x-wl, y-wt, x-wl+ERASERSIZE, y-wt+ERASERSIZE);  // Erase region
  mouse.show();                               // Restore the mouse cursor
}

// Initializes the random function to be used by the spraycantool
// before performing the spray painting
void spraycantool::draw(void)
{
  randomize();                         // Initializes random function
  drawingtool::draw();                 // Use spraycan
}

// Overrides drawingtool's updatedrawing() function so that the spraycan
// paints as long as the left mouse button is pressed--even if the
// mouse has not been moved
void spraycantool::updatedrawing(void)
{
  while (!mouse.buttonreleased(LEFT_BUTTON)) {
    mouse.getcoords(x, y);             // Get current mouse location
    show();                            // Spray paint
  }
}

// Sprays a small region of the screen. Two separate for loops are used
// to randomly paint a series of pixels using the global drawing color.
void spraycantool::show(void)
{
  mouse.hide();     // Remove the mouse before painting on the screen
  for (int i=0; i<8; i++)          // Randomly draw 8 pixels
```

```
      putpixel(x-random(SPRAYSIZE)+5-wl,
        y-random(SPRAYSIZE)+5-wt, globaldrawcolor);
    for (i=0; i<8; i++)            // Randomly draw another 8 pixels
      putpixel(x-random(SPRAYSIZE-2)+3-wl,
        y-random(SPRAYSIZE-2)+3-wt, globaldrawcolor);
    mouse.show();    // Restore the mouse cursor to the screen
}

// This routine enables you to change the line's style as
// well as the inherited drawing color
void linetool::setproperties(int code, int val)
{
  switch (code) {
    case LINESTYLEPROP: linestyle = val; break;
    default: drawingtool::setproperties(code, val);
  }
}

// Sets the line styles and color before drawing
void linetool::draw(void)
{
  setlinestyle(globallinestyle, 0, NORM_WIDTH); // Use global line style
  setcolor(globaldrawcolor);                    // Use global draw color
  linestyle = globallinestyle;                  // Save line style used
  drawingtool::draw();                          // Draw one or more lines
}

// Uses exclusive-ORed lines while the line is initially drawn
void linetool::startdrawing(void)
{
  drawingtool::startdrawing();
  setwritemode(XOR_PUT);         // Use exclusive-OR lines while drawing
  x1 = x;  y1 = y;  // This will be the stationary point of the line
}

// Draws a line from fixed point where the mouse was pressed (which
// was saved in startdrawing()) to its current location. Save the
// current location of the mouse in (x2,y2).
void linetool::show(void)
{
  mouse.hide();                     // Hide the mouse before drawing
  line(x1-wl, y1-wt, x-wl, y-wt); // Draw the line
  mouse.show();                     // Restore the mouse to the screen
  x2 = x;  y2 = y;                  // Save the line's other end point
}

// Erases the line by drawing it again. This works since the
// exclusive-OR mode is being used.
void linetool::hide(void)
{
  mouse.hide();                        // Hide the mouse cursor
  line(x1-wl, y1-wt, oldx-wl, oldy-wt); // Erase the line
  mouse.show();                        // Restore the mouse cursor
}
```

```
// The size of the line has been fixed, so switch out of exclusive-OR
// mode and draw the line in permanently by drawing it again
void linetool::finishdrawing(void)
{
  setwritemode(COPY_PUT);         // Get out of exclusive-OR mode
  show();                         // Draw the line in permanently
}


// Drawing a rectangle is similar to drawing a line, except that
// rectangle() is called rather than line()
void rectangletool::show(void)
{
  mouse.hide();                                // Hide the mouse cursor
  rectangle(x1-wl, y1-wt, oldx-wl, oldy-wt); // Draw the rectangle
  mouse.show();                                // Show the mouse cursor
}


// Removes the current rectangle by drawing it again. This method
// assumes that the exclusive-OR feature is being used.
void rectangletool::hide(void)
{
  mouse.hide();                           // Hide the mouse cursor
  rectangle(x1-wl, y1-wt, x-wl, y-wt);  // Erase the rectangle
  mouse.show();                           // Show the mouse cursor
}


// Sets the fill style or fill color as well as the properties
// supported for the inherited rectangletool class
void fillrectangletool::setproperties(int code, int val)
{
  switch (code) {
    case FILLSTYLEPROP: fillstyle = val; break;
    case FILLCOLORPROP: fillcolor = val; break;
    default: rectangletool::setproperties(code, val);
  }
}


// Sets up for drawing a filled rectangle by selecting fill settings
// before performing the drawing operation
void fillrectangletool::draw(void)
{
  fillcolor = globalfillcolor;  fillstyle = globalfillstyle;
  setfillstyle(fillstyle, fillcolor);
  rectangletool::draw();
}


// Uses a dashed rectangle while setting the size of the filled rectangle
void fillrectangletool::startdrawing(void)
{
  // Use a dashed rubber-banding rectangle to set the size of the
  // filled rectangle
  setlinestyle(DASHED_LINE, 0, NORM_WIDTH);
  rectangletool::startdrawing();
}
```

```
// Draws the filled rectangle
void fillrectangletool::finishdrawing(void)
{
  setlinestyle(globallinestyle, 0, NORM_WIDTH);
  setwritemode(COPY_PUT);           // Switch out of exclusive-OR mode
  mouse.hide();
  bar3d(x1-wl, y1-wt, x-wl, y-wt, 0, 0); // Draw the filled rectangle
  mouse.show();
}

// Sets the fill style or fill color as well as the properties
// supported for the inherited linetool class
void polygontool::setproperties(int code, int val)
{
  switch (code) {
    case FILLSTYLEPROP: fillstyle = val; break;
    case FILLCOLORPROP: fillcolor = val; break;
    default: linetool::setproperties(code, val);
  }
}

// Saves the starting location of the polygon. These coordinates are
// saved in the same array, poly.
void polygontool::startdrawing(void)
{
  linetool::startdrawing();
  fillcolor = globalfillcolor;  fillstyle = globalfillstyle;
  poly[0] = x-wl; poly[1] = y-wt;  // Save current location of mouse
  numpts = 2;                      // One coordinate pair is saved
}

// Overrides updatedrawing() so that the left mouse button is used to
// specify the location of vertices and the right mouse button ends
// the drawing of the polygon.
void polygontool::updatedrawing(void)
{
  do {
    mouse.getcoords(x, y);         // Get current location of mouse
    if (x != oldx || y != oldy) {  // If mouse hasn't moved, update
      hide();                      // current edge of polygon
      show();
      oldx = x;   oldy = y;        // Remember last location of edge
    }
    if (mouse.buttonreleased(LEFT_BUTTON)) {
      mouse.buttonpressed(LEFT_BUTTON);
      setwritemode(COPY_PUT); // Draw line in permanently
      show();
      setwritemode(XOR_PUT);  // Switch back to exlusive-OR mode
      x1 = x; y1 = y;         // Save the new vertice of the line
      poly[numpts++] = x-wl;  poly[numpts++] = y-wt;
    }
    // End drawing when right mouse button is pressed
  } while (!mouse.buttonpressed(RIGHT_BUTTON)) ;
}
```

```
// Closes off the polygon by drawing a line back to its beginning
void polygontool::finishdrawing(void)
{
  poly[numpts++] = x-wl;      poly[numpts++] = y-wt;
  poly[numpts++] = poly[0];   poly[numpts++] = poly[1];
  setwritemode(COPY_PUT);                 // Draw line in permanently
  mouse.hide();
  line(x1-wl, y1-wt, x-wl, y-wt);
  line(x-wl, y-wt, poly[0], poly[1]); // Close polygon
  mouse.show();
}

// Prepares for drawing a filled figure before calling the polygon routine
void fillpolygontool::startdrawing(void)
{
  setfillstyle(globalfillstyle, globalfillcolor);
  polygontool::startdrawing();
}

// Draws a filled polygon
void fillpolygontool::finishdrawing(void)
{
  poly[numpts++] = x-wl;      poly[numpts++] = y-wt;
  poly[numpts++] = poly[0];   poly[numpts++] = poly[1];
  setwritemode(COPY_PUT);     // Draw line in permanently
  mouse.hide();               // Hide the mouse cursor
  fillpoly(numpts/2, poly);   // Draw the filled polygon
  mouse.show();               // Show the mouse cursor
}

// The getimage() and putimage() functions are used to create a rubber-
// banding circle effect by popping up a "window" with a circle in it.
// This method allocates and frees the memory used to save the screen
// where the circle is displayed. Since some high-resolution modes
// consume more than 64K, the drawing window is saved in two pieces,
// covered1 and covered2.
void circletool::draw(void)
{
  halfx = (wr + wl) / 2;      // Split drawing window into two
  covered1 = malloc(imagesize(wl, wt, halfx, wb)); // Allocate memory
  covered2 = malloc(imagesize(halfx, wt, wr, wb));
  if (covered1 == NULL || covered2 == NULL) mallocerror();
  setcolor(globaldrawcolor);  // Prepare for drawing
  drawingtool::draw();        // Draw one or more circles
  free(covered2);             // Free the memory allocated earlier
  free(covered1);
}

// Starts drawing by saving the point where the mouse cursor is located
void circletool::startdrawing(void)
{
  drawingtool::startdrawing();
  centerx = x;  centery = y;
```

```
      oldleft = x;  oldtop = y;  oldright = x;
      mouse.hide();
      getimage(oldleft-wl, oldtop-wt, oldleft-wl, oldtop-wt, covered1);
      getimage(oldleft-wl, oldtop-wt, oldleft-wt, oldtop-wt, covered2);
      mouse.show();
   }

// Draws a circle while the left mouse button is pressed. We must
// calculate the bounds of the drawing window to be saved. These
// values are stored in cleft, cright, ctop, and cbottom. The radius
// of the circle is changed as the mouse is moved left and right.
void circletool::updatedrawing(void)
{
   while (!mouse.buttonreleased(LEFT_BUTTON)) {
     mouse.getcoords(x, y);
     absradiusx = abs(centerx - x);   // Calculate new radius of circle
     // Clip the region that must be saved below the circle
     // to the boundaries of the drawing window
     if (centerx-absradiusx < wl) cleft = wl;
       else cleft = centerx - absradiusx;
     if (centerx+absradiusx > wr) cright = wr;
       else cright = centerx + absradiusx;
     if (centery-absradiusx < wt) ctop = wt;
       else ctop = centery - absradiusx;
     if (centery+absradiusx > wb) cbottom = wb;
       else cbottom = centery + absradiusx;
     if (x != oldx) { // If the size of the circle has changed, redraw it
       hide();
       show();
       oldleft = cleft;  oldtop = ctop;   oldx = x;   oldright = cright;
     }
   }
}

// Removes the current circle by overwriting it with the stored screen
// image that was saved before the circle was drawn
void circletool::hide(void)
{
  mouse.hide();
  putimage(oldleft-wl, oldtop-wt, covered1, COPY_PUT);
  putimage((oldleft+oldright)/2-wl, oldtop-wt, covered2, COPY_PUT);
  mouse.show();
}

// Draws the circle, but first saves the screen region where the circle
// will be drawn. This screen image is used in hide() to erase the circle.
void circletool::show(void)
{
  mouse.hide();
  getimage(cleft-wl, ctop-wt, (cleft+cright)/2-wl, cbottom-wt, covered1);
  getimage((cleft+cright)/2-wl, ctop-wt, cright-wl, cbottom-wt, covered2);
  if (absradiusx != 0)  // Draw circle if its radius is not zero
    circle(centerx-wl, centery-wt, absradiusx);  // Draw circle
```

```
    mouse.show();
}

// Drawing an ellipse is similar to drawing a circle, except that
// when the mouse is moved up and down it also changes the vertical
// height of the figure
void ellipsetool::updatedrawing(void)
{
  while (!mouse.buttonreleased(LEFT_BUTTON)) {
    mouse.getcoords(x, y);
    absradiusx = abs(centerx - x);
    absradiusy = abs(centery - y);
    // Clip the region that must be saved below the ellipse
    // to the boundaries of the drawing window
    if (centerx-absradiusx < wl) cleft = wl;
      else cleft = centerx - absradiusx;
    if (centerx+absradiusx > wr) cright = wr;
      else cright = centerx + absradiusx;
    if (centery-absradiusy < wt) ctop = wt;
      else ctop = centery - absradiusy;
    if (centery+absradiusy > wb) cbottom = wb;
      else cbottom = centery + absradiusy;
    // If the size of the ellipse has changed, redraw it
    if (x != oldx || y != oldy) {
      hide();  show();
      oldleft = cleft;        oldtop = ctop;
      oldx = x;  oldy = y;    oldright = cright;
    }
  }
}

// Displays the ellipse, but first saves the screen region where the
// ellipse is to be drawn so that the ellipse can later be erased
// by overwriting the screen with these saved images
void ellipsetool::show(void)
{
  mouse.hide();
  getimage(cleft-wl, ctop-wt, (cleft+cright)/2-wl, cbottom-wt, covered1);
  getimage((cleft+cright)/2-wl, ctop-wt, cright-wl, cbottom-wt, covered2);
  if (absradiusx != 0 && absradiusy != 0)  // Draw ellipse
    ellipse(centerx-wl, centery-wt, 0, 360, absradiusx, absradiusy);
  mouse.show();
}

// The radius is changed by moving the mouse left and right. The
// sweep angle of the arc changes as the mouse is moved up and down.
void arctool::updatedrawing(void)
{
  while (!mouse.buttonreleased(LEFT_BUTTON)) {
    mouse.getcoords(x, y);
    radius = abs(centerx - x);
    angle = abs(centery - y);
    if (centerx-radius < wl) cleft = wl;
```

```
        else cleft = centerx - radius;
      if (centerx+radius > wr) cright = wr;
        else cright = centerx + radius;
      if (centery-radius < wt) ctop = wt;
        else ctop = centery - radius;
      if (centery+radius > wb) cbottom = wb;
        else cbottom = centery + radius;
      // If the size of the ellipse has changed, redraw it
      if (x != oldx || y != oldy) {
        hide();     show();
        oldleft = cleft;        oldtop = ctop;
        oldx = x;   oldy = y; oldright = cright;
      }
  }
}

// Draws the arc using the current radius and angle. See the
// discussions for the similar functions in circletool and ellipsetool
// for how this function works.
void arctool::show(void)
{
  mouse.hide();
  getimage(cleft-wl, ctop-wt, (cleft+cright)/2-wl, cbottom-wt, covered1);
  getimage((cleft+cright)/2-wl, ctop-wt, cright-wl, cbottom-wt, covered2);
  if (radius > 0 && angle > 0)
    arc(centerx-wl, centery-wt, 0, angle, radius);  // Draw the arc
  mouse.show();
}

// Writes text to the drawing window. A vertical line is used as a cursor.
// The text is saved in the field "string." Use the global drawing
// color as the color of the text.
void texttool::draw(void)
{
  setcolor(globaldrawcolor);
  settextjustify(LEFT_TEXT, TOP_TEXT);
  textstyle = globaltextstyle;  // Remember which font is being used
  drawingtool::draw();
}

// Prepares for interactively entering text
void texttool::startdrawing(void)
{
  while (!mouse.buttonreleased(LEFT_BUTTON)) ;
  drawingtool::startdrawing();
  setwritemode(XOR_PUT);
  mouse.hide();       // Exclusive-OR in a cursor where mouse was pressed
  line(x-wl, y-wt, x-wl, y+textheight("S")-wt);
  mouse.show();
  setwritemode(COPY_PUT);       // Make sure to use the right mode when
  moveto(x-wl, y-wt);           // displaying text
  leftx = x;   lefty = y;       // Save starting location of text
  len = 0;
}
```

```
// Main routine to enter text. This routine displays characters
// entered until the left mouse button or the Esc
// key is pressed.
void texttool::updatedrawing(void)
{
  int c;
  char buff[MAXSTRING];

  len = 0;
  while (1) {
    c = mouse.waitforinput(LEFT_BUTTON);
    if (c < 0 || c == 0x1B) break;   // Quit if mouse button or
                                     // the Esc key is pressed
    setwritemode(XOR_PUT);
    mouse.hide();                // Display a cursor
    line(x-wl, y-wt, x-wl, y+textheight("S")-wt);
    mouse.show();
    setwritemode(COPY_PUT);
    if (c == CR) {                // If input is a carriage return,
      y += textheight("S")+2;  // then move to another line and
      x = leftx;                // insert a newline character into
      moveto(x-wl, y-wt);       // the string array
      if (len < MAXSTRING-1) string[len++] = '\n';
    }
    else if (c == BS) {        // The Backspace key was pressed
      if (len > 0) {           // Make sure there's a character remaining
        len--;
        sprintf(buff, "%c", string[len]);
        // Subtract the width of the deleted character from the
        // cursor's x pixel location
        string[len] = '\0';
        if (buff[0] == '\n') {
          // If the user just deleted a carriage return, move the
          // y value of the cursor up too
          y -= textheight("S")+2;
          // Determine the width of the string back to the
          // next carriage return or the beginning of the string
          for (int i=len; i>0 && string[i-1] != '\n'; i--) ;
          strncpy(buff, &string[i], len-i);
          buff[len-i] = '\0';
          x = leftx + textwidth(buff);
        }
        else {
          x -= textwidth(buff);
          moveto(x-wl, y-wt);
          mouse.hide();
          setcolor(0);
          outtext(buff);        // Erase the deleted character
          mouse.show();
          setcolor(drawcolor);
        }
        moveto(x-wl, y-wt);
      }
    }
```

```
    else {
      sprintf(buff, "%c", c);
      mouse.hide();
      outtext(buff);              // Write the new character
      mouse.show();
      x += textwidth(buff);    // Keep track of the cursor location
      if (len < MAXSTRING-1) string[len++] = c; // Add character to string
    }
    mouse.hide();
    setwritemode(XOR_PUT);
    line(x-wl, y-wt, x-wl, y+textheight("S")-wt); // Display new cursor
    setwritemode(COPY_PUT);
    mouse.show();
  }
}

// Finishes the text input routine by adding a NULL character to the
// end of the string entered and erases the cursor
void texttool::finishdrawing(void)
{
  mouse.hide();                   // Erase the cursor
  setwritemode(XOR_PUT);
  line(x-wl, y-wt, x-wl, y+textheight("S")-wt);
  setwritemode(COPY_PUT);
  string[len] = '\0';             // NULL-terminate the text
  moveto(leftx-wl, lefty-wt);
  int liney = 0;
  char buff[2] = "0";
  for (int i=0; i<len; i++) { // Display the text
    if (string[i] == '\n') {   // Carriage return
      liney++;
      moveto(leftx-wl, lefty-wt+textheight("T")+2*liney);
    }
    else {
      buff[0] = string[len];
      outtext(buff);
    }
  }
  mouse.show();
}

// Erases the drawing window
void clearwindowtool::draw(void)
{
  viewporttype v;

  getviewsettings(&v);
  setviewport(wl, wt, wr, wb, 1); // Set viewport to drawing window
  mouse.hide();
  clearviewport();                // Erase the drawing window
  mouse.show();
  setviewport(v.left, v.top, v.right, v.bottom, 1); // Restore viewport
}
```

```
// If an error occurs in memory allocation, call this routine to display
// an error message and the program will quit
void mallocerror(void)
{
  closegraph();
  printf("Not enough memory to run program\n\n");
  exit(1);
}
```

A Paint Program

This chapter has two interconnected goals. First, it will show you how to create the paint program that we have been developing classes for in earlier chapters, and second, it will serve as the user's guide for the paint program. By now, you should be armed with a powerful package of graphics programming tools, and because building a useful paint program is not a trivial task, we'll be relying heavily on these tools to simplify the process. Before we complete this chapter, we'll also discuss several enhancements that you might want to try implementing so that you can create your own customized version of the paint program.

OVERVIEW OF THE PAINT PROGRAM

Although our paint program uses many tools that we have developed throughout this book, we'll still need to develop more code in this chapter to create the program. The missing ingredients are handled by a series of special files. The first set, which includes USERTOOL.H and USERTOOL.CPP, provides a handful of additional interactive tools that we'll need in the paint program, including classes to display pull-down menus, a set of fill patterns, and a palette. The second two source files we'll construct, INTERACT.H and INTERACT.CPP, tie together the tools in DRAW.CPP and USERTOOL.CPP with the icons and menu options on the screen. The third and last file we'll build is called PAINT.CPP. It is responsible for drawing the paint program's environment by arranging the icons, positioning the pull-down menus, and segmenting off a portion of the screen for the drawing window. It also initiates the loop that responds to any user input. You'll find all of the new files listed at the end of this chapter.

273

USING SCREEN OBJECTS

Figure 11.1 shows a screen shot of the paint program's environment. As indicated, a large portion of the screen is reserved for the drawing window, but what's of more interest right now are the other components of the drawing environment. The left side of the screen is reserved for the icons that represent the commands supported by the program. In addition, the top of the screen contains several keywords that are used to pull down various menus or select additional functions. And at the bottom of the screen is a list of the fill patterns and the colors that are accessible in the current video mode.

One important thing to realize is that each item described so far is designed to be handled as a separate graphics object that is managed by the INTERACT.CPP file. As a result, each of these screen objects (icons, menus, and so on) has a predefined functionality that can be accessed by clicking on it with the mouse. For instance, when you click on the spray can icon, **spraycantool** will be used to spray paint inside the drawing window. So before we continue, we need to build the INTERACT.CPP package that ties together these screen objects and their operations.

Figure 11.1 We will build several files in this chapter to produce the paint program shown here.

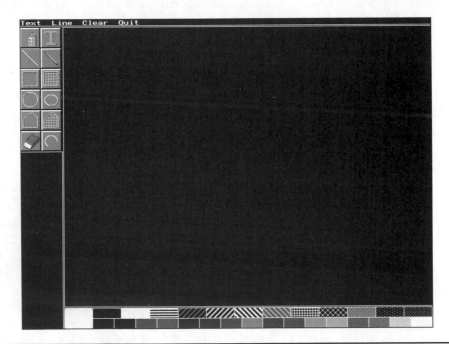

The INTERACT.CPP source file contains three new classes, which are listed in Table 11.1. The first class, **interact**, ties together a screen object with a particular drawing function. Here's its class definition:

```
class interact {
public :
  int cmd;               // Letter command that selects the object
  int left, right;       // Screen region where command is displayed
  int top, bottom;
  drawingtool *itool;
  interact(int c, int l, int t, int wd, int ht,
    drawingtool *tl, char *iconname=NULL);
  virtual void select(void);
  virtual void highlight(void);
};
```

The first instance variable in **interact** specifies a code or letter that can be used, in addition to the mouse, for selecting the drawing object. The next four variables, **left**, **right**, **top**, and **bottom**, define the screen region where the screen object resides. This region contains an icon or menu option that the user can click on to select a drawing tool. Next, lies the pointer, **itool**, which is set to the **drawingtool** object that is to be executed when the **interact** object is selected. Note that a pointer is used here so that we can fully exploit polymorphism to invoke any of the member functions in the hierarchy of drawing tools we created in Chapter 10. The last parameter is optional. If a string is passed as the parameter, it's assumed to be the name of an icon file that should be read and the resulting icon placed on the screen at the object's location. If the parameter isn't included, as would be the case for a menu selection, then no icon is read.

The **interact** class also contains three member functions. The first is a constructor that initializes a particular **interact** object. This function is passed the bounds of the screen region that defines the screen object, and a pointer to the drawing tool to be used when the screen object is selected. We'll need to create one **interact** object for each drawing tool used in the paint and CAD programs.

Table 11.1 Classes in INTERACT.CPP

Class	Description
interact	Ties together a screen object and an action
userinteract	Derived from the interact class and does everything that interact does except modify the screen when a screen object is selected
toolset	An array of interact tools and the code to select and process them

The **select( )** member function, which follows, is included in **interact** to invoke the **drawingtool** object that it contains:

```
void interact::select(void)
{
  highlight();           // Show that the option has been selected
  itool->draw();         // Execute the function selected
  highlight();           // Restore the option to its normal state
}
```

It is this member function that we want to call in order to select a particular drawing function. Recall that the **draw( )** function is the high-level member function that is to be used to initiate the drawing of a **drawingtool**. We'll also set up the menus and other user-interface tools so that they are derived from the **drawingtool** class and perform their actions in their **draw( )** functions. The calls to **highlight( )** in **select( )** highlight the screen object (icon or menu options) that the user has selected.

Currently, **highlight( )** merely reverses the image of the screen object. Therefore, the first call reverses the colors in an icon or menu option, while the second call restores the screen object to its original image.

The **interact** class provides everything we need to encapsulate a screen object with a drawing tool. But there are cases, like with the palette, where we don't want the screen object to be reversed when it is selected. For this reason, INTERACT.CPP also includes the derived class **userinteract**. This class inherits everything in **interact**, except that it overrides **select( )** so that only the nested **drawingtool**'s **draw( )** member function is called and the highlighting action does not take place:

```
virtual void select(void) { itool->draw(); }
```

You'll find this statement in the class declaration of **userinteract** in the INTERACT.H header file.

Now that we have a class hierarchy that allows us to select drawing tools from the screen, we need to build a class that ties a set of these together into one package. This is the job of the **toolset** class in INTERACT.CPP. As shown next, **toolset** contains an array of pointers to **interact** objects, called **tool**, and a set of three member functions that manage this array:

```
const int NUMTOOLS = 30;
class toolset {
public:
  interact *tool[NUMTOOLS];       // List of tools
  int numtools;                   // Number of tools in list
  toolset(void) { numtools=0; }
  void addtool(interact *t);
  void anytoprocess(int c);
};
```

Note that we have only allocated space for 30 interactive objects by using the integer constant **NUMTOOLS**. This is big enough for the paint, CAD, and three-dimensional graphics programs we'll be developing.

The **numtools** variable in **toolset** keeps track of the number of objects currently in the **tool** array. It is initialized to 0 in the **toolset** constructor. So how do objects get placed in the **tool** array? This is the job of the **addtool()** member function, shown here:

```
void toolset::addtool(interact *t)
{
  if (numtools >= NUMTOOLS) return;  // No more room in list
  tool[numtools++] = t;
}
```

We must call **addtool()** for every interactive tool we want included in an application program. For example, to add a spray can object and its icon that spans from (4,10) to (36,42), to the list of drawing tools, we first need to declare a **toolset** object and a spray can object

```
toolset tools;
drawingtool *spraycan = new spraycantool;
```

and then call **addtool()** to add the spraycan tool to the list maintained by **toolset**

```
tools.addtool(new interact('s', 4, 10, 36, 42, spraycan, "spray.icn"));
```

The last member function in **toolset**, **anytoprocess()**, is used in an application program to determine which drawing tool has been selected, if any, and then executes it. The member function is broken into two cases, which are built around an **if-else** statement. Which part of the **if** statement gets executed depends on the value of **c** passed into **anytoprocess()**. This variable is either a keyboard or mouse event code that was presumably returned from **waitforinput()** that we developed in the mouse tools in Chapter 7. If **c** is greater than 0, then a keyboard event has occurred; if its less than 0, then a mouse button was pressed; and finally, if it equals 0, then it means that no event has taken place, so nothing should be done.

The top part of **anytoprocess()** handles the situation in which the user has entered a character code to select an object. The second, which is quite similar, is used when a mouse action has occurred. The **anytoprocess()** function retrieves the current coordinates of the mouse and then searches through the tool array to find if any screen object is located where the mouse was pressed. If there is, then that tool's corresponding **select()** member function is executed:

```
else if (c < 0) {           // Mouse button pressed
  mouse.getcoords(x, y);    // Find which region was selected
```

```
    for (i=0; i<numtools; i++) {
      if (mouse.inbox(tool[i]->left, tool[i]->top,
                      tool[i]->right, tool[i]->bottom, x, y)) {
        tool[i]->select();          // Execute the function
        return;
      }
    }
}
```

For more on how ploymorphism is used to manage the array of drawing tools used in the paint program, refer *Polymorphism with Pointers* below.

SETTING UP THE ENVIRONMENT

All the components discussed in the last section are created in the function **setup_screen()**, which is located in PAINT.CPP. The first part of **setup_screen()** is responsible for setting up the main menu bar at the top of the screen, which is drawn by the following two statements:

```
h = textheight("H") + 2;
if (getmaxcolor() == 1) setfillstyle(SOLID_FILL, 0);
  else setfillstyle(SOLID_FILL, BLUE);
bar3d(0, 0, maxx, h, 0, 0);
outtextxy(2, 2, "Text  Line  Clear  Quit");
```

The processing of the menu bar is created in the lines that follow these two statements. The subsequent lines add each of the menu bar commands—Text,

---

POLYMORPHISM WITH POINTERS

We've already seen how inheritance can be used in a class hierarchy so that we can construct objects out of other objects and share common code. We did this, for example, in our interactive drawing toolkit by deriving the classes **penciltool** and **linetool** from the generic **drawingtool** class. It's fairly easy to see how we can declare objects of each of these derived types, but how can we handle arrays of **drawingtool** objects in which each array element is a different type like **penciltool**, **linetool**, and so on? Don't forget, we want to exploit polymorphism to call each object in the array with the same invocation—no matter what type it is.

To get the job done, we must resort to using *pointers* to the objects; and further, these pointers must be declared as the base class type. For example, to construct an array of ten **drawingtool**s, we could use the array declaration

```
drawingtool *toollist[10];
```

Line, Clear, and Quit—to the list of objects that are on the screen. This is accomplished by using the object-oriented utility, INTERACT.CPP, that was discussed in the last section. Here we're using a **toolset** object called **tools**, which is declared in INTERACT.CPP. Adding an object to the **tools** list is simply a matter of calling the **addtool( )** member function.

We will later write functions to pull down the appropriate menu when one of these text commands is selected. Note that the location under these words is saved in a pair of global variables in **setup_screen( )** so that later we'll know where to place the pull-down menus. For example, in the case of the Text command, the pull-down menu appears at **textmenux** and **textmenuy**. These variables are defined in USERTOOL.CPP. The **changefonttool** and **changelinetool** are **drawingtool** objects that manage the two menus. When their **draw( )** functions are called, a menu appears and the objects wait for a mouse click. The **startdrawing( )** member functions display the menus and **updatedrawing( )** magages the user input. If the user selects one of the menu options, the object's **finishdrawing( )** function is called to take the appropriate action. For instance, in the case of the line tool, the **globallinestyle** variable is set to the line style selected.

The next sequence of statements displays a series of icons on the left side of the screen and appends the corresponding drawing objects to the **tools** object. The **addtool( )** function performs these two tasks for the icons. The code presented in this chapter uses 32 x 32, sculpted icons. The icons are different than those presented in Chapter 8, however the newer icons are no more difficult to create with the ICONED program.

and assign a tool to each array element using statements like:

```
drawingtool *penciltoolptr = new penciltool;
toollist[0] = penciltoolptr;
```

Following this, we can access any of the member functions that the various tools in **toollist** inherited from the **drawingtool** class using the same notation—polymorphism at work. For instance, to call each of the **draw()** functions in the **toollist** one after another, we could use:

```
for (i=0; i<10; i++)
  toollist[i]->draw();
```

This is the same approach that we use in the paint and CAD programs, although we'll be building a list of pointers to **interact** objects instead of **drawingtool**s.

The next block of code in **setup_screen( )** creates the fill patterns and color palette located at the bottom of the screen. In order to keep our environment as consistent as possible, the fill patterns and palette are used by activating one of two new classes that are derived from **drawingtool**. These classes, called **changefillpatterntool** and **changefillcolortool**, are located in the USERTOOL.CPP source file, and their definitions are contained in the header file USERTOOL.H.

We'll add these objects to our tool list as we did earlier with the icon and menu objects. As mentioned earlier, their **draw( )** member functions are overridden to enable the user to select a fill pattern or color from the palette. The new **draw( )** functions call overridden versions of **finishdrawing( )** to actually set the proper global variables when the user clicks the mouse.

Because the size of the screen may vary according to the graphics mode in use, the **draw( )** member function in these classes is slightly more complicated than it would need to be otherwise. The primary thing to note is that each routine first calculates how wide each cell (for example, a single fill pattern) needs to be in order for all of the cells to fit across the screen. A **for** loop is then used to sequence through each of the patterns or colors until all of them have been displayed. Note also that we are not adding each cell individually to our list of objects; instead we add the complete block of fill patterns and the block of colors as two individual objects.

To the left of these fill styles in the paint program's environment is a rectangular region that displays the current fill pattern and color. This region is also added as an object through **changedrawcolortool**, and it serves as a platform for us to change the drawing color. Whenever you click on this region, the current fill color will become the current drawing color. The perimeter of the current fill color box is repainted with the new drawing color. As we did with the fill pattern and palette tools, this action is performed by the **draw( )** member function in **changedrawcolortool**.

One last operation that **setup_screen( )** performs is to calculate and draw the boundaries of the drawing window. As per the requirements of DRAW.CPP, these boundaries are saved in the global variables **wl**, **wt**, **wr**, and **wb**.

THE PAINT FUNCTIONS

Although we have the basic form of the paint program under control, there are a handful of functions that we still need to flush out. These will all be packaged in the USERTOOL.H and USERTOOL.CPP files. We've already touched on some of them briefly, like **changefillpatterntool** and **changefillcolortool**, but there are still more details in these and other member functions in USERTOOL.CPP that we need to cover.

Table 11.2 provides a list of the support classes in USERTOOL.CPP. We'll start by examining the function associated with the Quit command in the main

Table 11.2 Paint Program Support Classes in USERTOOL.CPP

Function	Description
changedrawcolortool	Sets the drawing color to the fill color
changefillcolortool	Selects a new painting color
changefillpatterntool	Selects a new painting pattern
changefonttool	Selects a new font style
changelinestyletool	Selects a new line style
quittool	Terminates the paint program

menu bar and then we'll proceed to the others. Remember, the drawing tools corresponding to the icons, the text entry option, and the clear window function, have already been taken care of by using the classes in the DRAW.CPP package from Chapter 10.

Quitting the Program

The **quittool** class provides the only path out of the paint program. When it is selected, it simply exits graphics mode and terminates the program by calling **exit( )**. The **quittool** class is implemented in USERTOOL.CPP as a derived **drawingtool** so that we can add it to our list of drawing operations and select it in the same way as all the other tools. Of course, **quittool** doesn't do any drawing. Instead, the **draw( )** function is overridden to execute the statements that terminate the program.

The Pull-Down Menus

As we stated earlier, the paint program uses pull-down menus for changing the text and line style. We could develop a general menu package to support pull-down menus, but this would lead to even more groundwork and would only delay our efforts to build a working paint program. Instead, we'll use a rather hard-coded approach in order to simplify the task of adding pull-down menus to our program.

The pull-down menus for the text and line styles are accessed by clicking on the words *Text* or *Line*. When one of these options is selected, either the class **changefonttool** or **changelinestyletool** is invoked through our object-oriented utility, INTERACT.CPP.

The **draw( )** functions in both of these classes are overridden to supply the user interaction in the pull-down menus. At the beginning of each of these functions are several statements that create the pull-down menus. The process

Figure 11.2 The Line pull-down menu allows the user to change line style.

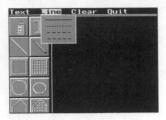

begins by using **gpopup( )** to pop up the window for the menu. Note that USERTOOL.CPP declares a global window object, called **w**, for it to use.

Next, a **for** loop is used to fill the window with the appropriate selections. For instance, if the Text command is selected, the different font styles are displayed so that you can select one. Similarly, if the user chooses the Line command, a set of available line styles is displayed in the corresponding pull-down menu. Figure 11.2 shows the paint environment with the Line pull-down menu visible.

The position of the pull-down menu commands are hard-coded and defined within the functions **changefonttool::draw( )** and **changelinestyletool::draw( )**. Therefore, when you click on one of the font styles (in the case of the Text pull-down menu) or one of the line segments (in the case of the Line pull-down menu), the program can determine which option has been selected and take the appropriate action.

Determining which menu selection has been chosen is performed by the second **for** loop in **changefonttool::draw( )** and **changelinestyletool::draw( )**. However, first both of the functions wait for the user to click the left mouse button with the statement:

```
while (!mouse.buttonpressed(LEFT_BUTTON));
```

Once the button is pressed, the mouse coordinates are retrieved and compared against the possible choices within the menu to see if one has been selected. If so, the routines call **finishdrawing( )** to set the appropriate text style or line style, and the function returns. If the mouse coordinates do not correspond to a menu selection, then **draw( )** returns without performing any action.

Changing the Fill Style

At the bottom of the screen are a series of fill patterns and colors that can be used in the paint program. To easily integrate these utilities into our existing packages, the fill patterns and the color palette are added to the object list as two objects and not as a series of smaller objects. Therefore, if the user clicks the mouse within one of the fill patterns, no matter which one has been selected, the **changefillpatterntool** class is used. Alternatively, if one of the color boxes is selected, then **changefillcolortool** is used.

These classes operate much like **changefonttool** and **changelinestyletool** in that they compare the mouse coordinates at the time of the button press with the locations of each of the regions. If the mouse has selected one of the boxes, the fill pattern or color from that box is used to set either **globalfillstyle** or **globalfillcolor**, which are two of the global drawing parameters defined in DRAW.CPP.

User Interaction

The code used to process and control the user's inputs to the paint program is placed in the **do** loop at the bottom of the **main( )** function in the PAINT.CPP file. This infinite loop calls the mouse member function **waitforinput( )** to get any user inputs, and then subsequently invokes **anytoprocess( )** to perform the appropriate action, if any.

```
do {
  c = mouse.waitforinput(LEFT_BUTTON);
  tools.anytoprocess(c);
} while(1);
```

The **waitforinput( )** member function is found in the file MOUSE.CPP that we developed in Chapter 7. As written, this function waits for either the left mouse button to be pressed or a key to be struck before it returns. The value of the action is returned in the integer variable **c**.

The input value is passed to **anytoprocess( )**, which is a member function of the class **toolset** that we defined in INTERACT.CPP. It steps through the list of objects in the object lists and tests whether the user has clicked in the region bounding the object or has pressed its quick access key. If either is true, the member function invokes the appropriate function associated with it.

Note that the **do** loop in **main( )** is an infinite loop. The infinite loop functions as what is commonly called an event-driven loop. (An event can be a mouse click or a keyboard action.) That is, the loop repeats as it waits for an event to occur. Remember that the **quittool** function provides a path for exiting the program. Therefore, one of the events that can occur is that the user can select the Quit command or type in the letter *q* which in turn calls **quittool::draw( )**.

Compiling the Paint Program

As mentioned before, our paint program uses several of the tools that we developed in earlier chapters of the book. A listing of these files and the chapters that they are discussed in is shown in Table 11.3. You will need to

Table 11.3 Files Needed to Compile the PAINT Program

Source File	From Chapter	Description
DRAW.CPP	Chapter 10	Interactive drawing utilities
DRAWTOOL.CPP	Chapter 10	Base class for drawing utilities
GPOPUP.CPP	Chapter 9	Pop-up window package
GTEXT.CPP	Chapter 3	Graphics mode text utilities
INTERACT.CPP	Chapter 11	Object-oriented utilities
KBDMOUSE.CPP	Chapter 7	Keyboard emulated mouse
MOUSE.CPP	Chapter 7	Mouse utilities
PAINT.CPP	Chapter 11	The main paint program
USERTOOL.CPP	Chapter 11	Miscellaneous environment tools

make a project file that contains each of these files in order to compile and link the paint program (you'll need the header files too). Note that because of the amount of memory required in the paint program and its size, you'll need to compile all of the files in the large memory model. You also must define the **MOUSE** compiler constant to enable the GTEXT.CPP and GPOPUP.CPP utilities to properly support the mouse.

USING THE **PAINT** PROGRAM

Once you have a compiled and linked the PAINT program, you are ready to try it out. After invoking PAINT, the first thing you should see is the environment shown earlier in Figure 11.1. If you have any difficulty, make sure you have all of the icon files and graphics libraries in their appropriate locations. The program shown in Figure 11.1 uses the 32 x 32 icon files listed in Table 11.4. If you're running in a low-resolution mode, you may want to modify the code to work with the smaller 16 x 16 icons. In addition, the icons assume that they will be displayed in a 16-color mode. Therefore, if you're going to support a monochrome display mode, you'll have to handle this condition.

The program is easy to run. You can use the mouse or keyboard, as outlined in Chapter 7, to move the cursor about the screen, and you can use the various quick keys that were defined for the icons. The drawing functions should all work as described in Chapter 10. Most of the other functions that we have added have been described earlier in this chapter. The only one remaining is how to change the drawing color.

Remember, the palette on the bottom of the screen is used to change the fill color directly. To change the drawing color, you need to click on the box just to the left of the fill patterns, which shows the current fill settings.

Table 11.4 Icons Used in PAINT.CPP

Icon Filename	Description
ARC32.ICN	Arc tool icon
BOX32.ICN	Rectangle tool icon
CIRCLE32.ICN	Circle tool icon
ELLPSE32.ICN	Ellipse tool icon
ERASE32.ICN	Erasing tool icon
FBOX32.ICN	Filled rectangle tool icon
FPOLY32.ICN	Filled polygon tool icon
LETTER32.ICN	Text tool icon
LINE32.ICN	Line tool icon
PENCIL32.ICN	Pencil tool icon
POLY32.ICN	Polygon tool icon
SPRAY32.ICN	The spray can tool icon

By clicking on this box, which also was added as an object in **setup_screen( )**, you will force the drawing color to be changed to the drawing color currently displayed within it.

ENHANCING THE PAINT PROGRAM

Although the complete paint program is large, there are many features you might want to add. First, let's look at what you need to do to add a new function that would be accessible through an icon. For instance, let's say you want to add a routine that will use the flood fill operation to fill selected regions. Basically, there are three things that you will need to do:

1. Use the Icon Editor from Chapter 8 to create an icon that reflects the functionality of the new feature.
2. Derive a class from **drawingtool** that implements the desired feature.
3. Add a call to **tools.addtool( )** within **setup_screen( )** to install your new function.

Some Additional Ideas

There are many additions you could make to the paint program. Probably the most useful would be to add functions to save the image of the current drawing window to disk and, similarly, read an image from disk. This way, you can work on various pictures intermittently and can begin to archive your work. To add this feature, you will need to write a function that captures the screen and writes it to disk, and a companion routine to read the saved screen image and display it. In addition, you'll need to supply a function that prompts the user for the filename to be written or read. We'll add a similar feature in Chapter 12; you may want to model your user interaction code after this feature.

Another possibility is to expand some of the existing member functions. For instance, you could modify the text member function, **typetexttool::draw( )**, so that it can type vertical text or text automatically scaled or justified. Each of these can be added with a minimal amount of effort.

A final idea is to add a function that allows the user to cut out a portion of the image and move it elsewhere. You could implement this feature by letting the user mark off a rectangular region of the drawing window and then use **getimage( )** and **putimage( )** to move it to another location.

• USERTOOL.H

```
// USERTOOL.H: User interface tools used in the paint program.
// Save the drawing window in the current screen.
#ifndef USERTOOLH
#define USERTOOLH
#include "draw.h"
#include "gpopup.h"

#define FILL_HEIGHT 16          // All 12 of the BGI fill patterns
#define NUM_FILLS_WIDE 12       // are 16 pixels high in size
#define BORDER 2                // Two-pixel border is used
extern int textmenux;           // Global values that specify where the
extern int textmenuy;           // Text pull-down menu should appear
extern int linemenux;           // Specify where the Line pull-down menu
extern int linemenuy;           // should appear
extern int maxx, maxy;          // Maximum coordinates of drawing area
extern int iconwd, iconht;      // Pixel dimensions of icons
extern gwindows w;              // A window object for pop-up menus

void read_icon(int x, int y, char *filename);

class quittool : public drawingtool {
public:
  virtual void draw(void);
};

// User has selected one of the fill patterns. Find which one it is
// and set globalfillstyle to this type
class changefillpatterntool : public drawingtool {
public:
  int filltype;                 // The new fill style
```

```
    virtual void draw(void);
    virtual void finishdrawing(void);
};

// User has selected one of the fill colors. Find which one it is
// and set globalfillcolor to this value
class changefillcolortool : public drawingtool {
public:
    int fillcolor;
    virtual void draw(void);
    virtual void finishdrawing(void);
};

// User has selected the drawcolor block. Change globaldrawcolor
// to the color used by globalfillcolor, which is the current color
// in the drawcolor block.
class changedrawcolortool : public drawingtool {
public:
    virtual void draw(void);
};

// User has selected Text main menu command. Pull down the Text menu
// and let the user select one of the fonts. Load this new font, if
// any is selected.
const WINDOW_LINES = 5;
class changefonttool : public drawingtool {
public:
    int fontstyle;
    virtual void draw(void);
    virtual void startdrawing(void);
    virtual void updatedrawing(void);
    virtual void finishdrawing(void);
};

// Pull down Line menu. Change globallinestyle to the line type
// selected from the menu, if any.
#define LINE_HEIGHT 10
#define LINE_WIDTH 40
#define MAX_LINESTYLES 4
class changelinestyletool : public drawingtool {
public:
    int linestyle;
    int maxlinestyles;
    virtual void draw(void);
    virtual void performdraw(void);
    virtual void startdrawing(void);
    virtual void updatedrawing(void);
    virtual void finishdrawing(void);
};

#endif
```

• USERTOOL.CPP

```
// USERTOOL.CPP: User interface tools used in the paint program.
#include <stdio.h>
#include <alloc.h>
#include <stdlib.h>
#include <graphics.h>
#include "draw.h"
#include "usertool.h"
#include "kbdmouse.h"
#include "gpopup.h"
#include "gtext.h"

int textmenux;          // Global values that specify where the
int textmenuy;          // Text pull-down menu should appear
int linemenux;          // Specifies where the Line pull-down menu
int linemenuy;          // should appear
int iconwd;             // The pixel width of icons
int iconht;             // The pixel height of icons
gwindows w;  // Declare a window object to be used in the pop-up menus

// This object terminates the program
void quittool::draw(void)
{
  closegraph();
  exit(0);
}

// This function is called when the left mouse button is pressed
// while the mouse is within the list of fill patterns. This
// code then determines which fill pattern was selected based
// on the mouse's coordinates and then sets this fill style
// as the global fill pattern.
void changefillpatterntool::draw(void)
{
  int x, i, fillwd, mx, my;

  filltype = 0;
  fillwd = (getmaxx()-1-iconwd*2+2) / (NUM_FILLS_WIDE+1);
  for (i=0, x=iconwd*2+2+fillwd; i<NUM_FILLS_WIDE; i++, x+=fillwd) {
    mouse.getcoords(mx, my);
    if (mouse.inbox(x, getmaxy()-FILL_HEIGHT*2, x+fillwd,
      getmaxy()-FILL_HEIGHT, mx, my)) {
      finishdrawing();
      return;
    }
    filltype++;
  }
}

// Sets the global fill style to the fill style the user has selected
// from the fill style palette (see the draw() member function). This
// code is separated from draw() so that we can change its behavior
// in the CAD porgram.
```

```
void changefillpatterntool::finishdrawing(void)
{
  globalfillstyle = filltype;
  setfillstyle(globalfillstyle, globalfillcolor);
  setlinestyle(SOLID_LINE, 0, THICK_WIDTH);
  mouse.hide();
  // Show the new fill style
  int fillwd = (getmaxx()-1-iconwd*2+2) / (NUM_FILLS_WIDE+1);
  bar3d(iconwd*2+2+2, getmaxy()-FILL_HEIGHT*2+2,
    iconwd*2+2+fillwd-2, getmaxy()-2, 0, 0);
  setlinestyle(SOLID_LINE, 0, NORM_WIDTH);
  mouse.show();
}


// User has selected one of the fill colors. Find which one it is
// and set globalfillcolor to this value.
void changefillcolortool::draw(void)
{
  int maxcolors, colorwd, fillwd, i, x, mx, my;

  fillcolor = 0;
  fillwd = (getmaxx()-1-iconwd*2+2) / (NUM_FILLS_WIDE+1);
  maxcolors = getmaxcolor();
  colorwd = (getmaxx()-1-iconwd*2+2-fillwd) / (maxcolors + 1);
  for (i=0, x=iconwd*2+2+fillwd; i<=maxcolors; i++, x+=colorwd) {
    mouse.getcoords(mx, my);
    if (mouse.inbox(x, getmaxy()-FILL_HEIGHT,
      x+colorwd, getmaxy(), mx, my)) {
      finishdrawing();
      return;
    }
    fillcolor++;
  }
}


// Sets the global fill color and displays the color in the box to
// the left of the color palette. This is a virtual function so that
// we can extend its code in the CAD program.
void changefillcolortool::finishdrawing(void)
{
  globalfillcolor = fillcolor;
  setfillstyle(globalfillstyle, globalfillcolor);
  setlinestyle(SOLID_LINE, 0, THICK_WIDTH);
  int fillwd = (getmaxx()-1-iconwd*2+2) / (NUM_FILLS_WIDE+1);
  mouse.hide();
  // Show the new fill color
  bar3d(iconwd*2+2+2, getmaxy()-FILL_HEIGHT*2+2,
    iconwd*2+2+fillwd-2, getmaxy()-2, 0, 0);
  setlinestyle(SOLID_LINE, 0, NORM_WIDTH);
  mouse.show();
}


// User has selected the drawcolor block. Change globaldrawcolor
// to the color used by globalfillcolor, which is the current color
```

```
// in the drawcolor block.
void changedrawcolortool::draw(void)
{
  int fillwd = (getmaxx()-1-iconwd*2+2) / (NUM_FILLS_WIDE+1);
  globaldrawcolor = globalfillcolor;
  setfillstyle(globalfillstyle, globalfillcolor);
  setlinestyle(SOLID_LINE, 0, THICK_WIDTH);
  setcolor(globaldrawcolor);
  mouse.hide();
  bar3d(iconwd*2+2+2, getmaxy()-FILL_HEIGHT*2+2, // Show new color as
    iconwd*2+2+fillwd-2, getmaxy()-2, 0, 0);      // border to the block
  setlinestyle(SOLID_LINE, 0, NORM_WIDTH);
  mouse.show();
}

// The user has selected the Text main menu command. Pull down the Text
// menu and let the user select one of the fonts. Load this new font, if
// any is selected.
void changefonttool::draw(void)
{
  startdrawing();
  updatedrawing();
}

// Paints the Text pull-down menu
void changefonttool::startdrawing(void)
{
  textsettingstype savetext;
  int windowwidth, windowheight, offs, i;
  char *strings[WINDOW_LINES] = {"Default", "Triplex",
    "Small", "Sans Serif", "Gothic"};

  gettextsettings(&savetext);
  settextstyle(DEFAULT_FONT,HORIZ_DIR,1);
  windowwidth = textwidth("Sans Serif") + BORDER;
  windowheight = (textheight("S")+2) * WINDOW_LINES + 3 * BORDER;
  settextstyle(savetext.font, savetext.direction, savetext.charsize);
  w.gpopup(textmenux, textmenuy, textmenux+windowwidth+BORDER,
    textmenuy+windowheight, SOLID_LINE, getmaxcolor(),
    SOLID_FILL, LIGHTGRAY, BLACK);
  mouse.hide();
  settextjustify(LEFT_TEXT,TOP_TEXT);
  settextstyle(DEFAULT_FONT,HORIZ_DIR,1);
  setcolor(getmaxcolor());
  offs = BORDER;
  for (i=0; i<WINDOW_LINES; i++) {
    gprintfxy(BORDER,offs,"%s",strings[i]);
    offs += textheight(strings[i]) + 2;
  }
  mouse.show();
}

// Waits for user input and then determines which font was selected
// from the Text menu. If a font is selected, the global settings
```

```
// are changed in the finishdrawing() function.
void changefonttool::updatedrawing(void)
{
  int offs, mx, my;
  char *strings[WINDOW_LINES] = {"Default", "Triplex",
    "Small", "Sans Serif", "Gothic"};

  while (!mouse.buttonpressed(LEFT_BUTTON)) {
    if (getkey() == 0x1B) {
      w.gunpop();
      return;     // Quit if Esc key was pressed
    }
  }
  mouse.getcoords(mx, my);
  offs = BORDER;
  // Determine which font style the user has clicked on
  for (fontstyle=0; fontstyle<WINDOW_LINES; fontstyle++) {
    if (mouse.inbox(textmenux+BORDER, offs,
      textmenux+textwidth(strings[fontstyle]),
      textmenuy+offs+textheight(strings[fontstyle])+2, mx, my)) {
      w.gunpop();     // Remove the Text menu
      finishdrawing(); // Use the font selected in the menu
      return;
    }
    offs += textheight(strings[fontstyle]) + 2;
  }
  w.gunpop();          // No font has been selected
}


// Sets the global font settings to those selected in the Text menu
void changefonttool::finishdrawing(void)
{
  settextstyle(fontstyle, HORIZ_DIR, 1);
  globaltextstyle = fontstyle;
  while (!mouse.buttonreleased(LEFT_BUTTON)) ;
}


// High-level routine for the Line pull-down menu
void changelinestyletool::draw(void)
{
  maxlinestyles = MAX_LINESTYLES;
  performdraw();
}


// Draws the Line pull-down menu and then gets the user input
void changelinestyletool::performdraw(void)
{
  startdrawing();     // Draw the menu
  updatedrawing();    // Get the user selection and process it
}


void changelinestyletool::startdrawing(void)
{
  int windowwd, windowht, offs, i;
```

```
  windowwd = LINE_WIDTH + BORDER*6;
  windowht = LINE_HEIGHT * MAX_LINESTYLES;
  w.gpopup(linemenux, linemenuy, linemenux+windowwd+BORDER,
    linemenuy+windowht+LINE_HEIGHT/2, SOLID_LINE, getmaxcolor(),
    SOLID_FILL, LIGHTGRAY, BLACK);
  setcolor(0);         // Use black to draw the lines
  offs = BORDER;
  mouse.hide();
  for (i=0; i<maxlinestyles; i++) {
    setlinestyle(i, 0, NORM_WIDTH);
    line(BORDER*3, offs+LINE_HEIGHT/2, BORDER*3+LINE_WIDTH,
      offs+LINE_HEIGHT/2);
    offs += LINE_HEIGHT;
  }
  mouse.show();
}

// Waits for the user to make a menu selection in the Line pull-down menu.
// The user can press Esc to abort or click on the desired line
// style. The for loop determines which line style was selected, and
// finishdrawing() sets the proper global settings for this line style.
void changelinestyletool::updatedrawing(void)
{
  int mx, my, offs;

  while (!mouse.buttonpressed(LEFT_BUTTON)) {    // Wait for the user
    if (getkey() == 0x1B) {                      // to do something
      w.gunpop();              // Remove the Line pull-down menu
      return;                  // Quit if the user pressed the Esc key
    }
  }
  mouse.getcoords(mx, my);     // The mouse button was pushed. Get the
  offs = BORDER;               // mouse's coordinates.
  // Determine which line style was selected. Each line style is
  // LINE_HEIGHT in the y direction
  for (linestyle=0; linestyle<maxlinestyles; linestyle++) {
    if (mouse.inbox(linemenux+BORDER*3, linemenuy+offs-LINE_HEIGHT,
      linemenux+BORDER*3+LINE_WIDTH, linemenuy+offs+LINE_HEIGHT, mx, my))
{
      w.gunpop();          // Remove the menu from the screen
      finishdrawing();     // Set the line style to the current value
      return;
    }
    offs += LINE_HEIGHT;
  }
  w.gunpop();               // No line style has been selected
}

// Once the line style is selected from the Line menu, save
// its value in the global line style variable and switch to that
// line style. Also, when using menus, wait for the mouse to be released.
void changelinestyletool::finishdrawing(void)
{
```

```
    setlinestyle(linestyle, 0, NORM_WIDTH);
    globallinestyle = linestyle;
    while (!mouse.buttonreleased(LEFT_BUTTON)) ;
}
```

• INTERACT.H

```
// INTERACT.H: Header file for INTERACT.CPP. Ties together a
// drawing tool and the screen region that the user selects to
// activate the function.

extern int iconwd, iconht;  // Size of icons

class interact {
public :
  int cmd;                   // Letter command that selects the object
  int left, right;           // Screen region where command is displayed
  int top, bottom;
  drawingtool *itool;
  interact(int c, int l, int t, int wd, int ht,
    drawingtool *tl, char *iconname=NULL);
  virtual void select(void);
  virtual void highlight(void);
};

// This class provides access to a user interface's action function
// without changing anything on the screen
class userinteract : public interact {
public:
  // Note call to the base class constructor
  userinteract(int c, int l, int t, int r, int b,
    drawingtool *tl, char *iconname=NULL) :
    interact(c, l, t, r, b, tl, iconname) {  }
  virtual void select(void) { itool->draw(); }
};

// The primary class used to provide the user interaction tools
// for the environment. It ties together a drawing function with
// a menu option, icon, and so on.
const int NUMTOOLS = 30;
class toolset {
public:
  interact *tool[NUMTOOLS];       // List of tools
  int numtools;                   // Number of tools in list
  toolset(void) { numtools=0; }
  void addtool(interact *t);
  void anytoprocess(int c);
};

extern toolset tools;

void readicon(int x, int y, char *filename);
```

• INTERACT.CPP

```
// INTERACT.CPP: Defines a class that ties together interface objects
// on the screen, such as icons and menu entries, with their operations.
#include <stdio.h>
#include <stdlib.h>
#include <graphics.h>
#include "kbdmouse.h"
#include "drawtool.h"
#include "interact.h"

// Specify a code that can be used to select the object and a
// screen region that can be selected using the mouse to activate
// the drawing tool passed in as t. Note that the last paramter is
// optional. If included, it specifies the name of an icon file
// to read and display for this tool.
interact::interact(int c, int l, int t,
  int wd, int ht, drawingtool *tl, char *iconname)
{
  cmd = c;   itool = tl;
  left = l;  top = t;  right = l+wd;  bottom = t+ht;
  if (iconname != NULL)            // Read and display an icon if the
    readicon(left, top, iconname);   // icon name is not NULL
}

// A particular drawing tool has been selected using the mouse. Call
// its highlight function to show that it has been activated and
// then call its draw() member function.
void interact::select(void)
{
  highlight();          // Show that the option has been selected
  itool->draw();        // Do the function selected
  highlight();          // Restore the option to its normal state
}

// Highlight the option on the screen by reversing the screen image
// where the option is placed. This action can be applied to both
// icons and menu options.
void interact::highlight(void)
{
  // Allocate memory to be used to reverse screen option
  void *region = malloc(imagesize(left, top, right, bottom));
  if (region != NULL) {                       // Not enough memory
    mouse.hide();
    getimage(left, top, right, bottom, region); // Get the option's image
    putimage(left, top, region, NOT_PUT);       // Reverse it
    mouse.show();
    free(region);                               // Free the memory used
  }
}

// This function is called to add an object to the user object list
void toolset::addtool(interact *t)
```

```
{
  if (numtools >= NUMTOOLS-1) return;  // No more room in list
  tool[numtools++] = t;
}

toolset tools;                          // Declare a list of tools

// After a button press, search the icon list to see if
// the mouse is positioned over an object. If an object
// is found, execute the function associated with the object.
// The argument c specifies what action has just taken place.
// If it is a letter, then the if statement is executed and
// the list is checked to see if any of the objects have a
// cmd code equal to c. If so, the function associated with
// that object is executed. The else part is executed when c<0,
// which occurs when a mouse button has been pressed. It is
// similar to the code described previously, except that it uses
// the mouse as the selector.
void toolset::anytoprocess(int c)
{
  int i, x, y;

  if (c > 0) {                          // A letter command is supplied
    for (i=0; i<numtools; i++) {        // Find which command the letter
      if (tool[i]->cmd == c) {          // corresponds to
        tool[i]->select();              // Execute the drawing function
        return;
      }
    }
  }
  else if (c < 0) {                     // Mouse button pressed
    mouse.getcoords(x, y);              // Find which region was selected
    for (i=0; i<numtools; i++) {
      if (mouse.inbox(tool[i]->left, tool[i]->top,
        tool[i]->right, tool[i]->bottom, x, y)) {
        tool[i]->select();             // Execute the function
        return;
      }
    }
  }
}
// Reads an icon from a file and displays it. Program quits if
// the icon file cannot be found.
void readicon(int x, int y, char *filename)
{
  FILE *iconfile;
  int i, j, width, height, iconpixel;

  if ((iconfile = fopen(filename,"r")) == NULL) {
    closegraph();
    printf("Could not find icon file=%s\n", filename);
    exit(1);
  }
```

```
  fscanf(iconfile, "%d %d", &width, &height);
  if (width != iconwd || height != iconht) {
    closegraph();
    printf("Incompatible icon file.\n");
    exit(1);
  }
  // Double the size of the icon so that it is a good size
  for (j=0; j<iconht; j++) {
    for (i=0; i<iconwd; i++) {
      fscanf(iconfile, "%x", &iconpixel);
      putpixel(i+x, y+j, iconpixel);
    }
  }
  fclose(iconfile);
}
```

• PAINT.CPP

```
// PAINT.CPP: A paint program that exploits many of the BGI's built-in
// drawing functions. Several of the tools built up earlier in the book
// are put to use in this program. The paint program will run, without
// modification in most modes, although in some low-resolution modes you
// may want to make the icons smaller. The program uses KBDMOUSE.CPP
// so it supports either the mouse or the keyboard automatically.
// Most of the drawing functions used in PAINT.CPP are discussed
// in Chapter 10. Make sure to define MOUSE in the Defines field of the
// Options | Compiler | Code generation dialog box in your IDE. This
// forces the code to support the mouse, which PAINT.CPP assumes exists.
#include <stdio.h>
#include <graphics.h>
#include <stdlib.h>
#include "kbdmouse.h"          // Keyboard/mouse support
#include "gtext.h"             // Text in graphics mode tools
#include "gpopup.h"            // Graphics pop-up window package
#include "draw.h"              // The interactive drawing classes
#include "interact.h"          // Object-oriented management of objects
#include "usertool.h"          // Miscellaneous routines needed

const int ICONWD = 32;         // Use 32 x 32 icons
const int ICONHT = 32;

// Sets up the environment for the paint program
void setup_screen(void)
{
  int h, i, x, fillwd, offs, space;
  int filltype, colorwd, maxcolors, fillcolor;
  // Declare a set of drawing tools. Note that late binding
  // is used to get the power of polymorphism.
  drawingtool *changefont = new changefonttool;
  drawingtool *changelinestyle = new changelinestyletool;
  drawingtool *clearworkarea = new clearwindowtool;
  drawingtool *quit = new quittool;
  drawingtool *pencil = new penciltool;
  drawingtool *eraser = new erasertool;
```

```
drawingtool *spraycan = new spraycantool;
drawingtool *linetl = new linetool;
drawingtool *rect = new rectangletool;
drawingtool *fillrect = new fillrectangletool;
drawingtool *poly = new polygontool;
drawingtool *fillpoly = new fillpolygontool;
drawingtool *circletl = new circletool;
drawingtool *ellipsetl = new ellipsetool;
drawingtool *arctl = new arctool;
drawingtool *text = new texttool;
drawingtool *changefillpattern = new changefillpatterntool;
drawingtool *changefillcolor = new changefillcolortool;
drawingtool *changedrawcolor = new changedrawcolortool;

// Draw a main menu bar across the top of the screen. Each of the
// words in the menu bar will act as a user-interface object that
// can be selected. Some of the words, such as Text and Line, will
// cause pull-down menus to appear if the user clicks on them.
h = textheight("H") + 2;
if (getmaxcolor() == 1) setfillstyle(SOLID_FILL, 0);
  else setfillstyle(SOLID_FILL, BLUE);
bar3d(0, 0, maxx, h, 0, 0);
outtextxy(2, 2, "Text  Line  Clear  Quit");
space = textwidth("  ");
offs = 2;
int iconl = ICONWD;       // Left column of right-most icons
int iconr = ICONWD*2;     // Left column of right-most icons
iconht = ICONHT;          // Height of icons
iconwd = ICONWD;          // Pixel width of icons

tools.addtool(new interact('t', offs, 1, textwidth("Text"),
  textheight("Text")-1, changefont));
textmenux = offs;    // Set the position of the text menu
textmenuy = textheight("Text") + BORDER;
offs += textwidth("Text") + space;
tools.addtool(new interact('l', offs, 1,
  textwidth("Line")-1, textheight("Line"), changelinestyle));
linemenux = offs;    // Set the position of the line menu
linemenuy = textheight("Line") + BORDER;
offs += textwidth("Line") + space;
tools.addtool(new interact('c', offs, 1,
  textwidth("Clear")-1, textheight("Clear"), clearworkarea));
offs += textwidth("Clear") + space;
tools.addtool(new interact('q', offs, 1,
  textwidth("Quit")-1, textheight("Quit"), quit));
h += 3;
// Now draw the icons on the left-hand side of the screen
tools.addtool(new interact('s', 0, h, iconwd, iconht,
  spraycan, "spray32.icn"));
tools.addtool(new interact('l', iconl, h, iconwd, iconht,
  text, "letter32.icn"));
tools.addtool(new interact('d', 0, h+iconht, iconwd, iconht,
  linetl, "line32.icn"));
tools.addtool(new interact('p', iconl, h+iconht, iconwd,
  iconht, pencil, "pencil32.icn"));
```

```
tools.addtool(new interact('b', 0, h+2*iconht, iconwd, iconht,
  rect, "box32.icn"));
tools.addtool(new interact('r', iconl, h+2*iconht, iconwd,
  iconht, fillrect, "fbox32.icn"));
tools.addtool(new interact('c', 0, h+3*iconht, iconwd,
  iconht, circletl, "circle32.icn"));
tools.addtool(new interact('g', iconl, h+3*iconht, iconwd,
  iconht, ellipsetl, "ellpse32.icn"));
tools.addtool(new interact('p', 0, h+4*iconht, iconwd, iconht,
  poly, "poly32.icn"));
tools.addtool(new interact('x', iconl, h+4*iconht, iconwd,
  iconht, fillpoly, "fpoly32.icn"));
tools.addtool(new interact('e', 0, h+5*iconht, iconwd,
  iconht, eraser, "erase32.icn"));
tools.addtool(new interact('a', iconl, h+5*iconht, iconwd,
  iconht, arctl, "arc32.icn"));

// Draw a backdrop below the icons
setfillstyle(SOLID_FILL, BLUE);
bar3d(0, h+6*iconht, iconr, maxy, 0, 0);

// Create the fill pattern box. This will appear on the lower portion
// of the screen.
fillwd = (maxx-1-iconr+2) / (NUM_FILLS_WIDE+1);
globalfillcolor = getmaxcolor(); // Start fill color at maxcolor
globaldrawcolor = globalfillcolor;
filltype = 0;
for (i=0, x=iconr+2+fillwd; i<NUM_FILLS_WIDE; i++,x+=fillwd) {
  setfillstyle(filltype, globalfillcolor);
  bar3d(x, maxy-FILL_HEIGHT*2, x+fillwd, maxy-FILL_HEIGHT, 0, 0);
  filltype++;
}
rectangle(iconr+2, maxy-FILL_HEIGHT*2, maxx, maxy);
tools.addtool(new userinteract('w', iconr+2+fillwd,
  maxy-FILL_HEIGHT*2, fillwd*NUM_FILLS_WIDE, FILL_HEIGHT,
  changefillpattern));
globalfillstyle = SOLID_FILL;

maxcolors = getmaxcolor();
colorwd = (maxx-1-iconr+2-fillwd) / (maxcolors + 1);
fillcolor = 0;
for (i=0, x=iconr+2+fillwd; i<=maxcolors; i++, x+=colorwd) {
  setfillstyle(SOLID_FILL, fillcolor);
  bar3d(x, maxy-FILL_HEIGHT, x+colorwd, maxy, 0, 0);
  fillcolor++;
}
tools.addtool(new userinteract('z', iconr+2+fillwd,
  maxy-FILL_HEIGHT, fillwd*maxcolors, FILL_HEIGHT, changefillcolor));
setlinestyle(SOLID_LINE, 0, THICK_WIDTH);
setfillstyle(globalfillstyle, globalfillcolor);
bar3d(iconr+4, maxy-FILL_HEIGHT*2+2, iconr+fillwd, maxy-2, 0, 0);
tools.addtool(new userinteract('y', iconr+2,
  maxy-FILL_HEIGHT*2, fillwd, FILL_HEIGHT*2, changedrawcolor));
setlinestyle(SOLID_LINE, 0, NORM_WIDTH);
```

```c
    // Draw main draw area window
    wl = iconr+2+1;    wt = h;
    wr = maxx-1;
    wb = maxy-FILL_HEIGHT*2-2-1;
    rectangle(wl-1, wt-1, wr+1, wb+1);
    globalfillstyle = SOLID_FILL;
    globallinestyle = SOLID_LINE;
    globaltextstyle = DEFAULT_FONT;
}

int main(void)
{
    int c, errcode, gmode, gdriver = DETECT;

    initgraph(&gdriver, &gmode, "\\tcpp\\bgi");
    if ((errcode=graphresult()) != grOk) {
        printf("Graphics error: %s\n", grapherrormsg(errcode));
        exit(1);                      // Return with error code
    }
    maxx = getmaxx();  maxy = getmaxy();
    setup_screen();
    mouse.init();
    do {
        c = mouse.waitforinput(LEFT_BUTTON);
        tools.anytoprocess(c);
    } while (1);
}
```

12

A CAD Program

The paint program we developed in Chapter 11 provides a graphics environment for drawing figures and shapes. In this chapter, we'll extend the paint program so that it becomes a working drawing or CAD package. The differences between the two graphics programs may seem minor based on appearance; however, internally the two differ in several important ways. We'll explore these differences throughout this chapter as we discuss how the CAD program is written and how it functions. We'll also outline several enhancements that you might want to add to the program to extend its capabilities further.

PAINTING VERSUS DRAFTING

The environment for the CAD program is shown in Figure 12.1. Although the program looks like last chapter's paint program, the two have significant differences. For instance, the paint program is designed to provide an environment for drawing pictures—much like an artist painting with watercolors. Once a scene is painted, it's difficult to change it. The CAD program, on the other hand, is designed so that each of the scenes it displays is constructed from individual components that can readily be moved, rotated, deleted, stored in a file, and so on.

The flexibility of the CAD program is due to the fact that it maintains a list of all the graphics objects that are in its drawing window. This list contains various attributes associated with each figure, such as its size, color, and location. In addition, the dimensioning information is saved in world coordinates so that it can more easily match the specifications of a real world object.

Figure 12.1 We will build several files in this chapter to create the environment of the CAD program.

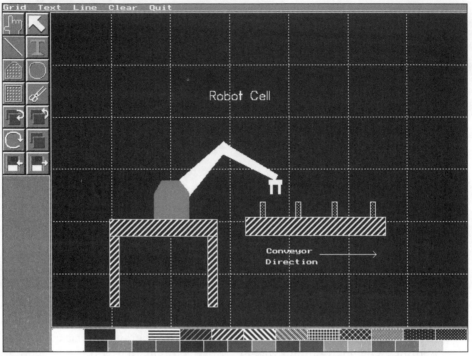

With this new object list, we can easily access, manipulate, and move each of the graphics objects in the drawing window.

Here is a summary of the major enhancements included in the CAD program:

- Stores all objects in real world coordinates
- Allows the user to select and move objects
- Uses an object list to internally represent graphics figures
- Supports a rotate and duplication feature
- Draws dimensioning lines
- Displays an alignment grid
- Allows the order in which objects are drawn to be changed
- Allows drawings to be saved to and read from a file
- Allows modification of the drawing parameters of each object

Table 12.1 Source Files Specific to the CAD Program

Filename	Description
CAD.CPP	Contains the main( ) function for the CAD program
CADDRAW.H	Contains class definitions and constants used in CADDRAW.CPP
CADDRAW.CPP	Supplies the user interaction and miscellaneous functions used in the CAD program
GOBJLIST.H	Contains class definitions and constants used in GOBJLIST.CPP
GOBJLIST.CPP	Maintains a list of figures in the drawing window
GOBJECT.H	Contains class definitions and constants used in GOBJECT.CPP
GOBJECT.CPP	Provides the objects used to represent the figures in the drawing window

In order to support each of these features, the CAD program will become rather large. Fortunately, we'll be able to exploit C++'s inheritance capability and build upon the code we used in the paint program. We will, however, have to develop seven new files that support the specialized functions for the CAD program. These files, discussed in this chapter, are listed in Table 12.1 along with a short description of each.

The CAD.CPP file is similar to the main source file developed for the paint program in Chapter 11, so it won't be the primary focus of this chapter. Instead, we'll devote the majority of this chapter to discussions of GOBJLIST.CPP, GOBJECT.CPP, and CADDRAW.CPP.

Because of the large size of the CAD program, the program only supports the line, polygon, circle, and text drawing functions. These functions provide enough power to make a useful CAD package. However, you could easily modify the CAD program to include several of the other drawing functions found in the paint program.

In addition, the program is currently designed to work best in one of the high-resolution EGA or VGA modes. You may want to adjust the sizing of the icons or the size of the drawing window if you use other modes.

SETTING UP THE SCREEN

In you look closely at Figure 12.1, you'll notice that the environment of the CAD program is slightly different than the paint program. There are a few new icons and a grid pattern added to the drawing window. Each of these changes can be found in the **setup_screen( )** function in CAD.CPP, which is used to create the environment of the CAD program.

Let's start by examining the new icon patterns and their corresponding functions. If you review CAD.CPP, you'll notice that several new or modified calls are being made to **addtool( )** in **setup_screen( )**. We are, however, using the same technique for maintaining a list of all the drawing tools. Therefore, the majority of the **setup_screen( )** function relates to adding the various drawing tools in the CAD program to the list of interactive tools that can be used.

A less visible change to **setup_screen( )** is that the drawing window is set up to reflect real world coordinates that are 7 units wide by 6 units high. (You can consider the units to be of any type—inches, feet, kilometers, and so on.) This is done by the following two statements in **setup_screen( )**:

```
set_window(0.0, 7.0, 0.0, 6.0);
set_viewport(wl, wt, wr, wb);
```

Both of these functions were introduced in Chapter 5. To refresh your memory, they are used to set the relationship between real world coordinates and screen coordinates. The function **set_window( )** defines the real world coordinate boundaries to be between (0.0, 0.0) and (7.0, 6.0). The **set_viewport( )** function (keep in mind that this function is different than the BGI's **setviewport( )** function), defines the bounds of the drawing window for the MATRIX.CPP package.

A new feature added to the CAD program is the grid displayed in the drawing window. It is drawn by the **draw_grid( )** function located in CADDRAW.CPP. You'll find a call to this function in **setup_screen( )** after the window and viewports are initialized. The grid is designed to help you align objects in the drawing window. It consists of a series of horizontal and vertical dashed lines, spaced 1 unit apart in real world coordinates. After the line style is temporarily changed to dotted lines, the grid is drawn in **draw_grid( )** with the two **for** loops:

```
for (j=1; j<6; j++) {
  WORLDtoPC(0.0, 0.0+j, x, y);
  line(wl, y, wr, y);
}
for (i=1; i<7; i++) {
  WORLDtoPC(0.0+i, 0.0, x, y);
  line(x, wt, x, wb);
}
```

The first **for** loop sequences through the horizontal lines extending across the screen, the second **for** loop draws the vertical lines. Notice that the index variables are added to real world coordinates, which are then converted to screen coordinates by **WORLDtoPC( )** and then drawn. This ensures that the lines are spaced according to the dimensions of the world coordinates. You may need to adjust the values passed to **set_window( )** and used in the **for** loops so that your grid pattern contains square-looking cells.

A global flag called **gridon** (defined in CAD.CPP) controls whether the grid is displayed. If **gridon** is set to a value of 1, the grid is displayed; if it's set to 0, however, the grid won't be displayed. To toggle the display of the grid, you can select the Grid menu command in the main menu bar. The CADDRAW package derives the **togglegridtool** class from **drawingtool** so that it can respond to the menu selection. In particular, CADDRAW.CPP overrides the **drawingtool**'s **draw( )** member function to turn the grid on or off and repaint the drawing window with the new setting. The **setup_screen( )** function adds a **togglegridtool** to the program's list of user-selectable tools.

Now that we've looked at the major changes that are visible in the environment, let's turn to the unique internal parts of the CAD program.

THE OBJECT LIST

One of the major differences between the paint program in Chapter 11 and the CAD program is that the CAD program maintains a list of all the objects in its drawing window. This list is much like the object-oriented list, found in INTERACT.CPP, that we used to tie together the icons, pull-down menus, and commands on the screen in the paint program with their operations.

As was the case in INTERACT.CPP, the list of objects is implemented as a class that contains an array of pointers to objects (we'll discuss these objects in a bit). Each figure on the screen will have an object associated with it in the list. The new class type, **gobjlist**, manages the list of graphics figures and is defined in GOBJLIST.H as:

```
// Maximum number of objects maintained in figure list
const int NUMGOBJECTS = 50;
class gobjlist {
public:
  drawingtool *gobjects[NUMGOBJECTS];  // List of graphics figures
  int nextobj;                         // Number of graphics objects
  int currentobj;                      // Currently active object
  int selectedobj;                     // Currently selected object
  gobjlist(void) { selectedobj = -1; }
  void addobj(drawingtool *obj);
  void deleteobj(void);
  void deleteall(void);
  void fliptoback(void);
  void fliptofront(void);
  void duplicate(void);
  void rotate(void);
  void select(void);
  void move(void);
  void mark(int obj);
  void displayall(void);
  int savefiglist(FILE *fp);
  int readfiglist(FILE *fp);
};
```

Table 12.2 Member Functions in the gobjlist Class

Member Function	Description
addobj()	Adds an object to the gobjects array
deleteall()	Deletes all objects from the gobjects array and clears the screen
deleteobj()	Deletes the current object from the gobjects array and removes its figure from the screen
displayall()	Displays all of the objects in the gobjects array on the screen
duplicate()	Duplicates the current object
fliptoback()	Moves the current object to the back of the screen
fliptofront()	Moves the current object to the front of the screen
mark()	Displays a bounding box around the current object
move()	Enables the user to interactively move the current object
readfiglist()	Reads a list of figures from a text file and displays them
rotate()	Rotates the current object by 45 degrees
savefiglist()	Saves the list of figures to a text file
select()	Enables the user to specify which object is the current object

---

Table 12.2 provides a short description of each of the member functions in **gobjlist**.

As this definition shows, a **gobjlist** object contains a list of pointers to **drawingtool**s in the array **gobjects**. Are these the same **drawingtool**s we developed in Chapter 10 and used in the paint program? Not quite. The objects in **gobjects** are specialized versions of the drawing tools. In other words, these objects are derived from the **drawingtool** objects we used in the paint program. We'll talk more about them in an upcoming section, but first let's get back to the details of **gobjlist**. You'll notice that **gobjects** is declared to be large enough to hold **NUMGOBJECTS** objects, which in turn is defined to be 50. You may want to increase this number if you want to have more than 50 graphics figures on the screen at a time. A global **gobjlist** object, called **figlist**, is declared in CADDRAW.CPP and is used throughout the CAD program to access the features of the **gobjlist** class and holds the list of graphics objects on the screen.

A graphics figure is added to the **gobjects** array by a call to the **gobjlist** member function **addobj()**. It appends the **drawingtool** object passed into the function to the **gobjects** array if there is room. In addition, **addobj()** increments the **nextobj** variable that specifies the next free location in the **gobjects** array. At the same time, the variable **currentobj**, which points to the object in the array that is currently being manipulated, is set to the object just added.

The remaining member functions in **gobjlist** are also used to manipulate the graphics figures in the **gobjects** list. These functions manage which objects are displayed and in what order. For instance, there are member functions to delete, duplicate, move, and select graphics objects on the screen. We'll look at these additional member functions when we discuss the various operations supported in the CAD program.

DRAWING OBJECTS

The CAD program supports a limited set of drawing functions. These include a line drawing routine, a polygon function, a text routine, and a circle drawing function. Each of these routines uses the same code we used in the paint program to draw their figures. (Recall that these drawing tools were implemented as classes that were derived from the base class **drawingtool**.) Actually, these tools won't be exactly the same. We've extended them by deriving a new set of tools so that they add the figures that they draw to **figlist**. For instance, we've derived a **lineobj** class from the **linetool** class that we used in Chapter 11. Figure 12.2 shows the new class hierarchy. The code for these new tools is included in GOBJECT.H and GOBJECT.CPP, which are listed at the end of this chapter.

Figure 12.2 The CAD drawing tools are derived from those in DRAW.CPP.

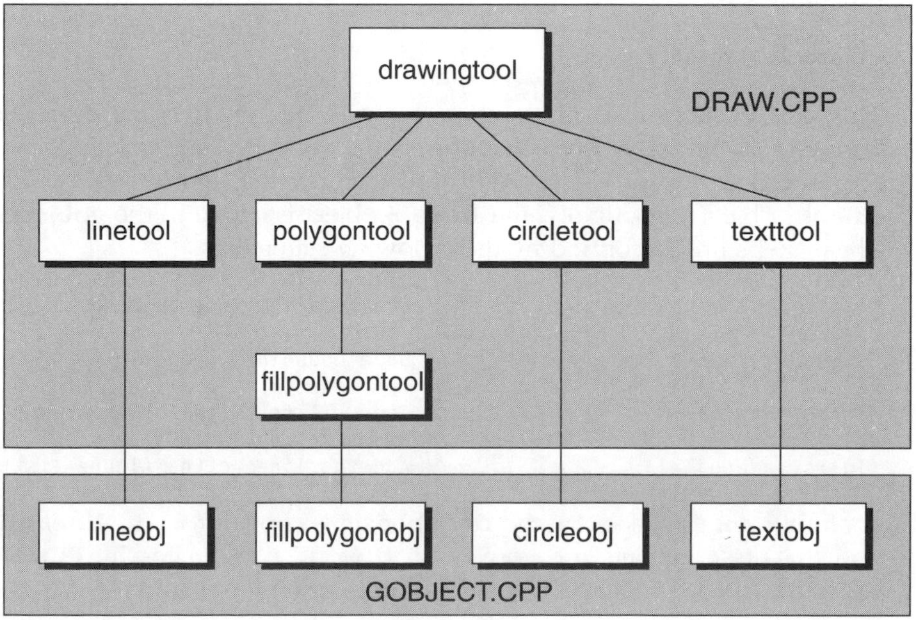

So what do these new classes contain and how are they used? Here's a brief list of the new features you'll find in them:

- Save the coordinates of their figures in world coordinates
- Provide member functions to select, move, duplicate, translate, save, load, and rotate a particular figure
- Override the inherited **finishdrawing( )** member function so figures are added to the object list after they are drawn

One important point to note is that all the graphics objects are saved in world coordinates. This is done so that the objects can easily be manipulated in the program. If you examine the various member functions in the derived **drawingtool** classes, you will see the conversions that are made between screen and world coordinates. In the next section, you'll learn how objects are drawn and added to the graphics object list.

Working with Lines

The new line drawing class, **lineobj**, is derived from DRAW.CPP's **linetool** class. We're overriding the original drawing tools so that we can add the new functionality outlined in the previous section. For instance, **finishdrawing( )** is overridden so that after a line is drawn, which is the only time it is called, we can add the figure to the **gobjects** array in **figlist**. Therefore, the first thing our new **finishdrawing( )** member function does is call its inherited member function:

```
linetool::finishdrawing();
```

This call ensures that all the finishing touches on the figure are handled correctly as before. Next, a **lineobj** is created, called **nl**, and the contents of the **linetool** object, which were used to draw the figure, are copied to the **lineobj** object. And, finally, the **lineobj** object is added to the **gobjects** array. These steps are performed by the following statements:

```
lineobj *nl = new lineobj;          // Create a new line object
getbounds(left, top, right, bottom);
PCtoWORLD(x1, y1, xw1, yw1);        // Save endpoints in world
PCtoWORLD(x2, y2, xw2, yw2);        // coordinates
nl->copy(this);                     // Copy all settings to new object
draw_arrows();                      // Draw arrows on new line
figlist.addobj(nl);                 // Add the line to the figure list
```

It's important to notice that the **lineobj** data is copied from the **linetool** object and that its endpoints are converted to world coordinates by **PCtoWORLD** (MATRIX.CPP), and saved in world coordinates.

The **getbounds()** member function, which is near the top of this sequence of statements, calculates the PC screen boundaries of the object. We'll use these screen boundaries later when we check whether the mouse has been clicked while over the object. Note that the boundary values in **lineobj::getbounds()** are offset by three pixels. This is done so that when the line is horizontal or vertical it appears slightly larger, making the line easier to select.

The **draw_arrows()** function appends arrowheads to the line segment if the user has selected this style. Three new line types have been added to the Line menu to support these arrows. The new pull-down menu for the Line menu command, which includes these new arrow line styles, is shown in Figure 12.3. The **CADchangelinestyletool** object, defined in CADDRAW.CPP, paints the Line menu and manages the user interaction. We've derived the object from the **changelinestyletool** in USERTOOL.CPP so that it can share as much of the paint program's Line menu code as possible.

The arrowhead lines require special attention. It is important to maintain which side of the line the arrowhead is to be placed on. Depending on the style of arrow selected, either **left_arrow**, **right_arrow**, or both are set to a value of 1. These values are then used in the function **draw_arrows()** to select which arrows are displayed. The arrow size is specified by **ARROWSIZE**, and is set in GOBJECT.CPP to be 3 pixels in width and height.

The one difficult part in dealing with arrows is that the arrowheads must be rotated so that they are oriented at the same angle as the line segment to which they are attached. These adjustments are done in **draw_arrows()**.

The **draw_arrows()** routine draws an arrow on the leading edge of the line segment, at (x1, y1) if **left_arrow** is non-zero, and an arrow on the trailing edge of the line segment, at (x2, y2) if **right_arrow** is non-zero. The arrowhead itself is made from two connected line segments that are joined to one of the ends of the line. The points describing this process are contained in the array **arrowhead**. The arrowhead figure is adjusted so that its angle matches that of the line segment by first translating its center to the origin, rotating it,

Figure 12.3 The Line menu in the CAD program has three additional line styles.

and then translating it back to the tip of the line segment. This process is performed by the lines:

```
PCtranslatepoly(3,arrowhead, -x1+wl, -y1+wt);
PCotatepoly(3, arrowhead, angle);
PCtranslatepoly(3, arrowhead, x1-wl, y1-wt);
```

Finally, the arrow is drawn by the statement:

```
drawpoly(3, arrowhead);
```

Drawing Polygons and Circles

Displaying and managing figures of polygons and circles is handled by the **fillpolygonobj** and **circleobj** classes. These classes are derived from the equivalent interactive drawing tools from DRAW.CPP. You'll find that they are quite similar to the **lineobj** class discussed in the last section; therefore, we'll focus on their differences.

You'll notice that the **getbounds( )** member functions for the two classes are quite different. The reason is that each object stores its figure information differently. For instance, we saw in **lineobj** that the endpoints readily gave us the dimensions of a bounding box. For a circle or polygon, however, the task is a bit more complicated, although only slightly so.

In the case of a circle, the bounding box is calculated by adding or subtracting the radius of the circle to its center. For example, the statement

```
r = centerx + absradiusx
```

calculates the right edge of the circle. Recall that **absradiusx** was saved by the **circletool** class when the figure was drawn. Calculating the top and bottom of the circle is a little different. In these instances, we need to account for the screen's aspect ratio. To calculate the top of the circle, therefore, we use the statement

```
t = centery - absradiusx * aspectratio;
```

where **aspectratio** is a global variable calculated in **main( )** and is based on the values returned by the BGI function **getaspectratio( )**.

Determining the bounds of the polygon is unique in that each of the vertices of the polygon must be tested to see whether it lies on the bounding box. The code, however, is fairly straightforward.

Text as a Graphics Object

In order to support text as a graphics object, we've had to make a few changes to the **texttool** class that appeared in the paint program. These changes appear in the derived class **textobj**, also included in GOBJECT.CPP. One modification is that **finishdrawing( )** is overridden so that **addobj( )** can be called to add the text string the user types to the object list. The string itself is saved in **texttool**'s **string** field. The starting screen coordinates of the text are stored in **leftx** and **lefty**. These are converted to world coordinates and saved in the **pointsw** component of the **textobj** class.

Displaying text stored in a **textobj** is handled by the **display( )** member function. It is somewhat complicated by the fact that the text string may contain newline characters. Therefore, we must check whether a newline character is present and then skip to the next lines by adjusting the current position (CP). This process is handled by the **for** loop in **display( )**:

```
for (i=0; i<len; i++)
  if (string[i] == '\n') {          // Newline character
    lefty += textheight("S");       // Skip to next line
    moveto(leftx-wl, lefty-wt);     // Adjust current position
  }
  else {
    c[0] = string[i];               // Write out the next character
    outtext(c);
  }
```

Displaying the Graphics Objects

Because the CAD program is designed so that you can modify the objects in the drawing window, it must have functions that are capable of redrawing the screen after the objects are changed. This is the purpose of many of the member functions in the **gobjlist** class and the tools in GOBJECT.CPP, which we have not touched on yet.

For instance, in the last section we saw how **textobj::display( )** was used to display one or more lines of text stored in a string. There are comparable member functions for the **lineobj**, **fillpolygonobj**, and **circleobj** classes. In addition, the **displayall( )** routine in **gobjlist** draws all the objects in the figure list. The heart of this routine is the **for** loop that sequences through the **gobjects** array—until the **nextobj** index is reached—and calls each object's **display( )** member function. Therefore, each graphics object draws itself:

```
for (obj=0; obj<nextobj; obj++)
  gobjects[obj]->display();
```

DELETING A GRAPHICS OBJECT

Now let's take a look at how to remove an object from the drawing window. Deleting an object from the screen involves two steps. First, the object is deleted from the internal **gobjects** array, then the whole screen is cleared and all remaining objects in **gobjects** are displayed.

The **deleteobj( )** member function in the GOBJLIST.CPP source file removes the object indexed by the global variable **currentobj**. The function starts by calling the destructor for the deleted **drawingtool**:

```
delete(gobjects[currentobj]);
```

Next, the array is rearranged so that the current object is moved to the end of the **gobjects** array and all objects that were above it are moved down one index location:

```
for (i=currentobj; i<nextobj-1; i++)
  gobjects[i] = gobjects[i+1];
```

Then, the index pointer, called **nextobj**, which points to the next available object location in **gobjects**, is decremented by 1. In addition, a test is made to see if the last object is the one being deleted. If so, the **currentobj** index is also decremented. Finally, the screen is cleared and all the objects in the object list are redrawn by calling these functions:

```
cleardrawingarea();
displayall();
```

The function **cleardrawingarea( )** clears the drawing window by using the BGI **clearviewport( )** function and, in addition, draws a grid if the flag **gridon** is 1. The second function, **displayall( )**, redraws all of the objects on the screen, except, of course, the object just deleted. Notice that after the delete operation, the **currentobj** normally becomes the next object in the array **gobjects**.

THE DUPLICATE( ) FUNCTION

The CAD program also includes the **duplicate( )** function to duplicate objects in the object list. This member function is included in the **gobjlist** class and copies the object indexed by **currentobj** to the next free location in **gobjects** pointed to by the variable **nextobj**.

Actually, each **drawingtool** object now has its own duplicate member function, called **dup( )**, that is called to have an object duplicate itself and return a pointer to the new object. Of course, simply duplicating all the information about an object will cause the new figure to be displayed over the original object. To avoid this, the **dup( )** member functions translate their figure's coordinates by 0.1 (in world coordinates) in the x and y directions. The translated copy of the current object, which now becomes the current object, is drawn at the end of **duplicate( )** by the call to:

```
gobjects[currenobj]->display();
```

The rotate() Function

Another function provided by the CAD program allows you to rotate objects about their center. This is accomplished by the **gobjlist** member function **rotate()** and the **rotate()** member functions in the new **drawingtool** objects. Once again, the **gobjlist** member function, actually calls **drawingtool**'s **rotate()** member function to perform the rotation.

These **drawingtool::rotate()** member functions use a series of calls to routines in MATRIX.CPP (Chapter 5) to rotate the current object clockwise by 45-degree increments about their center points.

If the object is a polygon or a line (circles, rectangles, and text cannot be rotated in the CAD program) then the object's center is translated to the origin, the object is rotated, and then it is translated back to its original location. Once the object is rotated, its new screen boundaries are determined by calling **getbounds()**. Finally, the screen is cleared and all objects are redrawn using **displayall()**.

Changing the Drawing Order

Each time **displayall()** is called, it draws each of the objects in the **gobjects** array, starting from the zero index and working toward the last location in the array, which is just before the index **nextobj**. Since this drawing order is always followed, objects at the beginning of the list are always drawn first. Consequently, if two objects overlap, the object closer to the beginning of the **gobjects** array is always drawn below the other.

The CAD program allows you to modify the order in which the objects are displayed by swapping the positions of objects in the **gobjects** array. For instance, to move an object behind all other objects, it is simply a matter of moving the object to the beginning of the list. This is what is done in the **gobjlist** member function **fliptoback()**. Similarly, the member function **fliptofront()** moves an object from its current location to the tail of the list so that it will be displayed last and, therefore, on top of all of the other objects. Since both are similar, let's just look at **fliptofront()**.

The function begins by testing whether the object list is empty. This is the case if **nextobj** is 0. If so, the function simply returns with no action taken:

```
if (nextobj == 0) return;
```

Next, a temporary pointer, called **temp**, is used to save the object pointed to by **currentobj**. This is the object that will be moved to the end of the **gobjects** array. Then each of the objects above **currentobj** are shifted down one position in the array by the **for** loop:

```
for (i=currentobj; i<nextobj-1; i++)
  gobjects[i] = gobjects[i+1];
```

Finally, the object, saved in **temp** is copied to the end of the object list, and the **currentobj** index is updated so it still points to the same object, even though now it is at the end of the list.

```
gobjects[i] = temp;
currentobj = i;
```

Once the object list is modified, the drawing window is updated by clearing the screen and displaying all objects in **gobjects** by executing these two statements:

```
cleardrawingarea();
displayall();
```

This action causes the current object to be displayed on top of all the other graphics objects in the drawing window.

SELECTING AN OBJECT

The CAD program enables you to select and move objects in the drawing window. To select an object, you must first click the mouse on the pointer icon. Then you can select an object by clicking the left mouse button while the mouse cursor is positioned within the bounds of the desired object. A dashed rectangle will appear around the figure. If another object shares the same area on the screen as the currently selected object, it can be selected instead by clicking on the mouse again in the same region. Similarly, if there are other objects in the same area, you can sequence through them by clicking the mouse several times. If an object is selected, you can unselect it by clicking on it again, or clicking somewhere in the drawing window where there aren't any objects.

The **select()** member function in the **gobjlist** class provides the user interaction to select figures in the drawing window. Rather than go through **select()**'s code line by line, let's take a high-level view of it. Its main purpose is to change the **currentobj** and **selectedobj**'s indices to the object pointed at by the mouse when the left mouse button is pressed. The **currentobj** variable specifies the index of the current, or most recently selected, object. The **selectedobj** variable also points to the currently selected object. However, if there isn't an object selected, **selectedobj** is set to -1. The object specified by **selectedobj** is the object manipulated by any subsequent calls to the functions, such as **dup()** and **rotate()**.

The **select()** function highlights the currently selected object by calling the **mark()** function. It uses the **left**, **top**, **right**, and **bottom** components of the **drawingtool** class to position a dashed rectangle around the object. The routine sets **setwritemode()** to **XOR_PUT** so that the rectangle can be exclusive-ORed on the screen and, therefore, easily moved.

Before we go on, we need to clear up one last issue. You may have noticed the following lines of code at the beginning of most of the user-interface functions:

```
if (selectedobj >= 0) {
  mark(selectedobj);
  selectedobj = -1;
}
```

These statements deselect an object if there is one selected. Recall, an object is selected if **selectedobj** contains a value other than -1. The code calls **mark()** to remove the bounding rectangle if there is a selected object. This step is taken so that the highlight box that appears around selected objects won't get in our way as we draw and manipulate objects. It's not always necessary to do this, but we're taking these steps to keep the code simple. You'll notice that the select and move operations don't remove the highlight box, since they use them.

Moving an Object

The user of the CAD program can move a selected object by clicking on the hand icon, positioning the mouse cursor over the dashed rectangle around the object, and then pressing the left mouse button and dragging the object to its new location. When the mouse button is released, the whole screen is redrawn with the object at its new location.

The figure list's **move()** function implements the code that moves the object. It keeps track of the amount that the mouse has been moved in the variables **movex** and **movey**, and maps them into world coordinates in order to translate the object. Once it is translated, the drawing window is erased and completely redrawn to reflect the object's new position.

Accessing Member Functions in gobjlist

So far, we have described several new operations that have been added to the CAD program. Most of these are included in the **gobjlist** class. But how are its member functions, like **deleteobj()**, accessed from the environment? Remember that all of our other drawing operations are linked to a **drawingtool** that is activated when an icon or some other screen object is selected. But since our **deleteobj()** function is a member of the **gobjlist** class, we can't simply add it to our list of **drawingtool** objects—it has the wrong base type. As a result, we have defined a series of **drawingtool** objects in CADDRAW.H and CADDRAW.CPP that call the appropriate actions in **gobjlist**. These classes serve as a bridge between the **drawingtool**s used in the environment and the functions provided in **gobjlist**. The **deleteobj()** member function, for example, is called within the class **deleteobjtool** that is derived from **drawingtool**. The declaration of **deleteobjtool**, therefore, is:

```
class deleteobjtool : public drawingtool {
public: virtual void draw(void);
}
```

The **draw( )** member function is overridden because this is the member function that gets called when the **drawingtool** is selected. In this case, we want **draw( )** to simply call the **deleteobj( )** member function in the global list **figlist**:

```
void deleteobjtool::draw(void) { figlist.deleteobj(); }
```

This new "drawing tool" then is added to our list of tools in the **setup_screen( )** function in CAD.CPP and is activated whenever its icon is clicked on. A similar technique is used to access the other functions in the **gobjlist** class like **fliptoback( )**, **rotate( )**, **move( )**, and so on.

SAVING THE OBJECT LIST TO A FILE

You can save your drawings to a text file by clicking on the save drawing icon. A pop-up window will appear, which prompts you for the filename to write to. The file is saved as a text file so that you can view and edit it with a text editor. The first line of the file is the string "CAD1.0." On the next line is an integer that specifies how many objects are in the file. This line is followed by the information for each figure. In particular, information for each object begins on a separate line. The first characters on each of these lines is a string that specifies which graphics object it represents. For instance, the saved data for a rectangle begins with the string "RECTANGLE."

The **savefiglistobjtool** class, defined in CADDRAW.CPP, provides the user interaction for the save operation. When the user clicks on the Save File icon, **savefiglistobjtool**'s **draw( )** function is called. The first part of the function pops up a window, shown in Figure 12.4, in the middle of the screen. It also paints a three-dimensional–looking box around the edit field where the user enters the filename. The code calls the **readstring( )** function in GTEXT.CPP to actually read the string and return the filename in the **fn** variable. Recall that

Figure 12.4 A pop-up window prompts the user for the name of a file to read.

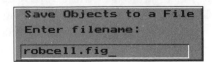

readstring( ) supports a variety of editing keys. If a filename is entered, the function calls **gobjlist**'s **savefiglist( )** function to actually save the drawing.

The **savefiglist( )** function, however, doesn't do that much. It writes the file header and the number of objects in the drawing to the file and then loops through each of the objects in the figure and tells them to save themselves. Here's the complete function:

```
// Saves all the object list to a file
int gobjlist::savefiglist(FILE *fp)
{
  int retval;

  if (selectedobj >= 0) {
    mark(selectedobj);
    selectedobj = -1;
  }
  fprintf(fp, "CAD1.0\n");          // Write a header to the file
  // Write the number of objects to the file
  fprintf(fp, "%d\n", figlist.nextobj);
  for (int obj=0; obj<nextobj; obj++)
    retval = gobjects[obj]->save(fp);
  return retval;  // Returns the status of the last save
}
```

The classes in GOBJECT.CPP extend each **drawingtool** so that they can save their drawing parameters and coordinates to a text file. Each object has a **save( )** member function that writes a single line of text with that object's information. The line object, for instance, has the following **save( )** function:

```
int lineobj::save(FILE *fp)
{
  return fprintf(fp, "LINE %d %d %d %d %lf %lf %lf %lf\n", drawcolor,
    linestyle, left_arrow, right_arrow, xw1, yw1, xw2, yw2);
}
```

The **save( )** function writes the line's information to the text file passed into the routine. The line begins with the identifying string "LINE." After this are the color, line style, and arrowhead settings for the line. The next four values are the real world coordinates of the line's endpoints. This is all the information that the CAD program needs to re-create the line.

Reading the Object List from a File

Reading the object information from a file is quite similar to the write operation. The **readfiglistobjtool** in CADDRAW.CPP hooks the code to the read file icon on the screen. It pops up a window, requesting the name of the file to read. If a valid filename is entered, it is opened and passed to **gobjlist**'s **readfiglist( )** function. As with saving the object list, each object actually reads its own information from the file. The routine reads the object type at the beginning of each line and creates an object of that type. For instance, if the code encounters the string "LINE," it creates a **lineobj** and eventually calls that object's **read( )** function to process the rest of the data. Here's the code for the **lineobj**'s **read( )** function.

```
int lineobj::read(FILE *fp)
{
  if (!fscanf(fp, "%d %d %d %d %lf %lf %lf %lf", &drawcolor,
    &linestyle, &left_arrow, &right_arrow, &xw1, &yw1, &xw2, &yw2))
    return 0;                           // Failed to read line data
  // Determine the screen positions of the object (x1,y1) and (x2,y2)
  // based on the world coordinates (xw1,yw1) and (xw2,yw2)
  WORLDtoPC(xw1, yw1, x1, y1);
  WORLDtoPC(xw2, yw2, x2, y2);
  getbounds(left, top, right, bottom);
  return 1;
}
```

The **fscanf( )** function reads the line's information, except for the "LINE" tag that **savefiglist( )** already read.

What do the other lines in the **read( )** function do? Since the files store the coordinates of the drawing in real world values, the **read( )** routines must take special care to ensure that the PC coordinates that we will use later to manipulate the object are properly initialized. The screen bounds used to select and highlight the object, for instance, must be valid PC coordinates. For this reason, the **read( )** functions typically convert the real-world coordinates to PC coordinates and then call **getbounds( )** to initialize the bounds of the figure.

CHANGING AN OBJECT'S DRAWING PARAMETERS

In Chapter 11's paint program, once you drew an object, you could not change its color or drawing settings. The CAD program extends the code in the paint program to provide this feature. It derives new classes from the paint program's three objects that control the drawing color, fill pattern, and fill color. These new classes are **CADchangedrawcolortool**, **CADchangefillpatterntool**, and **CADchangefillcolortool**, which are located in CADDRAW.CPP. The extended classes now enable you to modify the color, fill pattern, or fill color of the currently selected object. To change the fill pattern of an object, for instance, you must first select the object by clicking on the pointer tool and then on the object. Next, you must click on the desired fill pattern at the bottom of the screen. When you select one of the fill patterns, the object is redrawn with the new setting. To simplify the code, the whole scene is repainted. If no object is currently selected, the classes call the inherited code to modify the global drawing parameters, which affect the next object drawn. The other two tools work in a similar manner.

Compiling the CAD Program

The CAD program involves many source files from throughout this book. Table 12.3 list all the source files you'll need to add to a project file in order to compile and link the CAD program. Remember, as with the paint program, the CAD application is rather large, so you must compile it using the large memory model. In addition, you must define the **MOUSE** compiler constant when you compile the code so that GTEXT.CPP and GPOPUP.CPP properly support the mouse. Finally, you'll also need to create the 32 x 32 icons listed in Table 12.4.

Table 12.3 Files Needed to Compile the CAD Program

File	Header File	Chapter
CAD.CPP	None	2
CADDRAW.CPP	CADDRAW.H	12
DRAW.CPP	DRAW.H	10
DRAWTOOL.CPP	DRAWTOOL.H	10
GPOPUP.CPP	GPOPUP.H	9
GTEXT.CPP	GTEXT.H	3
INTERACT.CPP	INTERACT.H	11
KBDMOUSE.CPP	KBDMOUSE.H	7
MATRIX.CPP	MATRIX.H	5
MOUSE.CPP	MOUSE.H	7
USERTOOL.CPP	USERTOOL.H	11

Table 12.4 Icons Used in CAD.CPP

Icon Filename	Description
BACK32.ICN	Move object to back of list icon
CIRCLE32.ICN	Circle tool icon
CUT32.ICN	Delete tool icon
CW32.ICN	Rotate tool icon
DUP32.ICN	Duplicate tool icon
FBOX32.ICN	Fill rectangle tool icon
FPOLY32.ICN	Fill polygon tool icon
FRONT32.ICN	Move object to front of list icon
HAND32.ICN	Hand tool, used for moving objects

continued

Table 12.4 Icons Used in CAD.CPP (Continued)

Icon Filename	Description
LETTER32.ICN	Text tool icon
LINE32.ICN	Line tool icon
POINT32.ICN	Pointer tool icon, used for selecting objects
READ32.ICN	Load object list from file icon
SAVE32.ICN	Save object list to file icon

The following text file, TEST.FIG, renders the scene shown in Figure 12.5. To display the drawing, start the CAD program, then type **r** or click on the read file icon. In the pop-up window that appears, type **TEST.FIG**. The drawing should then appear.

```
CAD1.0
20
RECTANGLE 15 0 0 1 0.367776 0.361949 6.705779 5.554524
RECTANGLE 15 0 0 4 0.539405 2.283063 1.422067 3.591647
LINE 15 0 0 0 1.593695 1.809745 1.593695 5.540603
LINE 15 0 0 0 1.593695 1.795824 6.693520 1.795824
RECTANGLE 15 0 7 4 5.455342 0.361949 6.705779 1.795824
CIRCLE 15 1.189142 2.742459 -0.698774
CIRCLE 15 0.774256 2.745012 -0.698774
CIRCLE 15 1.192995 3.262645 -0.698774
CIRCLE 15 0.778109 3.251276 -0.698774
RECTANGLE 15 0 0 4 3.028021 0.612529 4.633975 1.600928
RECTANGLE 15 0 0 4 3.751313 0.515081 3.861646 0.946636
TEXT 15 0 5.406305 2.394432 12 Refrigerator
LINE 15 0 0 1 5.908932 2.283063 6.043783 1.851508
RECTANGLE 15 0 7 8 0.527145 3.897912 1.176883 5.095128
TEXT 15 0 1.875657 4.607889 9 Microwave
LINE 15 0 0 1 1.765324 4.635731 1.299475 4.635731
CIRCLE 15 5.418564 3.883991 0.110333
TEXT 15 0 5.161121 3.800464 5 Table
FILLPOLY 15 0 0 10 18 1.360771 4.900232 1.360771 4.900232 1.213660
    5.150812 1.176883 5.373550 1.262697 5.651972 1.446585 5.874710 2.795096
    5.359629 1.373030 4.900232 1.360771 4.900232
LINE 15 3 0 1 1.998249 5.540603 3.567426 5.540603
```

EXTENDING THE CAD PROGRAM

There are many ways to enhance the CAD program presented in this chapter. You might add functions to zoom in and out on the objects being displayed, group objects together, or resize the figures in the drawing.

Adding a zoom feature is probably the easiest. The basic idea is to change the window size of the world coordinates that are displayed on the screen. For

Figure 12.5 The TEST.FIG file displays this figure.

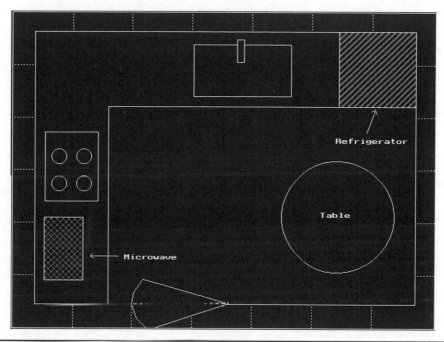

instance, to zoom in on objects in the drawing window, you can set the window to between (0.0, 0.0) and (3.0, 3.0) as follows:

```
void zoomin(void)
{
  set_window(0.0, 3.0, 0.0, 3.0);
  set_viewport(wl, wr, wt, wb);
  cleardrawingarea();
  displayall();
}
```

You might also consider adding routines that keep track of the connectivity of the object list. For instance, if you want to convert the CAD program into a flow-charting tool, you'd need to maintain a list that records which objects are connected to which. When you move an object and repaint the drawing, you'll want to use this connectivity list to determine how to redraw the objects.

● CAD.CPP

```
// CAD.CPP: A CAD program. This program exploits many of the BGI
// functions to build a simple yet powerful CAD program.
// Several of the tools built up earlier in the book are put to
```

```
// use in this program. The program will run in many of the
// graphics adapters supported by the BGI and supports many of
// their modes. However, it is currently configured so that it
// will appear best if run on an EGA or VGA display. The progam
// supports either the mouse or the keyboard automatically.
#include <stdio.h>
#include <graphics.h>
#include <stdlib.h>
#include <stdarg.h>
#include <math.h>
#include "kbdmouse.h"
#include "usertool.h"
#include "interact.h"
#include "gtext.h"                    // Text in graphics mode tools
#include "gpopup.h"                   // Graphics pop-up window package
#include "matrix.h"
#include "caddraw.h"
#include "draw.h"
#include "gobject.h"

#define ICONWD 32                      // Use 32 x 32 pixel icons
#define ICONHT 32

double aspectratio;              // Aspect ratio of the screen
int gridon;                      // Value of 1 if grid is to be displayed
extern int currentobj;           // Current graphics object in list
extern int nextobj;              // Next available slot in list of objects
int left_arrow;                  // If value of 1, adds left or right arrow
int right_arrow;                 // heads to the lines that are drawn

// Sets up the environment for the CAD program
void setup_screen(void)
{
  int h, i, x, fillwd, offset, space;
  int filltype, colorwd, maxcolors, fillcolor;
  // Declare a set of drawing tools. Note that late binding
  // is used to get the power of polymorphism.
  drawingtool *togglegrid = new togglegridtool;
  drawingtool *deleteallobj = new deleteallobjtool;
  drawingtool *changefont = new changefonttool;
  drawingtool *changelinestyle = new CADchangelinestyletool;
  drawingtool *quit = new quittool;
  drawingtool *linetl = new lineobj;
  drawingtool *fillpoly = new fillpolygonobj;
  drawingtool *circletl = new circleobj;
  drawingtool *text = new textobj;
  drawingtool *rectangletl = new fillrectangleobj;
  drawingtool *changefillcolor = new CADchangefillcolortool;
  drawingtool *changefillpattern = new CADchangefillpatterntool;
  drawingtool *changedrawcolor = new CADchangedrawcolortool;
  drawingtool *moveobj = new moveobjtool;
  drawingtool *selectobj = new selectobjtool;
  drawingtool *duplicateobj = new duplicateobjtool;
  drawingtool *deleteobj = new deleteobjtool;
```

```
drawingtool *fliptofront = new fliptofronttool;
drawingtool *fliptoback = new fliptobacktool;
drawingtool *rotateobj = new rotateobjtool;
drawingtool *savefiglistobj = new savefiglistobjtool;
drawingtool *readfiglistobj = new readfiglistobjtool;

// Draw a main menu bar across the top of the screen. Each of the
// words in the menu bar will act as a user-interface object that
// can be selected.
h = textheight("H") + 2;
if (getmaxcolor() == 1) setfillstyle(SOLID_FILL, 0);
  else setfillstyle(SOLID_FILL, BLUE);
bar3d(0, 0, maxx, h, 0, 0);
outtextxy(2, 2, "Grid  Text  Line  Clear  Quit");
space = textwidth("  ");
offset = 2;

tools.addtool(new interact('g', offset, 1,
  textwidth("Grid"), textheight("Grid")-1, togglegrid));
offset += textwidth("Grid") + space;
tools.addtool(new interact('x', offset, 1,
  textwidth("Text"), textheight("Text")-1, changefont));
textmenux = offset;    // Position of the Text pull-down menu
textmenuy = textheight("Text") + BORDER;
offset += textwidth("Text") + space;
tools.addtool(new interact('n', offset, 1,
  textwidth("Line"), textheight("Line") 1, changelinestyle));
linemenux = offset;    // Position of the Line pull-down menu
linemenuy = textheight("Line") + BORDER;
offset += textwidth("Line") + space;
tools.addtool(new interact('e', offset, 1,
  textwidth("Clear"), textheight("Clear")-1, deleteallobj));
offset += textwidth("Clear") + space;
tools.addtool(new interact('q', offset, 1,
  textwidth("Quit"), textheight("Quit")-1, quit));

// Draw the icons on the left-hand side of the screen and
// add their associated tools to the tool list
iconwd = ICONWD;   iconht = ICONHT;
int riconx = iconwd + 1;    // Leftmost column of right icon
h += 3; // Icons and the drawing window start 3 pixels below the menu bar

tools.addtool(new interact('h', 0, h, iconwd, iconht,
  moveobj, "hand32.icn"));
tools.addtool(new interact('p', riconx, h, iconwd,
  iconht, selectobj, "point32.icn"));

tools.addtool(new interact('l', 0, h+iconht, iconwd,
  iconht, linetl, "line32.icn"));
tools.addtool(new interact('t', riconx, h+iconht, iconwd,
  iconht, text, "letter32.icn"));

tools.addtool(new interact('y', 0, h+2*iconht, iconwd,
  iconht, fillpoly, "fpoly32.icn"));
```

```
      tools.addtool(new interact('c', riconx, h+2*iconht, iconwd,
        iconht, circletl, "circle32.icn"));

      tools.addtool(new interact('b', 0, h+3*iconht, iconwd,
        iconht, rectangletl, "fbox32.icn"));
      tools.addtool(new interact(DEL, riconx, h+3*iconht, iconwd,
        iconht, deleteobj, "cut32.icn"));

      tools.addtool(new interact('f', 0, h+4*iconht, iconwd,
        iconht, fliptofront, "front32.icn"));
      tools.addtool(new interact('b', riconx, h+4*iconht, iconwd,
        iconht, fliptoback, "back32.icn"));

      tools.addtool(new interact('a', 0, h+5*iconht, iconwd,
        iconht, rotateobj, "cw32.icn"));
      tools.addtool(new interact(INS, riconx, h+5*iconht, iconwd,
        iconht, duplicateobj, "dup32.icn"));

      tools.addtool(new interact('s', 0, h+6*iconht, iconwd,
        iconht, savefiglistobj, "save32.icn"));
      tools.addtool(new interact('r', riconx, h+6*iconht, iconwd,
        iconht, readfiglistobj, "read32.icn"));

      // Draw a backdrop below the icons
      setfillstyle(SOLID_FILL, BLUE);
      bar3d(0, h+7*iconht, iconwd*2, maxy, 0, 0);

      // Create the fill pattern box. This will appear on the lower
      // portion of the screen.
      fillwd = (maxx-1-iconwd*2+2) / (NUM_FILLS_WIDE+1);
      globalfillcolor = getmaxcolor();      // Start fill color and drawing
      globaldrawcolor = globalfillcolor;    // color as white
      filltype = 0;
      for (i=0, x=iconwd*2+2+fillwd; i<NUM_FILLS_WIDE; i++,
        x += fillwd) {
        setfillstyle(filltype, globalfillcolor);
        bar3d(x, maxy-FILL_HEIGHT*2, x+fillwd, maxy-FILL_HEIGHT, 0, 0);
        filltype++;
      }
      rectangle(iconwd*2+2, maxy-FILL_HEIGHT*2, maxx, maxy);
      tools.addtool(new userinteract('w', iconwd*2+2+fillwd,
        maxy-FILL_HEIGHT*2, fillwd*NUM_FILLS_WIDE, FILL_HEIGHT,
        changefillpattern));
      globalfillstyle = SOLID_FILL;
      maxcolors = getmaxcolor();
      colorwd = (maxx-1-iconwd*2+2-fillwd) / (maxcolors + 1);
      fillcolor = 0;
      for (i=0, x=iconwd*2+2+fillwd; i<=maxcolors; i++,x+=colorwd) {
        setfillstyle(SOLID_FILL, fillcolor);
        bar3d(x, maxy-FILL_HEIGHT, x+colorwd, maxy, 0, 0);
        fillcolor++;
      }
      tools.addtool(new userinteract('z', iconwd*2+2+fillwd,
        maxy-FILL_HEIGHT, fillwd*maxcolors, FILL_HEIGHT, changefillcolor));
```

```
      setlinestyle(SOLID_LINE, 0, THICK_WIDTH);
      setfillstyle(globalfillstyle, globalfillcolor);
      bar3d(iconwd*2+2+2, maxy-FILL_HEIGHT*2+2,
        iconwd*2+2+fillwd-2, maxy-2, 0, 0);
      tools.addtool(new userinteract('y', iconwd*2+4, maxy-FILL_HEIGHT*2+2,
        fillwd-2, FILL_HEIGHT*2, changedrawcolor));
      setlinestyle(SOLID_LINE, 0, NORM_WIDTH);

      // Draw main draw area window
      wl = iconwd*2+2+1;    wt = h;
      wr = maxx-1;          wb = maxy-FILL_HEIGHT*2-2-1;
      rectangle(wl-1, wt-1, wr+1, wb+1);

      // Set world coordinate to screen coordinate relationship. If
      // you change these values, change the corresponding ones in
      // draw_grid() located in CADDRAW.CPP. Pick numbers that make
      // the grid look square. These work well on a VGA.
      set_window(0.0, 7.0, 0.0, 6.0);
      set_viewport(wl, wr, wt, wb);

      globalfillstyle = SOLID_FILL;
      globallinestyle = SOLID_LINE;
      globaltextstyle = DEFAULT_FONT;
      gridon = 1;
      draw_grid();
      left_arrow = 0;
      right_arrow = 0;

      // Set the font here to what you want to use for the dimension labels.
      // On the CGA in medium-resolution mode, small font is good.
      settextstyle(globaltextstyle, HORIZ_DIR, 1);
}

int main()
{
  int c, errcode, gmode, gdriver = DETECT;
  int xasp, yasp;

  initgraph(&gdriver, &gmode, "\\tcpp\\bgi");
  if ((errcode=graphresult()) != grOk) {
    printf("Graphics error: %s\n", grapherrormsg(errcode));
    exit(1);                      // Return with error code
  }
  getaspectratio(&xasp, &yasp);
  aspectratio = (double)xasp / (double)yasp;
  maxx = getmaxx();   maxy = getmaxy();
  setup_screen();
  mouse.init();
  do {
    c = mouse.waitforinput(LEFT_BUTTON);
    tools.anytoprocess(c);
  } while (1);
}
```

• GOBJLIST.H

```
// GOBJLIST.H: Defines a class that maintains a list of all the
// graphics figure objects that have been drawn.
#ifndef GOBJLISTH
#define GOBJLISTH
#include "gobject.h"

// Maximum number of objects maintained in figure list
const int NUMGOBJECTS = 50;

// This class is used to maintain the list of figures currently
// displayed in the drawing window
class gobjlist {
public:
  drawingtool *gobjects[NUMGOBJECTS];   // List of graphics figures
  int nextobj;                          // Number of graphics objects
  int currentobj;                       // Currently active object
  int selectedobj;                      // Currently selected object
  gobjlist(void) { selectedobj = -1; }
  void addobj(drawingtool *obj);
  void deleteobj(void);
  void deleteall(void);
  void fliptoback(void);
  void fliptofront(void);
  void duplicate(void);
  void rotate(void);
  void select(void);
  void move(void);
  void mark(int obj);
  void displayall(void);
  int savefiglist(FILE *fp);
  int readfiglist(FILE *fp);
};
#endif
```

• GOBJLIST.CPP

```
// GOBJLIST.CPP: Member functions for the gobjlist class. These
// routines handle the management of the gobject graphics objects
// maintained in the CAD program. These are the objects that
// represent individual graphics figures on the screen.
#include <graphics.h>
#include <string.h>
#include "gobjlist.h"
#include "matrix.h"
#include "kbdmouse.h"
#include "caddraw.h"

// Adds an object to the list of graphics objects in the drawing window
void gobjlist::addobj(drawingtool *obj)
{
  if (nextobj >= NUMGOBJECTS) return;  // List is full. Do nothing.
```

```
    if (selectedobj >= 0) {
      mark(selectedobj);
      selectedobj = -1;
    }
    currentobj = nextobj;
    gobjects[nextobj++] = obj;
}

// Delete an object from the graphics object list. Make the next
// object in the gobjects array the currentobj. Update the screen
// after deleting the object from the list by erasing it and then
// redrawing all remaining objects.
void gobjlist::deleteobj(void)
{
  int i;

  if (nextobj == 0) return;              // Empty list. No objects.
  if (selectedobj >= 0) {
    mark(selectedobj);
    selectedobj = -1;
  }
  delete(gobjects[currentobj]);
  for (i=currentobj; i<nextobj-1; i++)
    gobjects[i] = gobjects[i+1];
  nextobj--;
  if (currentobj >= nextobj && currentobj)
    currentobj--;                         // Deleted last, but not first
  cleardrawingarea();
  displayall();
}

// Delete all objects in the object list
void gobjlist::deleteall(void)
{
  for (int i=0; i<nextobj; i++)
    delete(gobjects[i]);
  nextobj = 0;
  currentobj = 0;
  selectedobj = -1;
  cleardrawingarea();
}

// Move the current object to the back by copying it to the
// head of the object list. After the operation, the same object
// is the current object.
void gobjlist::fliptoback(void)
{
  if (nextobj == 0) return;
  if (selectedobj >= 0) {
    mark(selectedobj);
    selectedobj = -1;
  }
  drawingtool *temp = gobjects[currentobj];
  for (int i=currentobj; i>0; i--)
```

```
        gobjects[i] = gobjects[i-1];
     gobjects[0] = temp;
     currentobj = 0;
     cleardrawingarea();
     displayall();
}

// Move the object to the front by putting it at the end of the
// object list and redrawing all of the objects. After the operation,
// the same object is the current object.
void gobjlist::fliptofront(void)
{
  if (nextobj == 0) return;
  if (selectedobj >= 0) {
    mark(selectedobj);
    selectedobj = -1;
  }
  drawingtool *temp = gobjects[currentobj];
  for (int i=currentobj; i<nextobj-1; i++)
    gobjects[i] = gobjects[i+1];
  gobjects[i] = temp;
  currentobj = i;
  cleardrawingarea();
  displayall();
}

// Duplicate currentobj. Make a copy of the current object in the
// drawing window. New object appears offset from the original
// by translating it (.1, .1). Make sure the object is saved in
// world coordinates.
void gobjlist::duplicate(void)
{
  if (nextobj == 0) return;              // No objects in list
  if (nextobj >= NUMGOBJECTS) return;    // Object list is full
  if (selectedobj >= 0) {
    mark(selectedobj);
    selectedobj = -1;
  }
  gobjects[nextobj] = gobjects[currentobj]->dup();
  currentobj = nextobj;                  // New object becomes current object
  nextobj++;
  setviewport(wl, wt, wr, wb, 1);
  gobjects[currentobj]->display();
  setviewport(0, 0, getmaxx(), getmaxy(), 1);
}

// Rotate the current object about its center point. The object is
// rotated in 45-degree increments. Note that only polygon and line
// rotations are supported.
void gobjlist::rotate(void)
{
  if (nextobj == 0) return;              // No objects in list
  if (selectedobj >= 0) {
```

```
      mark(selectedobj);
      selectedobj = -1;
    }
    gobjects[currentobj]->rotate(45);
    cleardrawingarea();
    displayall();                          // Display updated objects
}

// Interactively move the current object on the screen
void gobjlist::move(void)
{
    int x, y, oldx, oldy, movex, movey;
    int l, t, r, b;
    double originalx, originaly, translatex, translatey;

    if (nextobj == 0 || selectedobj == -1) return; // No objects in list
    setviewport(wl, wt, wr, wb, 1);
    while (1) {
      while (!mouse.buttonpressed(LEFT_BUTTON)) {
        int c = getkey();
        if (c == 0x1B) {
          setviewport(0, 0, getmaxx(), getmaxy(), 1);
          return;    // Quit if Esc key was pressed
        }
      }
      mouse.getcoords(x, y);
      if (x <= wl || y <= wt || y > wb || x > wr) {
        setviewport(0, 0, getmaxx(), getmaxy(), 1);
        return;
      }
      l = gobjects[currentobj]->left;
      t = gobjects[currentobj]->top;
      r = gobjects[currentobj]->right;
      b = gobjects[currentobj]->bottom;
      if (mouse.inbox(l, t, r, b, x, y)) {
        oldx = x;     oldy = y;
        while (!mouse.buttonreleased(LEFT_BUTTON)) {
          mouse.getcoords(x, y);
          movex = x - oldx;   movey = y - oldy;
          if (movex != 0 || movey != 0) {
            mark(currentobj);
            gobjects[currentobj]->left += movex;
            gobjects[currentobj]->top += movey;
            gobjects[currentobj]->right += movex;
            gobjects[currentobj]->bottom += movey;
            mark(currentobj);
            oldx = x;   oldy = y;
          }
        }
        PCtoWORLD(l, t, originalx, originaly);
        PCtoWORLD(gobjects[currentobj]->left,
          gobjects[currentobj]->top, translatex, translatey);
        translatex -= originalx;   translatey -= originaly;
```

```
                gobjects[currentobj]->translate(translatex, translatey);
                cleardrawingarea();
                displayall();
                mark(currentobj);
            }
            else
                while (!mouse.buttonreleased(LEFT_BUTTON)) ;
    }
}

// Select an object by encompassing it with a rectangle. An object
// can be selected by pressing the left mouse button while over
// the object. To select another object in the same region, click
// the mouse button again. Upon exiting, the currently marked
// object becomes the currentobj, which is used in all succeeding
// operations.
void gobjlist::select(void)
{
    int x, y, testobj, found;

    if (nextobj == 0) return;        // No objects in list
    setviewport(wl, wt, wr, wb, 1);
    testobj = currentobj + 1;
    if (testobj >= nextobj) testobj = 0;
    if (selectedobj == -1) {
        selectedobj = currentobj;    // Select the current object
        mark(currentobj);            // Mark object
    }
    while (1) {
        while (!mouse.buttonpressed(LEFT_BUTTON)) {
            int c = getkey();
            if (c == 0x1B) {
                setviewport(0, 0, getmaxx(), getmaxy(), 1);
                return;                 // Quit if Esc key is pressed
            }
        }
        mouse.getcoords(x, y);
        if (x <= wl || y <= wt || y > wb || x > wr) {
            setviewport(0, 0, getmaxx(), getmaxy(), 1);
            return;
        }
        while (!mouse.buttonreleased(LEFT_BUTTON)) ;
        mouse.getcoords(x, y);
        found = -1;
        do {
            if (mouse.inbox(gobjects[testobj]->left,
                gobjects[testobj]->top, gobjects[testobj]->right,
                gobjects[testobj]->bottom, x, y)) {
                currentobj = testobj;
                found = testobj;
                testobj++;
                if (testobj >= nextobj) testobj = 0;
                break;
            }
```

```
      testobj++;
      if (testobj >= nextobj) testobj = 0;
    } while (testobj != currentobj);
    if (found == -1) {
      if (selectedobj >= 0)
        // No object selected. Remove the highlight from
        // the currently selected object.
        mark(selectedobj);
      selectedobj = -1;
    }
    else {
      if (found == selectedobj) {
        // If the object was selected again, deselect it
        mark(selectedobj);
        selectedobj = -1;
      }
      else {
        if (selectedobj >= 0)
          mark(selectedobj);
        mark(found);
        selectedobj = found;
      }
    }
  }
}

// Display all of the graphics objects in the drawing window
void gobjlist::displayall(void)
{
  viewporttype v;

  getviewsettings(&v);                 // Save viewport settings
  setviewport(wl, wt, wr, wb, 1);      // Use drawing window
  setwritemode(COPY_PUT);
  for (int obj=0; obj<nextobj; obj++)
    gobjects[obj]->display();
  // Restore viewport
  setviewport(v.left, v.top, v.right, v.bottom, v.clip);
}

// Highlight an object by drawing a dashed rectangle around its border
void gobjlist::mark(int obj)
{
  linesettingstype oline;
  viewporttype v;

  getviewsettings(&v);                 // Save viewport settings
  setviewport(wl, wt, wr, wb, 1);
  drawingtool *t = gobjects[obj];
  int savecolor = getcolor();
  getlinesettings(&oline);
  setwritemode(XOR_PUT);
  setcolor(getmaxcolor());
```

```
      setlinestyle(DASHED_LINE, 0, NORM_WIDTH);
      mouse.hide();
      rectangle(t->left-wl, t->top-wt, t->right-wl, t->bottom-wt);
      mouse.show();
      setlinestyle(oline.linestyle, oline.upattern, oline.thickness);
      setcolor(savecolor);
      setwritemode(COPY_PUT);
      setviewport(v.left, v.top, v.right, v.bottom, v.clip);
}

// Saves all the object list to a file
int gobjlist::savefiglist(FILE *fp)
{
    int retval;

    if (selectedobj >= 0) {
      mark(selectedobj);
      selectedobj = -1;
    }
    fprintf(fp, "CAD1.0\n");          // Write a header to the file
    // Write the number of objects to the file
    fprintf(fp, "%d\n", figlist.nextobj);
    for (int obj=0; obj<nextobj; obj++)
      retval = gobjects[obj]->save(fp);
    return retval;  // Returns the status of the last save
}

// Reads the object list from a file and displays it. The
// file should already be open. Returns negative if failure.
int gobjlist::readfiglist(FILE *fp)
{
    char buffer[80];
    drawingtool *obj;
    int numobj;

    if (selectedobj >= 0) {
      mark(selectedobj);
      selectedobj = -1;
    }
    // Read the header to make sure the file is okay. It should
    // say "CAD1.0."
    fscanf(fp, "%6s", buffer);
    if (stricmp(buffer, "CAD1.0") != 0) {
      return -1;
    }
    // Delete all existing objects
    for (int i=0; i<nextobj; i++)
      delete(gobjects[i]);
    nextobj = 0;
    currentobj = 0;
    // Read the number of objects in the file
    fscanf(fp, "%d", &numobj);
    // Read each of the objects in the file
    for (i=0; i<numobj; i++) {
```

```
      if (EOF == fscanf(fp, "%s", buffer)) {
        // Unexpected end of file. Force the program to show what it read.
        return 1;
      }
      // Add the appropriate object to the object list
      if (stricmp(buffer, "TEXT") == 0) {
        obj = new textobj;              // Create a new text object
      }
      else if (stricmp(buffer, "LINE") == 0) {
        obj = new lineobj;              // Create a new line object
      }
      else if (stricmp(buffer, "RECTANGLE") == 0) {
        obj = new fillrectangleobj; // Create a new rectangle object
      }
      else if (stricmp(buffer, "CIRCLE") == 0) {
        obj = new circleobj;         // Create a new cirlce object
      }
      else if (stricmp(buffer, "FILLPOLY") == 0) {
        obj = new fillpolygonobj;   // Create a new polygon object
      }
      else return -2;             // Unknown object type
      obj->read(fp);              // Read the line's information
      addobj(obj);               // Add the object to the object list
    }
    cleardrawingarea();          // Clear the screen
    displayall();                // Display the new list of objects
    return 0;                    // Signal success
}
```

• GOBJECT.H

```
// GOBJECT.H: Defines graphics objects, such as lines and circles,
// that are drawn in the CAD program. These objects, derived
// from the drawingtool classes in DRAW.CPP, supply the functions to
// draw, move, and rotate the graphics objects.
#ifndef GOBJECTH
#define GOBJECTH
#include "draw.h"

// Text object. Text rotation is not supported.
class textobj : public texttool {
public:
  double xw, yw;       // Top left of text in real-world coordinates
  virtual void draw(void);
  virtual void copy(textobj *f);
  virtual void translate(double transx, double transy);
  virtual void getbounds(int &l, int &t, int &r, int &b);
  virtual void display(void);
  virtual void finishdrawing(void);
  virtual drawingtool *dup(void);
  virtual int save(FILE *fp);
  virtual int read(FILE *fp);
};
```

```
class lineobj : public linetool {  // Line object
public:
  double xw1, yw1;
  double xw2, yw2;           // Other endpoints of line
  double rot;                // Angle of rotation
  int left_arrow, right_arrow; // Non-zero if the line has an arrowhead
  static const int ARROWSIZE;  // Size of arrowheads
  virtual void draw(void);
  virtual void translate(double transx, double transy);
  virtual void getbounds(int &l, int &t, int &r, int &b);
  virtual void copy(lineobj *f);
  virtual void display(void);
  virtual void finishdrawing(void);
  virtual void draw_arrows(void);
  virtual drawingtool *dup(void);
  virtual void rotate(double angle);
  virtual int save(FILE *fp);
  virtual int read(FILE *fp);
};

class fillrectangleobj : public fillrectangletool { // A filled rectangle
public:
  double xw1, yw1, xw2, yw2;  // Rectangle's world coordinates
  virtual void draw(void);
  virtual void translate(double transx, double transy);
  virtual void getbounds(int &l, int &t, int &r, int &b);
  virtual void copy(fillrectangleobj *f);
  virtual void display(void);
  virtual void finishdrawing(void);
  virtual drawingtool *dup(void);
  virtual void rotate(double angle);
  virtual int save(FILE *fp);
  virtual int read(FILE *fp);
};

class circleobj : public circletool {    // Circle object
public:
  double centerwx, centerwy;  // Center of circle in world coordinates
  double radiusw;             // Radius of circle in world coordinates
  virtual void draw(void);
  virtual void getbounds(int &l, int &t, int &r, int &b);
  virtual void copy(circleobj *f);
  virtual void translate(double transx, double transy);
  virtual void display(void);
  virtual void finishdrawing(void);
  virtual drawingtool *dup(void);
  virtual int save(FILE *fp);
  virtual int read(FILE *fp);
};

// A filled polygon object
class fillpolygonobj : public fillpolygontool {
public:
```

```
    double pointsw[MAXPOLYSIZE];   // Polygon in world coordinates
    double rot;                    // Angle of rotation
    ~fillpolygonobj(void);
    virtual void draw(void);
    void getbounds(int &l, int &t, int &r, int &b);
    virtual void copy(fillpolygonobj *f);
    virtual void display(void);
    virtual void translate(double transx, double transy);
    virtual void finishdrawing(void);
    virtual drawingtool *dup(void);
    virtual void rotate(double angle);
    virtual int save(FILE *fp);
    virtual int read(FILE *fp);
};
#endif
```

• GOBJECT.CPP

```
// GOBJECT.CPP: Defines the functions used to support graphics figures
// as objects in the CAD program. The classes here are derived from the
// tools developed in DRAW.CPP in Chapter 10. These objects are maintained
// in a list by the class gobjlist, which is defined in GOBJLIST.CPP.
#include <graphics.h>
#include <alloc.h>
#include <math.h>
#include <string.h>
#include "gobject.h"
#include "gobjlist.h"
#include "kbdmouse.h"
#include "matrix.h"
#include "gtext.h"
#include "caddraw.h"

// Override draw() so that it won't be called if the object list is full
void textobj::draw(void)
{
  if (figlist.selectedobj >= 0) {
    figlist.mark(figlist.selectedobj);
    figlist.selectedobj = -1;
  }
  if (figlist.nextobj < NUMGOBJECTS-1) texttool::draw();
}

// Create a new text object by making a copy of the current text
// object and then translating it in world coordinates by (0.1,0.1).
// Returns a pointer to the new object.
drawingtool *textobj::dup(void)
{
  textobj *nt = new textobj;             // Create new text object
  nt->copy(this);                        // Copy "this" to new object
  nt->xw += 0.1;    nt->yw += 0.1;       // Translate new text
  // Calculate screen position of duplicated text
  WORLDtoPC(nt->xw, nt->yw, nt->leftx, nt->lefty);
```

```
    nt->getbounds(nt->left, nt->top, nt->right, nt->bottom);
    return nt;                              // Return pointer to new object
}

// Display the text in the text object. It accounts for newline
// characters included in the string.
void textobj::display(void)
{
  int i;
  char c[] = "c";                          // String to hold a single character

  setcolor(drawcolor);                     // Use the stored drawing color
  WORLDtoPC(xw,yw, leftx, lefty);          // Using the world coordinates saved
  moveto(leftx-wl, lefty-wt);              // in the object, write the text out
  settextstyle(textstyle,HORIZ_DIR,1);
  mouse.hide();
  for (i=0; i<len; i++)
    if (string[i] == '\n') {               // Newline character
      lefty += textheight("S");            // Skip to next line
      moveto(leftx-wl, lefty-wt);          // Adjust current position
    }
    else {
      c[0] = string[i];                    // Write out the next character
      outtext(c);
    }
  mouse.show();
}

// Get bounding box of text object in screen coordinates. Since text
// can stretch across multiple lines, check for the newline character
// to get the real text block's width and height.
void textobj::getbounds(int &l, int &t, int &r, int &b)
{
  int i=0, linew=0, w=0, h=1, startofline=0, ptr;
  char buff[80];   // The longest line can't have more than 80 characters

  l = leftx-3;  t = lefty-3;               // The -3 adds a 3-pixel border
  for (i=0; string[i]; i++) {
    if (string[i] == '\n') {               // Newline encountered
      h++;                                 // Increment height count
      if (linew > w) {                     // Check whether this line is
        w = linew; ptr = startofline;      // the longest line so far
      }
      linew = 0;                           // Reset the line width counter
      startofline = i+1;                   // Remember where next line starts
    }
    else
      linew++;                             // Increment line width
  }
  if (linew > w) {                         // Check whether last line is
    w = linew; ptr = startofline;          // the longest line
  }
  settextstyle(textstyle, HORIZ_DIR, 1); // Use this object's font
```

```
    strncpy(buff, &string[ptr], w);  // Copy the longest line to a string
    buff[w] = 0;                      // so it can be used to get the
    r = leftx + textwidth(buff) + 3;  // width of the widest line
    b = lefty + (textheight("C")+2) * h + 3;
}

// Move the top-left location of the text by the amount (transx,transy)
void textobj::translate(double transx, double transy)
{
    xw += transx;   yw += transy;
}

// Copy the text object f to "this"
void textobj::copy(textobj *f)
{
    left = f->left;        top = f->top;
    right = f->right;      bottom = f->bottom;
    leftx = f->leftx;      lefty = f->lefty;
    xw = f->xw;            yw = f->yw;
    drawcolor = f->drawcolor;
    textstyle = f->textstyle;
    len = f->len;
    strcpy(string,f->string);
}

// After entering a text string, this function adds the string
// to the figure object list
void textobj::finishdrawing(void)
{
    texttool::finishdrawing();
    if (len == 0) return;            // Don't add object if string is empty
    textobj *nl = new textobj;       // Create a new object to add
    getbounds(left, top, right, bottom);
    PCtoWORLD(leftx, lefty, xw, yw); // Save things in world coordinates
    nl->copy(this);                  // Copy settings to new object
    figlist.addobj(nl);              // Add "this" to the list of objects
}

// Saves the text object to a file. The format is: color, textstyle,
// left, top, string length, string.
int textobj::save(FILE *fp)
{
    return fprintf(fp, "TEXT %d %d %lf %lf %d %s\n", drawcolor, textstyle,
        xw, yw, len, string);
}

// Reads the text object's information to a file
int textobj::read(FILE *fp)
{
    if (!fscanf(fp, "%d %d %lf %lf %d ", &drawcolor, &textstyle,
        &xw, &yw, &len)) return 0;
    for (int i=0; i<len; i++)
        fscanf(fp, "%c", &string[i]);
    string[len] = 0;    // Null-terminate the string
```

```
   // Determine the screen positions of the object
   WORLDtoPC(xw, yw, leftx, lefty);
   getbounds(left, top, right, bottom);
   return 1;
}

// Override draw() so that it won't be called if the object list is full
void lineobj::draw(void)
{
  if (figlist.selectedobj >= 0) {
    figlist.mark(figlist.selectedobj);
    figlist.selectedobj = -1;
  }
  if (figlist.nextobj < NUMGOBJECTS-1) linetool::draw();
}

// After drawing a line, append it to the figure list
void lineobj::finishdrawing(void)
{
  linetool::finishdrawing();          // Call inherited routine
  left_arrow = ::left_arrow;          // Remember the settings of
  right_arrow = ::right_arrow;        // the arrows
  lineobj *nl = new lineobj;          // Create a new line object
  getbounds(left, top, right, bottom);
  PCtoWORLD(x1, y1, xw1, yw1);        // Save endpoints in world
  PCtoWORLD(x2, y2, xw2, yw2);        // coordinates
  nl->copy(this);                     // Copy all settings to the new object
  draw_arrows();                      // Draw arrows on the new line
  figlist.addobj(nl);                 // Add the line to the figure list
}

// Create a new line object by making a copy of the current line
// object. Translate the new line in world coordinates by (0.1,0.1)
// and then set its bounding box size.
drawingtool *lineobj::dup(void)
{
  lineobj *nl = new lineobj;          // Create new line
  nl->copy(this);                     // Copy current object to new object
  nl->xw1 += 0.1;   nl->yw1 += 0.1;   // Translate new line
  nl->xw2 += 0.1;   nl->yw2 += 0.1;
  WORLDtoPC(nl->xw1, nl->yw1, nl->x1, nl->y1); // Calculate new line's
  WORLDtoPC(nl->xw2, nl->yw2, nl->x2, nl->y2); // screen position
  nl->getbounds(nl->left, nl->top, nl->right, nl->bottom);
  return nl;
}

// Copy line1 to line2
void lineobj::copy(lineobj *f)
{
  left = f->left;     top = f->top;
  right = f->right;   bottom = f->bottom;
  x1 = f->x1;         y1 = f->y1;
  x2 = f->x2;         y2 = f->y2;
```

```
    xw1 = f->xw1;        yw1 = f->yw1;
    xw2 = f->xw2;        yw2 = f->yw2;
    drawcolor = f->drawcolor;
    linestyle = f->linestyle;
    left_arrow = f->left_arrow;
    right_arrow = f->right_arrow;
}

// Display the line in the line object
void lineobj::display(void)
{
    int xpc1, ypc1, xpc2, ypc2;

    setcolor(drawcolor);
    setlinestyle(linestyle, 0, NORM_WIDTH);
    WORLDtoPC(xw1, yw1, xpc1, ypc1);
    WORLDtoPC(xw2, yw2, xpc2, ypc2);
    mouse.hide();
    line(xpc1-wl, ypc1-wt, xpc2-wl, ypc2-wt);
    mouse.show();
    draw_arrows();
}

// Translate the line in world coordinates by the amount (transx,transy)
void lineobj::translate(double transx, double transy)
{
    xw1 += transx;  yw1 += transy;
    xw2 += transx;  yw2 += transy;
}

// Get the bounding box for a line object. Note that the bounding box
// is expanded by 3 pixels to make it easier to select a line.
void lineobj::getbounds(int &l, int &t, int &r, int &b)
{
    if (x1 <= x2) {
        l = x1 - 3;      r = x2 + 3;
    }
    else {
        l = x2 - 3;      r = x1 + 3;
    }
    if (y1 <= y2) {
        t = y1 - 3;      b = y2 + 3;
    }
    else {
        t = y2 - 3;      b = y1 + 3;
    }
}

// Rotates a line an additional "angle" degrees
void lineobj::rotate(double angle)
{
    int cx, cy, PCpoints[4], numpoints = 2;
    double points[4], cwx, cwy;
```

```
      cx = (left + right) / 2;              // Get the center of the line
      cy = (top + bottom) / 2;
      PCtoWORLD(cx, cy, cwx, cwy);          // Translate to world coordinates
      points[0] = xw1;  points[1] = yw1;    // Store line endpoints in an
      points[2] = xw2;  points[3] = yw2;    // array
      WORLDtranslatepoly(numpoints, points, -cwx, -cwy);
      WORLDrotatepoly(numpoints, points, angle);
      WORLDtranslatepoly(numpoints, points, cwx, cwy);
      WORLDpolytoPCpoly(numpoints, points, PCpoints);
      xw1 = points[0];    yw1 = points[1];
      xw2 = points[2];    yw2 = points[3];
      x1 = PCpoints[0];   y1 = PCpoints[1];
      x2 = PCpoints[2];   y2 = PCpoints[3];
      getbounds(left, top, right, bottom);    // Calculate the new bounding box
}

// Draw arrows to the line if needed. The mouse is already hidden
// when this function is called. The arrows are displayed as an
// open-ended polygon.
const int lineobj::ARROWSIZE = 4;           // Size of an arrow

void lineobj::draw_arrows(void)
{
    double angle;                    // Calculated slope of line
    int x1, x2, y1, y2;
    int arrowhead[3*2];              // An arrow is made from two lines offset
                                     // 45 degrees on each side of the line
    WORLDtoPC(xw1, yw1, x1, y1);
    WORLDtoPC(xw2, yw2, x2, y2);
    if (left_arrow) {                // Draw an arrow at the start of the line
      arrowhead[0] = x1 + ARROWSIZE - wl;
      arrowhead[1] = y1 - ARROWSIZE - wt;
      arrowhead[2] = x1 - wl;
      arrowhead[3] = y1 - wt;
      arrowhead[4] = x1 + ARROWSIZE - wl;
      arrowhead[5] = y1 + ARROWSIZE - wt;
      angle = atan2((double)(y2-y1), (double)(x2-x1)) * 180.0 / M_PI;
      PCtranslatepoly(3, arrowhead, -x1+wl, -y1+wt);
      PCrotatepoly(3, arrowhead, angle);
      PCtranslatepoly(3, arrowhead, x1-wl, y1-wt);
      mouse.hide();
      drawpoly(3,arrowhead);          // Draw the arrow
      mouse.show();
    }
    if (right_arrow) {                // Draw an arrow at the end of the line
      arrowhead[0] = x2 - ARROWSIZE - wl;
      arrowhead[1] = y2 - ARROWSIZE - wt;
      arrowhead[2] = x2 - wl;
      arrowhead[3] = y2 - wt;
      arrowhead[4] = x2 - ARROWSIZE - wl;
      arrowhead[5] = y2 + ARROWSIZE - wt;
      angle = atan2((double)(y2-y1), (double)(x2-x1)) * 180.0 / M_PI;
```

```
        PCtranslatepoly(3, arrowhead, -x2+wl, -y2+wt);
        PCrotatepoly(3, arrowhead, angle);
        PCtranslatepoly(3, arrowhead, x2-wl, y2-wt);
        mouse.hide();
        drawpoly(3,arrowhead);                  // Draw the arrow
        mouse.show();
    }
}

// Saves the line information to a file. The format is: color,
// line style, left arrow, right arrow, x1, y1, x2, y2.
int lineobj::save(FILE *fp)
{
    return fprintf(fp, "LINE %d %d %d %d %lf %lf %lf %lf\n", drawcolor,
        linestyle, left_arrow, right_arrow, xw1, yw1, xw2, yw2);
}

// Reads the line information from a file
int lineobj::read(FILE *fp)
{
    if (!fscanf(fp, "%d %d %d %d %lf %lf %lf %lf", &drawcolor,
        &linestyle, &left_arrow, &right_arrow, &xw1, &yw1, &xw2, &yw2))
        return 0;                        // Failed to read line data
    // Determine the screen positions of the objects (x1,y1) and (x2,y2)
    // based on the world coordinates (xw1,yw1) and (xw2,yw2)
    WORLDtoPC(xw1, yw1, x1, y1);
    WORLDtoPC(xw2, yw2, x2, y2);
    getbounds(left, top, right, bottom);
    return 1;
}

// Override draw() so that it won't be called if the object list is full
void fillrectangleobj::draw(void)
{
    if (figlist.selectedobj >= 0) {
        figlist.mark(figlist.selectedobj);
        figlist.selectedobj = -1;
    }
    if (figlist.nextobj < NUMGOBJECTS-1) fillrectangletool::draw();
}

// After drawing a rectangle, append it to the figure list
void fillrectangleobj::finishdrawing(void)
{
    fillrectangletool::finishdrawing(); // Call inherited routine
    x2 = x;   y2 = y;
    getbounds(left, top, right, bottom);
    PCtoWORLD(x1, y1, xw1, yw1);      // Save corners of rectangle in world
    PCtoWORLD(x2, y2, xw2, yw2);      // coordinates
    fillrectangleobj *nr = new fillrectangleobj; // Create a new rectangle
    nr->copy(this);                   // Copy all settings to the new object
    figlist.addobj(nr);               // Add the line to the figure list
}
```

```
// Create a new rectangle object by making a copy of the current
// object. Translate the new rectangle in world coordinates by (0.1,0.1)
// and then set its bounding box size.
drawingtool *fillrectangleobj::dup(void)
{
  fillrectangleobj *nr = new fillrectangleobj;  // Create a new object
  nr->copy(this);                     // Copy current object to new object
  nr->xw1 += 0.1;    nr->yw1 += 0.1; // Translate new rectangle
  nr->xw2 += 0.1;    nr->yw2 += 0.1;
  WORLDtoPC(nr->xw1, nr->yw1, nr->x1, nr->y1);  // Calculate new object's
  WORLDtoPC(nr->xw2, nr->yw2, nr->x2, nr->y2);  // screen position
  nr->getbounds(nr->left, nr->top, nr->right, nr->bottom);
  return nr;
}

// Copy one rectangle object to another
void fillrectangleobj::copy(fillrectangleobj *f)
{
  left = f->left;      top = f->top;
  right = f->right;    bottom = f->bottom;
  x1 = f->x1;          y1 = f->y1;
  x2 = f->x2;          y2 = f->y2;
  xw1 = f->xw1;        yw1 = f->yw1;
  xw2 = f->xw2;        yw2 = f->yw2;
  drawcolor = f->drawcolor;
  linestyle = f->linestyle;
  fillcolor = f->fillcolor;
  fillstyle = f->fillstyle;
}

// Displays the rectangle represented by the object
void fillrectangleobj::display(void)
{
  setcolor(drawcolor);
  setlinestyle(linestyle, 0, NORM_WIDTH);
  setfillstyle(fillstyle, fillcolor);
  WORLDtoPC(xw1, yw1, x1, y1);
  WORLDtoPC(xw2, yw2, x2, y2);
  mouse.hide();
  bar3d(x1-wl, y1-wt, x2-wl, y2-wt, 0, 0); // Draw the filled rectangle
  mouse.show();
}

// Translates the rectangle in world coordinates by the (transx,transy)
void fillrectangleobj::translate(double transx, double transy)
{
  xw1 += transx;  yw1 += transy;
  xw2 += transx;  yw2 += transy;
}

// Gets the bounding box for a rectangle object. Note that the bounding
// box is expanded by 3 pixels to make it easier to select the object.
void fillrectangleobj::getbounds(int &l, int &t, int &r, int &b)
```

```
{
  if (x1 <= x2) {
    l = x1 - 3;     r = x2 + 3;
  }
  else {
    l = x2 - 3;     r = x1 + 3;
  }
  if (y1 <= y2) {
    t = y1 - 3;     b = y2 + 3;
  }
  else {
    t = y2 - 3;     b = y1 + 3;
  }
}

// Rotates a rectangle
void fillrectangleobj::rotate(double /*angle*/)
{
  // Currently not supported
}

// Saves the rectangle information to a file. The format is: color,
// line style, fill color, fill style, x1, y1, x2, y2.
int fillrectangleobj::save(FILE *fp)
{
  return fprintf(fp, "RECTANGLE %d %d %d %d %lf %lf %lf %lf\n",
    drawcolor, linestyle, fillcolor, fillstyle, xw1, yw1, xw2, yw2);
}

// Reads the rectangle's information from a file
int fillrectangleobj::read(FILE *fp)
{
  if (!fscanf(fp, "%d %d %d %d %lf %lf %lf %lf", &drawcolor,
    &linestyle, &fillcolor, &fillstyle, &xw1, &yw1, &xw2, &yw2))
    return 0;                      // Failed to read line data
  // Determine the screen positions of the object (x1,y1) and (x2,y2)
  // based on the world coordinates (xw1,yw1) and (xw2,yw2)
  WORLDtoPC(xw1, yw1, x1, y1);
  WORLDtoPC(xw2, yw2, x2, y2);
  getbounds(left, top, right, bottom);
  return 1;
}

// Overrides draw() so that it won't be called if the object list is full
void circleobj::draw(void)
{
  if (figlist.selectedobj >= 0) {
    figlist.mark(figlist.selectedobj);
    figlist.selectedobj = -1;
  }
  if (figlist.nextobj < NUMGOBJECTS-1) circletool::draw();
}
```

```
// Gets the bounding box of a circle object
void circleobj::getbounds(int &l, int &t, int &r, int &b)
{
  int tmp;
  WORLDtoPC(radiusw, 0, absradiusx, tmp);
  WORLDtoPC(centerwx, centerwy, centerx, centery);
  l = centerx - absradiusx;                    // centerx - radius
  t = centery - absradiusx * aspectratio;   // centery - radius
  r = centerx + absradiusx;                    // centerx + radius
  b = centery + absradiusx * aspectratio;   // centery + radius
}

// Make a copy of a circle object. The new circle is the same as
// "this" circle, except it is translated by (0.1,0.1). Returns
// pointer to new circle object.
drawingtool *circleobj::dup(void)
{
  circleobj *nc = new circleobj;    // Create a new circle object
  nc->copy(this);                   // Copy the circle settings
  nc->centerwx += 0.1;              // Translate the center (0.1,0.1)
  nc->centerwy += 0.1;
  // Calculate position and bounds of new circle
  WORLDtoPC(nc->centerwx, nc->centerwy, nc->centerx, nc->centery);
  nc->getbounds(nc->left, nc->top, nc->right, nc->bottom);
  return nc;                        // Return pointer to new circle
}

// Copy the settings in the f object to "this" circle
void circleobj::copy(circleobj *f)
{
  centerwx = f->centerwx;      centerwy = f->centerwy;
  centerx = f->centerx;        centery = f->centery;
  absradiusx = f->absradiusx;  radiusw = f->radiusw;
  left = f->left;              top = f->top;
  right = f->right;            bottom = f->bottom;
  drawcolor = f->drawcolor;
}

// Saves the circle's information to a file. The format is: color,
// radius, centerx, centery.
int circleobj::save(FILE *fp)
{
  return fprintf(fp, "CIRCLE %d %lf %lf %lf\n", drawcolor,
    centerwx, centerwy, radiusw);
}

// Reads a circle's information from a file
int circleobj::read(FILE *fp)
{
  if (!fscanf(fp, "%d %lf %lf %lf", &drawcolor,
    &centerwx, &centerwy, &radiusw))
    return 0;
  // Determine the screen positions of the object
```

```
    WORLDtoPC(centerwx, centerwy, centerx, centery);
    int tmp;
    WORLDtoPC(radiusw, 0, absradiusx, tmp);
    getbounds(left, top, right, bottom);
    return 1;
}

// Display the circle object
void circleobj::display(void)
{
    int tmp;
    setcolor(drawcolor);
    WORLDtoPC(centerwx, centerwy, centerx, centery);
    WORLDtoPC(radiusw, 0, absradiusx, tmp);
    mouse.hide();
    circle(centerx-wl, centery-wt, absradiusx); // Draw the circle
    mouse.show();
}

// After drawing a circle, append an object for it to the list of
// graphics figures on the screen
void circleobj::finishdrawing(void)
{
    double tmp;
    circletool::finishdrawing();          // Call the inherited routine
    circleobj *nc = new circleobj;        // Create a new circle object
    PCtoWORLD(centerx, centery, centerwx, centerwy);
                                          // Use world coordinates
    PCtoWORLD(absradiusx, 0, radiusw, tmp); // Use world coordinates
    getbounds(left, top, right, bottom);  // Save bounding box of circle
    nc->copy(this);                       // Copy settings to new object
    figlist.addobj(nc);                   // Add object to figure list
}

// Translate a circle in world coordinates
void circleobj::translate(double transx, double transy)
{
    centerwx += transx;
    centerwy += transy;
}

// Override draw() so that it won't be called if the object list is full
void fillpolygonobj::draw(void)
{
    if (figlist.selectedobj >= 0) {
        figlist.mark(figlist.selectedobj);
        figlist.selectedobj = -1;
    }
    if (figlist.nextobj < NUMGOBJECTS-1)
        fillpolygontool::draw();
}

// Duplicate the current polygon object by creating an identical
// polygon except that it is translated by (0.1,0.1). A pointer
```

```
// to the new object is returned.
drawingtool *fillpolygonobj::dup(void)
{
  fillpolygonobj *np = new fillpolygonobj;   // Create new polygon object
  np->copy(this);                            // Copy settings to new object
  WORLDtranslatepoly(np->numpts/2, np->pointsw, 0.1, 0.1);
  WORLDpolytoPCpoly(np->numpts/2, np->pointsw, np->poly);
  np->getbounds(np->left, np->top, np->right, np->bottom);
  return np;                                 // Return pointer to new object
}

// After drawing a polygon, add an object for it to the list of
// figures. Copy the polygon's settings that were used to draw
// the figure to the new object.
void fillpolygonobj::finishdrawing(void)
{
  fillpolygontool::finishdrawing();
  fillpolygonobj *np = new fillpolygonobj;     // Create a polygon object
  PCpolytoWORLDpoly(numpts/2, poly, pointsw);  // Use world coordinates
  getbounds(left, top, right, bottom);         // Get bounds of polygon
  np->copy(this);                              // Copy settings
  figlist.addobj(np);                          // Add polygon object
}

// Copy the polygon f to "this" polygon
void fillpolygonobj::copy(fillpolygonobj *f)
{
  left = f->left;        top = f->top;
  right = f->right;      bottom = f->bottom;
  numpts = f->numpts;
  for (int i=0; i<numpts; i++)                 // Copy PC points
    poly[i] = f->poly[i];
  copyWORLDpoly(f->numpts/2, f->pointsw, pointsw);
  drawcolor = f->drawcolor;
  linestyle = f->linestyle;
  fillcolor = f->fillcolor;
  fillstyle = f->fillstyle;
}

// Saves the polygon's information to a file. The format is:
// "FILLPOLY", outline color, line style, fill color, fill style,
// number of points, points.
int fillpolygonobj::save(FILE *fp)
{
  fprintf(fp, "FILLPOLY %d %d %d %d %d", drawcolor,
    linestyle, fillcolor, fillstyle, numpts);
  for (int i=0; i<numpts; i++)
    fprintf(fp, "% lf", pointsw[i]);
  return fprintf(fp, "\n");
}

// Reads the polygon's information from a file
int fillpolygonobj::read(FILE *fp)
```

```
{
  if (!fscanf(fp, "%d %d %d %d %d", &drawcolor,
    &linestyle, &fillcolor, &fillstyle, &numpts)) return 0;
  for (int i=0; i<numpts; i++)
    if (!fscanf(fp, "%lf", &pointsw[i])) return 0;

  // Determine the screen positions of the object (x1,y1) and (x2,y2)
  // based on the world coordinates (xw1,yw1) and (xw2,yw2)
  WORLDpolytoPCpoly(numpts/2, pointsw, poly);
  getbounds(left, top, right, bottom);
  return 1;
}

// Display a polygon
void fillpolygonobj::display(void)
{
  setcolor(drawcolor);
  setlinestyle(linestyle, 0, NORM_WIDTH);
  setfillstyle(fillstyle, fillcolor);
  WORLDpolytoPCpoly(numpts/2, pointsw, poly);
  mouse.hide();
  fillpoly(numpts/2, poly);
  mouse.show();
}

// Get bounding box of polygon object in screen coordinates
void fillpolygonobj::getbounds(int &l, int &t, int &r, int &b)
{
  l = getmaxx();  t = getmaxy();
  r = 0;          b = 0;
  WORLDpolytoPCpoly(numpts/2, pointsw, poly);
  for (int i=0; i<numpts; i+=2) {
    if (poly[i] < l) l = poly[i];
    if (poly[i] > r) r = poly[i];
    if (poly[i+1] < t) t = poly[i+1];
    if (poly[i+1] > b) b = poly[i+1];
  }
  l += wl;  r += wl;  t += wt;  b += wt;
}

// Translate a polygon in world coordinates
void fillpolygonobj::translate(double transx, double transy)
{
  WORLDtranslatepoly(numpts/2, pointsw, transx, transy);
}

// Rotate a polygon by the amount in "angle"
void fillpolygonobj::rotate(double angle)
{
  int cx = (left + right) / 2 - wl;
  int cy = (top + bottom) / 2 - wt;
  WORLDpolytoPCpoly(numpts/2, pointsw, poly);
  PCtranslatepoly(numpts/2, poly, -cx, -cy);
```

```
    PCrotatepoly(numpts/2, poly, angle);
    PCtranslatepoly(numpts/2, poly, cx, cy);
    for (int i=0; i<numpts; i+=2)
      PCtoWORLD(poly[i], poly[i+1], pointsw[i], pointsw[i+1]);
    getbounds(left, top, right, bottom);
}
```

• CADDRAW.H

```
// CADDRAW.H: Header file for CADDRAW.CPP.
#ifndef CADDRAWH
#define CADDRAWH
#include "gpopup.h"
#include "gobjlist.h"
#include "usertool.h"

extern gobjlist figlist;    // The list of figures on the screen

#define MAX_LINESTYLES2 7   // Number of line styles in the Line menu

// The following classes are provided so that we can provide
// access to various functions in the environment through the
// same drawing tool object list we created in Chapter 11 for
// the paint program
class togglegridtool : public drawingtool {
public:
  virtual void draw(void);
};

class deleteallobjtool : public drawingtool {
public:
  virtual void draw(void);
};

class moveobjtool : public drawingtool {
  virtual void draw(void);
};

class selectobjtool : public drawingtool {
  virtual void draw(void);
};

class duplicateobjtool : public drawingtool {
  virtual void draw(void);
};

class deleteobjtool : public drawingtool {
  virtual void draw(void);
};

class fliptofronttool : public drawingtool {
  virtual void draw(void);
};
```

```
class fliptobacktool : public drawingtool {
  virtual void draw(void);
};

class rotateobjtool : public drawingtool {
  virtual void draw(void);
};

class cadlinetool : public linetool {
  virtual void draw(void);
};

class cleardrawingareatool : public drawingtool {
public:
  virtual void draw(void);
};

class savefiglistobjtool : public drawingtool {
public:
  virtual void draw(void);
};

class readfiglistobjtool : public drawingtool {
public:
  virtual void draw(void);
};

class CADchangelinestyletool : public changelinestyletool {
public:
  virtual void draw(void);
  virtual void startdrawing(void);
  virtual void finishdrawing(void);
};

class CADchangefillpatterntool : public changefillpatterntool {
public:
  virtual void finishdrawing(void);
};

class CADchangefillcolortool : public changefillcolortool {
public:
  virtual void draw(void);
};

class CADchangedrawcolortool : public changedrawcolortool {
public:
  virtual void draw(void);
};

void draw_grid(void);
void cleardrawingarea(void);

extern int linewindowx;
extern int linewindowy;
```

```
        extern int left_arrow;
        extern int right_arrow;
        extern int gridon;
        extern gwindows w;
        extern double aspectratio;
        #endif
```

• CADDRAW.CPP

```cpp
// CADDRAW.CPP: Drawing and object support routines for the CAD program.
#include <stdio.h>
#include <graphics.h>
#include <stdlib.h>
#include <stdarg.h>
#include <math.h>
#include <string.h>
#include "kbdmouse.h"
#include "draw.h"
#include "gpopup.h"
#include "caddraw.h"              // Utilities specific to the CAD program
#include "matrix.h"
#include "gobject.h"
#include "gobjlist.h"
#include "gtext.h"

gobjlist figlist;               // Globally define a list of screen figures

// Clears the drawing window
void cleardrawingarea(void)
{
  viewporttype v;

  getviewsettings(&v);
  setviewport(wl, wt, wr, wb, 1); // Set viewport to drawing window
  mouse.hide();
  clearviewport();                // Clear the drawing window
  // Set viewport back to full screen
  setviewport(v.left, v.top, v.right, v.bottom, 1);
  if (gridon)                     // Draw a grid in the drawing
    draw_grid();                  // window if the gridon flag equals 1
  mouse.show();
}

// Interfaces the environment to the figure list's move() function
void moveobjtool::draw(void) {  figlist.move();  }

// Interfaces the environment to the figure list's select() function
void selectobjtool::draw(void) { figlist.select(); }

// Interfaces the environment to the figure list's duplicate() function
void duplicateobjtool::draw(void) { figlist.duplicate(); }
```

```
// Interfaces the environment to the figure list's delete() function
void deleteobjtool::draw(void) { figlist.deleteobj(); }

// Interfaces the environment to the figure list's fliptofront() function
void fliptofronttool::draw(void) { figlist.fliptofront(); }

// Interfaces the environment to the figure list's fliptoback() function
void fliptobacktool::draw(void) { figlist.fliptoback(); }

// Interfaces the environment to the figure list's rotate() function
void rotateobjtool::draw(void) { figlist.rotate(); }

// Sets the fill pattern of the current object to the new fill pattern,
// or sets the global fill pattern if there isn't an object selected
// If an object is selected, set that object's fill style.
void CADchangefillpatterntool::finishdrawing(void)
{
  if (figlist.selectedobj >= 0) {
    // If there was an object selected, set this object to the
    // specified fill pattern
    figlist.mark(figlist.selectedobj); // Remove the object's highlight
    figlist.gobjects[figlist.selectedobj]->
      setproperties(FILLSTYLEPROP, filltype);
    // Paint the object with its new fill style
    figlist.displayall();
    figlist.mark(figlist.selectedobj); // Restore highlight
  }
  else
    changefillpatterntool::finishdrawing();
}

// Sets the fill color of the current object to the new fill color,
// or sets the global fill color if there isn't an object selected
void CADchangefillcolortool::draw(void)
{
  if (figlist.selectedobj >= 0) {
    int maxcolors, colorwd, fillcolor=0, fillwd, i, x, mx, my;

    figlist.mark(figlist.selectedobj); // Remove the object's highlight
    fillwd = (getmaxx()-1-iconwd*2+2) / (NUM_FILLS_WIDE+1);
    maxcolors = getmaxcolor();
    colorwd = (getmaxx()-1-iconwd*2+2-fillwd) / (maxcolors + 1);
    for (i=0, x=iconwd*2+2+fillwd; i<=maxcolors; i++, x+=colorwd) {
      mouse.getcoords(mx, my);
      if (mouse.inbox(x, getmaxy()-FILL_HEIGHT,
        x+colorwd, getmaxy(), mx, my)) {
        // If there was an object selected, set this object to the
        // specified fill color
        figlist.gobjects[figlist.selectedobj]->
          setproperties(FILLCOLORPROP, fillcolor);
        // Paint the object with its new fill color
        setviewport(wl, wt, wr, wb, 1);
        figlist.displayall();
```

```
        setviewport(0, 0, getmaxx(), getmaxy(), 1);
        figlist.mark(figlist.selectedobj); // Restore highlight
        return;
      }
      fillcolor++;
    }
  }
  else      // Change the fill color globally
    changefillcolortool::draw();
}

// Sets the current object's color to the new color,
// or sets the global drawing color if there isn't an object selected
void CADchangedrawcolortool::draw(void)
{
  if (figlist.selectedobj >= 0) {
    figlist.mark(figlist.selectedobj); // Remove the object's highlight
    // If there was an object selected, set this object to the
    // specified color. Use the fill color as the new drawing color.
    figlist.gobjects[figlist.selectedobj]->
      setproperties(DRAWCOLORPROP, globalfillcolor);
    // Paint the object with its new color
    setviewport(wl, wt, wr, wb, 1);
    figlist.displayall();
    setviewport(0, 0, getmaxx(), getmaxy(), 1);
    figlist.mark(figlist.selectedobj); // Restore the object's highlight
  }
  else      // Change the drawing color globally
    changedrawcolortool::draw();
}

// Interfaces the environment to the figure list's savefiglist() function
void savefiglistobjtool::draw(void)
{
  const int MAXSTR = 128;
  const int TEXTSIZE = 8;
  static char *title = " Save Objects to a File ";
  char fn[MAXSTR], def[MAXSTR] = "";
  int ch, dlen=21;    // Set editing window size to 21 characters
  FILE *fp;
  textsettingstype oldfont;

  // Save the current font, and use the default font
  gettextsettings(&oldfont);
  settextstyle(DEFAULT_FONT, HORIZ_DIR, 1);

  w.gpopup(getmaxx()/2-textwidth(title)/2-BORDER,
    getmaxy()/2-3*textheight("H"),
    getmaxx()/2+textwidth(title)/2+BORDER,
    getmaxy()/2+4*textheight("H"),
    THREED, getmaxcolor(), SOLID_FILL, LIGHTGRAY, BLACK);
  gprintfxy(BORDER, BORDER, title);
  gprintfxy(BORDER, BORDER+2*textheight("H"), " Enter filename:");
```

```
      settextbkcolor(LIGHTGRAY);
      settextcolor(BLACK);

      // Draw an edit box for the text
      setcolor(DARKGRAY);
      linesettingstype oline;
      getlinesettings(&oline);
      setlinestyle(SOLID_LINE, 0, NORM_WIDTH);
      moveto(TEXTSIZE-3, (5+1)*TEXTSIZE+3);
      mouse.hide();
      lineto(TEXTSIZE-3, 5*TEXTSIZE-3);
      lineto((1+dlen)*TEXTSIZE+3, 5*TEXTSIZE-3);
      setcolor(getmaxcolor());
      moveto(TEXTSIZE-3+1, (5+1)*TEXTSIZE+3);
      lineto((1+dlen)*TEXTSIZE+3, (5+1)*TEXTSIZE+3);
      lineto((1+dlen)*TEXTSIZE+3, 5*TEXTSIZE-3+1);
      mouse.show();
      setlinestyle(oline.linestyle, oline.upattern, oline.thickness);

      readstring(1, 5, def, fn, dlen, MAXSTR, &ch, 0);

      // Restore the font setting
      settextstyle(oldfont.font, oldfont.direction, oldfont.charsize);
      if (strlen(fn) > 0 && ch != ESC) {
        w.gunpop();
        if ((fp=fopen(fn, "w")) == NULL) {
          return;
        }
        figlist.savefiglist(fp);
        fclose(fp);
      }
      else
        w.gunpop();
    }

    // Interfaces the environment to the figure list's readfiglist() function
    void readfiglistobjtool::draw(void)
    {
      const int MAXSTR = 128;
      const int TEXTSIZE = 8;
      static char *title = "  Read an Object File   ";
      char fn[MAXSTR], def[MAXSTR] = "";
      int ch, dlen=21;    // Set editing window size to 21 characters
      FILE *fp;
      textsettingstype oldfont;

      // Save the current font, and use the default font
      gettextsettings(&oldfont);
      settextstyle(DEFAULT_FONT, HORIZ_DIR, 1);

      w.gpopup(getmaxx()/2-textwidth(title)/2-BORDER,
        getmaxy()/2-3*textheight("H"),
        getmaxx()/2+textwidth(title)/2+BORDER,
```

```
        getmaxy()/2+4*textheight("H"),
      THREED, getmaxcolor(), SOLID_FILL, LIGHTGRAY, BLACK);
  gprintfxy(BORDER, BORDER, title);
  gprintfxy(BORDER, BORDER+2*textheight("H"), " Enter filename:");

  settextbkcolor(LIGHTGRAY);
  settextcolor(BLACK);

  linesettingstype oline;
  getlinesettings(&oline);
  setlinestyle(SOLID_LINE, 0, NORM_WIDTH);
  setcolor(DARKGRAY);
  moveto(TEXTSIZE-3, (5+1)*TEXTSIZE+3);
  mouse.hide();
  lineto(TEXTSIZE-3, 5*TEXTSIZE-3);
  lineto((1+dlen)*TEXTSIZE+3, 5*TEXTSIZE-3);
  setcolor(getmaxcolor());
  moveto(TEXTSIZE-3+1, (5+1)*TEXTSIZE+3);
  lineto((1+dlen)*TEXTSIZE+3, (5+1)*TEXTSIZE+3);
  lineto((1+dlen)*TEXTSIZE+3, 5*TEXTSIZE-3+1);
  mouse.show();

  setlinestyle(oline.linestyle, oline.upattern, oline.thickness);
  readstring(1, 5, def, fn, dlen, MAXSTR, &ch, 0);
  // Restore the font setting
  settextstyle(oldfont.font, oldfont.direction, oldfont.charsize);
  if (strlen(fn) > 0 && ch != ESC) {
    w.gunpop();
    if ((fp=fopen(fn, "r")) == NULL) {
      return;
    }
    figlist.readfiglist(fp);
    fclose(fp);
  }
  else
    w.gunpop();
}


// Interfaces the environment to the deleteall() function.
// Deletes all objects in the figure list.
void deleteallobjtool::draw(void) { figlist.deleteall(); }

// Selects a new line style from the Line pull-down menu.
// This class overrides the changelinestyletool class used in the
// paint program (Chapter 11) to create a pull-down menu with
// arrows.
void CADchangelinestyletool::draw(void)
{
  maxlinestyles = MAX_LINESTYLES2;   // There are now more line styles
  performdraw();
}


// Draws the line style menu
void CADchangelinestyletool::startdrawing(void)
```

```
{
  int windowwidth, windowheight, offs, i;

  windowwidth = LINE_WIDTH + BORDER*6;
  windowheight = LINE_HEIGHT * maxlinestyles;
  w.gpopup(linemenux, linemenuy, linemenux+windowwidth+BORDER,
    linemenuy+windowheight+LINE_HEIGHT/2,
    SOLID_LINE, getmaxcolor(), SOLID_FILL, LIGHTGRAY, BLACK);
  setcolor(0);              // Draw the lines with black
  offs = BORDER;
  mouse.hide();
  for (i=0; i<maxlinestyles; i++) {
    switch(i) {
      case SOLID_LINE:    // These are the standard line styles
      case DOTTED_LINE:
      case CENTER_LINE:
      case DASHED_LINE:
        setlinestyle(i, 0, NORM_WIDTH);
        line(BORDER*3, offs+LINE_HEIGHT/2, BORDER*3+LINE_WIDTH,
          offs+LINE_HEIGHT/2);
        break;
      default:        // Line types 4, 5, and 6 have arrowheads
        setlinestyle(SOLID_LINE, 0, NORM_WIDTH);
        line(BORDER*3, offs+LINE_HEIGHT/2, BORDER*3+LINE_WIDTH,
          offs+LINE_HEIGHT/2);
        switch(i) { // Draw the lines with the arrowheads
          case 4 : line(BORDER*3, offs+LINE_HEIGHT/2,
              BORDER*3+2, offs+LINE_HEIGHT/2-2);
            line(BORDER*3, offs+LINE_HEIGHT/2,
              BORDER*3+2, offs+LINE_HEIGHT/2+2);
            break;
          case 5 : line(BORDER*3+LINE_WIDTH, offs+LINE_HEIGHT/2,
              BORDER*3+LINE_WIDTH-2, offs+LINE_HEIGHT/2-2);
            line(BORDER*3+LINE_WIDTH, offs+LINE_HEIGHT/2,
              BORDER*3+LINE_WIDTH-2, offs+LINE_HEIGHT/2+2);
            break;
          case 6 : line(BORDER*3,offs+LINE_HEIGHT/2,
              BORDER*3+2, offs+LINE_HEIGHT/2-2);
            line(BORDER*3, offs+LINE_HEIGHT/2,
              BORDER*3+2, offs+LINE_HEIGHT/2+2);
            line(BORDER*3+LINE_WIDTH, offs+LINE_HEIGHT/2,
              BORDER*3+LINE_WIDTH-2, offs+LINE_HEIGHT/2-2);
            line(BORDER*3+LINE_WIDTH, offs+LINE_HEIGHT/2,
              BORDER*3+LINE_WIDTH-2, offs+LINE_HEIGHT/2+2);
            break;
        }
    }
    offs += LINE_HEIGHT;
  }
  mouse.show();
}

// Sets the proper global settings for the line style selected in
// the menu. We have to be a little careful here with the arrowhead
```

```
                    // lines because they aren't defined by the BGI.
                    void CADchangelinestyletool::finishdrawing(void)
                    {
                      changelinestyletool::finishdrawing(); // Do everything in the inherited
                      if (linestyle >= 4) {                 // function plus set the arrowhead
                        switch (linestyle) {                // flags
                          case 4 : left_arrow = 1; right_arrow = 0; break;
                          case 5 : left_arrow = 0; right_arrow = 1; break;
                          case 6 : left_arrow = 1; right_arrow = 1; break;
                        }
                        globallinestyle = SOLID_LINE;              // Lines with arrows use
                        setlinestyle(SOLID_LINE, 0, NORM_WIDTH);  // solid lines
                      }
                    }

                    // Turns grid off if on; otherwise, redraws screen with the grid
                    void togglegridtool::draw(void)
                    {
                      if (figlist.selectedobj >= 0) {    // Deselect any selected object
                        figlist.mark(figlist.selectedobj);
                        figlist.selectedobj = -1;
                      }
                      gridon = (gridon) ? 0 : 1;          // Toggle grid flag
                      cleardrawingarea();                 // Erase the drawing
                      figlist.displayall();               // Redraw all the figures
                    }

                    // Draw a background grid in the drawing window using six
                    // horizontal and vertical dotted lines. This function assumes
                    // that the mouse is not visible.
                    void draw_grid(void)
                    {
                      int i, j, x, y, savecolor;
                      linesettingstype oline;
                      viewporttype v;

                      getviewsettings(&v);
                      setviewport(0, 0, maxx, maxy, 1);
                      savecolor = getcolor();
                      getlinesettings(&oline);
                      setlinestyle(DOTTED_LINE, 0, NORM_WIDTH);
                      setcolor(getmaxcolor());
                      for (j=1; j<6; j++) {              // Place same number here as that
                        WORLDtoPC(0.0, 0.0+j, x, y);     // used in set_window() in
                        line(wl, y, wr, y);              // setup_screen()
                      }
                      for (i=1; i<7; i++) {              // Use same number here as that
                        WORLDtoPC(0.0+i, 0.0, x, y);     // in setup_screen()
                        line(x, wt, x, wb);
                      }
                      setlinestyle(oline.linestyle, oline.upattern, oline.thickness);
                      setcolor(savecolor);
                      setviewport(v.left, v.top, v.right, v.bottom, v.clip);
                    }
```

Three-Dimensional Graphics

I n this chapter, we will explore three-dimensional graphics. Our goal is to develop a graphics package that displays three-dimensional, wire-frame objects from any vantage point. We'll begin by defining some of the terminology used in three-dimensional graphics. Then, we'll discuss various components of the three-dimensional viewing package and explain how it works. Finally, we'll give you a few sample three-dimensional object files for you to display and suggest some extensions you might try adding to the program.

ADDING THE THIRD DIMENSION

In the preceding chapters, we have been limiting our discussion to programs with two-dimensional objects. For example, in the CAD program presented in Chapter 12, the objects that we created were all defined in world coordinates using only the x and y dimensions. This gave us objects with specific heights and widths. Now we will add depth to our objects by including a third dimension, z.

In the following sections, we'll develop a program called 3D.CPP that will allow us to view wire-frame objects. The 3D.CPP environment is shown in Figure 13.1. In order to develop the three-dimensional program, however, we'll be developing a handful of new tools and exploring various issues related to three-dimensional graphics.

Figure 13.1 We'll be building several new files in this chapter to create the environment for the 3D.CPP program.

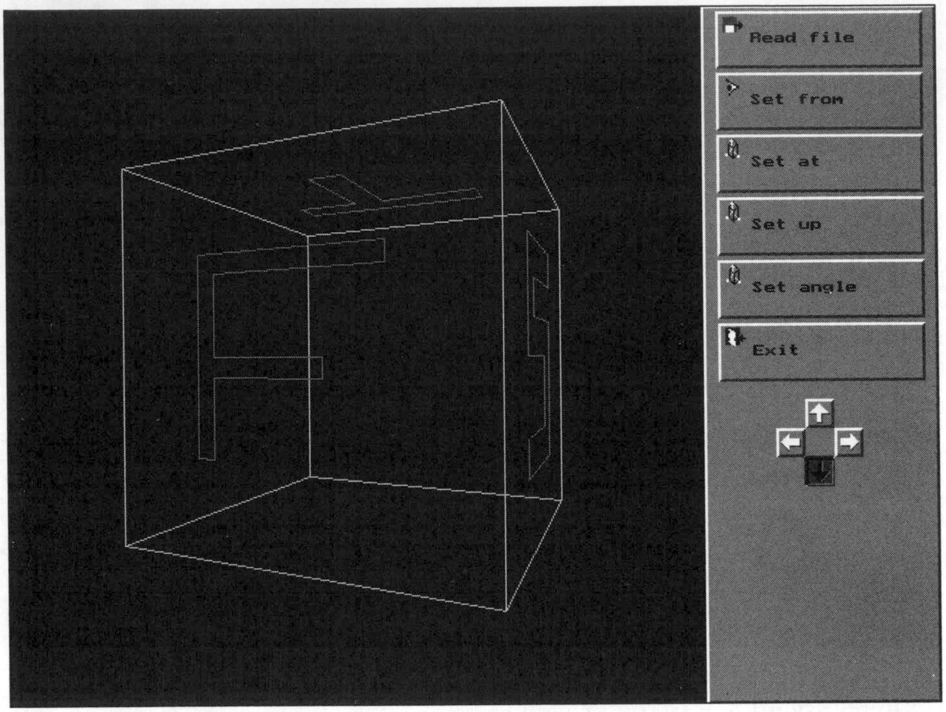

Using a Camera Model

Generating a scene of a three-dimensional object is a lot like taking a picture of an object with a camera in that they both create a two-dimensional view of a three-dimensional object. In fact, we'll be using a camera model to help us specify how objects are to be displayed.

Basically, we will assume that we are using a pinhole camera where everything in view is in focus. In addition, we'll assume that the camera is located somewhere in world coordinates at a location called the *from* point, and that it is looking directly toward a location called the *at* point. The camera model also specifies a viewing angle that acts much like a lens in that it defines how much of the scene will actually be displayed. Finally, our camera model includes a parameter called an *up* vector, which defines the orientation of the viewing plane in relation to the coordinate system. Figure 13.2 illustrates each of these viewing parameters as they appear in world coordinates.

Actually, since we are interested in how objects appear with respect to the screen, we will be using another coordinate system, called *eye coordinates*. It

Figure 13.2 This illustration shows the from, at, up, and viewing parameters in world coordinates.

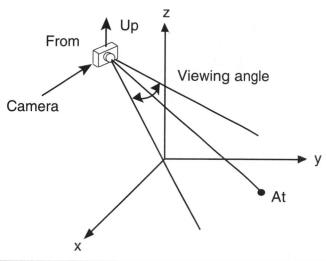

has its origin at the *from* point and the *at* point on the positive z axis, as shown in Figure 13.3. The name "eye coordinates" comes from the fact that the coordinate system is oriented with respect to the viewer—in our case, the camera.

Figure 13.3 These are the viewing parameters as they appear in eye coordinates.

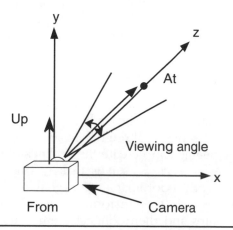

Figure 13.4 We will use perspective projection to project a three-dimensional object into two dimensions.

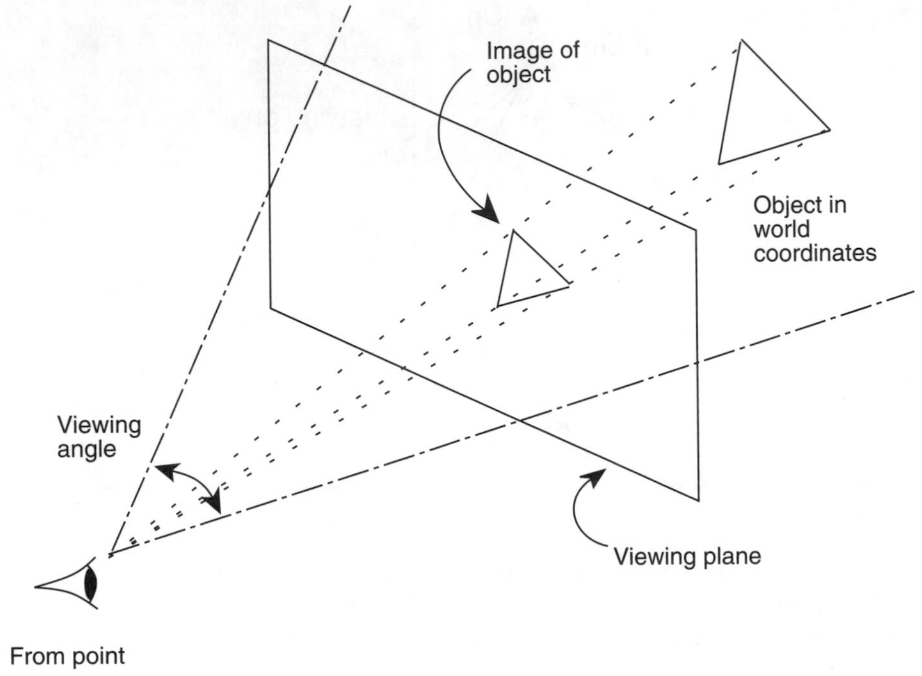

Image of object

Object in world coordinates

Viewing angle

Viewing plane

From point

Finally, our camera model uses a perspective projection of all objects. In other words, we will project all objects onto the viewing plane along rays that extend out from the *from* point, as shown in Figure 13.4. Because we will be using perspective projection, objects will appear distorted, as was illustrated in Figure 13.1; however, this technique gives a natural sensation of depth.

OBJECTS IN THREE DIMENSIONS

To keep things simple, we'll be dealing exclusively with three-dimensional, wire-frame objects like that shown in Figure 13.1. Consequently, each object is represented by a series of three-dimensional coordinate triplets that are connected by line segments to create the outlines of an object being displayed.

Each point, or *vertex*, as it is usually called, is specified as an (x,y,z) coordinate in world coordinates. The goal of a three-dimensional graphics package, therefore, is to transform these coordinates into two-dimensional screen coordinates and then connect them with line segments. This process requires numerous steps, which we'll cover in the next several sections.

TRANSFORMING FROM WORLD TO EYE COORDINATES

As mentioned before, we'll represent each object as a series of connected vertices where each point specifies an x, y, and z value in world coordinates. However, we are not so much interested in where these points are located in world coordinates as we are in where they are located with respect to the viewer—the eye coordinates. In fact, one of our first steps will be to transform object points from the world-coordinate system to an eye-coordinate system. By doing this we will easily be able to determine what objects are in view and how they appear.

Unfortunately, transforming a three-dimensional point from world coordinates to eye coordinates is not a trivial matter. Basically, what we need to do is apply a series of transforms that can align the world coordinate system with the eye coordinate system. This task can be broken up into the following steps:

1. Translate the world coordinate system so that the location of the viewer (the *from* point) is at the origin of the eye coordinate system.
2. Rotate the x axis so that the *at* point will lie on the positive z axis.
3. Rotate the y axis similarly.
4. Rotate the z axis.

At this point, objects can be projected onto the viewing plane, which is situated along the z axis. The projection process is described in greater detail later.

Although the steps just described can be used to transform between world and eye coordinates, they require numerous mathematical operations. On a PC these calculations can make a system too slow to be practical.

Instead, we'll use a vector algebra technique that reduces the number of mathematical operations that must be made. The process begins, as before, by translating the viewer in the world-coordinate system to the origin of the eye coordinates; however, to align the coordinate axes, we will not use a series of rotations. Instead, we'll replace the remaining three steps with one, as shown in Figure 13.5. We won't derive the matrix expression V that replaces the rotations described earlier, but let's look at what it is doing. Essentially, the matrix V specifies how the unit vectors A1, A2, and A3 can be aligned to the eye coordinate system, as Figure 13.6 illustrates. Therefore, by applying the matrix V, shown in Figure 13.5, after translating the world coordinates, we can transform all world coordinates to eye coordinates.

In addition, we will apply the matrix

```
D 0 0 0
0 D 0 0
0 0 1 0
0 0 0 1
```

where D is

$$\frac{1}{\texttt{tan(viewing\_angle/2)}}$$

after converting points to eye coordinates. The purpose of this matrix operation is to adjust the scene according to the viewing angle, so that the object extends between the lines y=z, y=–z, x=z, and x=–z, and as a result makes clipping a lot easier. We'll look at this operation in a minute.

Fortunately, we can combine the operations shown in Figure 13.5 and the matrix shown previously into a handful of equations. These resulting equations are used in the function **transformseg( )** to transform lines from world to eye coordinates in the three-dimensional program. Many of the values in **transformseg( )** are calculated in the function **seteye( )**, which must be called prior to transforming any line segments. You'll notice that **seteye( )** performs most of the calculations outlined in Figure 13.5. Since many of these operations are vector operations, we have included a separate utility called VECTOR.CPP to perform these operations. The source file for VECTOR.CPP and its header file VECTOR.H are listed near the end of this chapter. Table 13.1 shows the functions included in VECTOR.CPP.

Figure 13.5 Use these operations to convert world coordinates to eye coordinates.

Step 1: Translate points by $(-f_x, -f_y, -f_z)$

Step 2: Multiply result from Step 1 by V_{4x4} where

$$V = \begin{bmatrix} a_{1x} & a_{2x} & a_{3x} & 0 \\ a_{1y} & a_{2y} & a_{3y} & 0 \\ a_{1z} & a_{2z} & a_{3z} & 0 \\ 0 & 0 & 0 & 1 \end{bmatrix}$$

$$(A_1) \quad (A_2) \quad (A_3)$$

To compute A_1, A_2, and A_3, let A′ be a vector where A′=A–F

and
$$A_3 = \frac{A'}{\|A'\|} \qquad A_1 = \frac{A' \times U}{\|A' \times U\|}$$

$$A_2 = \frac{(A' \times U) \times A'}{\|(A' \times U) \times A'\|}$$

Figure 13.6 These are the vectors before and after the matrix V is applied.

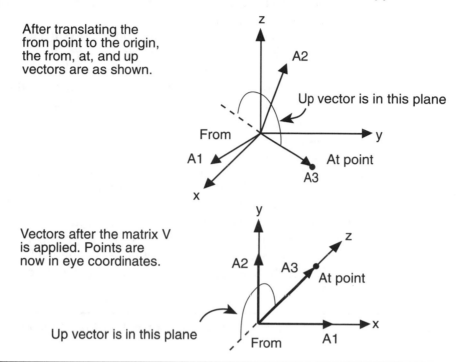

After translating the from point to the origin, the from, at, and up vectors are as shown.

Up vector is in this plane

Vectors after the matrix V is applied. Points are now in eye coordinates.

Up vector is in this plane

Table 13.1 Functions in VECTOR.CPP

Function	Description
cross()	Calculates the cross product of two vectors
divide()	Divides a vector by a scalar
dot()	Computes the dot product of two vectors
mag()	Returns the magnitude of a vector
normalize()	Normalizes a vector
subtract()	Subtracts two vectors

CLIPPING IN THREE DIMENSIONS

Thus far we have been fortunate in that the BGI has provided us with clipping algorithms to handle the clipping of graphics figures as they are displayed. However, now we must develop our own code to clip objects in three dimensions.

Essentially, what we want to do is to ignore all objects that do not project onto the projection plane and clip edges of objects that extend out beyond the border of the viewport on the projection plane.

To accomplish this, 3D.CPP includes the functions **clip3d( )** and **code( )**, which clip three-dimensional line segments in *eye coordinates* to a *viewing pyramid*, as shown in Figure 13.7. Note that all objects within the viewing pyramid will be projected onto the viewing plane and displayed on the screen.

After we transform a line segment from world coordinates to eye coordinates, we'll pass it through the clipping process, which begins by calling **clip3d( )**. In turn, **clip3d( )** calls **code( )** to determine on which side of the viewing pyramid the endpoints of the line segment fall. If one of the coordinates falls outside of the viewing pyramid, an appropriate bit in the variable **c** is set to indicate that the line may cross the edge of the viewing pyramid and must be clipped. The clipping is done in **clip3d( )** by calculating where the line segment intersects the viewing pyramid. This intersection is then used as the new endpoint of the line, and the resulting line is passed through the process again until it is broken up into a segment that is completely within the viewing pyramid. This is the line that the calling function should display.

Figure 13.7 The viewing pyramid is used to clip objects in three dimensions.

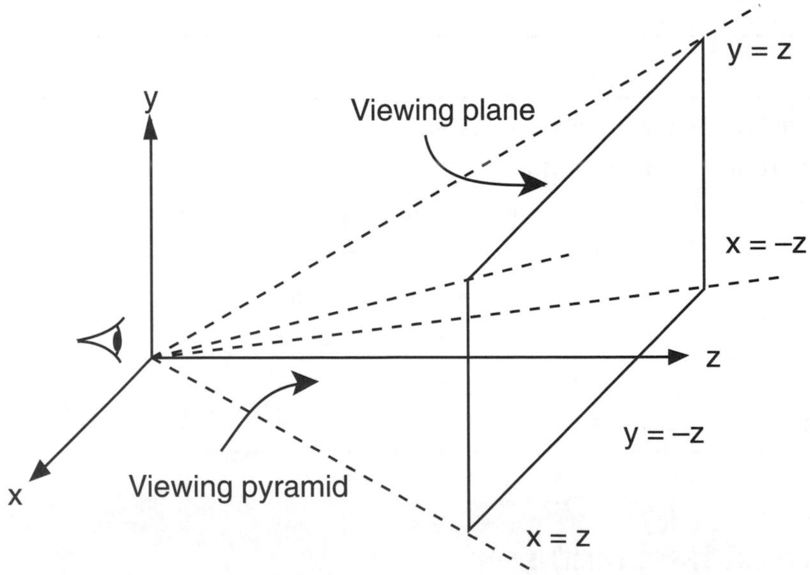

Objects are clipped to the viewing pyramid which is a region bounded by the planes y=z, y=−z, x=z, and x=−z.

PERSPECTIVE PROJECTION

All objects in the three-dimensional viewing program are displayed using *perspective projection*. The basic idea is to project all objects onto the viewing plane, as shown in Figure 13.8. Note that objects will only be displayed if a line connecting them and the viewer passes through the viewport on the viewing plane. Objects that do not intersect this region are clipped, as described in the last section.

Assuming that we have a line segment that is within the viewport on the viewing plane, how do we know what size to draw it? Fortunately, we can use

Figure 13.8 Perspective projection projects an object onto the viewing plane.

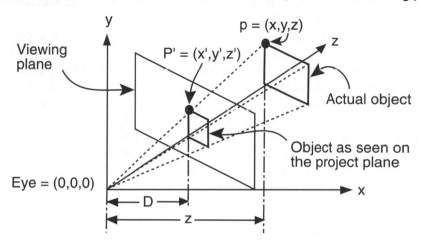

The cross-section of the yz plane from the figure above is shown below
From similar triangles:

$$y' = \frac{D \times y}{z}$$

Similarly:

$$x' = \frac{D \times x}{z}$$

where D is $\dfrac{1}{\tan(\Theta/2)}$ used in the matrix V

a simple geometric property of similar triangles, shown in the lower portion of Figure 13.8. Based on these values, a point (x,y,z) maps to (x/z,y/z) on the viewing plane. This point is then converted to PC coordinates using the function **WORLDtoPC( )**, as is done in **clip3d( )**. Note that we need to make sure z is not 0, so that we don't divide by 0! Once the points are converted to PC screen coordinates, the line segment is ready to be displayed.

OBJECTS FILES

The three-dimensional viewing program does not let you interactively create objects like the CAD program in Chapter 12. Instead, 3D.CPP is intended to only *display* three-dimensional objects. The program reads the objects that it displays from object files. This operation is performed in the **threedobj** member function **read3dobject( )**.

In order to save space and simplify modifications, 3D.CPP saves three-dimensional objects in a special format. The file begins with a header that specifies the number of independent objects in the scene. This is followed by the information for each object. Each object's description begins on a new line and includes the number of vertices in the object and the number of connections between the vertices, respectively. After this line is a list of the vertices that make up the object. Each vertex is represented as three floating-point values that correspond to the point's x, y, and z world coordinates. Next, is a series of indices into this preceding list of vertices. These indices specify how the vertices should be connected to one another. For example, if we had a triangle with the vertices

```
(0.0, 1.0, 0.1)    vertex 1
(1.0, 0.0, 0.1)    vertex 2
(1.0, 0.1, 1.0)    vertex 3
```

and we wanted these vertices connected in this order, then the list of connections would appear as:

```
1 2 3 -1
```

This list indicates that vertex 1 is connected to vertex 2, which is connected to vertex 3, which in turn is connected to vertex 1. Note that the last value is negative. This is a special marker in the connection list that indicates that the object has ended or, at least, that this face of the object is complete. The number of connections that must be read in is specified by the second number in the file header.

Actually, our connecting lists will have one more addition. Each sequence starts with an integer that specifies the color to use for that part of the object. This number can range from 0 to 15. The values correspond to the standard

---

Table 13.2 Global Variables That Store Objects

Variable	Description
connect	Array of indices into the pointarray that specifies how the vertices are to be connected
length	Number of connecting vertices in each object
numobjects	Number of objects in the scene
pointarray	Array of vertices that is stored in world coordinates for each object
vertices	Number of vertices in each object

16-color indices provided on an EGA or VGA display. Therefore, if we were to paint the previous triangle white, we'd specify a value of 15 before the connecting points:

```
15  1  2  3  -1
```

The function **read3dobject( )** reads these values into the global variables listed in Table 13.2. Later, the values in **pointarray** are accessed according to the order specified in the **connect** array to draw the object.

DISPLAYING A THREE-DIMENSIONAL OBJECT

Now that we know how a three-dimensional object is read from a file, let's see how **threedobj** uses **pointarray** and **connect** to display an object. This task is accomplished in the **view( )** member function in the following nested **while** loops:

```
i = 1;    // The arrays start at index position 1
while (i<objects[obj].numconnect) {
  // The first point is the polygon's color
  usecolor = objects[obj].connect[i++];
  startofside = i++;
  while (objects[obj].connect[i] > 0) {
    transformseg(objects[obj].pointarray[objects[obj].connect[i-1]],
      objects[obj].pointarray[objects[obj].connect[i]], usecolor);
  i++;
}
}
// The negative index specifies the last point in the polygon
transformseg(objects[obj].pointarray[objects[obj].connect[i-1]],
  objects[obj].pointarray[-objects[obj].connect[i]], usecolor);
// Connect the last point to the first
transformseg(objects[obj].pointarray[-objects[obj].connect[i]],
  objects[obj].pointarray[objects[obj].connect[startofside]], usecolor);
```

The outer **while** loop sequences through the list of vertex connections contained in **connect**. Note that the array starts at 1 and not the traditional zero index for C++ arrays. Since negative values are used to denote the end of a series of connected points, a negative 0 value would not be distinguishable from a positive 0. For this reason, the zero index is not used. The inner **while** loop sequences through the list of connected vertices until a negative marker is found. For each pair of connected points, **transformseg( )** is called as follows to transform the two points and display a line connecting them if it is visible:

```
transformseg(objects[obj].pointarray[objects[obj].connect[i-1]],
  objects[obj].pointarray[objects[obj].connect[i]], usecolor);
```

When a negative value is reached in the **connect** array, the current pair of points is displayed and then the last point is connected back to the first by the lines:

```
transformseg(objects[obj].pointarray[objects[obj].connect[i-1]],
  objects[obj].pointarray[-objects[obj].connect[i]], usecolor);
// Connect the last point to the first
transformseg(objects[obj].pointarray[-objects[obj].connect[i]],
  objects[obj].pointarray[objects[obj].connect[startofside]], usecolor);
```

This process continues until all values in the **connect** array are used.

Initializing the Viewing Parameters

There are several parameters that must be set for the three-dimensional viewing package to work properly. For instance, before an object can be viewed, the **from**, **at**, **up**, and **angle** variables must all be set. To simplify things, each of these is given a default value or is designed to automatically calculate a value that can be used. For example, the **at** location is set by **setat( )** each time a new object is read in. It calls the function **minmax( )** to determine the bounds of the object and then it sets the *at* point to the middle of the object. Similarly, **setfrom( )** sets the *from* point so that it is far enough away from the object that the whole object will appear in the viewport.

CREATING THE ENVIRONMENT

The **setup_environment( )** function in 3D.CPP sets up most of the user-interface elements in the program. It draws the viewing window and creates a series of icon-like buttons. The buttons are a hybrid between sculpted windows and simple icons.

Most of the program's user interaction is packed in the objects in USER3D.CPP. These classes are all derived from the **drawingtool** base class defined in Chapter 10's DRAWTOOL.CPP. As you might guess, the code for processing the user's interaction is located in each class' **draw( )** member function. This is the same approach that we used in the paint and CAD programs in Chapters 11 and 12. We'll add each of these tools to a tool list and associate them with buttons on the screen. Then, when the user clicks on a button, the corresponding object's **draw( )** function is executed. Table 13.3 provides a brief description of each of these new classes and hints at the menu items provided in the program.

The USER3D.CPP file also defines **mainview**, a pointer to **threedobj:**

```
threedobj *mainview;            // This is the 3D view
```

This file manages all the work necessary to display a three-dimensional scene. The **main( )** function in 3D.CPP allocates and initializes the **mainview** object so that it will draw in the window encompassed by the bounding coordinates (**pcl,pct**) and (**pcr,pcb**):

```
mainview = new threedobj();
mainview->init3dgraphics(pcl, pct, pcr, pcb);
```

The USER3D.CPP source file uses **mainview** to draw a three-dimensional scene to the screen.

Table 13.3 The User-Interface Objects in USER3D.CPP

Class	Description
quittool	Exits the program
readtool	Queries the user for a filename and then reads a scene file
setfromtool	Pops up a window that enables the user to set the from point
setattool	Pops up a window that enables the user to set the at point
setuptool	Pops up a window that enables the user to set the up vector
setangletool	Pops up a window that enables the user to change the viewing angle
forwardtool	Moves the viewer forward while the left mouse button is pressed on the up arrow icon or while the up arrow key is pressed
backwardtool	Moves the viewer backward while the left mouse button is pressed on the down arrow icon or while the down arrow key is pressed
cwtool	Rotates the viewer clockwise while the left mouse button is pressed on the left arrow icon or while the left arrow key is pressed
ccwtool	Rotates the viewer counterclockwise while the left mouse button is pressed on the right arrow icon or while the right arrow key is pressed

Moving the Viewer

The 3D program includes four arrow buttons that you can use to move the viewer. Currently, the viewer is restricted to a horizontal plane, however, you can extend the code to get around this. Each arrow button is really an icon painted on a sculpted window. When you press the left mouse button while on one of the arrows, it calls the corresponding **draw()** function of the tools defined in USER3D.CPP. For instance, if you click on the Up Arrow icon, the **forwardtool** advances the viewer as long as the left mouse button is pressed. Alternatively, you can reposition the viewer using the arrow keys. To move the viewer using the keyboard, first press and release the arrow key corresponding to the direction you want to move. For example, to move forward, you must press the Up Arrow key. The viewer's location will change each time you press the arrow key again. When you are ready to select another command, you must press the Esc key.

Changing the Viewing Parameters

The 3D program includes several menu options that enable you to modify the viewing parameters, such as the *from* point, *at* point, and *up* vector. Each of these operations is similar, so let's focus on the Set *from* menu option.

To change the *at* point, you can click on the Set *at* menu option with the mouse or press the letter *f.* This will trigger the **setattool::draw()** function, which is defined in USER3D.CPP. This function begins by popping up a sculpted window that prompts the user to enter the x, y, and z coordinates of a new *at* point. The user input is retrieved by the **readstring()** function in GTEXT.CPP. The values entered are then extracted by a call to the C++ library function **sscanf()** and used to generate a new version of the scene. This requires clearing the viewing window, recalculating the eye-coordinate system, and redisplaying the scene:

```
mainview->clear_viewport();
mainview->seteye();
mainview->view();
```

COMPILING THE 3D.CPP PROGRAM

To compile the 3D program you will need to build a project file that includes the files listed in Table 13.4. Since we're supporting the mouse, make sure that you place the compilation switch **MOUSE** in your compiler's list of defines. Otherwise, several of the routines won't work correctly with the mouse. To run the program, you'll also need to create the 16 x 16 icons shown in Figure 13.9.

Table 13.4 Files Needed to Compile the 3D Program

Source File	Header File	Chapter
3D.CPP	None	13
3DTOOL.CPP	3DTOOL.H	13
DRAWTOOL.CPP	DRAWTOOL.H	10
USER3D.CPP	USER3D.H	13
GPOPUP.CPP	GPOPUP.H	9
GTEXT.CPP	GTEXT.H	3
INTERACT.CPP	INTERACT.H	10
KBDMOUSE.CPP	KBDMOUSE.H	7
MOUSE.CPP	MOUSE.H	7
VECTOR.CPP	VECTOR.H	13

Figure 13.9 You'll need to create these icons for use with the 3D.CPP program.

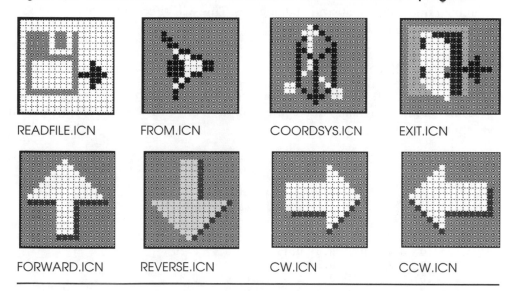

READFILE.ICN   FROM.ICN   COORDSYS.ICN   EXIT.ICN

FORWARD.ICN   REVERSE.ICN   CW.ICN   CCW.ICN

USING THE THREE-DIMENSIONAL PROGRAM

After you have 3D.CPP compiled, you're ready to try displaying an object. In the next section, the file listings for two three-dimensional objects are shown. To display each of these objects, first type the data into two separate files and name them as indicated. You can read the files into the three-dimensional program by selecting the read file command with the mouse or by typing the letter *r*. A pop-up window will appear in the center of the screen prompting you to enter the name of the file to be read. You should type this filename and press Enter. Once you press Enter, the object file is read and the object is displayed. You can then move the location of the viewer by pressing the left mouse button over the arrow icons. Alternatively, you can use the keyboard's Arrow keys. To move forward, press the Up Arrow key; to continue moving forward hold down the Up Arrow key. When you want to go another direction or select another command, you must first press the Esc key.

You may also want to experiment with each of the viewing parameters by selecting the appropriate menu options from the screen. For instance, to change the *from* point, type the letter *f* or click on the *from* button. This will cause a pop-up window to prompt you for a new *from* point. Try changing the *from* point to the world coordinate location (2, 2, 2) or even (0, 0, 0). The latter value should take you inside the object!

Another area that you might want to try experimenting with is changing the viewing angle. To select this feature, click on the Set angle menu option or type the letter *g*. The program will prompt you for a new viewing angle that must range between 0 and 180 degrees. This will effectively allow you to zoom in and out on the object.

Sample Objects

This section lists two data files for objects that you should try with your three-dimensional program. Here is the data file TEST1.DAT for the object shown in Figure 13.10:

```
1
38 63
1.0  1.0  1.0   1.0  1.0  0.0   1.0  0.0  0.0
1.0  0.0  1.0   0.0  1.0  1.0   0.0  1.0  0.0
0.0  0.0  0.0   0.0  0.0  1.0   0.25 0.0  0.25
0.25 0.0  0.75  0.75 0.0  0.75  0.75 0.0  0.7
0.3  0.0  0.7   0.3  0.0  0.5   0.6  0.0  0.5
0.6  0.0  0.45  0.3  0.0  0.45  0.3  0.0  0.25
1.0  0.3  0.2   1.0  0.3  0.3   1.0  0.6  0.3
1.0  0.6  0.5   1.0  0.3  0.5   1.0  0.3  0.8
1.0  0.7  0.8   1.0  0.7  0.7   1.0  0.4  0.7
1.0  0.4  0.6   1.0  0.7  0.6   1.0  0.7  0.2
0.4  0.3  1.0   0.4  0.6  1.0   0.2  0.6  1.0
0.2  0.7  1.0   0.8  0.7  1.0   0.8  0.6  1.0
0.5  0.6  1.0   0.5  0.3  1.0
14 1  5   8   -4
14 5  6   7   -8
14 6  2   3   -7
```

Figure 13.10 The TEST1.DAT file displays this scene.

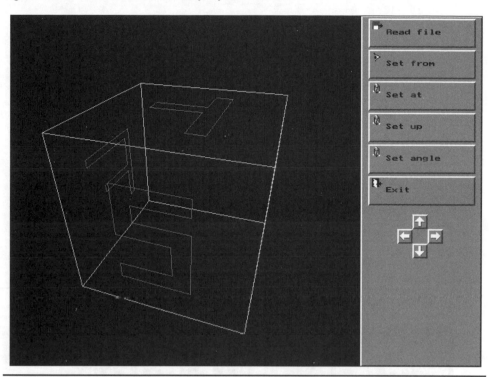

```
14 1   4   3   -2
14 8   7   3   -4
14 6   5   1   -2
13 9   10  11  12  13  14  15  16 17  -18
13 19  20  21  22  23  24  25  26 27  28  29  -30
13 31  32 33  34  35  36  37  -38
```

This data file, called TEST2.DAT, generates the three objects shown in Figure 13.11.

```
3
13 51
1.0  1.0  1.0   1.0  1.0  0.0   1.0  0.0  0.0
1.0  0.0  1.0   0.0  1.0  1.0   0.0  1.0  0.0
0.0  0.0  0.0   0.0  0.0  1.0   0.8  0.2  1.1
0.8  0.8  1.1   0.2  0.8  1.1   0.2  0.2  1.1
0.5  0.5  1.5
14 1   5   8   -4
14 5   6   7   -8
14 6   2   3   -7
14 1   4   3   -2
```

```
14 8   7    3   -4
14 6   5    1   -2
10 9   10  -13
10 10  11  -13
10 11  12  -13
10 12  9   -13
10 12  11  10  -9
13 51
3.0  3.0  1.0   3.0  3.0  0.0   3.0  2.0  0.0
3.0  2.0  1.0   2.0  3.0  1.0   2.0  3.0  0.0
2.0  2.0  0.0   2.0  2.0  1.0   2.8  2.2  1.1
2.8  2.8  1.1   2.2  2.8  1.1   2.2  2.2  1.1
2.5  2.5  1.5
12 1   5    8   -4
12 5   6    7   -8
12 6   2    3   -7
12 1   4    3   -2
12 8   7    3   -4
12 6   5    1   -2
11 9   10  -13
11 10  11  -13
```

Figure 13.11 The TEST2.DAT file displays this scene.

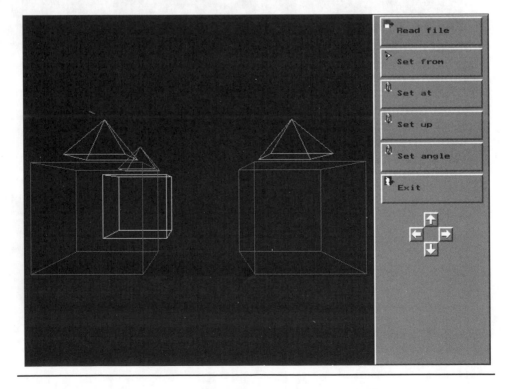

```
11 11 12  -13
11 12  9  -13
11 12 11  10 -9
13 51
3.0  1.0  1.0    3.0  1.0  0.0    3.0  0.0  0.0
3.0  0.0  1.0    2.0  1.0  1.0    2.0  1.0  0.0
2.0  0.0  0.0    2.0  0.0  1.0    2.8  0.2  1.1
2.8  0.8  1.1    2.2  0.8  1.1    2.2  0.2  1.1
2.5  0.5  1.5
12 1    5    8   -4
12 5    6    7   -8
12 6    2    3   -7
12 1    4    3   -2
12 8    7    3   -4
12 6    5    1   -2
11 9   10  -13
11 10  11  -13
11 11  12  -13
11 12   9  -13
11 12  11  10 -9
```

EXTENDING THE PROGRAM

There are several enhancements that you might try adding to the three-dimensional viewing package. The first thing you might try is to paint the objects so that the ones farthest from the viewer are painted first. This ensures that the objects will appear correctly on the screen. You'll notice that currently 3D may paint the objects so that more distant line segments overlap line segments that are actually closer.

You might also want to try adding routines that enable you to interactively draw three-dimensional objects on the screen. This is not a simple task. You will probably want to use several viewports that show the object at different perspectives in order to give yourself a good idea of the object that you are drawing.

In the next chapter, we'll add solid surfaces to our objects.

• 3DTOOL.H

```
// 3DTOOL.H: Header file for 3DTOOL.CPP.

#ifndef TOOL3DH
#define TOOL3DH

#include "vector.h"

const int NUMCONNECTIONS = 100;    // An object can have this many
const int NUMVERTICES = 100;       // vertices and connections
const int NUMOBJECTS = 3;          // Maximum number of objects allowed
```

```
struct ANOBJECT {
  int connect[NUMCONNECTIONS];      // Vertex connections
  VECTOR pointarray[NUMVERTICES];   // Vertices
  int numconnect;                   // Number of vertex connections
  int numvertices;                  // Number of vertices
};

class threedobj {
public:
  double a, b, c, d, dval;
  VECTOR from, at, up;              // Viewing parameters
  double angle;                     // The viewing angle
  VECTOR a1, a2, a3;                // Used in three-dimensional transform
  ANOBJECT objects[NUMOBJECTS];
  int numobjects;
  double objxmin, objxmax;          // Extent of three-dimensional object
  double objymin, objymax;
  double objzmin, objzmax;
  double t_from;                    // Controls from-at point dist
  double offsx, offsy, offsz;       // Transform variables
  VECTOR dist;                      // Distance to from-at point
  double theta, thetainc;
  double alpha, alphainc;
  double r;
  int left, right, top, bottom;     // PC screen boundaries of viewing area
  void init3dgraphics(int useleft, int usetop,
    int useright, int usebottom);
  void minmax(void);
  void setat(void);
  void setfrom(void);
  void seteye(void);
  int code(double x, double y, double z);
  void WORLDtoPC(double xw, double yw, int& xpc, int& ypc);
  void transformseg(VECTOR& v1, VECTOR& v2, int color);
  void clear_viewport(void);
  int clip3d(VECTOR *V1, VECTOR *V2, int& xpc1, int& ypc1,
  int& xpc2, int& ypc2, int& clippos1, int& clippos2, int& clip);
  virtual void view(void);
  virtual int read3dobject(char *filename);
};

#endif
```

• 3DTOOL.CPP

```
// 3DTOOL.CPP: Implements a wire-frame, three-dimensional viewing toolkit.
#include <graphics.h>
#include <math.h>
#include <stdio.h>
#include "vector.h"
#include "3dtool.h"
```

```
#ifdef MOUSE
#include "kbdmouse.h"
extern kbdmouseobj mouse;
#endif

// Returns the larger of two values
inline double maxof(double val1, double val2) {
  return (val1 > val2) ? val1 : val2;
}

// Converts an angle to radians
inline double torad(double degrees) {
  return degrees * 0.017453293;
}

// Converts clipped world coordinates to screen coordinates
void threedobj::WORLDtoPC(double xw, double yw, int& xpc, int& ypc)
{
  xpc = (int)(a * xw + b);
  ypc = (int)(c * yw + d);
}

// Must be called before program begins main execution. It sets
// up the dimensions of the screen and various default values.
void threedobj::init3dgraphics(int useleft, int usetop,
  int useright, int usebottom)
{
  // Set up the dimensions of the viewing region
  left = useleft;
  top = usetop;
  right = useright;
  bottom = usebottom;
  a = (right - left) / (1 + 1);      // Set viewport and window
  b = left - a * (-1);               // mapping variables
  c = (top - bottom) / (1 + 1);
  d = bottom - c * (-1);
  // Set default values for from, at, and up vectors
  from.x = 1.0;  from.y = 0.0;  from.z = 0.0;
  at.x = 0.0;    at.y = 0.0;    at.z = 0.0;
  up.x = 0.0;    up.y = 0.0;    up.z = 1.0;
  angle = torad(60.0); // Use a 60 degree viewing angle
  t_from = 1.0;
  thetainc = 0.0174;   // 1 degree
  alphainc = 0.0174;   // 1 degree
  numobjects = 0;      // There aren't any objects initially
}

// Returns the minimum and maximum values in the point array
// for the x, y, and z values. This function is used to determine
// where to place the viewer initially so that everything in
// the scene is in view.
void threedobj::minmax(void)
{
  int i, obj;
```

```
        objxmin = 32000;  objymin = 32000;  objzmin = 32000;
        objxmax = -32000; objymax = -32000; objzmax = -32000;
        for (obj=0; obj<numobjects; obj++) {
          for (i=1; i<=objects[obj].numvertices; i++) {
            if (objects[obj].pointarray[i].x > objxmax)
                objxmax = objects[obj].pointarray[i].x;
              else if (objects[obj].pointarray[i].x < objxmin)
                objxmin = objects[obj].pointarray[i].x;
            if (objects[obj].pointarray[i].y > objymax)
              objymax = objects[obj].pointarray[i].y;
              else if (objects[obj].pointarray[i].y < objymin)
              objymin = objects[obj].pointarray[i].y;
            if (objects[obj].pointarray[i].z > objzmax)
              objzmax = objects[obj].pointarray[i].z;
              else if (objects[obj].pointarray[i].z < objzmin)
              objzmin = objects[obj].pointarray[i].z;
          }
        }
      }

// Routine to provide a default value for the at point. It
// is set to the midpoint of the extents of the scene.
void threedobj::setat(void)
{
  minmax();
  at.x = (objxmin+objxmax) / 2.0;
  at.y = (objymin+objymax) / 2.0;
  at.z = (objzmin+objzmax) / 2.0;
}


// Routine that provides a default value for the from point. It
// is dependent on the at point and the view angle.
const double WIDTH = 1.8;   // Ratio used to determine from point
                            // It is based on size of object
void threedobj::setfrom(void)
{
  from.x = at.x + (objxmax-objxmin) / 2.0 + WIDTH *
    maxof((objzmax-objzmin)/2.0, (objymax-objymin)/2.0);
  from.y = at.y;
  from.z = at.z;
}

// There must be a valid object in pointarray before calling this
// function. It sets up the various variables used in transforming
// an object from world to eye coordinates.
void threedobj::seteye(void)
{
  double tempmag;
  VECTOR temp;

  dval = cos(angle/2.0) / sin(angle/2.0);
  dist = subtract(&at, &from);
  r = mag(&dist);
  a3 = divide(&dist, r);
```

```
    temp = cross(&dist, &up);
    tempmag = mag(&temp);
    a1 = divide(&temp, tempmag);
    temp = cross(&a1, &a3);
    tempmag = mag(&temp);
    a2 = divide(&temp, tempmag);
    offsx = -a1.x * from.x - a1.y * from.y - a1.z * from.z;
    offsy = -a2.x * from.x - a2.y * from.y - a2.z * from.z;
    offsz = -a3.x * from.x - a3.y * from.y - a3.z * from.z;
    theta = atan2(dist.y, dist.x);
    alpha = atan2(dist.z, dist.x);
}

const int NOEDGE = 0x00;
const int LEFTEDGE = 0x01;
const int RIGHTEDGE = 0x02;
const int BOTTOMEDGE = 0x04;
const int TOPEDGE = 0x08;
const int TOL = 0.001;

// Returns a code specifying which edge in the viewing
// pyramid was crossed. There may be more than one.
int threedobj::code(double x, double y, double z)
{
    Int c = NOEDGE;
    if (x < -z-TOL) c |= LEFTEDGE;
    if (x > z+TOL)  c |= RIGHTEDGE;
    if (y < -z-TOL) c |= BOTTOMEDGE;
    if (y > z+TOL)  c |= TOPEDGE;
    return c;
}

// Clips the line segment in 3D coordinates to the viewing pyramid.
// Returns 0 if at least part of the line segment is visible.
int threedobj::clip3d(VECTOR *V1, VECTOR *V2, int& xpc1, int& ypc1,
    int& xpc2, int& ypc2, int& clippos1, int& clippos2, int& clip)
{
    int c, c1, c2, clippos;
    double x, y, z, t;

    c1 = code(V1->x, V1->y, V1->z);
    c2 = code(V2->x, V2->y, V2->z);
    clippos1 = 0;
    clippos2 = 0;
    clippos = -1;
    clip = 0;
    while (c1 != NOEDGE || c2 != NOEDGE) {
        if ((c1 & c2) != NOEDGE) return 1;
        c = c1;
        if (c == NOEDGE) c = c2;
        if ((c & LEFTEDGE) == LEFTEDGE) {
            // Crosses left edge
            t = (V1->z + V1->x) / ((V1->x - V2->x) - (V2->z - V1->z));
            z = t * (V2->z - V1->z) + V1->z;
```

```
      x = -z;
      y = t * (V2->y - V1->y) + V1->y;
      clippos = 3;    // Remember the side that was clipped on
    }
    else if ((c & RIGHTEDGE) == RIGHTEDGE) {
      // Crosses right edge
      t = (V1->z - V1->x) / ((V2->x - V1->x) - (V2->z - V1->z));
      z = t * (V2->z - V1->z) + V1->z;
      x = z;
      y = t * (V2->y - V1->y) + V1->y;
      clippos = 1;    // Remember the side that was clipped on
    }
    else if ((c & BOTTOMEDGE) == BOTTOMEDGE) {
      // Crosses bottom edge
      t = (V1->z + V1->y) / ((V1->y - V2->y) - (V2->z - V1->z));
      z = t * (V2->z - V1->z) + V1->z;
      x = t * (V2->x - V1->x) + V1->x;
      y = -z;
      clippos = 2;    // Remember the side that was clipped on
    }
    else if ((c & TOPEDGE) == TOPEDGE) {
      // Crosses top edge
      t = (V1->z - V1->y) / ((V2->y - V1->y) - (V2->z - V1->z));
      z = t * (V2->z - V1->z) + V1->z;
      x = t * (V2->x - V1->x) + V1->x;
      y = z;
      clippos = 0;    // Remember the side that was clipped on
    }
    if (c == c1) {
      V1->x = x;  V1->y = y;  V1->z = z;
      clippos1 = clippos;
      clip |= 0x80;
      c1 = code(x, y, z);
    }
    else {
      V2->x = x;  V2->y = y;  V2->z = z;
      clippos2 = clippos;
      clip |= 0x08;
      c2 = code(x, y, z);
    }
  }
  // Convert the clipped world coordinates to screen coordinates
  if (V1->z != 0) {
    WORLDtoPC(V1->x/V1->z, V1->y/V1->z, xpc1, ypc1);
    WORLDtoPC(V2->x/V2->z, V2->y/V2->z, xpc2, ypc2);
  }
  else {
    WORLDtoPC(V1->x, V1->y, xpc1, ypc1);
    WORLDtoPC(V2->x, V2->y, xpc2, ypc2);
  }
  return 0;  // A clipped point is visible
}
```

```
// Transforms the segment connecting the two vectors into
// the viewing plane. 3dclip() clips and draws the line if visible.
void threedobj::transformseg(VECTOR& v1, VECTOR& v2, int color)
{
  VECTOR V1, V2;
  int xpc1, ypc1, xpc2, ypc2, t1, t2, t3;

  V1.x = (v1.x * a1.x + a1.y * v1.y + a1.z * v1.z + offsx)*dval;
  V1.y = (v1.x * a2.x + a2.y * v1.y + a2.z * v1.z + offsy)*dval;
  V1.z =  v1.x * a3.x + a3.y * v1.y + a3.z * v1.z + offsz;
  V2.x = (v2.x * a1.x + a1.y * v2.y + a1.z * v2.z + offsx)*dval;
  V2.y = (v2.x * a2.x + a2.y * v2.y + a2.z * v2.z + offsy)*dval;
  V2.z =  v2.x * a3.x + a3.y * v2.y + a3.z * v2.z + offsz;
  if (!clip3d(&V1, &V2, xpc1, ypc1, xpc2, ypc2, t1, t2, t3)) {
    setcolor(color);              // Draw the clipped line with
    line(xpc1, ypc1, xpc2, ypc2); // the color passed in
  }
}


// Increments through the pointarray which contains the vertices of the
// object and display them as you go. This will draw out the object.
void threedobj::view(void)
{
  int i, obj, startofside, usecolor;

#ifdef MOUSE
  mouse.hide();
#endif
  for (obj=0; obj<numobjects; obj++) {  // Draw each object
    i = 1;     // The arrays start at index position 1
    while (i<objects[obj].numconnect) {
      // The first point is the polygon's color
      usecolor = objects[obj].connect[i++];
      startofside = i++;
      while (objects[obj].connect[i] > 0) {
        transformseg(objects[obj].pointarray[objects[obj].connect[i-1]],
          objects[obj].pointarray[objects[obj].connect[i]], usecolor);

        i++;
      }
      // The negative index specifies the last point in the polygon
      transformseg(objects[obj].pointarray[objects[obj].connect[i-1]],
        objects[obj].pointarray[-objects[obj].connect[i]], usecolor);
      // Connect the last point to the first
      transformseg(objects[obj].pointarray[-objects[obj].connect[i]],
        objects[obj].pointarray[objects[obj].connect[startofside]],
          usecolor);
      i++;
    }
  }
#ifdef MOUSE
  mouse.show();
#endif
}
```

```
// Clears the drawing window
void threedobj::clear_viewport(void)
{
  viewporttype vu;

  getviewsettings(&vu);
  setviewport(left, top, right, bottom, 1);
#ifdef MOUSE
  mouse.hide();
#endif
  clearviewport();
#ifdef MOUSE
  mouse.show();
#endif
  setviewport(vu.left, vu.top, vu.right, vu.bottom, vu.clip);
}


// Reads in a file that adheres to the standard described in Chapter 13.
// Returns 1 if file is read successfully; otherwise, it returns 0.
int threedobj::read3dobject(char *filename)
{
  FILE *infile;
  int i, obj;

  if ((infile=fopen(filename,"r")) == NULL)
    return -1;    // Failed to open file
  fscanf(infile, "%d", &numobjects);      // Read the number of objects
  for (obj=0; obj<numobjects; obj++) {
    fscanf(infile, "%d %d", &objects[obj].numvertices,
      &objects[obj].numconnect);
    if (objects[obj].numvertices >= NUMVERTICES ||
        objects[obj].numconnect >= NUMCONNECTIONS) {
      fclose(infile);    // Object is too large
      return -2;
    }
    for (i=1; i<=objects[obj].numvertices; i++)
      fscanf(infile, "%lf %lf %lf",
        &objects[obj].pointarray[i].x,
        &objects[obj].pointarray[i].y,
        &objects[obj].pointarray[i].z);
    for (i=1; i<=objects[obj].numconnect; i++)
      fscanf(infile, "%d", &objects[obj].connect[i]);
  }
  fclose(infile);
  return 1;
}
```

• USER3D.H

```
// USER3D.H: Tools used in the 3D programs.

#ifndef USER3DH
#define USER3DH
```

```
#include "drawtool.h"
#include "3dtool.h"
#include "gpopup.h"

extern threedobj *mainview, *birdview;
extern gwindows w;

class quittool : public drawingtool {
public:
  virtual void draw(void);
};

class readtool : public drawingtool {
public:
  virtual void draw(void);
};

class setfromtool : public drawingtool {
public:
  virtual void draw(void);
};

class setattool : public drawingtool {
public:
  virtual void draw(void);
};

class setuptool : public drawingtool {
public:
  virtual void draw(void);
};

class setangletool : public drawingtool {
public:
  virtual void draw(void);
};

class forwardtool : public drawingtool {
public:
  virtual void draw(void);
};

class backwardtool : public drawingtool {
public:
  virtual void draw(void);
};

class cwtool : public drawingtool {
public:
  virtual void draw(void);
};

class ccwtool : public drawingtool {
public:
```

```
    virtual void draw(void);
};

void popuperror(char *message);
void menustr(int x, int y, int tc, int hc, int bc, char *str);

#endif
```

• USER3D.CPP

```
// USER3D.CPP: Provides the user interaction for the 3D programs
// in Chapters 13 and 14.
#include <graphics.h>
#include <stdlib.h>
#include <string.h>
#include <stdio.h>
#include <conio.h>
#include <math.h>
#include "gtext.h"
#include "gpopup.h"
#include "3dtool.h"
#include "mouse.h"
#include "user3d.h"

#define TEXTSIZE 8                  // Pixel size of the default font

int iconwd, iconht;                 // The dimensions of the icons
gwindows w;
threedobj *mainview;                // This is the 3D view

const int BORDER=10;                // Border placed around windows

// Converts an angle to radians
inline double torad(double degrees) {
  return degrees * 0.017453293;
}

// Exits the program
void quittool::draw(void)
{
  closegraph();
  exit(0);
}

// Draws a frame for an edit field
void draweditframe(int col, int row, int cols)
{
  setcolor(DARKGRAY);
  moveto(col*TEXTSIZE-3, (row+1)*TEXTSIZE+3);
  mouse.hide();
  lineto(col*TEXTSIZE-3, row*TEXTSIZE-3);
  lineto((col+cols)*TEXTSIZE+3, row*TEXTSIZE-3);
```

```
    setcolor(WHITE);
    moveto(col*TEXTSIZE-3+1, (row+1)*TEXTSIZE+3);
    lineto((col+cols)*TEXTSIZE+3, (row+1)*TEXTSIZE+3);
    lineto((col+cols)*TEXTSIZE+3, row*TEXTSIZE-3+1);
    mouse.show();
}

// Prompts for the filename of the file to be read and then calls
// read3dobject() to read it. If the file is successfully read, it is
// displayed by calling view() after setting the viewing parameters.
void readtool::draw(void)
{
  const int MAXSTR = 128;
  static char *title = "Read a 3D Object File";
  char fn[MAXSTR], def[MAXSTR] = "";
  int ch, dlen=21;          // Set editing window size to 21 characters
  int txtht = textheight("H");

  w.gpopup(getmaxx()/2-textwidth(title)/2-BORDER,
    getmaxy()/2-3*txtht, getmaxx()/2+textwidth(title)/2+BORDER,
    getmaxy()/2+5*txtht, THREED, WHITE, SOLID_FILL, LIGHTGRAY, BLACK);
  gprintfxy(BORDER, BORDER, title);
  gprintfxy(BORDER, BORDER+2*txtht, "Enter filename:");

  settextbkcolor(LIGHTGRAY);
  settextcolor(BLACK);
  draweditframe(1, 5, dlen);   // Draw a frame around the edit field
  readstring(1, 5, def, fn, dlen, MAXSTR, &ch, 0);

  if (strlen(fn) > 0 && ch != ESC && mainview->read3dobject(fn)==1) {
    w.gunpop();
    mainview->setat();
    mainview->setfrom();
    mainview->seteye();
    mainview->r = 10;
    mainview->clear_viewport();
    mainview->view();
  }
  else {
    w.gunpop();
  }
}

// Pops up a window that the user can use to enter a new from point
void setfromtool::draw(void)
{
  const int MAXSTR = 128;
  static char *title = " Change the From Point    ";
  char fn[MAXSTR], def[MAXSTR] = "";
  int ch, dlen=24;   // Set editing window size
  VECTOR nu;
  int txtht = textheight("H");
```

```
  w.gpopup(getmaxx()/2-textwidth(title)/2-5,
    getmaxy()/2-3*txtht, getmaxx()/2+textwidth(title)/2+5,
    getmaxy()/2+6*txtht, THREED, WHITE, SOLID_FILL, LIGHTGRAY, BLACK);
  gprintfxy(BORDER, BORDER, title);
  gprintfxy(BORDER, BORDER+2*txtht, "Enter x y z coordinates");
  gprintfxy(BORDER, BORDER+3*txtht, "for the new from point.");

  draweditframe(1, 6, dlen);  // Draw a frame around the edit field
  readstring(1, 6, def, fn, dlen, MAXSTR, &ch, 0);
  if (sscanf(fn, "%lf %lf %lf", &nu.x, &nu.y, &nu.z) < 3) {
    w.gunpop();
    return;
  }
  w.gunpop();
  if (nu.x == mainview->at.x && nu.y == mainview->at.y &&
    nu.z == mainview->at.z)
    popuperror(" Invalid From Point ");
  else {
    mainview->from.x = nu.x;
    mainview->from.y = nu.y;
    mainview->from.z = nu.z;
    mainview->clear_viewport();
    mainview->seteye();
    mainview->view();
  }
  mouse.show();
}

// Pops up an error message
void popuperror(char *message)
{
  int width;
  static char *press = " Press Enter to Continue ";

  width = textwidth(message);
  if (width < textwidth(press))
    width = textwidth(press);
  w.gpopup(getmaxx()/2, getmaxy()/2+20, getmaxx()/2+width+10,
    getmaxy()/2+20+3*(textheight("H")+2),
    THREED, WHITE, SOLID_FILL, LIGHTGRAY, RED);
  gprintfxy(5, 5, message);
  gprintfxy(5, 5+textheight("H"), press);
  getch();
  w.gunpop();
}

// Pops up a window that the user can use to enter a new at point
void setattool::draw(void)
{
  const int MAXSTR = 128;
  static char *title = "  Change the At Point   ";
  char fn[MAXSTR], def[MAXSTR] = "";
  int ch, dlen=23;  // Set editing window size
```

```
   double nux, nuy, nuz;
   int txtht = textheight("H");

   w.gpopup(getmaxx()/2-textwidth(title)/2-5,
     getmaxy()/2-3*txtht, getmaxx()/2+textwidth(title)/2+5,
     getmaxy()/2+6*txtht, THREED, WHITE, SOLID_FILL, LIGHTGRAY, BLACK);
   gprintfxy(BORDER, BORDER, title);
   gprintfxy(BORDER, BORDER+2*txtht, "Enter x y z coordinates");
   gprintfxy(BORDER, BORDER+3*txtht, "for the new at point.");

   draweditframe(1, 6, dlen);  // Draw a frame around the edit field
   readstring(1, 6, def, fn, dlen, MAXSTR, &ch, 0);
   if (sscanf(fn, "%lf %lf %lf", &nux, &nuy, &nuz) < 3) {
     w.gunpop();
     return;
   }
   w.gunpop();
   if ((nux==mainview->from.x &&
        nuy==mainview->from.y &&
        nuz==mainview->from.z) ||
      (nux==mainview->up.x && nuy==mainview->up.y && nuz==mainview->up.z))
     popuperror(" Invalid From Point ");
   else {
     mainview->at.x = nux;  mainview->at.y = nuy;  mainview->at.z = nuz;
     mainview->clear_viewport();
     mainview->seteye();
     mainview->view();
   }
}

// Pops up a window that the user can use to enter a new up vector
void setuptool::draw(void)
{
  const int MAXSTR = 128;
  static char *title = "  Change the Up Point  ";
  char fn[MAXSTR], def[MAXSTR] = "";
  int ch, dlen=23;  // Set editing window size
  VECTOR nu;
  int txtht = textheight("H");

  w.gpopup(getmaxx()/2-textwidth(title)/2-5,
    getmaxy()/2-3*txtht, getmaxx()/2+textwidth(title)/2+5,
    getmaxy()/2+6*txtht, THREED, WHITE, SOLID_FILL, LIGHTGRAY, BLACK);
  gprintfxy(BORDER, BORDER, title);
  gprintfxy(BORDER, BORDER+2*txtht, "Enter x y z coordinates");
  gprintfxy(BORDER, BORDER+3*txtht, "for the new up vector.");

  draweditframe(1, 6, dlen);  // Draw a frame around the edit field
  readstring(1, 6, def, fn, dlen, MAXSTR, &ch, 0);
  if (sscanf(fn, "%lf %lf %lf", &nu.x, &nu.y, &nu.z) < 3) {
    w.gunpop();
    return;
  }
```

```
      w.gunpop();
      if (nu.x==mainview->at.x && nu.y==mainview->at.y && nu.z==mainview->at.z)
        popuperror(" Invalid Up vector ");
      else {
        mainview->up.x = nu.x;  mainview->up.y = nu.y;  mainview->up.z = nu.z;
        mainview->seteye();
        mainview->clear_viewport();
        mainview->view();
      }
}

// Asks the user for a viewing angle. It must be between 0 and 180 degrees.
void setangletool::draw(void)
{
  const int MAXSTR = 128;
  static char *title = " Change the Viewing Angle ";
  char fn[MAXSTR], def[MAXSTR] = "";
  int ch, dlen=23;  // Set editing window size
  double nut;
  int txtht = textheight("H");

  w.gpopup(getmaxx()/2-textwidth(title)/2-5,
    getmaxy()/2-3*txtht, getmaxx()/2+textwidth(title)/2+5,
    getmaxy()/2+6*txtht, THREED, WHITE, SOLID_FILL, LIGHTGRAY, BLACK);
  gprintfxy(BORDER, BORDER, title);
  gprintfxy(BORDER, BORDER+2*txtht, "Enter a new angle between");
  gprintfxy(BORDER, BORDER+3*txtht, "0 and 180 degrees.");

  draweditframe(1, 6, dlen);  // Draw a frame around the edit field
  readstring(1, 6, def, fn, dlen, MAXSTR, &ch, 0);
  if (sscanf(fn, "%lf", &nut) < 1) {
    w.gunpop();
    return;
  }
  w.gunpop();
  if (nut > 0 && nut < 180) {
    mainview->angle = torad(nut);
    mainview->seteye();
    mainview->clear_viewport();
    mainview->view();
  }
  else
    popuperror(" Angle must be between 0 and 180 ");
}

// Interactively moves the from point forward. Supports the keyboard
// and mouse.
void forwardtool::draw(void)
{
  int c, mx, my, usekeys=0;
  double nufx, nufy, nufz, fromincx, fromincy;
  VECTOR oldatv;
```

```
    if (mainview->numobjects <= 0) return;  // Nothing to draw

  mainview->t_from = 1.0;
  fromincx = mainview->r * cos(mainview->theta);
  fromincy = mainview->r * sin(mainview->theta);
  // Use the keyboard if the mouse is not pressed
  if (!mouse.buttondown((unsigned)1)) usekeys = 1;
  c = getkey();
  while (!mouse.buttonreleased(LEFT_BUTTON) || c == UP) {
    if (usekeys) {
      while ((c=getkey()) != 0x1B && c != UP) ;
      if (c == 0x1B) return; // You can press Esc to quit
    }
    else {
      // The mouse button is down; get the new mouse location
      mouse.getcoords(mx, my);
      if (mx < left || mx > right || my < top || my > bottom) {
        while (!mouse.buttonreleased(LEFT_BUTTON));
        // The user pressed outside of the button
        return;
      }
    }
    nufx = mainview->from.x + fromincx / 20;
    nufy = mainview->from.y + fromincy / 20;
    nufz = mainview->from.z;

    oldatv.x = mainview->at.x - mainview->from.x;
    oldatv.y = mainview->at.y - mainview->from.y;
    oldatv.z = mainview->at.z - mainview->from.z;

    if (nufx == mainview->at.x && nufy == mainview->at.y &&
      nufz == mainview->at.z)
      popuperror(" Cannot move to here ");
    else {
      mainview->from.x = nufx;
      mainview->from.y = nufy;
      mainview->from.z = nufz;

      mainview->at.x = mainview->from.x + oldatv.x;
      mainview->at.y = mainview->from.y + oldatv.y;
      mainview->at.z = mainview->from.z + oldatv.z;
      mainview->r = 10;
      mainview->seteye();
      mainview->clear_viewport();
      mainview->view();
    }
  }
}

// Interactively moves the from point back. Supports the keyboard
// and mouse.
void backwardtool::draw(void)
{
```

```
int c, mx, my, usekeys=0;
double nufx, nufy, nufz, fromincx, fromincy;
VECTOR oldatv;

if (mainview->numobjects <= 0) return;  // Nothing to draw

mainview->t_from = 1.0;

fromincx = mainview->r * cos(mainview->theta);
fromincy = mainview->r * sin(mainview->theta);

// Use the keyboard if the mouse is not pressed
if (!mouse.buttondown(1)) usekeys = 1;
c = getkey();
while (!mouse.buttonreleased(LEFT_BUTTON) || c == DOWN) {
  if (usekeys) {
    while ((c=getkey()) != 0x1B && c != DOWN) ;
    if (c == 0x1B) return; // You can press ESC to quit
  }
  else {
    // The mouse button is down; get the new mouse location
    mouse.getcoords(mx, my);
    if (mx < left || mx > right || my < top || my > bottom) {
      while (!mouse.buttonreleased(LEFT_BUTTON));
      // The user pressed outside of the button
      return;
    }
  }
  nufx = mainview->from.x - fromincx / 20;
  nufy = mainview->from.y - fromincy / 20;
  nufz = mainview->from.z;

  oldatv.x = mainview->at.x - mainview->from.x;
  oldatv.y = mainview->at.y - mainview->from.y;
  oldatv.z = mainview->at.z - mainview->from.z;

  if (nufx == mainview->at.x && nufy == mainview->at.y &&
    nufz == mainview->at.z)
    popuperror(" Cannot move to here ");
  else {
    mainview->from.x = nufx;
    mainview->from.y = nufy;
    mainview->from.z = nufz;

    mainview->at.x = mainview->from.x + oldatv.x;
    mainview->at.y = mainview->from.y + oldatv.y;
    mainview->at.z = mainview->from.z + oldatv.z;
    mainview->r = 10;
    mainview->seteye();
    mainview->clear_viewport();
    mainview->view();
  }
 }
}
```

```cpp
// Interactively rotates the viewer clockwise. Supports the keyboard
// and mouse.
void cwtool::draw(void)
{
  int c, mx, my, usekeys=0, times=0;
  double nuatx, nuaty, nuatz, fromincx,fromincy;

  if (mainview->numobjects <= 0) return;  // Nothing to draw

  mainview->t_from = 1.0;

  fromincx = mainview->r * cos(mainview->theta);
  fromincy = mainview->r * sin(mainview->theta);

  // Use the keyboard if the mouse is not pressed
  if (!mouse.buttondown(1)) usekeys = 1;
  c = getkey();
  while (!mouse.buttonreleased(LEFT_BUTTON) || c == RIGHT) {
    if (usekeys) {
      while ((c=getkey()) != 0x1B && c != RIGHT) ;
      if (c == 0x1B) return;  // You can press Esc to quit
    }
    else {
      // The mouse button is down; get the new mouse location
      mouse.getcoords(mx, my);
      if (mx < left || mx > right || my < top || my > bottom) {
        while (!mouse.buttonreleased(LEFT_BUTTON));
        // The user pressed outside of the button
        return;
      }
    }
    if (times < 10) {
      // Keep track of the number of times through this loop.
      // If it's more than 10, then speed up the rotation.
      times++;
      mainview->theta -= mainview->thetainc;
    }
    else
      mainview->theta -= mainview->thetainc*4;

    fromincx = mainview->r * cos(mainview->theta);
    fromincy = mainview->r * sin(mainview->theta);
    nuatx = fromincx + mainview->from.x;
    nuaty = fromincy + mainview->from.y;
    nuatz = mainview->at.z;

    if (nuatx == mainview->from.x &&
        nuaty == mainview->from.y &&
        nuatz == mainview->from.z)
      popuperror(" Cannot move to here ");
    else {
      mainview->at.x = nuatx;
      mainview->at.y = nuaty;
      mainview->at.z = nuatz;
```

```
        mainview->seteye();
        mainview->r = 10;
        mainview->clear_viewport();
        mainview->view();
    }
  }
}

// Interactively rotates the viewer counterclockwise. Supports the
// keyboard and mouse.
void ccwtool::draw(void)
{
  int c, mx, my, usekeys=0, times=0;
  double nuatx, nuaty, nuatz, fromincx, fromincy;

  if (mainview->numobjects <= 0) return;   // Nothing to draw

  mainview->t_from = 1.0;
  fromincx = mainview->r * cos(mainview->theta);
  fromincy = mainview->r * sin(mainview->theta);

  // Use the keyboard if the mouse is not pressed
  if (!mouse.buttondown(1)) usekeys = 1;
  c = getkey();
  while (!mouse.buttonreleased(LEFT_BUTTON) || c == LEFT) {
    if (usekeys) {
      while ((c=getkey()) != 0x1B && c != LEFT) ;
      if (c == 0x1B) return;   // You can press Esc to quit
    }
    else {
      // The mouse button is down; get the new mouse location
      mouse.getcoords(mx, my);
      if (mx < left || mx > right || my < top || my > bottom) {
        while (!mouse.buttonreleased(LEFT_BUTTON));
        // The user pressed outside of the button
        return;
      }
    }
    // Keep track of the number of times through this loop.
    // If it's more than 10, then speed up the rotation.
    if (times < 10) {
      times++;
      mainview->theta += mainview->thetainc;
    }
    else
      mainview->theta += mainview->thetainc*4;

    fromincx = mainview->r * cos(mainview->theta);
    fromincy = mainview->r * sin(mainview->theta);
    nuatx = fromincx + mainview->from.x;
    nuaty = fromincy + mainview->from.y;
    nuatz = mainview->at.z;
```

```
        if (nuatx == mainview->from.x &&
            nuaty == mainview->from.y &&
            nuatz == mainview->from.z)
          popuperror(" Cannot move to here ");
        else {
          mainview->at.x = nuatx;
          mainview->at.y = nuaty;
          mainview->at.z = nuatz;
          mainview->seteye();
          mainview->r = 10;
          mainview->clear_viewport();
          mainview->view();
        }
      }
    }

    // Displays a string at the location (x,y). The string should
    // fit in the menu. If you want a highlighted (hot key) character,
    // you should precede the desired character with the & character.
    // (Therefore the & character cannot be used in the menu name.)
    // The text is displayed using the tc color and the highlight
    // is displayed with the hc color. The variable bc specifies
    // the background color.
    void menustr(int x, int y, int tc, int hc, int bc, char *str)
    {
      settextbkcolor(bc);          // Use the main color specified
      settextcolor(tc);
      moveto(x, y);                // Set the initial location of the text
      for (int i=0; str[i] != '\0'; i++) {
        if (str[i] == '&') {
          i++;                     // Skip the & character
          settextcolor(hc);        // Switch to the hot key character
          gputch(str[i]);          // Display the hot key
          settextcolor(tc);        // Switch back to the normal text color
        }
        else
          gputch(str[i]);          // Display the current character
      }
    }
```

● VECTOR.H

```
// VECTOR.H: Header file for VECTOR.CPP.

#ifndef VECTORH
#define VECTORH

struct VECTOR {
  double x,y,z;
};

double mag(VECTOR *v);
VECTOR subtract(VECTOR *v1, VECTOR *v2);
```

```
VECTOR cross(VECTOR *v1, VECTOR *v2);
VECTOR divide(VECTOR *v,double num);
void normalize(VECTOR *V);
double dot(VECTOR *V1, VECTOR *V2);
#endif
```

• VECTOR.CPP

```
// VECTOR.CPP: Vector operations for 3D.CPP (Chapter 13) and
// V3D.CPP (Chapter 14).
#include <stdio.h>
#include <math.h>
#include <stdlib.h>
#include "vector.h"

// Calculates the magnitude of the vector v
double mag(VECTOR *v)
{
   return sqrt(v->x * v->x + v->y * v->y + v->z * v->z);
}

// Subtracts two vectors
VECTOR subtract(VECTOR *v1, VECTOR *v2)
{
  VECTOR d;

  d.x = v1->x - v2->x;
  d.y = v1->y - v2->y;
  d.z = v1->z - v2->z;
  return d;
}

// Computes the cross product of the two vectors v1 and v2
VECTOR cross(VECTOR *v1, VECTOR *v2)
{
  VECTOR c;

  c.x = v1->y * v2->z - v2->y * v1->z;
  c.y = v1->z * v2->x - v2->z * v1->x;
  c.z = v1->x * v2->y - v2->x * v1->y;
  return c;
}

// Divides the scalar number into the vector v
VECTOR divide(VECTOR *v,double num)
{
  VECTOR result;

  if (num == 0) {
    printf("Divide by 0 in Matrix Divide Operation\n");
    exit(1);
  }
```

```
    result.x = v->x / num;
    result.y = v->y / num;
    result.z = v->z / num;
    return result;
}

// Normalizes a vector
void normalize(VECTOR *V)
{
    double D = sqrt(V->x * V->x + V->y * V->y + V->z * V->z);
    if (D != 0) {
        V->x = V->x / D;
        V->y = V->y / D;
        V->z = V->z / D;
    }
}

// Calculates the dot product of the two vectors V1 and V2
double dot(VECTOR *V1, VECTOR *V2)
{
    return V1->x * V2->x + V1->y * V2->y + V1->z * V2->z;
}
```

• 3D.CPP

```
// 3D.CPP: Wire-frame viewing package. Displays wire-frame, three-
// dimensional views of objects using perspective projection. Objects
// are read from files and displayed according to the settings of the
// from, at, up, and viewing angle.
#include <stdio.h>
#include <stdlib.h>
#include <graphics.h>
#include <string.h>
#include <math.h>
#include <conio.h>
#include "gtext.h"
#include "vector.h"
#include "gpopup.h"
#include "user3d.h"
#include "3dtool.h"
#include "interact.h"

const int PCL = 1;              // Top left pixel coordinate of
const int PCT = 1;              // the viewing window
const int ICONWD = 16;          // The dimensions of the icons
const int ICONHT = 16;

int pcl, pct, pcr, pcb;         // Coordinates of the viewing window

// Creates an arrow tool that you can use to navigate around
// the world with. The key variable is the keyboard hot key that
// you can use to initiate the command. It also adds the drawing
```

```
// tool passed in to the list of tools. This is the tool that gets
// called when the user clicks on the arrow. The arrow symbol is
// read from the specified icon file. A three-dimensional window
// is painted behind the arrow icon to make it a little bigger.
// However, this last step isn't really necessary.
void setuparrowtool(int key, int left, int top, int wd, int ht,
  drawingtool *tool, char *iconfilename)
{
  tools.addtool(new interact(key, left-1, top-1, wd-1, ht-1, tool));
  tools.tool[tools.numtools-1]->itool->left = left;
  tools.tool[tools.numtools-1]->itool->top = top;
  tools.tool[tools.numtools-1]->itool->right = left+wd;
  tools.tool[tools.numtools-1]->itool->bottom = top+ht;
  w.paintwindow(left, top, left+wd-1,
    top+ht-1, THREED, LIGHTGRAY, SOLID_FILL, BLACK);
  readicon(left+2, top+2, iconfilename);
}


// Creates a menu button at the location specified. "key" is
// the hot key the user can use to activate the menu command.
// "tool" is the object that gets called when the button is
// activated. "str" is the string that gets drawn on the button.
// The icon specified by "iconfilename" is displayed at the
// top-left of the button. If it is NULL, an icon is not displayed.
void setupbutton(int key, int left, int top, int wd, int ht,
  drawingtool *tool, char *iconfilename, int Txty, char *str)
{
  tools.addtool(new interact(key, left, top, wd-1, ht-1, tool));
  // The button is made from a gray, three-dimensional window
  w.paintwindow(left, top, left+wd, top+ht,
    THREED, LIGHTGRAY, SOLID_FILL, BLACK);
  if (str != NULL)
    readicon(left+4, top+2, iconfilename);
  menustr(left+iconwd+8, top+Txty, BLACK, RED, LIGHTGRAY, str);
}


// Sets up the program's environment
void setup_environment(void)
{
  drawingtool *quit = new quittool;
  drawingtool *readfile = new readtool;
  drawingtool *setfrom = new setfromtool;
  drawingtool *setat = new setattool;
  drawingtool *setup = new setuptool;
  drawingtool *setangle = new setangletool;
  drawingtool *forward = new forwardtool;
  drawingtool *backward = new backwardtool;
  drawingtool *clockwise = new cwtool;
  drawingtool *counterclockwise = new ccwtool;

  int MenuWd = getmaxx() - pcr;
  int ButtonX=MenuWd/16;
  int ButtonWd=MenuWd-ButtonX*2;
  int NumButtons = 12;
```

```
    int ButtonSp = 4;
    int ButtonHt = (getmaxy() - ButtonSp*2) / NumButtons;
    int Offset = 4;
    iconwd = ICONWD;
    iconht = ICONHT;
    if (ButtonHt < iconht) ButtonHt = iconht+4;

    // Create the backdrop to the menu
    w.paintwindow(pcr+1, 0, getmaxx(), getmaxy(),
      THREED, LIGHTGRAY, SOLID_FILL, BLACK);
    ButtonX += pcr+1;
    int Txty = (ButtonHt - textheight("T")) / 2;

    // Create the menu buttons
    setupbutton('r', ButtonX, Offset, ButtonWd, ButtonHt, readfile,
      "READFILE.ICN", Txty, "&Read file");
    Offset += ButtonHt + ButtonSp;
    setupbutton('f', ButtonX, Offset, ButtonWd, ButtonHt, setfrom,
      "FROM.ICN", Txty, "Set &from");
    Offset += ButtonHt + ButtonSp;
    setupbutton('a', ButtonX, Offset, ButtonWd, ButtonHt, setat,
      "COORDSYS.ICN", Txty, "Set &at");
    Offset += ButtonHt + ButtonSp;
    setupbutton('u', ButtonX, Offset, ButtonWd, ButtonHt, setup,
      "COORDSYS.ICN", Txty, "Set &up");
    Offset += ButtonHt + ButtonSp;
    setupbutton('g', ButtonX, Offset, ButtonWd, ButtonHt, setangle,
      "COORDSYS.ICN", Txty, "Set an&gle");
    Offset += ButtonHt + ButtonSp;
    setupbutton('x', ButtonX, Offset, ButtonWd, ButtonHt, quit,
      "EXIT.ICN", Txty, "E&xit");

    // Add four arrow buttons that the user can use to navigate
    // through the scene
    int Midx = (getmaxx()+pcr)/2;
    Offset += ButtonHt+ButtonSp;
    int Midy = Offset+ButtonHt;
    ButtonHt = iconht+4;
    ButtonWd = iconwd+4;

    setuparrowtool(UP, Midx-ButtonWd/2, Midy-ButtonHt*3/2,
      ButtonWd, ButtonHt, forward, "FORWARD.ICN");
    setuparrowtool(DOWN, Midx-ButtonWd/2, Midy+ButtonHt/2,
      ButtonWd, ButtonHt, backward, "REVERSE.ICN");
    setuparrowtool(LEFT, Midx-ButtonWd*3/2, Midy-ButtonHt/2,
      ButtonWd, ButtonHt, counterclockwise, "CCW.ICN");
    setuparrowtool(RIGHT, Midx+ButtonWd/2, Midy-ButtonHt/2,
      ButtonWd, ButtonHt, clockwise, "CW.ICN");
}

main()
{
    int gmode, gdriver=DETECT, errcode, c;
```

```
initgraph(&gdriver, &gmode, "");
if ((errcode=graphresult()) != grOk) {
  printf("Graphics error: %s\n", grapherrormsg(errcode));
  exit(1);       // Return with an error code
}

mouse.init();
pcl = PCL;
pcb = getmaxy()-1;
int xasp, yasp;
getaspectratio(&xasp, &yasp);
pcr = pcb * (float)yasp / xasp;
pct = PCT;
mainview = new threedobj();
mainview->init3dgraphics(pcl, pct, pcr, pcb);
rectangle(pcl-1, pct-1, pcr+1, pcb+1);
setup_environment();

// Process the user input until the user selects the Quit command
do {
  c = mouse.getinputpress(LEFT_BUTTON);
  if (c != -2)  // Ignore button releases
    tools.anytoprocess(c);
} while (c != 'q');

closegraph();
return 0;
}
```

Solid Modeling

14

Displaying objects as wire frames is a quick way to render three-dimensional scenes. However, to make the scenes more realistic, we need to display the surfaces of the objects as well. In this chapter, we'll extend the **threedobj** class from Chapter 13 so that we can display solid objects. This new toolkit can form the foundation for your own virtual reality environment.

We'll begin by describing what's necessary to make the transition from wire-frame to solid objects. Then, we'll get into the application-level details of a new solid modeling program, V3D. We'll also present two object data files that are specially designed to illustrate the features of the new program.

ADDING SOLID MODELING

We already have the basic code for displaying three-dimensional objects contained in the **threedobj** class. However, to display solid, three-dimensional objects, we'll need to make the following changes:

- Add a color value for each polygon in the object file
- Display objects using filled polygons rather than line segments
- Shade the polygons that make up the object according to the color of the object and the angle of its surface with respect to the light source
- Paint the polygons in the correct order so that closer surfaces overlap more distant surfaces

REMOVING HIDDEN SURFACES

Rendering solid objects is more difficult than displaying wire frames. A key reason is that you simply can't display the object surfaces in any order that you choose. You must display the objects so that surfaces behind closer ones are not displayed, or are, at least, covered. This process is called *hidden surface removal.*

You can take several approaches to remove hidden surfaces. One sensible technique is to sort an object's polygons based on their distance from the viewer, the *from* point. Then, the polygons can be painted one at a time, starting from the polygon farthest away. This technique is known as the *painters algorithm.* Although simple, the painters algorithm is not guaranteed. Figure 14.1 illustrates two potential pitfalls. One problem occurs when several polygons overlap so that no single polygon is clearly behind all the others. Similiarly, the painters algorithm may not work correctly if one polygon pierces another. In addition, from a computational standpoint, the painters algorithm is not the best approach because the polygons must be re-sorted every time the viewer's location is changed.

Another technique is called *Z Buffering.* Often implemented in hardware, this approach uses an extensive two-dimensional array that stores the distance to each point in the generated image. A pixel on the screen is painted and the Z buffer is updated only if its distance is closer than the current distance stored in the Z buffer. To use this technique, we would need to write our own polygon display routine so that it would use a Z buffer.

To avoid these problems, we'll implement an algorithm known as *Binary Space Partitioning (BSP).* This technique avoids each of the problems that the painters and Z buffer algorithms suffer from.

The BSP Approach

The BSP algorithm consists of two parts. In the first stage, the object's polygons are organized into a specially ordered binary tree. Then, the tree is traversed according to the location of the viewer in order to display the correct scene.

Figure 14.1 The painters algorithm cannot display these two scenes correctly.

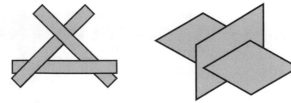

The technique revolves around the notion of *separation planes*. Polygons behind a separation plane are drawn first and those in front are painted last. Each node of the binary tree represents one polygon of the object and doubles as a separation plane. Two branches extend from each node of the BSP tree: One branch points to the polygons on the back side of the separation plane and the other branch points to the polygons on the front side. Displaying the scene requires traversing the binary tree in the correct order. For each node, it is determined whether the viewer is in front of or behind the separation plane and traverses its branches accordingly—displaying the polygons behind the separation plane (with respect to the viewer) first.

This probably sounds much like a painters algorithm. It is. However, the BSP algorithm goes one step further. If a polygon is not completely on one side of the separation plane, then the polygon is divided into two. The part behind the separation plane is placed on one branch of the tree and the other piece is placed on the branch that corresponds with the polygons on its front side.

Let's look at an example. Assume you want to build a BSP tree for the four polygons shown in the upper portion of Figure 14.2. You can select any of the polygons as the first separation plane. We'll choose polygon A and create a node for it. Next, we'll select polygon B. Since it is behind A, polygon B is placed on A's back list. Now let's consider polygon C; it's on the front side of

---

Figure 14.2 This figure illustrates the technique for building a BSP tree.

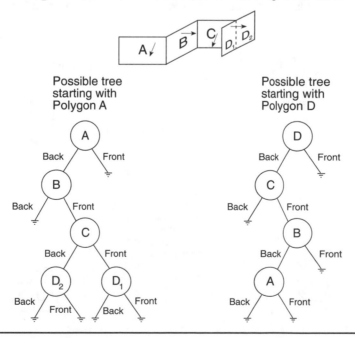

B, so it is placed on B's back pointer. Polygon D, however, is split by C into two pieces, D1 and D2, since it is neither completely in front of or behind polygon C. Polygons D1 and D2, therefore, are added to the front and back pointers of C, respectively.

This process would be repeated if there were any other polygons. Notice that the tree created depends on the order in which we consider the polygons. For instance, the other tree in Figure 14.2 is a valid BSP tree for the same scene; however, the polygons were processed in the order D, C, B, and then A.

Painting the scene is simply a matter of traversing the tree correctly. At each node of the tree, you determine whether the viewer (the *from* point) is in front of or behind the polygon represented by the node. The result of this calculation selects which branch of the tree we'll take. Whichever branch is on the side opposite the viewer is traversed first and its polygons are displayed. Then, the polygon for the node itself is painted, followed by the polygons in front. In this way, the scene is drawn in the correct order. Figure 14.3 walks you through the display process for building the BSP tree and the resulting view.

One advantage of the BSP algorithm: The tree only needs to be built once for each collection of objects. You do not have to rebuild the tree each time the view changes. The order in which the tree is traversed depends on the location of the viewer; when the viewers position changes, the program generates a different scene.

Figure 14.3 This is the process for displaying a scene using a BSP tree.

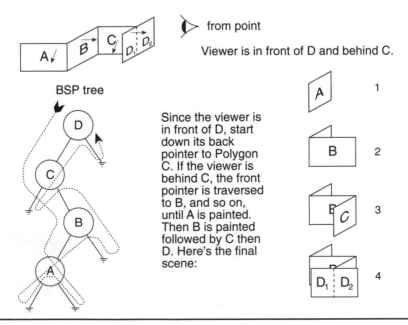

As you might guess, the BSP algorithm is not trivial and requires an extensive amount of code. If you are at all cautious about working with pointers, you may find the code a challenge. In addition, BSP trees can get quite large for complex scenes. The size of a tree depends on two factors: the number of polygons in the scene and the number of polygons that are split. The latter number tends to vary greatly with the order in which the polygons are added to the tree. Another problem with the technique: The polygon splitting can give the scene a "shattered glass" appearance. A suggestion on how to fix this problem is given at the end of this chapter.

There are also a few restrictions on the scenes that you can display. First, the polygons that make up the object must be planar. Therefore, we'll break up the figures into triangles so that we're always guaranteed planar polygons. In addition, the objects must be convex—in other words, they can't have depressions.

THE THREEDSOLID CLASS

The details of the BSP algorithm are encapsulated in the **threedsolid** class. This class is derived from **threedobj** and inherits much of its ability for handling three-dimensional objects. The new functions in **threedsolid** are provided to support the rendering of solids.

The **threedsolid** class also contains a handful of new data members. The **tril** pointer holds a linked list of the triangles in the scene, and the **tree** pointer points to the root of the BSP tree. Both of these structures are built into the overridden **read3dobject( )** function. In addition, **threedsolid** contains several new variables to control the lighting. We'll discuss these in a later section.

The bulk of the **threedsolid** class is dedicated to its numerous functions that support the BSP tree. These functions are listed in Table 14.1. Rather than review their code in detail, we'll take the high road and discuss in general terms what the important functions do.

Working with Triangles

To keep our code simple, objects will always be represented as a series of triangular polygons. By using triangles, we'll be assured that the polygons are always planar, which is a requirement of the BSP algorithm.

A key part of the BSP algorithm determines whether polygons are in front of or behind the current polygon being considered as the separation plane. But what do "in front of" and "behind" really mean? We'll assume that a polygon is in front of another if it is in the direction of the triangle's *normal*. (A normal is a vector that is perpendicular to the triangle's surface.) To be consistent in the way normals are used, we'll always specify the triangles in our data file by listing the vertices of the triangle in a counter-clockwise direction and calculate the normal, as shown in Figure 14.4.

Table 14.1 Member Functions in the threedsolid Class

Function	Description
read3dobject()	Reads an object file and builds the BSP tree
view()	Overridden in order to call traversetree()
calcplaneeqs()	Precomputes the D term of the plane equation for each triangle
disposeBSP()	Frees the nodes of a BSP tree
makeBSPnode()	Creates and initializes a BSP node
addlist()	Adds a triangle node to a temporary list
calcsign()	Determines which side of a plane a point is on
intersect()	Calculates where a line intersects a plane
inserttriangle()	Adds a triangle and its data to a temporary list of triangles
split()	Splits a triangle polygon into two or more pieces
makeBSPtree()	High-level function to create a BSP tree
calctrinormals()	Precomputes the normal for each triangle
precomputecentroids()	Precomputes the centroid of each triangle
worldtodisplay()	Calculates where a world point is located in the display window
computecolor()	Computes the shade of a color to use for a polygon
displaytriangle()	Displays a triangle patch
traversetree()	Traverses the BSP tree and displays the scene based on the current from point

Figure 14.4 We'll use this technique to calculate the normal of a triangle.

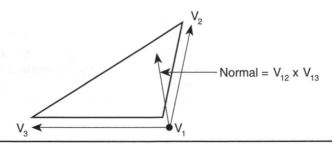

Solid Modeling ▲ 405

Adding Color to the Object Files

The **read3dobject( )** function in **threedobj** is overridden in order to read object files that contain a list of RGB colors. At the beginning of the object files, we'll now require a color table. The first number of the file will be a number that specifies the number of colors in the table. Following this table will be a list of red, green, and blue triples. The last change is that we'll now use the negative number to signal the end of the polygon connect list as an index into the list of colors. For instance, the following header defines a palette of three colors:

```
3
255  0  0
0  255  0
0  0  255
```

In this example, the first color is red, the second green, and the last blue. Then, to display a blue triangle, you might use the polygon sequence

```
1  2  3 -3
```

where the numbers 1, 2, and 3 point to the vertext list, and -3 instructs V3D that it should use the third color in the list of colors—blue. The colors are stored in the **colorpal** array starting at index location 1.

The rest of the file format is the same as before. Notice, however, that **read3dobject( )** cannot read the object files from Chapter 13 because the polygons are not specified as triangles.

Building a BSP Tree

The **read3dobject( )** routine takes the steps necessary to build and initialize the BSP tree. First, it builds a linked-list copy of the triangles in the scene. Then, **read3dobject( )** passes this list to **makeBSPtree( )**, which actually constructs the BSP tree. In addition, **read3dobject( )** precomputes the normals, centroids, and part of the plane equation for each triangle so that, when displaying a view, they don't have to be recomputed.

The **makeBSPtree( )** function labels the first triangle in the list of triangles passed to it as the current separation plane. It then sorts the remaining polygons into the **frontlist** and **backlist** linked lists, depending on whether the polygons are in front of or behind the separation plane. Next, the separation plane is added to the BSP tree, and **makeBSPtree( )** is called again to process the **frontlist** and **backlist** lists and return their BSP subtrees:

```
node = makeBSPnode(root->t);  // Add node for the root triangle
node->front = makeBSPtree(frontlist);
node->back = makeBSPtree(backlist);
```

Figure 14.5 A triangle is split into three pieces when calc() returns different signs.

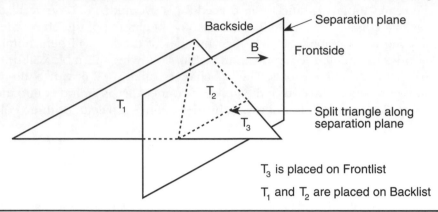

The **calcsign( )** function helps to determine which side of the separation plane the polygons are on. It is called once for each vertex in a triangle to solve the plane equation for the separation plane using the vertex coordinate. The sign of the result reveals which side of the separation plane the vertex is on.

If **calcsign( )** returns values with different signs for vertices in the same triangle, then that triangle crosses over the separation plane. In this case, the triangle is split into two or three pieces, as illustrated in Figure 14.5, by the function **split( )**. These new triangular pieces are added to the front and back lists and processed like the other polygons. Notice that the splitting is performed so that it always creates triangles. This explains why a single triangle is split into three pieces, rather than two.

Displaying the Triangles

Displaying a scene is still initiated by the **view( )** member function in **threedobj**. However, **view( )** is overridden in **threedsolid** in order to call **traversetree( )**, which recursively winds its way through the BSP tree, displaying the triangles in the BSP tree as it proceeds. The key to the function is the calculation of the dot product between the triangle's normal and vector **s**—the line of sight to the triangle. Figure 14.6 shows the relationship between these two vectors. The sign of the dot product indicates on which side of the polygon the viewer is located. If the *from* point is on the front side, the back polygons are displayed first. Otherwise, the front polygons are displayed first.

```
if (tree != NULL) {
  s.x = from.x - tree->tri->v1.x;
  s.y = from.y - tree->tri->v1.y;
```

Figure 14.6 The line of sight and the triangle's normal determine which side of the polygon the viewer is located.

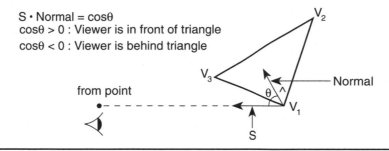

```
s.z = from.z - tree->tri->v1.z;
normalize(&s);
costheta = dot(&s, &tree->tri->normal);
if (costheta > 0) {  // The eye is in front of the polygon
  traversetree(tree->back);
  displaytriangle(tree->tri);
  traversetree(tree->front);
}
else {   // The eye is in back of the polygon
  traversetree(tree->front);
  displaytriangle(tree->tri);
  traversetree(tree->back);
}
}
```

The **displaytriangle( )** function handles the details required to paint each triangle. This function first calls **computecolor( )**—we'll get to this function in a bit—to retrieve the polygon's color. Then, it calls **worldtodisplay( )** to convert each of the triangle's vertices, which are in world coordinates, to the window's coordinates. Next, it creates and selects a solid fill pattern that matches the color returned by **computecolor( )**. Finally, it displays a filled triangle by calling **fillpoly( )**:

```
// Create the correct fill color and display the triangle
setfillstyle(SOLID_FILL, colorndx);
setcolor(colorndx);
setviewport(left, top, right, bottom, 1);
fillpoly(outlen/2, outpt);   // Display the triangle
```

As you look through the **displaytriangle( )** function, you'll also notice an extensive amount of code that has several calls to the **clip3d( )** routine. Although our base class, **threedobj**, can clip line segments to the viewing pyramid, it won't work for clipping our triangles. It might seem like all we

Figure 14.7 When you clip a triangle to the viewing pyramid, the process requires special attention.

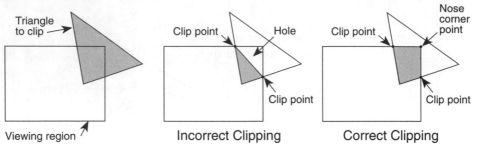

need to do is call **clip3d( )** for each edge of the triangle and display the resulting figure. We can't. A problem occurs when the triangle extends beyond more than one edge of the viewing pyramid, as shown in Figure 14.7. If we simply connect the clipped sides of the triangle, we'll render a triangle like that shown in the middle of Figure 14.7—leaving a gap in the scene. Instead, we must keep track of where the edges are clipped and add points to the output polygon if the clipped edges extend across adjacent planes of the viewing pyramid. The polygon at the right of Figure 14.7 shows the correctly clipped triangle.

Adding a Lighting Model

The BSP algorithm enables you to paint the polygons that represent a three-dimensional object in the correct order. However, to render realistic scenes, you must account for the shading of surfaces as well. If an object is green, for instance, and you paint all sides of the object the same green, the sides will merge and you won't have any sense of depth.

We'll introduce a lighting model to determine the shade of each polygon. The brightness of the color depends on how bright an imaginary light is, the orientation of the surfaces, and how reflective the object is supposed to be. All of these factors are encapsulated in the lighting model we'll use.

We'll assume that a single, distant light source illuminates the scene evenly. The position of the light is stored in the vector **light** in the **threedsolid** class. The overall amount that the light source illuminates the scene is known as the *ambient light* portion of the illumination. In general, the brighter the light is, the brighter the surface must be drawn.

The surface shade also depends on the properties of the surface and how much it scatters light at various angles—with respect to the light source. This is the *diffuse* component of the light. The closer the surface's normal points to the light source, the brighter the object should be drawn. A smoother, mirror-like object, for instance, would reflect more light when directly facing a light than a rough surface. The lighting model also darkens objects that face away from the light.

The V3D program contains two parameters that enable you to specify the contribution that the ambient and diffuse light make. These two variables, which must be between 0 and 1, are called **ambient** and **diffuse**, and are located in the **threedsolid** class. Their values are initialized in **threedsolid**'s constructor. Typically, the ambient light contribution is greater than the diffuse contribution.

The **computecolor( )** function applies the lighting model and returns an RGB color to use for a triangle. Although in the real world the color of an object would vary across its surface, we'll calculate the color for the centroid of the triangle and set the whole triangle to this color. The first step is to determine where the light is in relation to the surface of the triangle:

```
L = subtract(&light, &p); // Find vector from light to point P
normalize(&L);
```

Next, the code calculates the dot product of the normalized vector to the light and the triangle's surface normal. This calculation effectively gives us the cosine of the angle between the surface normal and the direction of the light source. As a result, this calculation returns its largest result when the two vectors align. This is exactly what we want for the diffuse lighting:

```
L_N = dot(&L, &normal);
// Calculate diffuse lighting contribution to object's color
if (L_N <= 0) L_N *= -diffuse * NUM_SHADES;
  else L_N *= diffuse * NUM_SHADES;
```

The **NUM_SHADES** constant specifies how many shades of colors we can have. As a result, the diffuse lighting contribution, **L_N**, will range between 0 and **NUM_SHADES**.

Finally, the function adds in the ambient portion of the light and clips the results to 255, since anything larger than this is too big:

```
int Red = (int)(colorpal[colorndx].r + ambient * NUM_SHADES + L_N);
int Green = (int)(colorpal[colorndx].g + ambient * NUM_SHADES + L_N);
int Blue = (int)(colorpal[colorndx].b + ambient * NUM_SHADES + L_N);
if (Red > 255) Red = 255;
if (Green > 255) Green = 255;
if (Blue > 255) Blue = 255;
```

Calculating these color shades only makes sense if you can display them. In a 16-color mode, this isn't possible. Therefore, if the program detects that you are using a video mode with 16 colors, it doesn't bother going through these calculations. Instead, the program simply uses the color index in the **connect** array as the color. This doesn't produce a correct color, but at least it will provide a range of colors. Because of this problem, we'll be targeting V3D for 256-color modes.

Compiling and Using V3D

The complete code for the BSP algorithm and the V3D program is located in the source files 3DSOLID.H, 3DSOLID.CPP, and V3D.CPP. Table 14.2 lists all the files you'll need to compile V3D. Because the program is so large, you can't compile the program with the small memory model. Since the program uses the mouse, you must also define **MOUSE** so that your compiler uses the mouse code in the text and pop-up window toolkits. In addition, the program works the best—in terms of colors and speed—if you use the 320 x 200 256-color VGA mode. This is a standard VGA mode, however, you'll need a third-party BGI driver, such as the VGA256.BGI driver discussed in Chapter 2. If you use the VGA256 driver, you'll also need to define the macro constant **HICOLOR**. In addition, if you run the program and don't see a mouse cursor, you should define a third macro constant, called **HIRESMOUSE**. In Borland's integrated development environment (IDE) you can place all three of these macro constants together, separated by semicolons. Recall, if you don't have access to a 256-color mode, V3D will paint the objects using psuedocolors rather than shading their surfaces.

Figure 14.8 shows the environment of the V3D program. In many ways, it is similar to its wire-frame counterpart in Chapter 13. Depending on your

---

Figure 14.8 This figure shows the V3D program output.

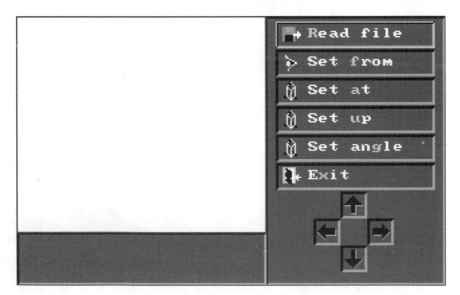

Table 14.2 Files Required to Compile the V3D Program

Source File	Include File	Chapter
3DSOLID.CPP	3DSOLID.H	14
3DTOOL.CPP	3DTOOL.H	13
DRAWTOOL.CPP	DRAWTOOL.H	10
GPOPUP.CPP	GPOPUP.H	9
GTEXT.CPP	GTEXT.H	3
INTERACT.CPP	INTERACT.H	11
KBDMOUSE.CPP	KBDMOUSE.H	7
MOUSE.CPP	MOUSE.H	7
USER3D.CPP	USER3D.H	13
V3D.CPP	None	14
VECTOR.CPP	VECTOR.H	13

equipment and screen resolution, you may have some problems with the program's speed. Running this program on a fast computer with a math co-processor is almost a necessity. If your PC updates the screen too slowly, try reducing the size of the display window.

Sample Solid Objects

This section provides two sample object files that adhere to the special file format described in this chapter. Remember, the scene is divided into triangles. The first object file, STEST1.DAT, generates a scene with two pyramids, as shown in Figure 14.9. Here is its data:

```
1
255 0 0
2
5 16
0.0   0.0   0.0    10.0   0.0   0.0    10.0   10.0   0.0
0.0   10.0   0.0    5.0   5.0   10.0
1 5 2 -1
2 5 3 -1
3 5 4 -1
4 5 1 -1
5 16
0.0   20.0   0.0    10.0   20.0   0.0    10.0   30.0   0.0
0.0   30.0   0.0   5.0   25.0   10.0
1 5 2 -1
2 5 3 -1
3 5 4 -1
4 5 1 -1
```

Figure 14.9 The STEST1.DAT file produces this output.

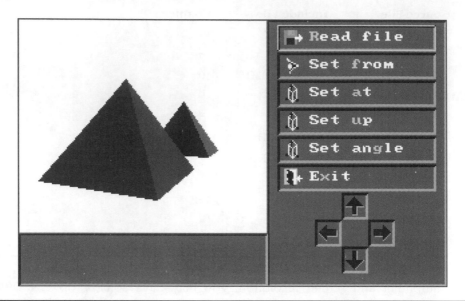

The next object file, STEST2.DAT, contains a plane and two cubes. Figure 14.10 shows the scene from two vantage points.

```
3
196 0 0
0 196 0
0   0 196
3
8 48
1.0  1.0  1.0     1.0  1.0  0.0     1.0  0.0  0.0
1.0  0.0  1.0     0.0  1.0  1.0     0.0  1.0  0.0
0.0  0.0  0.0     0.0  0.0  1.0
1   3   2  -1
1   4   3  -1
7   6   3  -1
2   3   6  -1
5   1   6  -1
1   2   6  -1
8   5   6  -1
8   6   7  -1
4   7   3  -1
4   8   7  -1
4   5   8  -1
4   1   5  -1
4 8
-1.5  -1.5   -0.2    2  -1.5  -0.2
 2    2    -0.2    -1.5   2    -0.2
```

```
3   2 4 -2
4   2 1 -2
8 48
1.0   1.0   3.0     1.0   1.0   2.0     1.0   0.0   2.0
1.0   0.0   3.0     0.0   1.0   3.0     0.0   1.0   2.0
0.0   0.0   2.0     0.0   0.0   3.0
1   3   2 -3
```

Figure 14.10 Here are two views of the objects in STEST2.DAT.

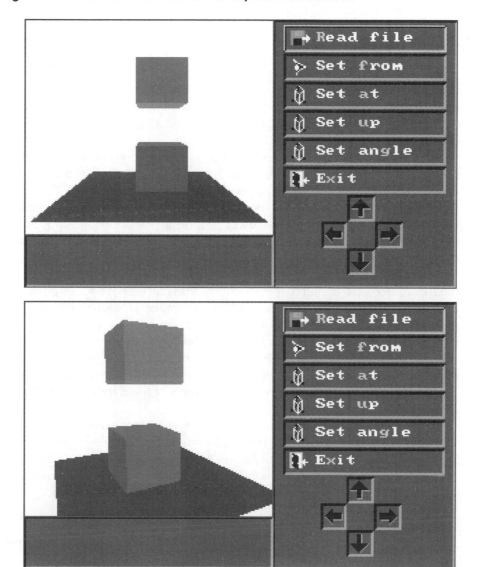

```
1   4   3   -3
7   6   3   -3
2   3   6   -3
5   1   6   -3
1   2   6   -3
8   5   6   -3
8   6   7   -3
4   7   3   -3
4   8   7   -3
4   5   8   -3
4   1   5   -3
```

ENHANCING V3D

There are many ways you can expand upon the V3D program. The most visually dramatic would be to provide better control over the shading of objects. First, you'll probably want to add menu options and pop-up windows that enable you to set the light paramters and maybe even the color of the objects.

Currently, the viewer is restricted to one plane, you'll probably want to remove this restriction and add code that enables the viewer to move up and down. Once you take this step, you'll probably also realize that it would be nice to provide other ways of moving the viewer. For instance, sometimes its more convenient to move the viewer around an object or the *at* point rather than steering the viewer around the screen. These additions aren't hard, but they do deserve quite a bit of forethought and extra code.

Another area that may cause problems is with the size of the object database. Because of memory restrictions, you can't have a lot of objects in the database. One solution is to use a DOS extender. However, this only solves part of the problem. As the object list gets bigger, the display routines get slower. This isn't good, especially when you consider the fact that most of the objects probably aren't in view anyway. If you're goal is to build a flight simulator-like program, you'll probably want to divide your world database into bricks or chunks, so that only one portion of the database is really loaded at one time.

This brings up another problem. What if you want your objects to be able to move? The easy part is creating a list of animated objects and inbetweening their positions like we did in Chapter 6. Once you free your objects, you'll probably want to redefine the ways objects are stored (or at least managed) so that they have their own coordinate system. This will simplify the process of moving the objects.

Finally, when viewing complex scenes, you may notice a lot of screen flicker as you move around the scene. This is caused by the triangular patches being painted one at a time. What we really need is the ability to paint the scenes to memory, and then copy the final, complete image to the screen. The results would be dramatic. Unfortunately, the BGI doesn't provide a way to do this. Therefore, if you want to fix this problem, you'll have to write your own fill operations that paint to memory.

▲ ● **3DSOLID.H**

```
// 3DSOLID.H: Header file for 3DSOLID.CPP.

#ifndef SOLIDH
#define SOLIDH

#define TOL 0.001
#define NUM_SHADES 254
#define NUMCOLORS 8     // Number of unique colors allowed in file

struct RGBCOLOR {
  int r, g, b;          // Red, green, and blue color components
};

extern RGBCOLOR palette[255];
extern int maxcolorsused;

typedef VECTOR Point;
struct TRIANGLE {
  Point v1, v2, v3;   // The three vertices of the triangle
  VECTOR normal;      // The normal of the triangle
  double d;   // The d term of the plane that contains the triangle
  Point centroid;     // Centroid of the triangle
  int colorndx;       // Index of triangle's color
  TRIANGLE *next;
};

struct TLIST {        // Points to the triangle list data in the tril
  TRIANGLE *t;        // Points to a specific triangle in the tril
  TLIST *next;        // Next TLIST structure
};

struct BSPNode {
  TRIANGLE *tri;
  BSPNode *inside, *outside;
};

class threedsolid : public threedobj {
public:
  TRIANGLE *tril;                   // List of triangles in drawing
  BSPNode *tree;                    // Pointer to the root of the BSP tree
  RGBCOLOR colorpal[NUMCOLORS];  // Color palette for polygons
  int numcolors;                    // Number of colors in colorpal
  double ambient, diffuse;          // Contributions of light: 0 <= >= 1.0
  VECTOR light;                     // Location of light
  threedsolid();
  virtual int read3dobject(char *filename);
```

```
    virtual void view(void);
    void calcplaneeqs();
    void disposeBSP(BSPNode *tree);
    BSPNode *makeBSPnode(TRIANGLE *tri);
    void addlist(TLIST **tlist, TRIANGLE *tri);
    double calcsign(Point& p, TRIANGLE* tri);
    void intersect(TRIANGLE *tri, Point& v1, Point& v2, Point& loc);
    void inserttriangle(TLIST **tlist, Point& v1, Point& v2,
      Point& v3, TRIANGLE* copyfrom);
    void split(TLIST **frontlist, TLIST **backlist, double signv1,
      double signv2, double signv3, TRIANGLE *sepplane, TRIANGLE *tri);
    BSPNode* makeBSPtree(TLIST *l);
    void calctrinormals();
    void precomputecentroids();
    void worldtodisplay(double x, double y, double z, int& xr, int& yr);
    RGBCOLOR computecolor(Point& p, VECTOR& normal, int colorddx);
    void displaytriangle(TRIANGLE *tri, unsigned char dir);
    void traversetree(BSPNode *tree);
};


#endif
```

• 3DSOLID.CPP

```
// 3DSOLID.CPP: This file extends the threed object in 3DTOOL.CPP
// so that it can display solid objects. The new object, threedsolid,
// uses the BSP algorithm described in Chapter 14.
#include <stdio.h>
#include <graphics.h>
#include <stdlib.h>
#include <string.h>
#include <math.h>
#include "vector.h"
#include "3dtool.h"
#include "user3d.h"
#include "3dsolid.h"

const int POLYLEN = 3;
const int NUMEDGES = 4;

struct POINT {
  int x, y;
};

struct CLIPPED {
  int len;
  int v[POLYLEN*4];
};

RGBCOLOR palette[255];
int maxcolorsused;
int maxcolorsavail;
```

```
// Sets up the dimensions of the window and various default values
void threedsolid::threedsolid() : threedobj()
{
  ambient = 0.30;  // Larger values make the object brighter
  diffuse = 0.80;  // Larger values add more shading
  // Set the light location to (-10,75,75)
  light.x = -10.0;  light.y = 75;  light.z = 75;
}

// Reads in a file describing a polygon that adheres to the
// standard described above. Returns 1 if file is read
// successfully; otherwise, it returns an error flag.
int threedsolid::read3dobject(char *filename)
{
  int i, obj;
  FILE *infile;

  if ((infile=fopen(filename,"r")) == NULL)
    return -1;
  // Read the list of RGB colors used in the objects
  fscanf(infile, "%d", &numcolors);
  if (numcolors >= NUMCOLORS) return -2;
  if (numcolors > 0)    // No color palette if 0 or negative
    for (i=1; i<=numcolors; i++)
      fscanf(infile, "%d %d %d", &colorpal[i].r,
        &colorpal[i].g, &colorpal[i].b);

  fscanf(infile, "%d", &numobjects);
  if (numobjects > NUMOBJECTS) {  // Too many objects in the file
    fclose(infile);
    return -3;
  }
  for (obj=0; obj<numobjects; obj++) {
    fscanf(infile, "%d %d", &objects[obj].numvertices,
      &objects[obj].numconnect);
    if (objects[obj].numvertices >= NUMVERTICES ||
        objects[obj].numconnect >= NUMCONNECTIONS) {
      fclose(infile);    // Object is too large
      return -2;
    }
    for (i=1; i<=objects[obj].numvertices; i++)
      fscanf(infile, "%lf %lf %lf",
        &objects[obj].pointarray[i].x,
        &objects[obj].pointarray[i].y,
        &objects[obj].pointarray[i].z);
    for (i=1; i<=objects[obj].numconnect; i++)
      fscanf(infile, "%d", &objects[obj].connect[i]);
  }
  fclose(infile);

  TRIANGLE *tri, *t;
  TLIST *nu, *trilist = NULL;
```

```
    // Create the list of triangle data for the BSP tree
    tril = NULL;
    for (obj=0; obj<numobjects; obj++) {
      i=1;
      while (i<objects[obj].numconnect) {
        t = new TRIANGLE;
        if (t == NULL) {
          popuperror("Out of Memory");
          return 0;
        }

        t->v1 = objects[obj].pointarray[objects[obj].connect[i]];
        t->v2 = objects[obj].pointarray[objects[obj].connect[i+1]];
        t->v3 = objects[obj].pointarray[objects[obj].connect[i+2]];
        t->colorndx = -objects[obj].connect[i+3];
        i += 4;
        t->next = tril;
        tril = t;
      }
    }
    // Create a TLIST list of all the triangles in tril
    tri = tril;
    while (tri != NULL) {
      nu = new TLIST;
      if (nu == NULL) {
        popuperror("Out of Memory");
        return 0;
      }
      nu->t = tri;
      nu->next = trilist;
      trilist = nu;           // Insert at head of list
      tri = tri->next;
    }
    calctrinormals();
    calcplaneeqs();
    tree = makeBSPtree(trilist);
    // Free the TLIST structures
    nu = trilist;
    while (nu != NULL) {
      trilist = nu->next;
      free(nu);
      nu = trilist;
    }
    // Precompute values so that it's faster to display the objects
    precomputecentroids();
    return 1;
}

// Precomputes the d term in the plane equation for each polygon.
// The normal of the plane and a point on the plane--one of
// its vertices--are used to solve for d.
void threedsolid::calcplaneeqs()
{
  TRIANGLE *tri = tril;
```

```
    while (tri != NULL) {
      tri->d = -(tri->normal.x * tri->v1.x +
        tri->normal.y * tri->v1.y + tri->normal.z * tri->v1.z);
      tri = tri->next;
    }
}

// Disposes of the BSP tree
void threedsolid::disposeBSP(BSPNode *tree)
{
  if (tree != NULL) {
    disposeBSP(tree->outside);
    disposeBSP(tree->inside);
    free(tree);
  }
}

// Creates a new node for the BSP tree
BSPNode *threedsolid::makeBSPnode(TRIANGLE *tri)
{
  BSPNode *node = new BSPNode;
  node->tri = tri;   // Point to the triangle's data
  node->outside = NULL;  node->inside = NULL;
  return node;
}

void threedsolid::addlist(TLIST **tlist, TRIANGLE *tri)
{
  TLIST *L = *tlist, *nuL, *back = *tlist;

  nuL = new TLIST;
  if (nuL == NULL) {
    popuperror("Out of Memory");
    return;
  }
  nuL->t = tri;
  nuL->next = NULL;
  if (L != NULL) {
    while (L != NULL) {
      back = L;
      L = L->next;
    }
    back->next = nuL;
  }
  else              // List is empty. This is the first node.
    *tlist = nuL;
}

// Calculates the sign that indicates which side of the separation
// plane vertex V is on. Note that a tolerance value is used to
// account for arithmetic round-off errors by the computer.
// This function uses the fact that a plane equation is:
// ax + by + cz + d = 0. If V is plugged into the equation,
// the result will be 0. If not, the sign of the result indicates
```

```
// which side of the plane the point is on.
double threedsolid::calcsign(Point& P, TRIANGLE* tri)
{
  double Value = P.x * tri->normal.x + P.y * tri->normal.y +
    P.z * tri->normal.z + tri->d;
  if (labs(Value) < TOL) return 0.0; // The point is on the plane
    else return Value;  // The sign of the value indicates which
}                       // side V is on

// Uses a parameteric equation to determine where a line
// intersects the plane. The two vertices v1 and v2 are the
// endpoints of the line.
void threedsolid::intersect(TRIANGLE *tri, Point& v1,
  Point& v2, Point& Loc)
{
  double T = -(tri->normal.x * v1.x + tri->normal.y * v1.y +
    tri->normal.z * v1.z + tri->d) / (tri->normal.x * (v2.x - v1.x) +
    tri->normal.y * (v2.y - v1.y) + tri->normal.z * (v2.z - v1.z));
  if (T >= -TOL && T <= 1 + TOL) {
    Loc.x = v1.x + T * (v2.x - v1.x);
    Loc.y = v1.y + T * (v2.y - v1.y);
    Loc.z = v1.z + T * (v2.z - v1.z);
  }
}

// Insert the triangle formed by the vertices v1, v2, and v3 to
// the beginning of the triangle list, trilist. Add an appropriate
// pointer to this TRIANGLE structure to the end of tlist.
void threedsolid::inserttriangle(TLIST **tlist,
  Point& v1, Point& v2, Point& v3, TRIANGLE* copyfrom)
{
  // Add a new triangle structure to the beginning of the
  // list of triangles in the figure
  TRIANGLE* nut = new TRIANGLE;
  nut->next = tril;
  tril = nut;
  nut->v1 = v1;    nut->v2 = v2;    nut->v3 = v3;
  nut->normal = copyfrom->normal;
  nut->d = copyfrom->d;  nut->colorndx = copyfrom->colorndx;
  // Append a pointer to this triangle data in the list of
  // triangles. This triangle must be appended because
  // the head of the list is being used.
  addlist(tlist, nut);
}

// Splits the triangle by the plane specified
void threedsolid::split(TLIST **frontlist, TLIST **backlist,
  double signv1, double signv2, double signv3,
  TRIANGLE *sepplane, TRIANGLE *tri)
{
  Point P, P2;

  if (signv1 == 0) {        // The plane goes through vertex v1
    intersect(sepplane, tri->v2, tri->v3, P);
```

```
    if (signv2 > 0) {          // Make right half on front side
      inserttriangle(frontlist, tri->v1, tri->v2, P, tri);
      inserttriangle(backlist, tri->v1, P, tri->v3, tri);
    }
    else {
      inserttriangle(backlist, tri->v1, tri->v2, P, tri);
      inserttriangle(frontlist, tri->v1, P, tri->v3, tri);
    }
  }
  else if (signv2 == 0) {    // The plane goes through vertex v2
    intersect(sepplane, tri->v1, tri->v3, P);
    if (signv1 > 0) {          // Make right half on front side
      inserttriangle(frontlist, tri->v1, tri->v2, P, tri);
      inserttriangle(backlist, P, tri->v2, tri->v3, tri);
    }
    else {
      inserttriangle(backlist, tri->v1, tri->v2, P, tri);
      inserttriangle(frontlist, P, tri->v2, tri->v3, tri);
    }
  }
  else if (signv3 == 0) {     // The plane goes through vertex v3
    intersect(sepplane, tri->v1, tri->v2, P);
    if (signv1 > 0) {          // Make right half on front side
      inserttriangle(frontlist, tri->v1, P, tri->v3, tri);
      inserttriangle(backlist, P, tri->v2, tri->v3, tri);
    }
    else {
      inserttriangle(backlist, tri->v1, P, tri->v3, tri);
      inserttriangle(frontlist, P, tri->v2, tri->v3, tri);
    }
  }
  else if (signv1 > 0 && signv3 > 0) {  // Vertex v2 on other side
    intersect(sepplane, tri->v1, tri->v2, P);
    intersect(sepplane, tri->v2, tri->v3, P2);
    inserttriangle(frontlist, tri->v1, P, tri->v3, tri);
    inserttriangle(frontlist, P, P2, tri->v3, tri);
    inserttriangle(backlist, P, tri->v2, P2, tri);
  }
  else if (signv1 < 0 && signv3 < 0) {  // Vertex v2 on other side
    intersect(sepplane, tri->v1, tri->v2, P);
    intersect(sepplane, tri->v2, tri->v3, P2);
    inserttriangle(backlist, tri->v1, P, tri->v3, tri);
    inserttriangle(backlist, P, P2, tri->v3, tri);
    inserttriangle(frontlist, P, tri->v2, P2, tri);
  }
  else if (signv2 > 0 && signv3 > 0) {  // Vertex v1 on other side
    intersect(sepplane, tri->v1, tri->v2, P);
    intersect(sepplane, tri->v1, tri->v3, P2);
    inserttriangle(frontlist, P, tri->v3, P2, tri);
    inserttriangle(frontlist, P, tri->v2, tri->v3, tri);
    inserttriangle(backlist, tri->v1, P, P2, tri);
  }
  else if (signv2 < 0 && signv3 < 0) {  // Vertex v1 on other side
    intersect(sepplane, tri->v1, tri->v2, P);
```

```
          intersect(sepplane, tri->v1, tri->v3, P2);
          inserttriangle(backlist, P, tri->v3, P2, tri);
          inserttriangle(backlist, P, tri->v2, tri->v3, tri);
          inserttriangle(frontlist, tri->v1, P, P2, tri);
      }
      else if (signv1 > 0 && signv2 > 0) {   // Vertex v3 on other side
          intersect(sepplane, tri->v2, tri->v3, P);
          intersect(sepplane, tri->v1, tri->v3, P2);
          inserttriangle(frontlist, tri->v1, tri->v2, P, tri);
          inserttriangle(frontlist, tri->v1, P, P2, tri);
          inserttriangle(backlist, P2, P, tri->v3, tri);
      }
      else if (signv1 < 0 && signv2 < 0) {   // Vertex v3 on other side
          intersect(sepplane, tri->v2, tri->v3, P);
          intersect(sepplane, tri->v1, tri->v3, P2);
          inserttriangle(backlist, tri->v1, tri->v2, P, tri);
          inserttriangle(backlist, tri->v1, P, P2, tri);
          inserttriangle(frontlist, P, P2, tri->v3, tri);
      }
    }
}

// Makes the BSP tree structure
BSPNode* threedsolid::makeBSPtree(TLIST *L)
{
    TLIST *backlist=NULL, *frontlist=NULL, *root, *tri;
    double signv1, signv2, signv3;
    BSPNode *node;

    if (L == NULL) return NULL;
    else {
      root = L;  // Set the root as the first triangle in the list
      tri = root->next;
      while (tri != NULL) {
        signv1 = calcsign(tri->t->v1, root->t);
        signv2 = calcsign(tri->t->v2, root->t);
        signv3 = calcsign(tri->t->v3, root->t);
        if (signv1 >= 0 && signv2 >= 0 && signv3 >= 0)
          addlist(&frontlist, tri->t);   // triangle is in front of root
        else if (signv1 <= 0 && signv2 <= 0 && signv3 <= 0)
          addlist(&backlist, tri->t);    // triangle is in back of root
        else
          split(&frontlist, &backlist, signv1, signv2, signv3,
            root->t, tri->t);
        tri = tri->next;
      }
      node = makeBSPnode(root->t);  // Add node for the root triangle
      node->outside = makeBSPtree(frontlist);
      node->inside = makeBSPtree(backlist);

      TLIST *p = frontlist;
      while (p != NULL) {
        frontlist = p->next;  free(p);  p = frontlist;
      }
```

```
      p = backlist;
      while (p != NULL) {
        backlist = p->next;    free(p);   p = backlist;
      }
    }
    return node;
}

// Converts world coordinates to display coordinates
void threedsolid::worldtodisplay(double x, double y, double z,
  int& xr, int& yr)
{
  double xc = (x * a1.x + a1.y * y + a1.z * z + offsx) * dval;
  double yc = (x * a2.x + a2.y * y + a2.z * z + offsy) * dval;
  double zc = x * a3.x + a3.y * y + a3.z * z + offsz;
  double xm = xc / zc;
  double ym = yc / -zc;
  xr = a * xm + b;
  yr = c * ym + d;
}

// Calculates the normals of the triangles
void threedsolid::calctrinormals()
{
  TRIANGLE *tri = tril;
  VECTOR d1, d2;

  while (tri != NULL) {
    d1 = subtract(&tri->v1, &tri->v2);
    d2 = subtract(&tri->v1, &tri->v3);
    tri->normal = cross(&d1, &d2);
    normalize(&tri->normal);
    tri = tri->next;
  }
}

// Precomputed the centroids of all the triangles
void threedsolid::precomputecentroids()
{
  TRIANGLE *t = tril;
  while (t != NULL) {
    t->centroid.x = (t->v1.x + t->v2.x + t->v3.x) / 3.0;
    t->centroid.y = (t->v1.y + t->v2.y + t->v3.y) / 3.0;
    t->centroid.z = (t->v1.z + t->v2.z + t->v3.z) / 3.0;
    t = t->next;
  }
}

// Returns the color to paint a polygon. Only ambient and diffuse
// lighting is used. You are looking at point P. normal is the
// normal of the polygon. colorndx indicates the color of the polygon.
RGBCOLOR threedsolid::computecolor(Point& p, VECTOR& normal,
  int colorndx)
```

```
{
  VECTOR L;
  double L_N;

  L = subtract(&light, &p); // Find vector from light to point P
  normalize(&L);
  L_N = dot(&L, &normal);
  // Calculate diffuse lighting contribution to object's color
  if (L_N <= 0) L_N *= -diffuse * NUM_SHADES;
    else L_N *= diffuse * NUM_SHADES;
  // Add ambient coefficient
  int Red = (int)(colorpal[colorndx].r + ambient * NUM_SHADES + L_N);
  int Green = (int)(colorpal[colorndx].g + ambient * NUM_SHADES + L_N);
  int Blue = (int)(colorpal[colorndx].b + ambient * NUM_SHADES + L_N);
  if (Red > 255) Red = 255;
  if (Green > 255) Green = 255;
  if (Blue > 255) Blue = 255;

  RGBCOLOR c;
  c.r = Red;
  c.g = Green;
  c.b = Blue;
  return c;
}

// Returns a positive value if ndx is in the list
int inlist(int ndx, int list[], int listlen)
{
  int i=0;

  for (i=0; i<listlen; i++)
    if (list[i] == ndx)
      return i;
  return -1;
}

void inserttoclip(int cliptoedge1, CLIPPED clippts[],
  POINT v[], int vlen, int xpc3b, int ypc3b, int Enter)
{
  int i, j;

  switch(cliptoedge1) {
    case 0:    // Sort on min x
      for (i=0; i<clippts[cliptoedge1].len; i++) {
        if (Enter) {  // Append to list
          i = clippts[cliptoedge1].len;
          break;
        }
        else {
          if (v[clippts[cliptoedge1].v[i]].x > xpc3b) {
            // Insert before this point
            for (j=i; j<clippts[cliptoedge1].len; j++) {
              clippts[cliptoedge1].v[j+1] = clippts[cliptoedge1].v[j];
            }
```

```
          break;
        }
      }
    }
    break;
case 1:        // Sort on min y
  for (i=0; i<clippts[cliptoedge1].len; i++) {
    if (Enter) {  // Append to list
      i = clippts[cliptoedge1].len;
      break;
    }
    else {
      if (v[clippts[cliptoedge1].v[i]].y > ypc3b) {
        // Insert before this point
        for (j=i; j<clippts[cliptoedge1].len; j++) {
          clippts[cliptoedge1].v[j+1] = clippts[cliptoedge1].v[j];
        }
        break;
      }
    }
  }
  break;
case 2:        // Sort on max x
  for (i=0; i<clippts[cliptoedge1].len; i++) {
    if (Enter) {    // Append
      i = clippts[cliptoedge1].len;
      break;
    }
    else {
      if (v[clippts[cliptoedge1].v[i]].x < xpc3b) {
        // Insert before this point
        for (j=i; j<clippts[cliptoedge1].len; j++) {
          clippts[cliptoedge1].v[j+1] = clippts[cliptoedge1].v[j];
        }
        break;
      }
    }
  }
  break;
case 3:        // Sort on max y
  for (i=0; i<clippts[cliptoedge1].len; i++) {
    if (Enter) {
      i = clippts[cliptoedge1].len;
      break;
    }
    else {
      if (v[clippts[cliptoedge1].v[i]].y < ypc3b) {
        // Insert before this point
        for (j=i; j<clippts[cliptoedge1].len; j++) {
          clippts[cliptoedge1].v[j+1] = clippts[cliptoedge1].v[j];
        }
        break;
      }
    }
  }
```

```
        }
      break;
  }
  clippts[cliptoedge1].v[i] = vlen;
  clippts[cliptoedge1].len++;
}

unsigned char inptlist(int x, int y, POINT v[], int vlen)
{
  int i;

  for (i=0; i<vlen; i++)
    if (v[i].x == x && v[i].y == y)
      return 1;
  return 0;
}

int findcolor(RGBCOLOR Color)
{
  int i;

  for (i=16; i<maxcolorsused; i++)
    if (palette[i].r == Color.r &&
        palette[i].g == Color.g &&
        palette[i].b == Color.b)
      return i;
  return -1;
}

// Returns a color in the palette that matches the RGB color
// specified
int RGBtopalette(RGBCOLOR Color)
{
  static int newcolor=0;

  if ((newcolor=findcolor(Color)) >= 0)
    return newcolor;
  else {
    // Add a new color to the palette until it is full.
    // Don't use the last entry; it should remain white.
    if (maxcolorsused < 254) {
      setrgbpalette(maxcolorsused, Color.r, Color.g, Color.b);
      palette[maxcolorsused].r = Color.r;
      palette[maxcolorsused].g = Color.g;
      palette[maxcolorsused].b = Color.b;
      maxcolorsused++;
      return maxcolorsused-1;
    }
  }
  return 0;
}

// Displays the triangle. This lengthy routine clips the triangle
// to the viewing pyramid, computes its color, and then displays
```

```
// it on the screen.
void threedsolid::displaytriangle(TRIANGLE *tri, unsigned char dir)
{
  int xpc1a, ypc1a, xpc1b, ypc1b;
  int xpc2a, ypc2a, xpc2b, ypc2b;
  int xpc3a, ypc3a, xpc3b, ypc3b, i=0;
  VECTOR v1, v2, v3;
  int colorndx;

  if (maxcolorsavail > 16) {
    // Compute an RGB color when in a 256-color mode
    RGBCOLOR color = computecolor(tri->centroid, tri->normal,
      tri->colorndx);
    colorndx = RGBtopalette(color);
  }
  else {
    // In 16-color mode, use the red component of the object's
    // color as a psuedocolor. Don't apply a color model.
    colorndx = colorpal[tri->colorndx].r;
  }

  POINT v[POLYLEN*4];  // List of polygon's original and clipped points
  int vlen=0, visible[POLYLEN*4], vislen = 0;
  int clipped[POLYLEN*4], cliplen = 0, j;
  CLIPPED clippts[NUMEDGES];
  int cliptoedge1, cliptoedge2, startpt, pt;
  int outpt[POLYLEN*6], outlen=0, enter[POLYLEN*4];
  int enterlen=0, leave[POLYLEN*4], leavelen=0;
  int clip;

  for (i=0; i<NUMEDGES; i++) clippts[i].len = 0;
  // Initialize the clipped points with the four corners of
  // the viewing window too.
  v[0].x = left;  v[0].y = top;
  clippts[0].v[0] = 0;
  clippts[0].len = 1;
  v[1].x = right;  v[1].y = top;
  clippts[1].v[0] = 1;
  clippts[1].len = 1;
  v[2].x = right;  v[2].y = bottom;
  clippts[2].v[0] = 2;
  clippts[2].len = 1;
  v[3].x = left;  v[3].y = bottom;
  clippts[3].v[0] = 3;
  clippts[3].len = 1;
  vlen = 4;

  v1.x = (tri->v1.x*a1.x + a1.y*tri->v1.y + a1.z*tri->v1.z + offsx)*dval;
  v1.y = (tri->v1.x*a2.x + a2.y*tri->v1.y + a2.z*tri->v1.z + offsy)*dval;
  v1.z =  tri->v1.x*a3.x + a3.y*tri->v1.y + a3.z*tri->v1.z + offsz;
  v2.x = (tri->v2.x*a1.x + a1.y*tri->v2.y + a1.z*tri->v2.z + offsx)*dval;
  v2.y = (tri->v2.x*a2.x + a2.y*tri->v2.y + a2.z*tri->v2.z + offsy)*dval;
  v2.z =  tri->v2.x*a3.x + a3.y*tri->v2.y + a3.z*tri->v2.z + offsz;
  if (!clip3d(&v1, &v2, xpc1a, ypc1a, xpc2a, ypc2a,
```

```
                cliptoedge1, cliptoedge2, clip)) {
            // Add point to the list of points
            v[vlen].x = xpc1a;  v[vlen].y = ypc1a;
            if ((clip&0x80) == 0x80) {
              // First point was clipped
              // Insert the clipped point in the list of clipped vertices
              // Exiting
              inserttoclip(cliptoedge1, clippts, v, vlen, xpc1a, ypc1a, dir);
              enter[enterlen++] = vlen;
              visible[vislen++] = vlen;
            }
            else {
              visible[vislen++] = vlen;
            }
            vlen++;
            // Add point to the list of points
            v[vlen].x = xpc2a;  v[vlen].y = ypc2a;
            if ((clip&0x08) == 0x08) {
              // First point was clipped
              // Insert the clipped point in the list of clipped vertices
              inserttoclip(cliptoedge2, clippts, v, vlen, xpc2a, ypc2a, (!dir));
              leave[leavelen++] = vlen;
              visible[vislen++] = vlen;
            }
            else {
              visible[vislen++] = vlen;
            }
            vlen++;
          }
          v2.x = (tri->v2.x * a1.x + a1.y * tri->v2.y + a1.z * tri->v2.z + offsx)*dval;
          v2.y = (tri->v2.x * a2.x + a2.y * tri->v2.y + a2.z * tri->v2.z + offsy)*dval;
          v2.z =  tri->v2.x * a3.x + a3.y * tri->v2.y + a3.z * tri->v2.z + offsz;
          v3.x = (tri->v3.x * a1.x + a1.y * tri->v3.y + a1.z * tri->v3.z + offsx)*dval;
          v3.y = (tri->v3.x * a2.x + a2.y * tri->v3.y + a2.z * tri->v3.z + offsy)*dval;
          v3.z =  tri->v3.x * a3.x + a3.y * tri->v3.y + a3.z * tri->v3.z + offsz;
          if (!clip3d(&v2, &v3, xpc2b, ypc2b, xpc3a, ypc3a, cliptoedge1,
            cliptoedge2, clip)) {
            // Only add a point if it doesn't exist yet
            if (!inptlist(xpc2b, ypc2b, v, vlen)) {
              // Add point to the list of points
              v[vlen].x = xpc2b;  v[vlen].y = ypc2b;
              if ((clip&0x80) == 0x80) {
                // First point was clipped
                // Insert the clipped point in the list of clipped vertices
                inserttoclip(cliptoedge1, clippts, v, vlen, xpc2b, ypc2b, dir);
                enter[enterlen++] = vlen;
                visible[vislen++] = vlen;
              }
              else {
                visible[vislen++] = vlen;
              }
              vlen++;
            }
```

```
    if (!inptlist(xpc3a, ypc3a, v, vlen)) {
      // Add point to the list of points
      v[vlen].x = xpc3a;  v[vlen].y = ypc3a;
      if ((clip&0x08) == 0x08) {
        // First point was clipped
        // Insert the clipped point in the list of clipped vertices
        inserttoclip(cliptoedge2, clippts, v, vlen, xpc3a, ypc3a, (!dir));
        leave[leavelen++] = vlen;
        visible[vislen++] = vlen;
      }
      else {
        visible[vislen++] = vlen;
      }
      vlen++;
    }
  }
}

v3.x = (tri->v3.x * a1.x + a1.y * tri->v3.y + a1.z * tri->v3.z + offsx)*dval;
v3.y = (tri->v3.x * a2.x + a2.y * tri->v3.y + a2.z * tri->v3.z + offsy)*dval;
v3.z =  tri->v3.x * a3.x + a3.y * tri->v3.y + a3.z * tri->v3.z + offsz;
v1.x = (tri->v1.x * a1.x + a1.y * tri->v1.y + a1.z * tri->v1.z + offsx)*dval;
v1.y = (tri->v1.x * a2.x + a2.y * tri->v1.y + a2.z * tri->v1.z + offsy)*dval;
v1.z =  tri->v1.x * a3.x + a3.y * tri->v1.y + a3.z * tri->v1.z + offsz;
if (!clip3d(&v3, &v1, xpc3b, ypc3b, xpc1b, ypc1b, cliptoedge1,
  cliptoedge2, clip)) {
 if (!inptlist(xpc3b, ypc3b, v, vlen)) {
    // Add point to the list of points
    v[vlen].x = xpc3b;  v[vlen].y = ypc3b;
    if ((clip&0x80) == 0x80) {
      // First point was clipped
      // Insert the clipped point in the list of clipped vertices
      inserttoclip(cliptoedge1, clippts, v, vlen, xpc3b, ypc3b, dir);
      enter[enterlen++] = vlen;
      visible[vislen++] = vlen;
    }
    else {
      visible[vislen++] = vlen;
    }
    vlen++;
  }
  if (!inptlist(xpc1b, ypc1b, v, vlen)) {
    // Add point to the list of points
    v[vlen].x = xpc1b;  v[vlen].y = ypc1b;
    if ((clip&0x08) == 0x08) {
      // First point was clipped
      // Insert the clipped point in the list of clipped vertices
      inserttoclip(cliptoedge2, clippts, v, vlen, xpc1b, ypc1b, (!dir));
      leave[leavelen++] = vlen;
      visible[vislen++] = vlen;
    }
    else {
      visible[vislen++] = vlen;
    }
    vlen++;
```

```
      }
    }
    // If vislen equals 0, there's nothing to display. If
    // vislen equals 1, then only one point of the triangle
    // is sitting on the edge of the window. Ignore it.
    if (vislen < 2) return;  // Nothing is visible

    // To simplify the code below, copy the clipped points
    // into a single-dimensioned array
    // If the viewer is "behind" the object, reverse the
    // order of the clipped points to compenstate
    if (!dir) {
      for (j=NUMEDGES-1; j>=0; j--)
        for (i=clippts[j].len-1; i>=0; i--)
          clipped[cliplen++] = clippts[j].v[i];
    }
    else
    {
      for (j=0; j<NUMEDGES; j++)
        for (i=0; i<clippts[j].len; i++)
          clipped[cliplen++] = clippts[j].v[i];
    }
    // Only valid clippings have the same number of entering
    // and leaving points
    if (leavelen != enterlen) {
      leavelen = 0;
      enterlen = 0;
      cliplen = 0;
    }
    // Now that we have a list of the original points and the
    // points on the triangle that intersect the bounds of the viewing
    // rectangle, we'll build a list of the points that form the
    // perimeter of the viewable portion of the triangle.
    startpt = visible[0];
    int visndx=0, clipndx=0;
    do {
      if (visndx >= vislen) exit(1);
      do {
        pt = visible[visndx];
        // Add this point to the output list of vertices
        outpt[outlen++] = v[pt].x;
        outpt[outlen++] = v[pt].y;
        visndx++;
      } while (inlist(pt, leave, leavelen) < 0 && visndx < vislen);
      if ((clipndx=inlist(pt, clipped, cliplen)) >= 0) {
        clipndx++;
        if (clipndx >= cliplen) clipndx = 0;  // Circular list
        pt = clipped[clipndx];
        outpt[outlen++] = v[pt].x;
        outpt[outlen++] = v[pt].y;

        while (inlist(pt, enter, enterlen) < 0) {
          // Get the next point in the clip list
          clipndx++;
```

```
          if (clipndx >= cliplen) clipndx = 0;   // Circular list
          pt = clipped[clipndx];

          // Add this point to the output list of vertices
          outpt[outlen++] = v[pt].x;
          outpt[outlen++] = v[pt].y;
        }
        visndx = inlist(pt, visible, vislen);
      }
    } while(startpt != pt && visndx < vislen-1);

    if (outlen > 0) {
      // At least part of the triangle is visible
      // Wrap the array back to the beginning
      outpt[outlen++] = outpt[0];
      outpt[outlen++] = outpt[1];
      // Create the correct fill color and display the triangle
      setfillstyle(SOLID_FILL, colorndx);
      setcolor(colorndx);
      setviewport(left, top, right, bottom, 1);
      fillpoly(outlen/2, outpt);    // Display the triangle
    }
}

// Displays the figure stored in the BSP tree
void threedsolid::view(void)
{
  maxcolorsavail = getmaxcolor();
  traversetree(tree);
}

// Traverses a BSP tree, rendering a three-dimensional scene
void threedsolid::traversetree(BSPNode *tree)
{
  VECTOR s;
  double costheta;

  if (tree != NULL) {
    s.x = from.x - tree->tri->v1.x;
    s.y = from.y - tree->tri->v1.y;
    s.z = from.z - tree->tri->v1.z;
    normalize(&s);
    costheta = dot(&s, &tree->tri->normal);
    if (costheta > 0) {  // The eye is in front of the polygon
      traversetree(tree->inside);
      displaytriangle(tree->tri, 0);
      traversetree(tree->outside);
    }
    else {    // The eye is in back of the polygon
      traversetree(tree->outside);
      displaytriangle(tree->tri, 1);
      traversetree(tree->inside);
    }
  }
}
```

● **V3D.CPP**

```cpp
// V3D.CPP: A virtual reality-like program that enables you to
// move around in a three-dimensional world.
#include <stdio.h>
#include <stdlib.h>
#include <graphics.h>
#include <string.h>
#include <math.h>
#include <conio.h>
#include "gtext.h"
#include "vector.h"
#include "gpopup.h"
#include "user3d.h"
#include "3dtool.h"
#include "interact.h"
#include "3dsolid.h"

const int PCL = 1;                 // Top left pixel coordinate of
const int PCT = 1;                 // the viewing window
const int ICONWD = 16;             // The dimensions of the icons
const int ICONHT = 16;

int pcl, pct, pcr, pcb;            // Coordinates of the viewing window

// Retrieves the desired mode from the user
#ifdef HICOLOR
int huge DetectVGA256(void)
{
#ifdef SVGA256
  int Vid;

  printf("Which video mode would you like to use? \n");
  printf("  0) 320x200x256\n");
  printf("  1) 640x400x256\n");
  printf("  2) 640x480x256\n");
  printf("  3) 800x600x256\n");
  printf("  4) 1024x768x256\n\n>");
  scanf("%d",&Vid);
  return Vid;
#else
  return 0;    // Selects VGA's 320 x 200 256-color mode
#endif
}
#endif

// Creates an arrow tool that you can use to navigate around
// the world with. The key variable is the keyboard hot key that
// you can use to initiate the command. It also adds the drawing
// tool passed in to the list of tools. This is the tool that gets
// called when the user clicks on the arrow. The arrow symbol is
// read from the specified icon file. A three-dimensional window
// is painted behind the arrow icon to make it a little bigger.
// However, this last step isn't really necessary.
```

```
void setuparrowtool(int key, int left, int top, int wd, int ht,
  drawingtool *tool, char *iconfilename)
{
  tools.addtool(new interact(key, left-1, top-1, wd-1, ht-1, tool));
  tools.tool[tools.numtools-1]->itool->left = left;
  tools.tool[tools.numtools-1]->itool->top = top;
  tools.tool[tools.numtools-1]->itool->right = left+wd;
  tools.tool[tools.numtools-1]->itool->bottom = top+ht;
  w.paintwindow(left, top, left+wd-1,
    top+ht-1, THREED, LIGHTGRAY, SOLID_FILL, BLACK);
  readicon(left+2, top+2, iconfilename);
}


// Creates a menu button at the location specified. "key" is
// the hot key the user can use to activate the menu command.
// "tool" is the object that gets called when the button is
// activated. "str" is the string that gets drawn on the button.
// The icon specified by "iconfilename" is displayed at the
// top left of the button. If it is NULL, an icon is not displayed.
void setupbutton(int key, int left, int top, int wd, int ht,
  drawingtool *tool, char *iconfilename, int Txty, char *str)
{
  tools.addtool(new interact(key, left, top, wd-1, ht-1, tool));
  // The button is made from a gray, three-dimensional window
  w.paintwindow(left, top, left+wd, top+ht,
    THREED, LIGHTGRAY, SOLID_FILL, BLACK);
  if (str != NULL)
    readicon(left+4, top+2, iconfilename);
  menustr(left+iconwd+8, top+Txty, BLACK, RED, LIGHTGRAY, str);
}


// Sets up the environment for the solid modelling program
void setup_environment(void)
{
  drawingtool *quit = new quittool;
  drawingtool *readfile = new readtool;
  drawingtool *setfrom = new setfromtool;
  drawingtool *setat = new setattool;
  drawingtool *setup = new setuptool;
  drawingtool *setangle = new setangletool;
  drawingtool *forward = new forwardtool;
  drawingtool *backward = new backwardtool;
  drawingtool *clockwise = new cwtool;
  drawingtool *counterclockwise = new ccwtool;

  // Normally place the menu to the right of the location pcr.
  // If this makes the menu too wide, then decrease it.
  int Menux = pcr+1;
  int MenuWd = getmaxx() - Menux;
  int ButtonX = MenuWd / 16;
  int ButtonWd = MenuWd - ButtonX*2;
  int NumButtons = 10;
  int ButtonSp = 2;
  int ButtonHt = (getmaxy() - ButtonSp*2) / NumButtons;
```

```
      // There won't be enough room for the bird's eye view,
      // so set its height to 0
      int Offset = 4;
      iconwd = ICONWD;
      iconht = ICONHT;
      int IconMult = 2;   // Normally double the size of icons
      if (iconwd*IconMult > ButtonHt)
        IconMult = 1;     // Don't double the size of icons
      if (ButtonHt < iconht*IconMult) ButtonHt = iconht*IconMult+4;

      w.paintwindow(Menux, 0, getmaxx(), getmaxy(),
        THREED, LIGHTGRAY, SOLID_FILL, BLACK);
      ButtonX += Menux;
      int Txty = (ButtonHt - textheight("T")) / 2;

      setupbutton('r', ButtonX, Offset, ButtonWd, ButtonHt, readfile,
        "READFILE.ICN", Txty, "&Read file");
      Offset += ButtonHt + ButtonSp;
      setupbutton('f', ButtonX, Offset, ButtonWd, ButtonHt, setfrom,
        "FROM.ICN", Txty, "Set &from");
      Offset += ButtonHt + ButtonSp;
      setupbutton('a', ButtonX, Offset, ButtonWd, ButtonHt, setat,
        "COORDSYS.ICN", Txty, "Set &at");
      Offset += ButtonHt + ButtonSp;
      setupbutton('u', ButtonX, Offset, ButtonWd, ButtonHt, setup,
        "COORDSYS.ICN", Txty, "Set &up");
      Offset += ButtonHt + ButtonSp;
      setupbutton('g', ButtonX, Offset, ButtonWd, ButtonHt, setangle,
        "COORDSYS.ICN", Txty, "Set an&gle");
      Offset += ButtonHt + ButtonSp;
      setupbutton('x', ButtonX, Offset, ButtonWd, ButtonHt, quit,
        "EXIT.ICN", Txty, "E&xit");

      Offset += ButtonHt+ButtonSp;
      ButtonHt = iconht+4;
      int Midy = Offset+ButtonHt*3/2;
      ButtonWd = iconwd+4;
      int Midx = (getmaxx()+pcr)/2;

      // Set up the four arrows used to move around the world
      setuparrowtool(UP, Midx-ButtonWd/2, Midy-ButtonHt*3/2,
        ButtonWd, ButtonHt, forward, "FORWARD.ICN");
      setuparrowtool(DOWN, Midx-ButtonWd/2, Midy+ButtonHt/2,
        ButtonWd, ButtonHt, backward, "REVERSE.ICN");
      setuparrowtool(LEFT, Midx-ButtonWd*3/2, Midy-ButtonHt/2,
        ButtonWd, ButtonHt, counterclockwise, "CCW.ICN");
      setuparrowtool(RIGHT, Midx+ButtonWd/2, Midy-ButtonHt/2,
        ButtonWd, ButtonHt, clockwise, "CW.ICN");
    }

main()
{
  int gmode, gdriver=DETECT, c;
```

```
#ifdef HICOLOR
  // This code uses Borland's undistributed VGA256.BGI driver to access
  // the VGA's 320x200 256-color mode. To select this driver, you must
  // define HICOLOR for your compiler. If you are using Borland's IDE,
  // place HICOLOR in the Defines field of the Options | Compiler |
  // Code generation menu options. If you want to use the SVGA256.BGI
  // driver instead, define both HICOLOR and SVGA256.
#ifdef SVGA256
  installuserdriver("Svga256", DetectVGA256);  // Install the driver
#else
  installuserdriver("vga256", DetectVGA256);
#endif
  //
  initgraph(&gdriver, &gmode, "");  // Initialize the graphics system

  maxcolorsused = 16;  // Count the first default 16 colors as used
#else
  initgraph(&gdriver, &gmode, "");
  if ((errcode=graphresult()) != grOk) {
    printf("Graphics error: %s\n", grapherrormsg(errcode));
    exit(1);       // Return with an error code
  }
#endif

  mouse.init();

  pcl = PCL;
  // The following statement controls, indirectly, the size
  // of the viewing window. Increase the size of the constant
  // to make the window smaller.
  pcb = getmaxy()-textheight("T")*5;
  // Set the right side of the viewing window so that it is
  // square with the height of the window
  int xasp, yasp;
  getaspectratio(&xasp, &yasp);
  pcr = pcb * (float)yasp / xasp;
  pct = PCT;
  mainview = new threedsolid();
  // Make the coordinates of this window smaller if the
  // update rate is too slow
  mainview->init3dgraphics(pcl, pct, pcr, pcb);

  setup_environment();
  w.paintwindow(pcl-1, pcb+1, pcr+1, getmaxy(),
    THREED, LIGHTGRAY, SOLID_FILL, BLACK);
  rectangle(pcl-1, pct-1, pcr+1, pcb+1);

#ifdef HIRESMOUSE
  // If your mouse doesn't appear--which may happen if you are
  // using a Super VGA mode unsupported by your mouse driver--
  // define the HIRESMOUSE compiler constant.
  mouse.drawmouse = 1;
  // Set the mouse to the full screen
```

```
      mouse.sethorizlimits(0, getmaxx()+1);
      mouse.setvertlimits(0, getmaxy()+1);
      mouse.oldx = 3000;  mouse.oldy = 3000;
#endif


   do {
     c = mouse.getinputpress(LEFT_BUTTON);
     if (c != -2 && c != 0)  // Ignore button releases
       tools.anytoprocess(c);
   } while (1);

   closegraph();
   return 0;
}
```

Index

Disk Order Form

If you want to avoid typing in the programs in this book, you can order the *Power Graphics C++ Companion Disk*. This disk includes all the source code presented in the book, ready for you to experiment with.

To receive your disk, fill out the form below (or write the information on a separate sheet of paper) and mail it along with $15 in check or money order to Robots Etc, P.O. Box 122, Tempe, AZ 85280. Make checks payable to Robots Etc.

For phone orders or further information, call (602) 966-0695 or fax (602) 966-0769. This offer may change without notice.

Please send me _____ copies of the *Power Graphics C++ Companion Disk* at $15 each. Make checks payable to Robots Etc. (Checks must be in U.S. funds drawn on a U.S. bank.)

Diskette Size: ___ 5-1/4" (1.2MB)   ___ 5-1/4" (360K)   ___ 3-1/2" (1.44MB)

_____

Name

_____

Address

_____

City   State   Zip

_____

Country   Telephone

Send to: Robots Etc, P.O. Box 122, Tempe, AZ 85280
Please allow 2-4 weeks for delivery

John Wiley & Sons, Inc., is not responsible for orders placed with Robots Etc.